AF248702

Transatlantic Radicalism

Socialist and Anarchist Exchanges
in the 19th and 20th Centuries

STUDIES IN LABOUR HISTORY 16

Studies in Labour History

'…a series which will undoubtedly become an important force in
re-invigorating the study of Labour History.' *English Historical Review*

Studies in Labour History provides reassessments of broad themes along
with more detailed studies arising from the latest research in the field
of labour and working-class history, both in Britain and throughout the
world. Most books are single-authored but there are also volumes of essays
focussed on key themes and issues, usually emerging from major conferences
organized by the British Society for the Study of Labour History. The
series includes studies of labour organizations, including international ones,
where there is a need for new research or modern reassessment. It is also
its objective to extend the breadth of labour history's gaze beyond conven-
tionally organized workers, sometimes to workplace experiences in general,
sometimes to industrial relations, but also to working-class lives beyond the
immediate realm of work in households and communities.

Transatlantic Radicalism

Socialist and Anarchist Exchanges in the 19th and 20th Centuries

edited by
Frank Jacob and Mario Keßler

LIVERPOOL UNIVERSITY PRESS

First published 2021 by
Liverpool University Press
4 Cambridge Street
Liverpool
L69 7ZU

British Library Cataloguing-in-Publication data
A British Library CIP record is available

ISBN 978-1-800-85960-9

Typeset by Carnegie Book Production, Lancaster
Printed and bound by CPI Group (UK) Ltd, Croydon CR0 4YY

Contents

List of Figures   vii

1 Transatlantic Radicalism: A Short Introduction   1
   Frank Jacob and Mario Keßler

I Organizational Ties and Radical Press Networks

2 An Entangled World at the Beginning of the Twentieth
   Century: Russian Socialist Revolutionary Terrorism,
   Transatlantic Public Sphere and American Capital   23
   Lutz Häfner

3 The Italian Anarchists' Network in São Paulo at the Beginning
   of the Twentieth Century   57
   Carlo Romani and Bruno Corrêa de Sá e Benevides

4 The Panama Papers: Anarchist Press Networks between Spain
   and the Canal Zone in the Early Twentieth Century   83
   James Michael Yeoman

5 *Man!* and the International Group: Anti-Radicalism, Immigrant
   Solidarity and Depression-Era Transnational Anarchism   109
   Hillary Lazar

II Individual Perspectives

6 Global Master Workman: Terence Powderly (1849–1924),
   Transatlantic Radicalism and the Global History of the Knights
   of Labor, 1880–1900   129
   Steven Parfitt

7   Transatlantic Workers' Solidarity: The Kuzbas Autonomous
    Industrial Colony (1920–1926)   151
        Frank Jacob

8   "Alles z'Unterobsi": Hannes Meyer and German Communist
    Exiles in Mexico   171
        Georg Leidenberger

9   Damned to Do Nothing: The Transnational Network of Rosi
    Wolfstein and Paul Frölich in American Exile (1941–1950)   191
        Riccardo Altieri

10 Ossip K. Flechtheim (1909–1998): Political Scientist and
    Futurologist between Europe and North America   221
        Mario Keßler

11 Concluding Remarks   249
        Frank Jacob

List of Contributors   255

Index   259

Figures

9.1 Rosi Wolfstein, 1921, Berlin, in the Minute Book of the
Prussian Landtag
© Salomon-Ludwig-Steinheim Institute, Essen, Gidal Photo
Archive 3875   195

9.2 Paul Frölich, 1921, Berlin, in the Minute Book of the
German Reichstag
© Bureau of the Reichstag, 1924 (638)   199

9.3 The Transnational Wolfstein/Frölich Network between 1941
and 1950
© R. Altieri.   202

9.4 Willy Brandt, Rosi Frölich and Max Diamant in the AWO
retirement home, Frankfurt am Main
© Max Mannheimer (Frank Ahland)   213

1

Transatlantic Radicalism

A Short Introduction

Frank Jacob and Mario Keßler

The Atlantic has been an ocean of exchange, in a positive and negative sense, ever since Christopher Columbus (1451–1506) crossed it for the first time and thereby created the "prelude to a fearful saga." The European expansion that followed "[i]n next to no time … enriched [the Europeans, while] non-European populations and ecologies [were] destroyed, indigenous states and economies overthrown, a peculiarly European violence introduced into lands previously innocent of such ways, and the yoke of European colonial rule and hegemony eventually imposed."[1] From the beginning of transatlantic relations on, however, it was also knowledge that crossed the ocean in both directions.[2] That said, the nature of the Atlantic, as an ocean of slavery and trade, changed due to history's course. It very quickly transformed into an ocean of radicalism and different networks of radicals spanned it, especially during the nineteenth and twentieth centuries. Along with the exchange of commodities, the exchange of ideas and moral values through and by intellectuals educated in and related to both worlds connected by the Atlantic became more and more important, creating impacts that are still felt in our globalized world today.[3] The present volume addresses questions related to the genesis of these networks, taking a closer look at party ties, transatlantic press networks[4] and individual perspectives of the transatlantic left, which had not

---

[1] Geoffrey V. Scammell, "After Da Gama: Europe and Asia since 1498," *Modern Asian Studies* 34, no. 3 (2000): 513.

[2] For a more detailed discussion of knowledge exchange related to trade commodities, see Martina Kaller and Frank Jacob, eds., *Transatlantic Trade and Global Cultural Transfers since 1492: More than Commodities* (London: Routledge, 2019).

[3] To name just one example for the impact of the exchange of ideas, see Frank Jacob and Helmut Reinalter, eds., *Masonic Lodges and Their Impact in North and South America* (Würzburg: Königshausen & Neumann, 2019).

[4] Transatlantic communication networks, including the circulation of newspapers and other periodicals, had existed much earlier—for example, in relation to the abolitionist discourse in the Atlantic world. See John R. Oldfield, *Transatlantic Abolitionism in the Age*

been taken into consideration before. As will be shown, a lot of the relationships that determine the character of transatlantic radicalism are strongly tied to individual experiences of exile and the necessity to find a new home, not only as an individual but especially as a radical. The relatively high mobility of individuals within the existent world system[5] is important in understanding the genesis of on ocean-surpassing radicalism, which is transported as a kind of migrant knowledge.[6] The present volume will show who such individuals were, how and where they moved and which consequences their individual experiences had for the establishment of networks in larger contexts, i.e., party networks or press networks alike. It is consequently important to look at the transatlantic left not only as a functioning connection between radicals but as a construct that was very often created by accident and not always on purpose. Why these accidents could happen will also be shown, as they are related to national histories of suppression, persecution and refuge in the first place.

Furthermore, transnational events were also responsible for the establishment of transatlantic ties, especially when international solidarity was requested by the left radicals. When we look back at the "revolutionary left of a hundred or more years ago," including all kinds of left thinkers, i.e., anarchists, communists, socialists etc., it is not only, as Lewis Mates argues, "inspiring in some respects"[7] but it also highlights the transatlantic perspective of political radicalism that has characterized the history of the Atlantic since the late eighteenth century, being most intense in the years between the late nineteenth century and the end of World War II, when political radicals were often motivated to move to assist in international ventures that demanded transatlantic or transnational solidarity.[8]

In her seminal book *The Transatlantic Century: Europe and America, 1890–2010*, U.S. historian Mary Nolan also investigates capitalist economies as subjects of transatlantic exchanges, but she emphasizes that

---

of Revolution: An International History of Anti-Slavery, c.*1787–1820* (New York: Cambridge University Press, 2013).

[5] For discussions about the world system from a labor perspective, see Marcel van der Linden, *Workers of the World: Essays Toward a Global Labor History* (Leiden: Brill, 2011).

[6] Simone Lässig and Swen Steinberg, "Knowledge on the Move: New Approaches toward a History of Migrant Knowledge," *Geschichte und Gesellschaft* 43, no. 3 (2017): 313–346. An interesting study on the transnationality of workers' organizations is also provided in Richard Stoenescu, "Syndikalismus in Deutschland und den USA, 1897–1937" (Ph.D. thesis, University of Potsdam, 2020).

[7] Lewis Mates, "Syndicalism and the 'Transnational Turn,'" *Capital & Class* 40, no. 2 (2016): 354.

[8] One example would be the Spanish Civil War, which mobilized the participation from radicals all over the globe. Lewis Mates, *The Spanish Civil War and the British Left: Political Activism and the Popular Front* (London: I.B. Tauris, 2007); Gerben Zaagsma, *Jewish Volunteers, the International Brigades and the Spanish Civil War* (London: Bloomsbury, 2017).

[s]ocial and cultural ideas, goods, policies, and practices moved between Europe and America, and individuals and institutions developed dense networks to share ideas and experiences and foster international cooperation. Education and social reform, urban development and poverty, the status of labor and the rights of women were central to these multiple "Atlantic crossings."[9]

While radical ideas were existent on both sides of the Atlantic and often stimulated each other, there were multiple and multidimensional connections among as well as striking differences between organized left movements, i.e., anarchism, socialism, communism etc., in Europe and the Americas around 1900. Working-class parties from both sides of the Atlantic eventually formed the Second International,[10] which provided a platform for workers and leftist parties to debate every issue from the mass strike, colonialism and national questions to the relationship of trade unions and labor parties. After 1890, *Vorwärts*, the SPD national newspaper, regularly printed letters from German workers in America, where their influence within the left movement and its organization was definitely felt.[11] Very often, European socialist leaders showed more interest in the United States than their American comrades did towards Europe, and leading European socialists, such as Edward Aveling (1849–1898),[12] Eleanor Marx (1855–1898),[13] Keir Hardie (1856–1915)[14] and Wilhelm Liebknecht (1826–1900),[15] as well as the aging Friedrich Engels (1820–1895),[16] visited the United States.

---

[9] Mary Nolan, *The Transatlantic Century: Europe and America, 1890–2010* (Cambridge: Cambridge University Press, 2012), 36.

[10] George D. H. Cole, *The Second International, 1889–1914*, 2 vols. (London: Macmillan 1956); James Joll, *The Second International, 1889–1914* (London: Routledge 1974).

[11] With regard to the U.S. anarchist movement, see Tom Goyens, *Beer and Revolution: The German Anarchist Movement in New York City, 1880–1914*, paperback ed. (Urbana: Illinois University Press, 2014).

[12] Edward Aveling and Eleanor Marx-Aveling, *The Working-Class Movement in America* (London: Swan Sonnenschein, Lowrey & Co., 1888).

[13] Edward Aveling and Eleanor Marx-Aveling, "Die Lage der Arbeiterklasse in Amerika," *Die neue Zeit* 6 (1887): 241–246 and 7 (1888): 307–313.

[14] Kenneth O. Morgan, *Keir Hardie: Radical and Socialist* (London: Weidenfeld & Nicolson, 1975).

[15] Liebknecht even thought about emigration to the United States, specifically Wisconsin. Wilhelm Liebknecht, *Erinnerungen eines Soldaten der Revolution* (Berlin: Dietz, 1976), 16 and 82, cited in Hartmut Keil, "German Working-Class Radicalism after the Civil War," in *The German–American Encounter: Conflict and Cooperation between Two Cultures, 1800–2000*, eds. Frank Tommler and Elliott Shore (Oxford: Berghahn Books, 2001), 46. Liebknecht describes his journey to the United States between September and November 1886 in Wilhelm Liebknecht, *Ein Blick in die neue Welt* (Stuttgart: J.H.W. Dietz, 1887).

[16] Engels, like Karl Marx (1818–1883), also had some interest in American developments, especially during the Civil War. Wolfgang Freund, "Das 'Größte, was jetzt in der Welt

Some of the founding fathers of American socialism, like Joseph Weydemeyer (1818–1866),[17] and anarchism, like Johann Most (1846–1906),[18] were transatlantic socialists in the strictest sense; Daniel de Leon (1852–1914), an important thinker and an advocate of revolutionary industrial unionism, to name another example, was born in the Caribbean, but went to school in Hildesheim, Germany, before starting his political work in the United States.[19] Victor L. Berger (1860–1929), a founding member of the American Socialist Party, came to the United States from a small town in Transylvania (then Austro-Hungary), and Morris Hillquit (1869–1933), a famous socialist and candidate for Mayor of New York City in 1917, was born in Riga.[20] Abraham Cahan (1860–1951), the Jewish-American socialist newspaper editor, was born near Vilna, Lithuania. This short list of foreign-born political radicals in the United States could, of course, be extended, but the point should be clear. Many of them gathered in radical hubs in North and South America. The city of Chicago, birthplace of the International May Day and also of the Industrial Workers of the World (IWW), was, next to New York City, the most cosmopolitan place of international socialism in the northern hemisphere outside of Paris.[21]

The transnational history of the nineteenth and twentieth centuries' political radicalism consequently provides a fruitful field of research for those who are interested in the role of networks and the individuals who move and are active within them.[22] With regard to transnational anarchism,

---

vorgeht': Marx und Engels über die Erste und die Zweite Amerikanische Revolution, die Unabhängigkeit und den Bürgerkrieg," in *Revolution: Beiträge zu einem historischen Phänomen der globalen Moderne*, eds. Frank Jacob and Riccardo Altieri (Berlin: WVB, 2019), 41–68.

[17] Karl Obermann, *Joseph Weydemeyer: Pioneer of American Socialism* (New York: International Publishers, 1947); Karl Obermann, "Weydemeyer in Amerika: Neues zur Biographie von Joseph Weydemeyer (1854–60)," *International Review of Social History* 25, no. 2 (1980): 176–208. It should be mentioned as a sidenote here that the biography of the left German historian Karl Obermann was a transatlantic one, too.

[18] Tom Goyens, "Johann Most and the German Anarchists," in *Radical Gotham: Anarchism in New York City from Schwab's Saloon to Occupy Wall Street*, ed. Tom Goyens (Urbana: Illinois University Press, 2017), 12–32.

[19] Stephen Coleman, *Daniel De Leon* (Manchester: Manchester University Press, 1990).

[20] Norma Fain Pratt, *Morris Hillquit: A Political History of an American Jewish Socialist* (Westport, CT: Greenwood Press, 1979). On the candidacy for Mayor of New York City, see Frederick C. Giffin, "Morris Hillquit and the War Issue in the New York Mayoralty Campaign of 1917," *International Social Science Review* 74, nos. 3–4 (1999): 115–128.

[21] These radical hubs had transnational impacts as well. One example, namely the revolutionary impact of the Paris Commune on American memory, is discussed in J. Michelle Coghlan, *Sensational Internationalism: The Paris Commune and the Remapping of American Memory in the Long Nineteenth Century* (Edinburgh: Edinburgh University Press, 2016).

[22] Constance Bantman and Bert Altena, "Introduction: Problematizing Scales of Analysis in Network-Based Social Movements," in *Reassessing the Transnational Turn: Scales of Analysis*

the British-French historian Constance Bantman, however, warns scholars not to be too simplistic in their evaluations and therefore careful not to overemphasize the transnational perspective when studying it:

> The years between 1880 and 1914 saw the emergence of anarchism as an organised political movement in Western Europe and the United States. From its very inception, anarchism was regarded as *essentially internationalist*, and … the temptation to disregard or downplay the international dimension of the late nineteenth century anarchist movement is understandably great. First, [there is] the fact that anarchism was usually the product of very *specific national and even local contexts* … There is also the fact that anarchism was sometimes connected with nationalism and xenophobia … Lastly, views of international anarchism … have inevitably been tainted by the *collapse of militant unity* at the outbreak of World War I.[23]

When highlighting the most well-known individuals of the transatlantic radical scene and their movement within existent networks of political radicalism and their organizations, the focus is "too often reduced"[24] and the danger is to use the famous case studies for an oversimplified generalization. While some kind of internationalism seems to be inevitable for the achievement of the necessary revolution,[25] many individual cases of transatlantic radicalism show that the foreign experiences were often not planned or undertaken voluntarily.[26]

Radical and often revolutionary ideas were, however, transported not only by individuals and their networks across the Atlantic but also as words, printed in the journals, newspapers, pamphlets and radical announcements that were widely circulated on both sides of the radicals' ocean. Sian Byrne and Lucien van der Walt have highlighted the impact of these publications and correctly remark that "a widely circulating press facilitated the exchange of ideas, struggle repertoires and key militants, which in turn linked and created international activist communities."[27]

---

in Anarchist and Syndicalist Studies, eds. Constance Bantman and Bert Altena (London: Routledge, 2014), 3.

[23] Constance Bantman, "Internationalism without an International? Cross-Channel Anarchist Networks, 1880–1914," *Revue belge de philologie et d'histoire* 84, no. 4 (2006): 961 (emphasis added).

[24] Ibid., 962.

[25] Ibid., 964.

[26] For some examples of such biographies, see Allan Antliff and Matthew S. Adams, "George Woodcock's Transatlantic Anarchism," *Anarchist Studies* 23, no. 1 (2015): 6–14 and Nadine Willems, "Transnational Anarchism, Japanese Revolutionary Connections, and the Personal Politics of Exile," *Historical Journal* 61, no. 3 (2018): 719–741.

[27] Sian Byrne and Lucien van der Walt, "Worlds of Western Anarchism and Syndicalism: Class Struggle, Transnationalism, Violence and Anti-Imperialism, 1870s–1940s," *Canadian*

Considering the above-mentioned role of German immigrants in the socialist movement in the United States, it is hardly surprising that the *Arbeiter-Zeitung* (*Workers' Daily*) "had become the flagship of revolutionary anarchism in Chicago,"[28] nor that anarchist papers like *El Productor* (*The Producer*) from Barcelona found many readers on the other side of the Atlantic in the Spanish-speaking countries of Latin America.[29] The immigrant communities might have been ideal environments for the cultivation of radical ideas, although radicalism was not always a foreign import but a consequence of the immigrant experience in the new national context,[30] and where important multipliers for transatlantic radicalism could also be found as well. While anarchism in Buenos Aires at the end of the nineteenth century was "exotic"[31] because it had been associated with immigrants from Spain and Italy,[32] it was soon to be reconfigured into something specifically Argentinian, although it had foreign roots.[33] When considering the role of individuals, acting within networks or transnational organizations, often living within exile communities abroad and reading press publications due to the possibilities for global distribution, it is important to define how one wants to study the transnational perspective, without simply reproducing the already known narratives of the "big names" of transatlantic radicalism.

Journal of History 50, no. 1 (2015): 99. A similar evaluation is provided in Pietro Di Paola, "Anarchism and Transnational Networks in North and South America," *Labour/Le Travail* 81 (2018): 247.

[28] Timothy Messer-Kruse, *The Haymarket Conspiracy: Transatlantic Anarchist Networks* (Urbana: University of Illinois Press, 2012), 1.

[29] Susana Sueiro Seoane, "Prensa y redes anarquistas transnacionales: El olvidado papel de J. C. Campos y sus crónicas sobre los mártires de Chicago en el anarquismo de lengua hispana," *Cuadernos de Historia Contemporánea* 36 (2014): 262.

[30] For a more detailed discussion of the radical identity within immigrant communities, see Frank Jacob, "Radical Trinity: Anarchist, Jew, or New Yorker?", in *Jewish Radicalisms: Historical Perspectives on a Phenomenon of Global Modernity*, eds. Frank Jacob and Sebastian Kunze (Berlin: De Gruyter Oldenbourg, 2019), 153–180.

[31] Martín Albornoz, "Policías, cónsules y anarquistas: la dimensión transatlántica de la lucha contra el anarquismo en Buenos Aires (1889–1913)," *Iberoamericana* 17, no. 64 (2017): 58.

[32] James A. Baer, *Anarchist Immigrants in Spain and Argentina* (Urbana: University of Illinois Press, 2015); María Migueláñez Martínez, "Diego Abad de Santillán (1897–1983): Los viajes doctrinarios de un anarquista trasnacional," in *Trayectorias trasatlánticas (siglo XX): Personajes y redes entre España y América*, ed. Manuel Pérez Ledesma (Madrid: Polifemo 2013), 163–219.

[33] Ángel J. Cappelletti, *Anarchism in Latin America*, trans. Gabriel Palmer-Fernández (Chico, CA: AK Press, 2017), 45–114.

Transnational Radicalism

The so-called "transnational turn in labour and migration studies," as historian Pietro Di Paola has pointed out, "produced stimulating developments in the history of the anarchist and radical movements in the North and South Americas and has raised a considerable number of methodological and epistemological challenges."[34] While the already-mentioned networks play an important role, recent works have also shown and "emphasized the role of native-born militants in the emergence and shaping of libertarian and radical movements in colonial and postcolonial countries."[35] It is not necessary to doubt the transnationalism of socialism or anarchism as such, which were organized or active in many different ways,[36] and that is why it is wrong to argue that "[a]narchism in the late 19th and early 20th century can only be understood if considered as a transnational network, where a small number of qualified anarchists played a liaison role among the various national movements in Europe and America."[37] Regardless of the fact that anarchism "emerged as an active political movement within the First International"[38] and thereby relied on a global self-image, as did many socialists, from the beginning, the initial rise of these political movements on both sides of the Atlantic was related to the logistical possibilities that were provided by the period of globalization between the 1880s and World War I, "a period characterized by massive international flows of labour and capital, a transportation and telecommunications revolution, and the rapid spread of industrialization."[39]

The transnationality of the political radicals and their lives, however, was not only achieved by the possibilities and the wish for internationalization. Very often, the transnational momentum was created by forced migration and state power intervention. When Italian anarchists were widely active within

---

[34] Di Paola, "Anarchism and Transnational Networks," 245.

[35] Ibid. Examples of such works would be Benedict Anderson, *Under Three Flags: Anarchism and the Anti-Colonial Imagination* (London: Verso, 2007); Steven Hirsch and Lucien van der Walt, eds., *Anarchism and Syndicalism in the Colonial and Postcolonial World, 1870–1940: The Praxis of National Liberation, Internationalism, and Social Revolution* (Leiden: Brill, 2010); Maia Ramnath, *Decolonizing Anarchism: An Antiauthoritarian History of India's Liberation Struggle* (Chico, CA: AK Press, 2011).

[36] José Moya, "Anarchism," in *The Palgrave Dictionary of Transnational History: From the mid-19th Century to the Present Day*, eds. Akira Iriye and Pierre-Yves Saunier (London: Palgrave Macmillan, 2009), 39–41.

[37] Sueiro Seoane, "Prensa y redes anarquistas transnacionales," 260.

[38] Constance Bantman, *The French Anarchists in London, 1880–1914: Exile and Transnationalism in the First Globalisation* (Liverpool: Liverpool University Press, 2013), 1.

[39] Byrne and van der Walt, "Worlds of Western Anarchism and Syndicalism," 99.

anarchist movements abroad[40] and German socialists were influential in the foundational period of the American Socialist Party, they were so because they had been forced to live abroad by political circumstances at home as well. In addition, one has to take into consideration which role forced exiles played in the ideological development of the radicals who involuntarily lived abroad but at the same time got in contact with intellectual input that was mostly inaccessible to their fellow radicals in their original environments.[41]

With regard to the transnational approach of political radicalism in general, and anarchism in particular, Constance Bantman and Bert Altena have provided a survey of the "diversity of genres and levels of analysis" for the study of radical transnationality or transnational radicalism:

> They include *national or regional studies* on areas where transnational forces are at play, largely in connection with migratory phenomena. ...
> Studies on *movements in transnational configurations* rather than specific locales: Italian anarchists may be the most striking case in this respect. ...
> Studies at the *urban level*, focusing on the depiction and analysis of anarchist metropolises, global cities, or "hubs," as they are increasingly often called...
> The *biographical genre* (and its variant, prosopographical studies), which continues to garner considerable interest, all the more as anarchism is a very individualized movement, with a principled lack of hierarchical organization.[42]

That said, studies of transnational radicalism in general, and the transatlantic left movements, organizations and individuals in particular, will have to deal with an overlap of these levels of analysis to provide an accurate insight into the factors that create, determine and impact on a radical

---

[40] Federico Ferretti, "Organisation and Formal Activism: Insights from the Anarchist Tradition," *International Journal of Sociology and Social Policy* 36, nos. 11/12 (2016): 730. For more details on Italian anarchist activities in London, see Pietro Di Paola, *The Knights Errant of Anarchy: London and the Italian Anarchist Diaspora (1880–1917)* (Liverpool: Liverpool University Press, 2013).

[41] Constance Bantman writes concerning Pouget's British experiences: "Pouget became truly interested in trade unions during his stay in Britain, thereafter becoming one of the leading exponents of anarcho-syndicalism; however, little attention has been paid to the detail of his years in exile and the subsequent progression of his international militant career. This has resulted in obscuring not only the international and transnational dimensions of Pouget's impact, but also interpretations of *fin-de-siècle* French anarchism in general." See Constance Bantman, "The Militant Go-between: Émile Pouget's Transnational Propaganda (1880–1914)," *Labour History Review* 74, no. 3 (2009): 274–287.

[42] Bantman and Altena, "Introduction," 3–4 (emphasis added). Davide Turcato even identified eight levels for such an analysis. Davide Turcato, "Italian Anarchism as a Transnational Movement, 1885–1915," *International Review of Social History* 52, no. 3 (2007): 407–444.

life, no matter which side of the Atlantic in the late nineteenth and the early twentieth centuries, or even beyond, is being considered. Since these radicals not only have an impact on their host societies but often re-import new ideas, their lives provide, to quote Bantman and Altena once more, "an early example of anti-hegemonic globalization/transnational advocacy networks."[43] Two factors seem especially important for this globalization process. One is radical mobility, be it voluntary or enforced, and the other is the ties, organizational or individual, that connect the radical representatives of different countries with each other.

Radical Mobilities and Transatlantic Ties

Many radicals, no matter if they were Marxists, socialists or anarchists, crossed the Atlantic because they had to. The so-called German Forty-Eighters were refugees who sought a new home after the failed revolution in 1848.[44] Similarly, many anarchists had to leave their home countries because they were forced to. For many who had encountered anarchist violence between the 1870s and 1930s, it was obvious, as Richard Jensen Bach highlights, "to claim that anarchism was the terrorism of the era."[45] The internationalism of the socialist and anarchist movements was consequently not only based on the voluntary wish to overcome nationalism, but also often on the necessity to escape state repression at home. That the radicals continued their work in their host countries is hardly surprising, especially since they were often entering an already existent sphere of radicalism, whether it was local and genuine, or foreign and adopted.[46] French scholar Isabelle Felici describes the exiles' perspective very accurately as follows:

> like all migrants, they [the radicals] experience a literal rite of passage (one of the stages of the migratory journey), taking cultural and linguistic baggage with them, which is shaped by additions and borrowings with every new movement. They use these previous experiences for the interactions to which their condition as migrants increasingly exposes them, both in

---

[43] Bantman and Altena, "Introduction," 5.

[44] Carl Wittke, *Refugees of Revolution: The German Forty-Eighters in America* (Philadelphia: University of Pennsylvania Press, 1952).

[45] Richard Bach Jensen, *The Battle against Anarchist Terrorism: An International History, 1878–1934* (Cambridge: Cambridge University Press, 2014), 1. On the Russian state's reactions towards terrorism, including anarchist violence, see Tim-Lorenz Wurr, *Terrorismus und Autokratie: Staatliche Reaktionen auf den Russischen Terrorismus, 1870–1890* (Paderborn: Ferdinand Schöningh, 2017).

[46] Isabelle Felici, "Anarchists as Emigrants," in Bantman and Altena, *Reassessing the Transnational Turn*, 83. For a more detailed discussion of such a radical milieu, its establishment and change, see Jacob, "Radical Trinity."

their homeland and in their host countries. Eventually, they will consider returning; this is another stage inherent in the migratory journey, whether it be a true return, a fantasized one that never occurs, or a metaphorical return, so to speak, insofar as the person who has travelled can never fully shed this "elsewhere" from which they hail.[47]

Within the multicultural radical hubs like San Francisco, where "more than 20 anarchist periodicals in eight different languages"[48] were published between 1890 and 1930, the radicals would not only encounter fellow anarchists or socialists they knew, but also had to overcome existent national preconditions, especially language, to get access to existent networks in their new environment. Kenyon Zimmer therefore accurately highlights that "the very diversity of this movement [*anarchism, but also socialism*, F. J.] resulted in the fragmentation of its history into virtual oblivion."[49] Within the foreign environment, "ideas, individuals, and resources ... radiated outward, traveling through well-worn grooves of radical networks or forging new linkages,"[50] often simply due to the necessity of exiled radicals to reconnect to a network they had been personally unfamiliar with in the past. There is much room left to study those who were not the figureheads of their movement, like Emma Goldman (1869–1940)[51] and Errico Malatesta (1853–1932), for international anarchism.

The internationalization of anarchism and socialism, however, was paralleled by a development related to the attempt of multiple states better to control the radicals and their networks. After the anarchist bombings in Paris in 1892,[52] and especially after the assassination of U.S. President William McKinley (1843–1901),[53] anti-anarchist violence and state actions increased.[54] President Theodore Roosevelt (1858–1919) even declared that

> Anarchy is a crime against the whole human race; and all mankind should band against the anarchist. His crime should be made an offense against

---

[47] Felici, "Anarchists as Emigrants," 84.

[48] Kenyon Zimmer, "A Golden Gate of Anarchy: Local and Transnational Dimensions of Anarchism in San Francisco, 1880s–1930s," in Bantman and Altena, *Reassessing the Transnational Turn*, 100.

[49] Ibid.

[50] Ibid.

[51] Emma Goldman's interpretation of anarchism and its relation to the Russian Revolution was also changed due to the experiences of a forced migration. See Frank Jacob, "From Aspiration to Frustration: Emma Goldman's Perception of the Russian Revolution," *Amercian Communist History* 17, no. 2 (2018): 185–199.

[52] Richard Bach Jensen, "The United States, International Policing and the War against Anarchist Terrorism, 1900–1914," *Terrorism and Political Violence* 13, no. 1 (2001): 16.

[53] Jensen, *The Battle against Anarchist Terrorism*, 237–258.

[54] Emma Goldman, *Living My Life* (New York: AMS Press 1970), 301 and 307.

the law of nations, like piracy and that form of manstealing known as the slave trade; for it is of far blacker infamy than either. It should be so declared by treaties among all civilized powers. Such treaties would give to the Federal Government the power of dealing with the crime.[55]

Eventually, multiple countries signed a protocol in St. Petersburg in 1904 that was supposed to prevent such crimes in the future.[56] However, the United States and Italy did not sign the protocol: "America's traditions of isolationism, its abhorrence of European entanglements and its antipathy for an increasingly overbearing Germany and despotic Russia dissuaded it from adhering to the St. Petersburg Protocol." Italy, in contrast, had a more practical reason, namely "the fear that, if it joined the anti-anarchist accord, thousands of Italian anarchists residing abroad might be expelled back to Italy, and Rome would have no legal means of preventing their unwelcome homecoming."[57]

Regardless of such state attempts to root out the transnational and thereby both the intra-European as well as transatlantic freedom of movement for radicals, they were not really successful. Although the U.S. (with active measures like the Palmer Raids[58]) and Italian governments tried to repress radicalism at the end of World War I, the networks still functioned: "In December 1919 Errico Malatesta returned to Italy from his exile in London. ... Malatesta soon launched a major anarchist daily in Milan, *Umanita Nova*, and ... followers in New England ... raised funds to buy a linotype machine for the paper."[59] The networks that could be used by radicals of all flags and colors were also used on both sides of the Atlantic, and all of them were connected to each other by the necessities of migration eventually.[60] It was the actual experience of the other side of the Atlantic that

[55] Congress, Senate, President Roosevelt's Message to the Senate and House of Representatives, 57th Cong., 1st sess., Congressional Record, vol. 35 (3 Dec. 1901), 82, cited in Jensen, "International Policing," 19.

[56] Ibid., 15.

[57] Ibid., 15–16.

[58] On the raids, named after U.S. Attorney General A. Mitchell Palmer (1872–1936), see the older but still recommended Robert K. Murray, *Red Scare: A Study in National Hysteria, 1919–1920* (Minneapolis: University of Minnesota Press, 1955). See also with a broader perspective on the American mind, David M. Kennedy, *Over Here: The First World War and American Society,* 25th anniversary edition (New York: Oxford University Press, 2004), 45–92.

[59] Philip V. Cannistraro, "Mussolini, Sacco-Vanzetti, and the Anarchists: The Transatlantic Context," *Journal of Modern History* 68, no. 1 (1996): 37.

[60] For the American networks, see Marcella Bencivenni, *Italian Immigrant Radical Culture: The Idealism of the Sovversivi in the United States, 1890–1940* (New York: New York University Press, 2011); Geoffroy de Laforcade and Kirwin Shaffer, eds., *In Defiance of Boundaries: Anarchism in Latin American History* (Gainesville: University Press of Florida,

cured many radicals of Eurocentric concepts about their own exclusiveness with regard to the movements to which they belonged.

To name one example, Werner Sombart (1863–1941), in his 1906 study *Why There is no Socialism in the United States*, emphasized the higher standard of living of American workers, concluding that "[a]ll socialist utopias came to nothing on roast beef and apple pie."[61] Even he saw a rising gap between the rich and the poor. At the same time, the Belgian socialist Émile Vandervelde (1866–1938) observed that American workers lived better than European ones. However, he may have neglected New York's sweatshops and the living conditions of the black sharecroppers in the south.[62] Others, like August Bebel (1840–1913) and Karl Kautsky (1854–1938), felt that it was American capitalist development, rather than its workers' movement, that put socialism on the political agenda. As Kautsky wrote:

> The United States are today unquestionably the most important and the most interesting of the modern culture lands. Not England, but America shows us our future, insofar as one country can reveal it at all to another, since each has its own peculiar development. In America, capitalism is making its greatest progress; it rules there more absolutely than anywhere else.[63]

Until 1914 and even during the interwar period, Europe still dominated what Mary Nolan called the transatlantic high culture. This included the political culture of the international left. Therefore, future studies need to de-centralize this image by further studying the actual ties and connections of transnational and transatlantic radicalism, especially on the individual level.

Americans often saw themselves as many Europeans saw their country, as a nation of business and materialism, not of art, music and architecture. Many European travelers to the United States, socialists and non-socialists alike, wanted to see the America of steel mills and assembly lines.

2015); Travis Tomchuk, *Transnational Radicals: Italian Anarchists in Canada and the U.S., 1915–1940* (Winnipeg: University of Manitoba Press, 2015); Kenyon Zimmer, *Immigrants against the State: Yiddish and Italian Anarchism in America* (Urbana: University of Illinois Press, 2015).

[61] Werner Sombart, *Warum gibt es in den Vereinigten Staaten keinen Sozialismus?* (Tübingen: Mohr, 1906), cited and discussed in Miquel Requena, "Socialism, Roast Beef, and Apple Pie. Werner Sombart on Socialism a Hundred Years Later," *Sociologica* 2–3 (2009): 1–16.

[62] Jacob A. Riis, *How the Other Half Lives: Studies among the Tenements of New York* (New York: Charles Scribner's Sons, 1890) provided an early description of poverty in New York City.

[63] Quoted in Laurence A. Moore, *European Socialists and the American Promised Land* (New York: Oxford University Press, 1970), 58–59.

They consequently visited Chicago's slaughterhouses and New York's skyscrapers.

Regardless of such shortsightedness on behalf of many European radicals, the U.S. experience, especially when forced upon them, demanded a reconsideration of such opinions. While many European radicals tended to ignore the emerging American high culture, including jazz, they were eventually intrigued by the modernity of everyday life and the possibilities the United States offered, maybe because the existence of radicalism there was partly accepted. Before he set foot on the American continent, Bertolt Brecht (1898–1956) included strong Anglo-Saxon elements in his work. As his translator John Willett wrote, America provided "unforgettable images for [Brecht's] poetic fantasy to work on."[64] Even though Brecht's stay in the United States between 1941 and 1947 proved to be one of the most difficult periods in his life, it also turned out to be one of his most prolific. The poetry, prose and dramas that he wrote in Hollywood and which were published or performed in post-war East Germany established his global fame. None of his film scripts made it onto the screen, however, with the one exception of *Hangmen Also Die*. However, the collaboration of three prominent refugees from Nazi Germany—Bertolt Brecht, Fritz Lang (1890–1976) and Hanns Eisler (1898–1962)—for this movie is an example of the influence this generation of German exiles had on American culture. There were also other enormous contributions by other anti-Nazi refugees and political radicals to American culture and scholarship during and after World War II; however, for reasons of space we cannot make even brief references to them here.

The Contributions

In 2014, Constance Bantman announced a transnational turn and new demands for the study of anarchism and syndicalism:

> After a decade-long golden age for the study of anarchist and syndicalist internationalism and transnationalism, the time for reassessment has arrived. Many of the semantic debates and caveats that have populated studies on transnationalism and other "trans-" or "cross-" approaches since the early 1990s' transnational turn in the social and historical sciences have highlighted or even hinged on the fact that the emphasis on successful connections, border crossings, cultural transfers, and unfettered movement often results in an inaccurate depiction of historical realities, insofar as it obliterates the importance of other scales of analysis, the

---

[64] John Willett's foreword to Patty Lee Parmalee, *Brecht's America* (Columbus: Ohio State University Press, 1981), x.

permanence of simultaneous and occasionally conflicting affiliations, and the bourgeois assumptions underpinning these approaches.[65]

The present volume tries to address the demands of Bantman's announcement for the study of transnational radicalism in the Atlantic world. It closely analyzes rather understudied ties between radicals in the European and American contexts and tries to highlight the problems individuals faced with regard to the genesis and use of existent networks or transnational organizations. The volume looks at socialists and anarchists alike and presents the results of the workshop "Transatlantic Socialists and Anarchists in the 19th and 20th Centuries: Between New Freedom and Forced Integration" held in Würzburg, Germany on 30 June and 1 July 2017.[66]

The first section deals with organizational ties between party organizations and radical press networks connecting Europe and the Americas, and shows how individuals used their existence to follow their own political agenda, and how exactly press networks and organizations created interactions between the radical worlds they connected. The press networks especially had been steadily providing an extensive and transnational web through which not only information and ideas were exchanged by radicals on both sides of the Atlantic. The press-related exchange also created close personal ties and friendships that in a way allowed the radicals—whether in forced exile abroad or just interested in the news and events of another national context—to get involved in "politics from a distance."[67] In Chapter 2, Lutz Häfner highlights the interrelationship between Russian Socialist Revolutionary terrorism, the Transatlantic Public sphere and American capital. He therefore also focuses on a fundraising trip to the United States by one of the most famous Russian revolutionaries of the early period: Ekaterina Konstantinovna Breshko-Breshkovskaya (1844–1934). This chapter therefore shows how individuals could cross the Atlantic to

---

[65] Constance Bantman, "The Dangerous Liaisons of Belle Epoque Anarchists: Internationalism, Transnationalism, and Nationalism in the French Anarchist Movement (1880–1914)," in Bantman and Altena, *Reassessing the Transnational Turn*, 174.

[66] The obvious gender imbalance of the present volume was not intended by the editors. However, since neither the open call for a workshop in Würzburg, Germany, in 2017 nor the further recruitment attempts for the volume could solve this problem, the editors eventually decided to publish this volume in its current form. We nevertheless wish to emphasize that there are many female colleagues working in the field of anarchist studies and the history of the international labor movement as well, whose important and often extraordinary works deserve to be acknowledged and which are, of course, cited in the separate chapters.

[67] Constance Bantman and Ana Cláudia Suriani da Silva, eds., *The Foreign Political Press in Nineteenth-Century London: Politics from a Distance* (London: Bloomsbury, 2017). For an exemplary discussion of the radical Italian press in the United States, see Bencivenni, *Italian Immigrant Radical Culture*, 67–98.

use existent radical networks not only to arouse attention for their own cause but also to gain financial support for it. How anarchists from Italy were involved in the formation of early working-class organizations in São Paulo is then discussed by Carlo Romani and Bruno Corrêa de Sá e Benevides in Chapter 3. They show why the early history of the Brazilian labor movement must be considered a transnational one and demonstrate the role that leftist immigrants played in this. They then go on to examine the extent to which their radicalism changed in exchanges with the local radicals or created something new. In the fourth chapter, James Michael Yeoman discusses the networks between the Spanish anarchist press and the Panama Canal Zone. His analysis shows that a loose transatlantic network existed, but that personal and ideological disputes were responsible for its fragmentation once the Panama Canal had been finished. Yeoman therefore provides a close reading for a radical "hub" that only existed for a limited time span. The other chapter in this section, by Hillary Lazar, analyzes the internationalism of the anarchist journal *Man! A Journal of the Anarchist Ideal and Movement* by showing how the publication connected radical immigrant groups in the United States.

The second section takes a closer look at the role of individuals as representatives of a radical transnationalism that linked both sides of the Atlantic. The chapters in this section consequently continue the attempt to combine biographical studies with a historical analysis of the international labor movement.[68] It was the connections and cooperative attempts by individuals, who physically or ideally surpassed the limitations of their own national contexts, whether it was forced or voluntary, who eventually laid the foundations for the internationalism of the labor movement. Consequently, an approach that considers such individuals, especially from a rather "second- or third-row"-oriented perspective, will offer new insights into the establishment of transatlantic radical networks. In Chapter 6, Steven Parfitt highlights the role of Terence Powderly (1849–1924), linking it to transatlantic radicalism in general and the global history of the Knights of Labor during the 1880s and 1890s in particular. The chapter consequently looks at the impact of Powderly's work and his role as a global leader of the workers' movement. Afterward, Frank Jacob looks at the roles of individuals and idealists in the creation of the Kuzbas Autonomous Industrial Colony in the early 1920s. Despite not being supported by or officially connected to any radical organization in the United States, a committee was founded to recruit American workers to work in the mines of Kemerovo in Soviet Russia. The chapter shows how this quest was shaped by the individualism

---

[68] See, for example, Neville Kirk, *Transnational Radicalism and the Connected Lives of Tom Mann and Robert Samuel Ross* (Liverpool: Liverpool University Press, 2017).

of a few, before failing due to the political realities in Moscow and the hardships of the climate in Siberia.

The exile of European communists during World War II and the effect of this experience on their own radicalism as well as their connections with new American networks of radicalism are discussed by Georg Leidenberger, Riccardo Altieri and Mario Keßler. While Leidenberger takes a closer look at the exile experience of the architect and communist Hannes Meyer and his family in Mexico during the 1940s, Altieri discusses the New York years of the German communists Rosi Wolfstein (1888–1987) and Paul Frölich (1884–1953). The German exiles lived in the United States but kept in touch with their European friends, knowing that World War II would end and hoping for a return to their own national radical environment. Altieri therefore shows that the exile of radicals did not necessarily lead to a reconnection with foreign radical networks. The final chapter, by Mario Keßler, highlights how the radical life of the leftist political scientist and futurologist Ossip K. Flechtheim (1909–1998) was determined by his experience of exile in the United States and the ideas the radical confronted during these years that would have a permanent impact on him.

Works Cited

Albornoz, Martín. "Policías, cónsules y anarquistas: la dimensión transatlántica de la lucha contra el anarquismo en Buenos Aires (1889–1913)." *Iberoamericana* 17, no. 64 (2017): 57–79.

Anderson, Benedict. *Under Three Flags: Anarchism and the Anti-Colonial Imagination.* London: Verso, 2007.

Antliff, Allan and Matthew S. Adams. "George Woodcock's Transatlantic Anarchism." *Anarchist Studies* 23, no. 1 (2015): 6–14.

Aveling, Edward and Eleanor Marx-Aveling. "Die Lage der Arbeiterklasse in Amerika." *Die neue Zeit* 6 (1887): 241–246 and 7 (1888): 307–313.

——. *The Working-Class Movement in America.* London: Swan Sonnenschein, Lowrey & Co., 1888.

Baer, James A. *Anarchist Immigrants in Spain and Argentina.* Urbana: University of Illinois Press, 2015.

Bantman, Constance. "The Dangerous Liaisons of Belle Epoque Anarchists: Internationalism, Transnationalism, and Nationalism in the French Anarchist Movement (1880–1914)." In *Reassessing the Transnational Turn: Scales of Analysis in Anarchist and Syndicalist Studies,* eds. Constance Bantman and Bert Altena, 174–192. London: Routledge, 2014.

——. *The French Anarchists in London, 1880–1914: Exile and Transnationalism in the First Globalisation.* Liverpool: Liverpool University Press, 2013.

——. "Internationalism without an International? Cross-Channel Anarchist Networks, 1880–1914." *Revue belge de philologie et d'histoire* 84, no. 4 (2006): 961–981.

——. "The Militant Go-between: Émile Pouget's Transnational Propaganda (1880–1914)." *Labour History Review* 74, no. 3 (2009): 274–287. http://epubs. surrey.ac.uk/534406/. unpag. Accessed Sept. 15, 2019.

Bantman, Constance and Bert Altena. "Introduction: Problematizing Scales of Analysis in Network-Based Social Movements." In *Reassessing the Transnational Turn: Scales of Analysis in Anarchist and Syndicalist Studies*, eds. Constance Bantman and Bert Altena, 3–22. London: Routledge, 2014.

Bantman, Constance and Ana Cláudia Suriani da Silva, eds. *The Foreign Political Press in Nineteenth-Century London: Politics from a Distance*. London: Bloomsbury, 2017.

Bencivenni, Marcella. *Italian Immigrant Radical Culture: The Idealism of the Sovversivi in the United States, 1890–1940*. New York: New York University Press, 2011.

Byrne, Sian and Lucien van der Walt. "Worlds of Western Anarchism and Syndicalism: Class Struggle, Transnationalism, Violence and Anti-imperialism, 1870s–1940s." *Canadian Journal of History* 50, no. 1 (2015): 98–123.

Cannistraro, Philip V. "Mussolini, Sacco-Vanzetti, and the Anarchists: The Transatlantic Context." *Journal of Modern History* 68, no. 1 (1996): 31–62.

Cappelletti, Ángel J. *Anarchism in Latin America*, trans. Gabriel Palmer-Fernández. Chico, CA: AK Press, 2017.

Coghlan, J. Michelle. *Sensational Internationalism: The Paris Commune and the Remapping of American Memory in the Long Nineteenth Century*. Edinburgh: Edinburgh University Press, 2016.

Cole, George D. H. *The Second International, 1889–1914*, 2 vols. London: Macmillan, 1956.

Coleman, Stephen. *Daniel De Leon*. Manchester: Manchester University Press, 1990.

Di Paola, Pietro. "Anarchism and Transnational Networks in North and South America." *Labour/Le Travail* 81 (2018): 245–264.

——. *The Knights Errant of Anarchy: London and the Italian Anarchist Diaspora (1880–1917)*. Liverpool: Liverpool University Press, 2013.

Fain Pratt, Norma. *Morris Hillquit: A Political History of an American Jewish Socialist*. Westport, CT: Greenwood Press, 1979.

Felici, Isabelle. "Anarchists as Emigrants." In *Reassessing the Transnational Turn: Scales of Analysis in Anarchist and Syndicalist Studies*, eds. Constance Bantman and Bert Altena, 83–99. London: Routledge, 2014.

Ferretti, Federico. "Organisation and Formal Activism: Insights from the Anarchist Tradition." *International Journal of Sociology and Social Policy* 36, nos. 11/12 (2016): 726–740.

Freund, Wolfgang. "Das 'Größte, was jetzt in der Welt vorgeht': Marx und Engels über die Erste und die Zweite Amerikanische Revolution, die Unabhängigkeit und den Bürgerkrieg." In *Revolution: Beiträge zu einem historischen Phänomen der globalen Moderne*, eds. Frank Jacob and Riccardo Altieri, 41–68. Berlin: WVB, 2019.

Giffin, Frederick C. "Morris Hillquit and the War Issue in the New York Mayoralty Campaign of 1917." *International Social Science Review* 74, nos. 3–4 (1999): 115–128.

Goldman, Emma. *Living My Life.* New York: AMS Press 1970.

Goyens, Tom. *Beer and Revolution: The German Anarchist Movement in New York City, 1880–1914.* Urbana: University of Illinois Press, 2014.

———. "Johann Most and the German Anarchists." In *Radical Gotham: Anarchism in New York City from Schwab's Saloon to Occupy Wall Street*, ed. Tom Goyens, 12–32. Urbana: Illinois University Press, 2017.

Hirsch, Steven and Lucien van der Walt, eds. *Anarchism and Syndicalism in the Colonial and Postcolonial World, 1870–1940: The Praxis of National Liberation, Internationalism, and Social Revolution.* Leiden: Brill, 2010.

Jacob, Frank. "From Aspiration to Frustration: Emma Goldman's Perception of the Russian Revolution." *American Communist History* 17, no. 2 (2018): 185–199.

———. "Radical Trinity: Anarchist, Jew, or New Yorker?" In *Jewish Radicalisms: Historical Perspectives on a Phenomenon of Global Modernity*, eds. Frank Jacob and Sebastian Kunze, 153–180. Berlin: De Gruyter Oldenbourg, 2019.

Jacob, Frank and Helmut Reinalter, eds. *Masonic Lodges and Their Impact in North and South America.* Würzburg: Königshausen & Neumann, 2019.

Jensen, Richard Bach. *The Battle against Anarchist Terrorism: An International History, 1878–1934.* Cambridge: Cambridge University Press, 2014.

———. "The United States, International Policing and the War against Anarchist Terrorism, 1900–1914." *Terrorism and Political Violence* 13, no. 1 (2001): 15–46.

Joll, James. *The Second International, 1889–1914.* London: Routledge 1974.

Kaller, Martina and Frank Jacob, eds. *Transatlantic Trade and Global Cultural Transfers since 1492: More than Commodities.* London: Routledge, 2019.

Keil, Hartmut. "German Working-Class Radicalism after the Civil War." In *The German–American Encounter: Conflict and Cooperation between Two Cultures, 1800–2000*, eds. Frank Tommler and Elliott Shore, 37–48. Oxford: Berghahn Books, 2001.

Kennedy, David M. *Over Here: The First World War and American Society*, 25th anniversary edition. New York: Oxford University Press, 2004.

Kirk, Neville. *Transnational Radicalism and the Connected Lives of Tom Mann and Robert Samuel Ross.* Liverpool: Liverpool University Press, 2017.

Laforcade, Geoffroy de and Kirwin Shaffer, eds. *In Defiance of Boundaries: Anarchism in Latin American History.* Gainesville: University Press of Florida, 2015.

Lässig, Simone and Swen Steinberg. "Knowledge on the Move: New Approaches toward a History of Migrant Knowledge." *Geschichte und Gesellschaft* 43, no. 3 (2017): 313–346.

Liebknecht, Wilhelm. *Ein Blick in die neue Welt.* Stuttgart: J.H.W. Dietz, 1887.

———. *Erinnerungen eines Soldaten der Revolution.* Berlin: Dietz, 1976.

Mates, Lewis. *The Spanish Civil War and the British Left: Political Activism and the Popular Front.* London: I.B. Tauris, 2007.

———. "Syndicalism and the 'Transnational Turn.'" *Capital & Class* 40, no. 2 (2016): 344–354.

Messer-Kruse, Timothy. *The Haymarket Conspiracy: Transatlantic Anarchist Networks.* Urbana: University of Illinois Press, 2012.

Migueláñez Martínez, María. "Diego Abad de Santillán (1897–1983): Los viajes doctrinarios de un anarquista trasnacional." In *Trayectorias trasatlánticas (siglo xx): Personajes y redes entre España y América*, ed. Manuel Pérez Ledesma, 163–219. Madrid: Polifemo 2013.

Moore, Laurence A. *European Socialists and the American Promised Land.* New York: Oxford University Press, 1970.

Morgan, Kenneth O. *Keir Hardie: Radical and Socialist.* London: Weidenfeld & Nicolson, 1975.

Moya, José. "Anarchism." In *The Palgrave Dictionary of Transnational History: From the mid-19th Century to the Present Day*, eds. Akira Iriye and Pierre-Yves Saunier, 39–41. London: Palgrave Macmillan, 2009.

Murray, Robert K. *Red Scare: A Study in National Hysteria, 1919–1920.* Minneapolis: University of Minnesota Press, 1955.

Nolan, Mary. *The Transatlantic Century: Europe and America, 1890–2010.* Cambridge: Cambridge University Press, 2012.

Obermann, Karl. *Joseph Weydemeyer: Pioneer of American Socialism.* New York: International Publishers, 1947.

———. "Weydemeyer in Amerika: Neues zur Biographie von Joseph Weydemeyer (1854–60)." *International Review of Social History* 25, no. 2 (1980): 176–208.

Oldfield, John R. *Transatlantic Abolitionism in the Age of Revolution: An International History of Anti-Slavery, c.1787–1820.* New York: Cambridge University Press, 2013.

Parmalee, Patty Lee. *Brecht's America.* Columbus: Ohio State University Press, 1981.

Ramnath, Maia. *Decolonizing Anarchism: An Antiauthoritarian History of India's Liberation Struggle.* Chico, CA: AK Press, 2011.

Requena, Miquel. "Socialism, Roast Beef, and Apple Pie: Werner Sombart on Socialism a Hundred Years Later." *Sociologica* 2–3 (2009): 1–16. www.rivisteweb.it/download/article/10.2383/31375. Accessed May 15, 2019.

Riis, Jacob A. *How the Other Half Lives: Studies among the Tenements of New York.* New York: Charles Scribner's Sons, 1890.

Scammell, Geoffrey V. "After Da Gama: Europe and Asia since 1498." *Modern Asian Studies* 34, no. 3 (2000): 513–543.

Sombart, Werner. *Warum gibt es in den Vereinigten Staaten keinen Sozialismus?* Tübingen: Mohr, 1906.

Stoenescu, Richard. "Syndikalismus in Deutschland und den USA, 1897–1937." Ph.D. thesis, University of Potsdam, 2020.

Sueiro Seoane, Susana. "Prensa y redes anarquistas transnacionales: El olvidado papel de J. C. Campos y sus crónicas sobre los mártires de Chicago en el anarquismo de lengua hispana." *Cuadernos de Historia Contemporánea* 36 (2014): 259–295.

Tomchuk, Travis. *Transnational Radicals: Italian Anarchists in Canada and the U.S., 1915–1940.* Winnipeg: University of Manitoba Press, 2015.

Turcato, Davide. "Italian Anarchism as a Transnational Movement, 1885–1915." *International Review of Social History* 52, no. 3 (2007): 407–444.

van der Linden, Marcel. *Workers of the World: Essays Toward a Global Labor History.* Leiden: Brill, 2011.

Willems, Nadine. "Transnational Anarchism, Japanese Revolutionary Connections, and the Personal Politics of Exile." *Historical Journal* 61, no. 3 (2018): 719–741.

Wittke, Carl. *Refugees of Revolution: The German Forty-Eighters in America.* Philadelphia: University of Pennsylvania Press, 1952.

Wurr, Tim-Lorenz. *Terrorismus und Autokratie: Staatliche Reaktionen auf den Russischen Terrorismus, 1870–1890.* Paderborn: Ferdinand Schöningh, 2017.

Zaagsma, Gerben. *Jewish Volunteers, the International Brigades and the Spanish Civil War.* London: Bloomsbury, 2017.

Zimmer, Kenyon. "A Golden Gate of Anarchy: Local and Transnational Dimensions of Anarchism in San Francisco, 1880s–1930s." In *Reassessing the Transnational Turn: Scales of Analysis in Anarchist and Syndicalist Studies*, eds. Constance Bantman and Bert Altena, 100–117. London: Routledge, 2014.

——. *Immigrants against the State: Yiddish and Italian Anarchism in America.* Urbana: University of Illinois Press, 2015.

I

Organizational Ties
and Radical Press Networks

2

An Entangled World at the Beginning of the Twentieth Century

Russian Socialist Revolutionary Terrorism, Transatlantic Public Sphere and American Capital

Lutz Häfner

In mid-August of 1904, the *New York Times* published an appeal of the Central Committee of the Russian Socialist Revolutionary Party (the SRs) to the "Citizens of the Civilized World." The appeal avowed full responsibility "before history and the conscience of the civilized peoples" for the assassination of Minister of the Interior Viacheslav Konstantinovich Pleve (1846–1904). The deed was characterized as a "bloody act of justice."

> The execution of the public man in whom were incarnated all the abominations and all the horrors of Czarism has caused public opinion of the civilized world, despite its habitual and conventional reticence, to utter the cry of relief of a conscience at last set free. … And now we address this appeal to the citizens of the civilized world, and we say to them: To you falls the task of propagating in the free countries the true notion of the meaning of the duel which is being fought between autocracy and modern Russia. This duel will end only with the disappearance of one of the adversaries, and that will be Czarism, vanquished by the revolution, by the Russian nation, free at last. … More than anybody, we reprove … terrorist tactics in the free countries, but in Russia, where despotism precludes the possibility of an open political struggle, where there is no recourse against the irresponsibility of absolute power in all degrees of the omnipotent bureaucracy, we shall be obliged to oppose to the violence of tyranny the strength of revolutionary right.[1]

---

[1] "Take Responsibility of de Plehve Killing; Russian Revolutionary Socialists Issue Address to 'Civilized World,'" *New York Times*, Aug. 14, 1904, 4. The SRs reiterated their disapproval of terrorism as a means of politics in democratic states. Cf. *Boevyia predpriiatiia sotsialistov-revoliutsionerov v osveshchenii okhranki* (Moscow: Revoliutsionnyi sotsializm, 1918), 5; "Tragic Experiences of Two Russian Women Nihilists," *Washington Times*, Dec. 4, 1904, Magazine Features, 4.

This special letter claims responsibility for the assassination of Pleve. It highlighted three aspects of the SRs' communicative strategies: first, they addressed the "civilized world" to discredit the Tsarist system as inhumane, corrupt, defunct and rotten; second, they aimed to inform the Transatlantic Public about their democratic outlook; and third, they sought to recruit a solid support base among the international liberal society in order to acquire logistic and financial aid for their political endeavors.

The concept of the Transatlantic Public provides the analytical frame to explore the communicative strategies of the Russian SRs. It can be understood as a transnational normative authority that serves as an intermediary agency of the European public and its transnational communication structures. Historically speaking, it has functioned as an addressee of appeals of marginalized social players—especially of less developed countries of the Eastern European periphery—who lacked participatory rights or political power in their own states. Appealing to the Transatlantic Public, these players got access to an important forum of international bargaining, which might compensate for their weakness on a national scale.[2] On the one hand, the Transatlantic Public is created by events,[3] and is therefore ephemeral and fragile, but, on the other hand, the public is able to generate events via their medial imparting.[4]

Using asymmetric counter concepts in their appeals to the Transatlantic Public, the SRs aimed to win the moral and in the best case even financial support of European societies for their struggle for democracy against atavistic and arbitrary Russian Tsarism. The SRs' appeals to the international public can be seen as a means to influence societal conditions at home. The "interested Transatlantic Public" constituted an important factor in international relations. Concerning Russian socialist revolutionary terrorism at the beginning of the twentieth century, one considers there to be a very solid international support base such as via the international worker's movement, the socialist parties and trade unions of each country, as well as the Socialist International. It was further enhanced by the financial, logistic and journalistic support of liberal circles in Tsarist Russia and in many European countries, as well as in the United States.

---

[2] Jörg Requate and Martin Schulze-Wessel, "Europäische Öffentlichkeit: Realität und Imagination einer appellativen Instanz," in *Europäische Öffentlichkeit: Transnationale Kommunikation seit dem 18. Jahrhundert*, eds. Jörg Requate and Martin Schulze-Wessel (Frankfurt am Main: Campus, 2002), 13–14.

[3] Ibid., 17, 22.

[4] Carola Dietze, "Von Kornblumen, Heringen und Drohbriefen: Ereignis und Medienereignis am Beispiel der Attentate auf Wilhelm I.," in *Medienereignisse der Moderne*, eds. Friedrich Lenger and Ansgar Nünning (Darmstadt: Wissenschaftliche Buchgesellschaft, 2008), 40.

The present chapter is organized into four sections: the first defines terror and terrorism in late Tsarist Russia. The second section deals with the causes of terrorism, while the third is devoted to institutional aspects of the Transatlantic Public and its reactions to terrorist acts. Methodologically, I focus very briefly on five terrorist acts against high level Russian bureaucrats: the Minister of Enlightenment Nikolai Pavlovich Bogolepov (1846–1901) in 1901, the Minister of the Interior Dmitriĭ Sergeevich Sipiagin (1853–1902) in 1902, the Governor-General of Finland Nikolai Ivanovich Bobrikov (1839–1904) and the Minister of the Interior Viacheslav Konstantinovich Pleve in summer 1904, and finally the Moscow Governor-General and uncle of the Last Tsar Grand Duke Sergei Aleksandrovich (1857–1905) in February of 1905. Four of these assassinations were committed by members of the "Fighting Organization" [*Boevaia organizatsiia*] of the Socialist Revolutionary Party, while one—against Bobrikov—was individually executed by a Finnish civil servant who had no organizational affiliation of any kind but acted solely on his own convictions. I use this sample, which covers a period of five years and leads well into the turmoil of the First Russian Revolution, as a foil to analyze the waxing international media coverage, the interactions of Socialist Revolutionary terrorists with its solid support base in the ranks of international liberal society and, last but not least, the changes of societal perceptions of legitimate and illegitimate violence in Transatlantic Public opinion.

To illustrate this international entanglement of terrorism and the public sphere in more detail, I will finally deal with a case study: the fundraising trip of Ekaterina Konstantinovna Breshko-Breshkovskaya (1844–1934) to the United States, which lasted from October of 1904 to mid-March of 1905. She was a member of the Central Committee of the Party of Socialist Revolutionaries and well known as an "apostle of terrorism." However, she became the beloved darling of the U.S. public and the North American civil society that did not hesitate to subsidize Russian political terrorism.[5]

The contemporary U.S. media echo of Breshkovskaya's trip and lectures was wide-ranging and included not only articles of the well-inclined socialist[6] and women's movement's journals[7] but also of the leading major dailies of cities like New York, Philadelphia,[8] Boston, Chicago,[9] Cleveland,

---

[5] "Terrorists Hope to Win with Bombs: Believe Russian Public Opinion Will Not Condemn Them," *San Francisco Call*, Feb. 18, 1905, 2.

[6] See e.g. *The Comrade, The Labor World, Social-Democratic Herald.*

[7] See e.g. *The Woman's Journal.*

[8] See e.g. Chaim Leib Weinberg, *Forty Years in Struggle: The Memories of a Jewish Anarchist,* trans. Naomi Cohen, ed. Robert P. Helms (Duluth, MN: Litwin Books, 2001), 65–66. Breshkovskaya lectured in Philadelphia thrice: at the end of November, Christmas 1904 and at the beginning of March 1905.

[9] Breshkovskaya stayed as a guest of Jane Addams at Hull House in Chicago for a

St. Louis[10] and Washington. Even the press in provincial backwaters occasionally reported on Breshkovskaya's trip to the United States.[11] A biography of Breshkovskaya had already been published before the end of her stay in America.[12] Moreover, she wrote a few articles for American printed media: *The Chicago Daily Tribune, The Independent* and the socialist journal *The Comrade*.[13] Well-known emigrants such as the leading anarchist Emma Goldman—who participated in the plot of Alexander Berkman to kill the steel baron Henry Clay Frick in Pittsburgh in summer 1892[14]—introduced Breshkovskaya to leading American liberals[15] and important American members of the women's movement and of the Society of Friends of Russian Freedom, both being venues of influential intellectuals and politicians.[16] One may assume that the Society of Friends of Russian Freedom served as Breshkovskaya's quartermaster and was thus responsible for this highly successful

----

month. However, she complained that the inhabitants of this city showed less interest in the Russian Revolution than, for example, those in New York. Cf. "Mme. Breshkovsky Goes East: Is Disappointed With Interest Shown by Chicagoans in the Cause of the Russian People," *Chicago Daily Tribune*, Feb. 13, 1905, 2.

[10] On Feb. 11, 1905, Breshkovskaya headed for St. Louis for a few days and then for Cleveland. Cf. "Mrs. Katherine Breshkovskaya," *Woman's Journal* 36, no. 5 (Feb. 4, 1905): 17; "Assassination is Pleasing to Mme. Breshkovsky," *St. Louis Republic*, Feb. 18, 1905, 5.

[11] See e.g. "Chat about Women," *Omaha Daily Bee*, Dec. 4, 1904, 6.

[12] Ernest Poole, "Katharine Bereshkovsky [*sic*]: A Russian Revolutionist," *Outlook* 79 (Jan. 17, 1905): 78–88; Ernest Poole, *Katharine Breshkovsky: For Russia's Freedom* (Chicago: Charles H. Kerr & Co., 1905).

[13] Kathrine Breshkovsky, "Believes Revolution Will End in Romanoff's Expulsion from Russia," *Chicago Daily Tribune*, Jan. 24, 1905, 3; Catherine Breschkovsky, "The Internal Condition of Russia: Catherine Breschkovsky in *New York Independent*," *Comrade* 4, no. 2 (1905): 34–36.

[14] Steven Cassedy, *To the Other Shore: The Russian Jewish Intellectuals Who Came to America* (Princeton, N.J.: Princeton University Press, 1997), 120.

[15] Emma Goldman, *Gelebtes Leben* (Berlin: Karin Kramer, 1979), ii. 418. See Jane E. Good and David R. Jones, *Babushka: The Life of the Russian Revolutionary Ekaterina K. Breshko-Breshkovskaya (1844–1934)* (Newtonville, MA: Oriental Research Partners 1991), 81.

[16] Among the members of this Society were Indiana Republican William Dudley Foulke (1848–1935), journalists and writers like William Dean Howells (1837–1920) or George Kennan the Elder (1845–1924), the suffragettes Julia Ward Howe (1819–1910) and Alice Stone Blackwell. During Breshkovskaya's U.S. trip several branches were founded in different cities. See International Institute of Social History, Amsterdam, Partija Socialistov-Revoljucionerov Archives, Folder 696: Letters received by Breškovskaja after her visit to the USA, of which two from A. Stone Blackwell. 1905: [1–33], [26]; "Russian Freedom Society: Monster Meeting in Cooper Union," *Daily Morning Journal and Courier*, Nov. 23, 1904, 8; "Start Russian Aid Society: Chicago People Take Action After Hearing Mme. Breshkovsky Speak at Mrs. Coonley Ward's," *Chicago Daily Tribune*, Jan. 25, 1905, 2; David S. Foglesong, *The American Mission and the "Evil Empire": The Crusade for a "Free Russia" since 1881* (New York: Cambridge University Press, 2007), 19–20, 40.

socialist revolutionary propaganda venture.[17] In this way, Breshkovskaya got acquainted with U.S. businessmen, civic leaders and intellectuals.[18]

Terror and Terrorism in Late Imperial Russia

Typologically, we can distinguish three terrorist types in Russia, the first being anti-autocratic revolutionary terrorism. The second type it is necessary to focus on is "a form of state terror directed against its own citizens" such as the punitive expeditions of Tsarist military forces in order to suppress peasant and ethnic disobedience or martial law courts, operating to suppress revolution from summer 1906 to spring 1907.[19] With these sometimes illegitimate measures, the confidence of society in their government was affected. Finally, one has to focus on the violence within the society of the Old Regime like the pogroms and assassinations of ideological opponents, which were often committed by monarchists. Terror was thus a ubiquitous phenomenon afflicting both the government and society. This typology shows that the negation of an existing political order cannot be an integral part of a definition of terror/ism since it would not include right-wing political violence. Therefore, terrorism is understood as a teleological phenomenon. It has at its disposal a political program that is executed by means of symbolic acts by individuals or groups. These persons consciously infringe prevailing legal and moral conventions with a minimum of personal and material sources in order to achieve maximum political effect. The purpose of terrorism is to disorganize and destabilize the ruling system, to intimidate and to produce a state of panic within the higher echelons of the bureaucracy.

Communication is an important factor in terrorism. Terrorists seem compelled not only to explain but also to justify their actions in special letters claiming responsibility. These two aspects can be seen as a strategy of communication, as an appeal for sympathy, with the aim to impress an audience and "to create a public image of virtuous sincerity."[20] In Russia, terrorism cannot be discussed when disconnected from the political environment.

Imperial Russia was no "police state."[21] However, it was no *Rechtsstaat* either. The autocracy suppressed almost every public expression of moderate

---

[17] See Jane E. Good, "America and the Revolutionary Movement, 1888–1905," *Russian Review* 41, no. 2 (1982): 283.

[18] Tony Michels, *A Fire in Their Hearts: Yiddish Socialists in New York* (Cambridge, MA: Harvard University Press, 2005), 125.

[19] Abraham Ascher, *The Revolution of 1905*, vol. 1, *Russia in Disarray* (Stanford, CA: Hoover Institution Press, 1988), 330.

[20] Martha Crenshaw, "The Causes of Terrorism," *Comparative Politics* 13 (1981): 395–396.

[21] *Hamburger Fremdenblatt*, July 30, 1904, 1; "Rußland," *Vossische Zeitung*, Aug. 5, 1904, 9; Richard Pipes, *Russia under the Old Regime* (New York: Charles Scribner's Sons, 1974), 305.

liberal opinion all over the Empire. It dismissed all suggestions of concession or compromise forwarded by the educated society and the organs of self-administration and ruled out any opportunity for their political participation on a national scale. In late Imperial Russia there was no outlet, and no resource. Moreover, there was no law or justice that could not have been overridden at its pleasure by the administrative order.

Those who turned into revolutionaries in the 1860s and 1870s terrified officialdom. In order to stop the revolutionary peril, the rights of police and gendarmes were enlarged. Because of the law of 4 June 1874, the latter were even allowed to detain arrested persons under investigation for membership of secret societies for an unlimited period of time, since the law did not mention any specific term.[22] Moreover, because of an unpublished imperial act of 1 September 1878, any person of dubitable "political reliability" could be administratively exiled. Between 1881 and 1904, more than 11,870 people were subjected to this kind of exile.[23]

The emergency legislation was a terrifying weapon, especially in the hands of local administrators. It gave them a wide scope for settling personal scores and for revenge. It was the source of complete arbitrariness and lawlessness. The main defect of the emergency legislation was that the freedom and inviolability of the individual were entrusted to minor police officials.[24] The restrictions imposed on the Russian people were severe and even hampered the rights proclaimed in the manifesto of 17 October 1905 from coming into force. Because of the emergency, fundamental civil rights such as personal inviolability and the freedom of conscience, speech, assembly and association thus only existed on paper. Moreover, the newly granted Russian parliament, the State Duma, did not even have full-fledged budgetary rights. The contemporary German sociologist Max Weber (1864–1920) coined this setting "sham constitutionalism" [*Scheinkonstitutionalismus*].[25]

A formula that has been falsely attributed to the German poet and author Bertolt Brecht (1898–1956) aptly fits the conclusion contemporaries had drawn to overcome the political impasse between the *ancien régime* and society: "Where justice turns into injustice, resistance turns into a [moral] obligation."[26] This quote explains terrorism in Tsarist Russia. The suppression of any critics by the Tsarist State led the opposition to its single alternative: in Marx's terminology,

[22] Jonathan W. Daly, "On the Significance of Emergency Legislation in Late Imperial Russia," *Slavic Review* 54, no. 3 (1995): 606.

[23] Ibid., 606, 615.

[24] P. Kalinin, "Po povodu usilennoi okhrany," *Pravo* 48 (Nov. 11, 1904): 3304–3305.

[25] Max Weber, *Zur Russischen Revolution von 1905: Schriften und Reden, 1905–1912*, eds. Wolfgang J. Mommsen and Dittmar Dahlmann (Tübingen: J. C. B. Mohr, 1996), 102–103.

[26] See e.g. https://de.wikiquote.org/wiki/Diskussion:Bertolt_Brecht#%22Wo_Unrecht_zu_Recht_wird,_wird_Widerstand_zur_Pflicht.%22.

it turned from the weapon of critique to the critique of the weapon. It was the tyranny and oppression with which the Russian Government tried to suppress society's dissenting views and aspirations, leading to "repeated outbursts of indignation in other countries, especially the United States."[27] Because the *ancien régime* denied any expression of dissent, terrorism was without an alternative. Furthermore, terrorism could be considered as legitimate whereas the autocracy, because their actions were intolerably unjust, forfeited its own legitimacy. The end excused the terrorist means.

Terrorism and Russian Public Opinion

The division of labor between the Socialist Revolutionaries and the liberal society was a very important feature of the Russian *liberation movement* [*Osvoboditel'noe dvizhenie*]. Whereas the Socialist Revolutionaries functioned as practitioners of terrorist acts, the liberals among the educated classes solicited funds and thus financed the execution of terrorism, and with their articles published in their widespread and influential periodicals—such as the Moscow-based daily *Russkiia Vedomosti*, the prestigious weekly law journal *Pravo* and, from 1905, *Nasha zhizn'* and the like—had a deep impact in shaping public opinion to accept revolutionary violence as a justified response to an arbitrary, illegitimate and oppressive autocratic regime. Not only were moral considerations dismissed as irrelevant, but terrorism was accepted as a justifiable instrument and a legitimate political means of societal self-defense versus a despotic state, which granted neither civil rights nor a *Rechtsstaat*, nor parliamentary participation. The positions of prominent figures of the liberal camp such as the opponent of any terrorist violence like the important *zemstvo*-delegate Dmitrii Ivanovich Shakhovskoi (1861–1939), who uttered "Pleve has to be killed," or Ariadna Vladimirovna Tyrkova-Williams (1869–1962),[28] who wrote in her diary in February 1905 that the Tsar should be killed to prevent him from throttling Russia,[29] indicate the societal acceptance of terrorism as a weapon of the weak.[30]

The French diplomat and, during World War I, ambassador to Russia, Maurice Paléologue (1859–1944), remembered the conversation he had with ten members of the high society of the city of Moscow, "a sound mixture of

---

[27] "Terrorists of Unhappy Russia," *Bemidji Daily Pioneer*, Sept. 27, 1906, 4.

[28] In 1906, A. V. Tyrkova married Harold Williams (1876–1928), a British Slavist from New Zealand, who was working as a journalist in Saint Petersburg for the conservative London-based daily *Morning Post*.

[29] Ariadna Tyrkova-Vil'iams, *Na putiakh k svobode* (Moscow: Moskovskaia shkola politicheskikh issledovanii, 2007), 161, 170.

[30] Crenshaw, "Causes," 387; Laura Engelstein, "Weapon of the Weak (Apologies to James Scott): Violence in Russian History," *Kritika* 4, no. 3 (2003): 679–693.

liberal and conservative elements in their outlook," right after the assassination of the Grand Duke Sergei Aleksandrovich in February 1905:

> I was struck by the indifference, not to say complacency, shown in their comments on the Moscow drama. In the interests of decency they denounced the "hateful wickedness of the terrorists," but, under their breath, they admitted that, all things considered, the Grand Duke Sergei had deserved his fate. They thought it only natural that, in a state of society in which the government rules with the rifle, the opposition should reply with the bomb.[31]

Of Paléologue's interlocutors, no one was fully committed to the Old Regime. All of them were waiting for a political change for the better. The nucleus of the quote is best understood as a mirror of the public opinion of the Russian and international press, hinting at the missing quality of the *Rechtsstaat* in Tsarist Russia and a government that seemed to be dealing illegitimately with its own population. Who sows the wind of state terrorism must reap the terrorist whirlwind of the SRs.[32] The Berlin-based correspondent of *The Times* keenly commentated: "The Russian Nihilists are not Anarchists, but merely relatively moderate Republicans longing for a Constitution."[33] What seems to be a totally confused blend of different political outlooks is actually close to the truth: the Socialist Revolutionaries, as well as the moderates that cooperated in the Russian liberation movement, strived for both a constitution and a constituent assembly. Whereas the former were inclined to do the violent and bloody work to throttle Tsarism, the latter radicalized more and more, as can be seen in the articles published in their joint journal *Osvobozhdenie*, which was printed in the German city of Stuttgart. As a consequence of the intransigence, arbitrariness, unlawfulness and "terror" of the Tsarist State, the liberals did accept obstruction and strikes as political means but initially dismissed insurrection and terror. The latter means, however, became totally accepted after a process that lasted several months, including raids by peasants on noble estates. This was a liberal tribute to socialist coalition partners as a consequence of an adamant State and the radicalization of society. One caveat should be made, however: the liberals did more or less clandestinely accept societal terror but never committed to terrorist acts on their own.[34]

---

[31] Maurice Paléologue, *Three Critical Years: 1904–05–06* (New York: Robert Speller, 1957), 171.

[32] See "Gerichtet! Das Attentat gegen den russischen Polizeiminister von Plehwe," *Vorwärts*, July 29, 1904, 1.

[33] *The Times*, July 30, 1904, 3.

[34] *Osvobozhdenie*, no. 1 (June 18, 1902): 5; *Osvobozhdenie*, no. 7 (Sept. 18, 1902): 104; *Osvobozhdenie*, no. 13 (Dec. 19, 1902): 202, 207; *Osvobozhdenie*, no. 52 (July 19, 1904): 33–35.

One could argue, as John Keep did in a very thoughtful and intriguing article, that revolutionary terrorism executed by the Party of the Socialist Revolutionaries lost its *raison d'être* with the concessions of the *ancien régime* in mid-October, i.e., the October Manifesto.[35] With this important historical divide, the political constellation in Russia decisively changed. In the "days of freedom," right after the October Manifesto, all political parties could now operate openly. It is true, however, that the situation had already deteriorated after a few weeks. Nevertheless, the Socialist Revolutionaries opted for the suspension of any terrorist act because of the elections and the convocation of the State Duma. Two important members of the party's Fighting Organization, Evno F. Azef and Boris V. Savinkov, thought that terrorism was now superfluous. They even intended to disband the Fighting Organization because the Party now had other successful means of agitation and propaganda at its disposal to influence the masses.[36] This never took place. Quite the opposite happened: in 1906, terrorism became more and more ubiquitous and indistinguishable from common criminal acts. Thus, the terrorists lost their support they had initially enjoyed among the progressive educated society and the liberally inclined public.

Russian Terrorism and International Public Opinion

Initially, the international public did not pay much attention to terrorist activities that took place in the early twentieth century. For example, we can find only a few lines on the Bogolepov murder, published only on one day and mostly in the form of agency reports.

As a rule, the media coverage of the assassination of Sipiagin was broader, but not very thorough. The articles on the assassinations in most cases appeared on the inner pages.[37] A new quality was reached, however, after the European public had been sensitized through a whole series of terrorist acts from 1901 to

---

See Lutz Häfner, "'Die historischen Tage des 6.-8. November haben wie die Veče-Glocke die russische Gesellschaft aufgerüttelt': Zemcy und intelligenty als liberale Akteure der Russischen Revolution von 1905," in *Russland 1905: Perspektiven auf die erste Russische Revolution*, eds. Ludwig Steindorff and Martin Aust (Frankfurt am Main: Peter Lang, 2007), 78.

[35] John L. H. Keep, "Terror in 1905," in *Reinterpreting Revolutionary Russia: Essays in Honour of James D. White*, ed. Ian D. Thatcher (London: Palgrave Macmillan, 2006), 21.

[36] Viktor Mikhailovich Chernov, "Iz istorii Partii S.-R. Pokazaniia V. M. Chernova po delu Azefa v sledstvennoi komissii Partii S.-R. 2 fevr. 1910 g.," *Novyi Zhurnal* 101 (1970), 173–174.

[37] "L'attentat de Saint-Pétersbourg: conspiration nihiliste," *L'Ouest-Éclair*, Mar. 12, 1901, 1 informed on the front page; "Killed by a Student: M Sipiaguine, Russian Minister of the Interior, Shot So Badly He Died an Hour After," *Boston Globe*, Apr. 16, 1902, 14.

1904. The terrorist assaults in 1904 and 1905, to a lesser degree on Bobrikov but more noticeably on Pleve and Grand Duke Sergei Aleksandrovich, altered the whole situation fundamentally. More and more newspapers featured their articles prominently, with an eye-catching layout and big, spreading headlines with incredible details such as "Blown" or "Torn to Atoms" and "Bodies in the Debris,"[38] photographs,[39] clichés and sometimes even maps,[40] which allowed the reader to trace the last minutes of the life of the prominent victims. The media coverage of the latter assassinations was intense, continued on several pages,[41] lasted for a couple of days and was probably caused by the highly critical situation of Imperial Russia, not only because of waxing workers' and peasants' movements and the existence of the Russian liberation movement but also because of the Russo-Japanese war. Russia appeared on the pages of newspapers all over Europe and the United States every day. Against the background of economic and financial entanglement between Russia and the Great Powers, the public of these countries was interested in both the military and internal affairs of the Empire.

However, the Transatlantic Public was not homogeneous. Until the 1890s, it was not only conservatives who feared leftist ideologies and especially anarchist assassinations.[42] They tended therefore to sympathize with Tsarist Russia. In the following decade, as a consequence of diplomatic rivalry in world politics, some deeply rooted prejudices of a democratic state versus the autocratic system, and more recent aspects of interior politics (such as the relentless suppression of liberty in all forms, the brutal and uncivilized treatment of the Jews, especially the pogrom at Kishinev in 1903, and the domestic regime of Russification inaugurated in Finland) Russophobia in the United States became widespread.[43] The Russian Minister of the Interior was accused of direct responsibility for the horrors of Kishinev.[44]

[38] "Blown to Atoms," "Bodies in the Debris," *Washington Times*, July 28, 1904, 1; "Torn to Atoms," *Los Angeles Herald*, Feb. 18, 1905, 1.

[39] "Assassin Kills Czar's Minister: M. Sipiaguine Shot by Kieff Student Inside Palace in Russian Capital," *Chicago Daily Tribune*, Apr. 16, 1902, 3; *New-York Daily Tribune*, July 29, 1904, 1; "Plehve Assassinated by Explosion of Bomb," *Washington Times*, July 29, 1904, 1; *Los Angeles Herald*, Feb. 18, 1905, 2.

[40] "Map of the Kremlin and Environments," *Chicago Daily Tribune*, Feb. 18, 1905, 3; "Sergius' Route to Fatal Spot," *Washington Times*, Feb. 18, 1905, 1.

[41] "Sudden and Terrible: Death Came to Sergius as It Came to Von Plehve—Assassin Was Wounded—Captured but Defiant," *Boston Globe*, Feb. 18, 1905, 1, 7.

[42] Frederick F. Travis, *George Kennan and the American–Russian Relationships, 1865–1924* (Athens: Ohio University Press, 1990), 222.

[43] "Fiery Speeches from Peace Delegates at Cooper Union," *New-York Daily Tribune*, Oct. 14, 1904, 4; see Foglesong, *Mission*, 7–11, 28–31; Good, "America," 280.

[44] "Deplored in Washington: Fear Had Long Been Felt in Washington for de Pleve," *New York Times*, July 29, 1904, 2.

The sympathy for those who struggled to democratize autocratic Russia was widespread after George Kennan (1845–1924) and others wrote about the horrifying details of the Siberian exile system or hair-raising crimes committed by the Russian police, the secret police or other Tsarist officials against innocent people. In this respect, workers' associations such as the Society of Friends of Russian Freedom tried "to arouse public opinion throughout America in favour of representative government in Russia" as well as to ease the needs and sufferings of the people there.[45]

The Times had already portrayed the murder of Bobrikov as a "terrible crime … which must cause horror throughout the civilized world."[46] The paper, however, was not inclined to accept Russian politics in Finland. It characterized the Governor-General "as the symbol and chief instrument of Russian oppression" and as "the incarnation of Russian tyranny." Especially in the Finnish case, the oppressed people, who were neither socialists nor anarchists but had only love for free institutions, tried to fight versus a military dictator and his politics of enforced Russification.[47] *The Times* shared the almost unanimous opinion of quite a lot of European newspapers that "murder is always hateful" and "immoral." It added, however, a point of view very similar to the above-quoted slogan by Bertolt Brecht: "But history confirms … that, when oppression, whether in private life or in the domain of politics, reaches a certain degree of intensity, murder is but too likely to be the remedy of the oppressed."[48] In the same vein, the socio-politically active Prussian historian and influential editor of the *Preußische Jahrbücher*, Hans Delbrück, argued the following: "When despotism assumes absolutely intolerable forms, or a system of violence becomes so terrible as to violate all the laws of humanity … murder appears to be the last resource for the salvation, or at least the vengeance of mankind."[49] The essence of Delbrück's argument referred to a monograph published by Professor Theodor Lipps, chair of systematic philosophy at the University of Munich, in 1899. Lipps emphasized a morally legitimate right of self-defense, justified in itself by natural law.[50]

[45] Columbia University, New York, Butler Library, Lillian D. Wald Collection, Box 93: Russia II, Folder Friends of Russian Freedom, pamphlet "Society of the Friends of Russian Freedom," *Aims and Methods* (New York 1907), 1; "$15 for Russian Freedom," *The Sun*, Feb. 6, 1905, 3. See Ron Grant, "The Society of Friends of Russian Freedom (1890–1917): A Case Study in Internationalism," *Journal of the Scottish Labour History Society* 3, no. 3 (1970): 3–24.

[46] *The Times*, June 17, 1904, 9.

[47] *The Times*, June 18, 1904, 7.

[48] *The Times*, June 17, 1904, 9.

[49] D. [Hans Delbrück], "Politische Korrespondenz: Der Königsberger Prozeß wegen Hochverrats gegen den Zaren. Der Krieg, Die Zukunft Rußlands," *Preußische Jahrbücher* 117, no. 1 (July–Sept. 1904): 376.

[50] Theodor Lipps, *Die ethischen Grundfragen: Zehn Vorträge* (Hamburg: Voß, 1899), 239.

"Murder as a political weapon is universally condemned by civilized men."[51] What seems to be an eternal truth was refuted in many newspapers. They did not include any note of blame or horror, but rather a registration of the murder as an event regarded as startling in itself, but not such as to arouse feelings of execration or even pity. Some papers discounted the assassination as inevitable, while others expressed wonder that violent death had not reached Pleve earlier. *The Sun* (New York) wrote: "It is no paradox to say that the murder of … Plehve is a salutary crime."[52] The newspapers quite often mentioned the excitement and even jubilation in Russian émigré circles in Geneva, Paris, Boston and New York on hearing the news of Pleve's murder.[53] Thus, indifference or even approval were on the agenda, while at the same time the Tsarist regime was considered savage, pitiless and adamantine. The former U.S. ambassador to Germany, Andrew D. White (1832–1918), who knew Pleve well, having met him frequently in the course of his official business in St. Petersburg from 1892 to 1894, explained that Pleve's internal politics were "atrocious, reactionary and despotic."[54]

It is obvious that international public opinion, except for the French, tended to excuse Russian terrorism. The public took terrorism as a mirror image of Tsarist tyranny. As the saying goes, "Russian Tsarism was tempered by assassination."[55] Therefore, *The Times* seemed to accept terrorism against Russian bureaucrats as a legitimate and most effective means of political protest. The liberal *New York Times* went a step further. It drew a classical comparison and praised the murderer of Bobrikov as a modern Brutus. Although the American public disapproved of political assassinations in general, it equally could not approve of despotic cruelties that provoked them and it showed no pity for the victim.[56] The argumentation of the international press showed these assassinations as a consequence of the denial of the freedom of speech and civil rights.[57] Brutal internal Tsarist politics created a state of lawlessness, leaving the people with only one way to deal

---

[51] *The Times*, July 29, 1904, 7.

[52] *The Sun*, July 29, 1904, 2.

[53] "Boston Was Excited," *Boston Daily Globe*, July 29, 1904, 2; "Jubilation in Geneva," *Boston Daily Globe*, July 30, 1904, 2 and "Assassin Glorified: Mass Meeting of United Russian Revolutionists at the Cooper Union in New York," *Boston Daily Globe*, July 30, 1904, 10; *Boston Daily Globe*, Feb. 19, 1905, 2. See also *Berliner Tageblatt*, July 29, 1904, 2; *Münchner Neueste Nachrichten*, July 30, 1904, 1; *Vossische Zeitung*, July 29, 1904, 1.

[54] *New York Times*, July 29, 1904, 2.

[55] "Destiny and Assassination," *Morning Astorian*, Sept. 4, 1904, 4; *The Times*, July 29, 1904, 3; "The Killing of Plehve," *New York Times*, July 29, 1904, 6.

[56] *The Times*, June 20, 1904, 6. Cf. *The Times*, June 18, 1904, 7.

[57] "Destiny and Assassination," *Morning Astorian*, Sept. 4, 1904, 4.

with the situation and to act in self-defense: "The remedy is violent, but it is the only one."[58]

Except for most of the French papers, European public opinion concurred on the subject of Russian terrorism. The international press depicted the situation in the country before summer 1906 as a unique case. In Tsarist Russia, terrorist acts were regrettably necessary in the people's struggle for justice and democratization. The killing of a cruel and arbitrary representative of a despotic and corrupt regime seemed to be acceptable because it was held that they deserved their fate. Their death was regarded not only as retaliation to brutal repression by the State but as a moral act, as the vengeance of a highly ethical, heroic person who displayed self-devotion and did not hesitate to sacrifice their own life for the sake of the well-being of the people. These deeds were even more justified because in most cases there was no "collateral damage," i.e., no persons suffered but the depicted victim. Political violence was evidently acceptable and considered as a legitimate means under certain circumstances in Russia: the *New York Times* characterized it as the "one effective method of political agitation or of political criticism which the Russian form of government leaves open" to the people.[59]

"Russia's Most Famous Woman Now in America: Katherine Breshkovsky [...]"

Breshkovskaya's lecture tour lasted about half a year. She came to the United States in October 1904 and was detained for some time upon her arrival at Ellis Island. She left the country one day after having a Russian *vecherinka* and a huge banquet with more than 200 participants organized by the United League of New York Revolutionists on 17 March 1905.[60] Her tour through major cities on the U.S. East Coast and on the shores of the Lakes in 1904/1905 became important events in her personal revolutionary career promoting the SR Party, as well as in the Russian revolutionary movement itself. Her presentations strongly impacted on American public opinion concerning Russian internal affairs. Breshkovskaya strove to acquire moral and financial aid and the sympathy of American society to back

---

[58] *The Times*, June 21, 1904, 5, citing the letter of Schauman published in the Swedish newspaper *Aftenbladet*.

[59] "The Killing of Plehve," *New York Times*, July 29, 1904, 6.

[60] On Mar. 2, 1905, she was in New York City and wrote to her friend Feliks Vladimirovich Volkhovskiĭ that she would return to Europe soon. Cf. Stanford University, California, Hoover Institution Archives, Felix Vladimirovich Volkhovskiĭ Papers, Box 1, Folder 9: Breshko-Breshkovskaia, Ekaterina Konstantinovna, 1904–1905, letter of Mar. 2, 1905; "Mrs. Breshkovskaya's Farewell," *Woman's Journal* 36, no. 11 (Mar. 11, 1905): 41; "Mme. Breshkowsky Dined," *The Sun*, Mar. 18, 1905, 5.

up the efforts of the Russian socialists "to throw off the yoke of Tsarist tyranny."[61] Even almost thirty years later, Alexander Kerensky highlighted the importance of this event in his obituary of Breshkovskaya: "She carried out a great campaign in the United States for the Russian movement of liberation."[62] Perhaps the most important overarching task of Breshkovskaya in the United States was—as the party's leading theorist Viktor Mikhailovich Chernov bluntly admitted—to win over the very influential and compassionate Jewish public sphere [*evreiskoi obshchestvennosti*] of the United States.[63]

It is hardly surprising that a socialist journal lavishly praised Breshkovskaya, running with the title "Russia's Most Famous Woman Now in America: Katherine Breshkovsky, 'The Little Grandmother' of the Russian Peasantry. Comes to America to Create Public Opinion and Raise Funds for Liberty."[64] However, this ardor was no matter of political outlook as the following quote of a provincial paper shows: "At 61, still heart and soul afire with zeal for the revolutionary cause in Russia."[65] It is quite obvious that the U.S. newspapers were anything but neutral in their reporting of Russian affairs in general and of the U.S. trip of Breshkovskaya in particular as the above-given quotations emphasize. The opposite was closer to the truth. U.S. papers adored Breshkovskaya right from the beginning. Although being portrayed as a heroine, a "Russian Joan of Arc,"[66] and the embodiment of the Russian revolutionary movement,[67] the reporting of this socialist VIP

---

[61] "Russkoe dvizhenie v Amerike," *Revoliutsionnaia Rossiia* 62 (Mar. 25, 1905): 15; "To Uplift Peasantry: Mme. Breshkovskaya Tells Twentieth Century Club Members of Her Struggle in Russia," *Boston Daily Globe*, Dec. 18, 1904, 13; "Send Sympathy to Slav Masses: Chicago People in Massmeeting Adopt Resolutions," *Chicago Daily Tribune*, Jan. 30, 1905, 2; "Sympathy For Russian People," *Providence Journal*, Feb. 23, 1905, unpag. Expressions such as "Tsarist" or "Russian tyranny" were widely used by members of the Society of Friends of Russian Freedom. See "For Freedom: Meeting in Behalf of Russian People. Mme. Breshkoosky [*sic*] Says the Outlook is Bright," *Boston Daily Globe*, Dec. 15, 1904, 11; "Mme. Kathrine Breshkovsky," *Free Press*, Feb. 4, 1905, 4; "Mme. Kathrine Breshkovsky," *Chickasha Daily Express*, Feb. 11, 1905, 6.

[62] Alexander Kerensky, "Catherine Breshkovsky (1844–1934)," *Slavonic and Eastern European Review* 13 (1934–1935), 428.

[63] Viktor Mikhailovich Chernov, *Pered bureĭ* (New York: Izd-vo im. Chekhova, 1953), 204.

[64] "Russia's Most Famous Woman Now in America: Katherine Breshkovsky, 'The Little Grandmother' of the Russian Peasantry. Comes to America to Create Public Opinion and Raise Funds for Liberty," *The Labor World: Devoted to the Industrial Welfare of the Head of the Lakes*, no. 41 (Feb. 11, 1905), 3. See "For Freedom: Meeting in Behalf of Russian People," 11.

[65] Katherine Pope, "What Has Been Going On Recently," *Virginia Enterprise*, Feb. 17, 1905, 6.

[66] Ibid.

[67] Poole, *Katharine Breshkovsky*, 3.

was intimate: the *New York Sun* portrayed her face as "sweet."[68] The *New York Times* went into more detail:

> There was nothing about the appearance or demeanor of Mme. Catharina Breshkovskaya to indicate a character so dangerous as to compel the Czar's Government to keep her imprisoned or exiled for more than twenty-two years. Nor did she have the looks of one accustomed to brave the indescribable hardships of Siberian winters. The reporter who found her in a small east side flat saw before him a white-haired and mild-eyed woman, broad of face and body ... but with intelligent and pleasantly smiling features.[69]

It was with these words that the *New York Times* portrayed one of the staunchest apostles of terrorism[70] in the period of late Tsarist Russia. In a letter from the beginning of March 1905, Breshkovskaya expressed her delight that more and more Americans "gravitate towards socialism and terror is no longer a mortal sin but as a matter of fact to be excused depending on the circumstances."[71] Taking the public opinion—expressed in the U.S. newspapers in 1904/1905—concerning the assassinations of Pleve or Grand Duke Sergei Aleksandrovich into consideration, one could easily accept Breshkovskaya's conclusion. This process, however, did not consolidate itself. This consent completely faded away after the Tsar proclaimed the October manifesto in 1905 that guaranteed civil rights. Thus, the autocracy seemed to be on the way to a constitutional monarchy.

Breshkovskaya's task was to inform the U.S. public about the abuses of Tsarist officials, to justify Russian socialist (revolutionaries') methods and to appeal to the civilized world for support.[72] As it turned out, she was

---

[68] "A Woman's Exile in Siberia," *The Sun*, Dec. 25, 1904, sect. 3, 1.

[69] "Woman, Long an Exile, to Talk on Russia: Mme. Breshkovskaya to Lecture Here To-morrow Night," *New York Times*, Dec. 21, 1904, 8. For similar characterization by the journalists Ernest Poole and Kellogg Durland, see Ernest Poole, *The Bridge: My Own Story* (New York: Macmillan, 1940), 112; Margaret Maxwell, *Narodniki Women: Russian Women Who Sacrificed Themselves for the Dream of Freedom* (Elmsford, N.Y.: Pergamon Press, 1990), 147.

[70] Breshkovskaya touched upon terrorism in some of her speeches. See "Socialist Queen Is in New York: 'Grandma' Breshkovsky, Who Has Spent Twenty-two Years in Siberian Mines, Arrives Here from Russia," *Evening World*, Nov. 11, 1904, evening edition, 3; "Babushka Arrives Here: Noted Woman Socialist. Russian Says Defeat Will Be the Best for Her Country," *New-York Daily Tribune*, Nov. 12, 1904, 2; "Assassination is Pleasing to Mme. Breshkovsky," *St. Louis Republic*, Feb. 18, 1905, 5.

[71] Hoover Institution Archives, Felix Vladimirovich Volkhovskiĭ Papers, Box 1, Folder 9: Breshko-Breshkovskaia, Ekaterina Konstantinovna, letter of Mar. 2, 1905.

[72] "Babushka Arrives Here: Noted Woman Socialist," 2; "A Woman's Exile in Siberia"; "Suffered for the People: Mme. Breshkovsky, Russian Patriot, Who Was a Siberian Exile," *The Caucasian*, Feb. 26, 1905, 6; *Ocala Evening Star*, Mar. 17, 1905, 4.

perfectly suited for her mission, which she accomplished brilliantly. She had an outstanding record of serving the people for many years. For that she was imprisoned, exiled to Siberia and sentenced to penal servitude in the Kara Mines in 1876. It was during her exile that she was interviewed by the American journalist George Kennan. His account—published in the *Century Magazine* in the United States—made Breshkovskaya an internationally known socialist celebrity and a legend among radical Russian and Jewish emigrants.[73] She even tried to escape from her Siberian exile but failed.[74] After serving her sentence of more than twenty years she was released in 1896.[75] She returned to European Russia being called "babushka" [grandmother]—now much revered as a heroine and martyr of the people's cause.[76] During her stay in the United States, Breshkovskaya gratefully admitted that although Kennan had not been able to open her prison doors, he had helped her to win "the sympathy of the world."[77]

Breshkovskaya's versatility was one of her most characteristic traits. On the one hand, one has to praise her ability to speak passionately to great audiences: at her very first presentation at Cooper Union in New York City on 12 November, she started quite nervously. After a little while, she got a grip of herself, grabbed the audience and literally ripped them out of their seats.[78] There, as well as at the West Side Auditorium in Chicago and at Faneuil Hall in Boston, she attracted audiences of more than 3,000 people.[79]

[73] George Kennan, "Prison Life of the Russian Revolutionists," *Century Magazine* 35 (Dec. 1887): 285–297; George Kennan, "Siberia and the Exile System: Across the Russian Frontier," *Century Magazine* 36 (May 1888): 3–23; George Kennan, "A Ride Through the Trans-Baikal," *Century Magazine* 37 (May 1889): 76–78; George Kennan, *Siberia and the Exile System* (New York, 1891); George Kennan, "A Voice for the People of Russia," *Century Magazine* 41 (July 1893): 461–472; Lillian D. Wald, *The House on Henry Street* (New York, 1915), 238–239; Michels, *Fire*, 125.

[74] Kennan, "A Ride," 76.

[75] "A Russian Agitator: Mme. Breshkovskaya to Speak at Cooper Union To-night—Her Career," *New-York Daily Tribune*, Dec. 22, 1904, 5; "A Woman's Exile in Siberia"; "Aids Peasants. Mme Breshkoosky [*sic*] to Bostonians," *Boston Daily Globe*, Dec. 14, 1904, 11.

[76] See Maxwell, *Narodniki*, 140.

[77] "America a Fairy Tale," *Woman's Journal* 36, no. 11 (Mar. 18, 1905): 41.

[78] Goldman, *Leben*, ii. 420; "Russkoe dvizhenie v Amerike," 22.

[79] "Russian Freedom Society: Monster Meeting in Cooper Union," *Daily Morning Journal and Courier*, Nov. 23, 1904, 8; "Mrs. Katherine Breshkovskaya," *Woman's Journal* 36, no. 5 (Feb. 4, 1905): 17; Pope, "What Has Been Going On Recently," 6; "Welcome to a Russian Woman," *Woman's Journal* 35, no. 51 (Dec. 17, 1904): 401; Good and Jones, *Babushka*, 85–86. Two thousand listeners were present according to "Chicago Russians Show Sympathy: Cheer Mme. Breshkovsky and Give Liberally to Cause of Freedom," *Chicago Daily Tribune*, Jan. 23, 1905, 5; "Russkoe dvizhenie v Amerike," 18, 21. Good and Jones (*Babushka*, 87) claim that more than 6,000 people attended the lecture at West Side Auditorium.

Her speech evoked storms of enthusiasm and standing ovations lasting for several minutes.[80] These scenes recurred in other places such as Pennsylvania Hall in Philadelphia, where she was carried around on the shoulders of some strong listeners.[81] On the other hand, and this was even more important, she performed well in a wide array of different sociable forums: at public receptions with dances[82] as well as at informal meetings of the civil society, i.e., in clubs and associations[83] or private receptions at the houses of rich women belonging to the local society.[84] She was humble, cordial and able to thrill all audiences as an exceptionally gifted storyteller of her past life.[85] Lydia Ward Howe (1819–1910) recalled in a private letter: "She was splendid at both meetings [*i.e., at great assemblages and at private meetings*, L.H.]. We all love her dearly."[86]

The perfect timing of Breshkovskaya's journey is another clue to explain the enthusiasm of the U.S. public that she aroused. Previously, two other left-liberal actors had prepared the ground for Breshkovskaya's success. The old *narodnik* Nikolai Vasil'evich Chaikovskii (1851–1926) lectured in the United States in 1875 and at the beginning of 1904 and the important liberal and future leader of the Constitutional Democratic Party, the Kadets, Pavel Nikolaevich Miliukov (1859–1943), spoke almost simultaneously with her in Chicago and Boston. Both parties, the SRs and future Kadets, belonged to the *Soyuz Osvobozdeniia* [Union of Liberation] that formed a lib-lab alliance and cooperated politically. Miliukov even translated one of Breshkovskaya's lectures in Boston.[87] Bloody Sunday, taking place in front of the Winter Palace in St. Petersburg on 9 January 1905, signaled the beginning of

---

[80] Chernov, *Pered bureiĭ*, 204.

[81] "Russkoe dvizhenie v Amerike," 18; Maxwell, *Narodniki*, 146. See also the description of a similar scene, which took place in New York City: Wald, *House*, 240. One thousand five hundred were present at Breshkovskaya's lecture in Philadelphia at Christmas 1904. "Anarchist Poetess Quits Hospital to See Rally," *Philadelphia Press*, Dec. 26, 1904, 3. See "Woman Anarchist's Nerve," *New York Times*, Dec. 26, 1904, 1.

[82] "Mme. Breshkovsky's Friends to Dance," *Chicago Daily Tribune*, Feb. 3, 1905, 16.

[83] "To Uplift Peasantry: Mme. Breshkovskaya Tells Twentieth Century Club Members of Her Struggle in Russia," *Boston Daily Globe*, Dec. 18, 1904, 13; "Russian Woman Will Return: Mme. Breshkovsky at Banquet Says Her Help Is Needed by the Revolutionists," *Chicago Daily Tribune*, Jan. 27, 1905, 2; "Russkoe dvizhenie v Amerike," 17.

[84] "Mrs. Katherine Breshkovskaya," *Woman's Journal* 36, no. 5 (Feb. 4, 1905): 17; "Russkoe dvizhenie v Amerike," 17.

[85] See Goldman, *Leben*, ii. 420; Florence Brooks, "New York End of the Russian Uprising," *New York Times*, Jan. 29, 1905, sect. SM, 3; Maxwell, *Narodniki*, 124; Good and Jones, *Babushka*, 85.

[86] "Mrs. Katherine Breshkovskaya," *Woman's Journal* 36, no. 5 (Feb. 4, 1905): 17.

[87] "Aids Peasants," 11; Pavel Nikolaevich Miliukov, "Pamiati E. K. Breshko-Breshkovskoi," *Posledniia Novosti*, Sept. 28, 1934, 2.

the first Russian Revolution, and Breshkovskaya immediately figured as a first-hand expert on Russian affairs in the United States. Her prestige became unsurpassed and she gained in credibility even in the eyes of those who had been skeptical about the truth of her reports on Tsarist Russia.[88]

The American press considerably enhanced Breshkovskaya's popularity. Many articles not only in socialist papers but also in journals of the women's liberation movement portrayed her as a pleasant, charming, intelligent and outstanding person: "Mrs. Breshkovskaya has impressed all who have met her here as one of the most remarkable women they have ever seen."[89]

What is more, the U.S. press conveyed the resolution of the assemblies, which were basically attended by a biased audience. In Boston, the resolution adopted expressed a "protest to Russia because of discrimination against citizens of America on the fanatical pretext of race and religion" and that "we extend such aid as may be ours to give to help in the momentous labor through which a great people is struggling to emerge from darkness of cruel autocracy to the light of progressive constitutional government."[90] Another resolution equated the endeavors of these "brave, enlightened Russians" with the American struggle for human rights, independence, liberty and a Republic some 130 years previously.[91]

The institutional and organizational background, as well as the existence of intense personal networks, explain the success of Breshkovskaya's trip. The Society of the Friends of Russian Freedom, the women's liberation movement, several women's clubs and also certain clubs of Russian emigrants such as the Russian Circle of Boston are to be mentioned.[92] About a dozen men and women organized the meetings at which Breshkovskaya lectured: Isabel Hayes Chapin Barrows (1845–1913), assistant editor of the *Christian Register*, who worked as a translator, interpreter and a kind of *liaison-officer*, helped to acquaint Breshkovskaya with distinguished and influential Americans.[93] Among them were the well-known American feminist Alice Stone Blackwell (1857–1950), who became a kind of secretary to Breshkovskaya during her U.S. sojourn; the founder of the Hull House

---

[88] Goldman, *Leben*, ii. 422.

[89] "Mrs. Katherine Breshkovskaya," *Woman's Journal* 35, no. 51 (Dec. 17, 1904): 401.

[90] "For Freedom: Meeting in Behalf of Russian People," 11.

[91] "Hon. W. D. Foulke Presides at Meeting of Friends of Russian Freedom," *Daily Palladium*, Dec. 16, 1904, 3.

[92] Alice Stone Blackwell, ed., *The Little Grandmother of the Russian Revolution: Reminiscences and Letters of Catherine Breshkovsky* (Boston: Little, Brown & Co., 1919), 125; "Sympathy For Russian People," unpag.; "For Russian Freedom: Chicago Women Take Practical Interest in the Work," *Washington Post*, Mar. 20, 1905, 9.

[93] Stone Blackwell, *Little Grandmother*, 128.

settlement in Chicago, Jane Addams (1860–1935); the influential leader of the early settlement movement, co-organizer of the Women's Trade Union League in 1903 and director of Denison House in Boston, Helena Stuart Dudley (1858–1932);[94] the well-known poet, women's rights activist and long-time president of the New England Woman Suffrage Association, Julia Ward Howe; Rabbi Charles Fleischer (1871–1942) from Boston; and Henry Browne Blackwell (1825–1909), the husband of Lucy Stone and, together with her, editor of the *Woman's Journal* since 1870.[95]

When Breshkovskaya entered the United States in the fall of 1904, she was not able to lecture in English. Her mother tongue was Russian, and she had a good command of French, which she used for her presentations at first.[96] Breshkovskaya was accompanied by a young and promising SR of Jewish origin, Khaim Osipovich Zhitlovskii (1865–1943). He was fluent in German, Yiddish and Russian, had great rhetorical skills and could thus address a segment of the U.S. public that Breshkovskaya would have reached only with difficulty.[97] They proceeded collaboratively: Breshkovskaya was a well-known agitator; however, the subtleties of socialist theory and political philosophy were not her forte. It was Zhitlovskii who would take on the theoretical issues, as well as who would take care of contacts with other parties, such as the Russian Social Democrats or the Jewish Bund. Zhitlovskii had also started a series of ten lectures attended by more than 700 participants, but he was more and more absorbed by the ongoing events of the Russian Revolution of 1905 such that he did not finish his originally intended concept. However, Zhitlovskii managed to get into contact with Jewish trade union officials as well as different Jewish Masonic lodges.[98]

---

[94] Breshkovskaya stayed with her for six weeks. Ibid., 123.

[95] "Sympathy For Russian People," unpag.; Maxwell, *Narodniki*, 147.

[96] Stone Blackwell, *Little Grandmother*, 111–112, 125–126; Vida Dutton Scudder, *On Journey* (New York: E. P. Dutton & Co., 1937), 158; "Sympathy For Russian People," unpag.; "Russian Nihilists. Mme. Breshkovsky Addresses 'Friends of Russia,'" *New York Daily Tribune*, Mar. 9, 1905, 7.

[97] Nikolai Dmitrievich Erofeev, "Zhitlovskii Khaim Osipovich," in *Politicheskie partii Rossii. Konets XIX–pervaia tret' XX veka, Entsiklopediia*, ed. Valentin Valentinovich Shelokhaev (Moscow: ROSSPEN, 1996), 209; Kay Schweigmann-Greve, *Chaim Zhitlowsky: Philosoph, Sozialrevolutionär und Theoretiker einer säkularen nationaljüdischen Identität* (Hanover: Wehrhahn, 2012), 179; Arthur William Thompson and Robert A. Hart, *The Uncertain Crusade: America and the Russian Revolution of 1905* (Amherst: University of Massachusetts Press, 1970), 38.

[98] Hoover Institution Archives, Felix Vladimirovich Volkhovskiĭ Papers, Box 1, Folder 9: Breshko-Breshkovskaia, Ekaterina Konstantinovna, letter of Mar. 2, 1905; "Russkoe dvizhenie v Amerike," 22; Chernov, *Pered bureĭ*, 205; "Jews Cheer on Revolt: A Thousand Hail the Scenes in St. Petersburg as a Popular Uprising at Last," *The Sun*, Jan. 24, 1905, 2. At this meeting in New York's Clinton Hall, the Russian audience donated more than $230.

By the turn of the year 1904/1905, both well-known SRs had recruited a group of young and devoted comrades from the expatriates from Tsarist Russia. The aim was to establish an autonomous organization of the Socialist Revolutionary Party in the United States.[99]

Breshkovskaya did also lecture in academic milieus, where huge assembly halls were available—such as in College Chapel Hall at Wellesley College in mid-December of 1904, in Sayles Hall on the campus of Brown University in Providence, Rhode Island, and in the Auditorium of Chicago University.[100]

The response to Breshkovskaya's lectures and appeals in the U.S. press was a positive one throughout. Critical articles were almost entirely absent. The *New York Times*, for example, noted on the occasion of a mass gathering in Cooper Union just before Christmas 1904: "There were not a few of the votaries of the physical force propaganda that has figured so largely in the latter destinies of Russia. Emma Goldman and some of her following were on hand."[101] The U.S. police kept a close eye on Goldman and the anarchists, and sometimes even barred them or dissolved their gatherings. The *St. Louis-Post Dispatch* informed its readers that "Russians in America are all extremists."[102] It remains open to question, however, whether this was alarming news. Critical remarks concerning Russian socialist tendencies in the United States were rare exceptions.

Breshkovskaya lectured on different topics: on education and enlightenment, on arbitrary and despotic Tsarist Russia, on the forthcoming revolution, and on the prospects of a democratic and perhaps even a future socialist Russia.[103] Besides the articles in the U.S. press, we have a single transcript of one of her speeches she gave in Boston in mid-December of 1904[104] and her article published in the American socialist journal *The Comrade*.

Key topics on Breshkovskaya's political agenda were the cultural awakening and development of the people, gender and "racial" equality and the social

---

[99] Hoover Institution Archives, Felix Vladimirovich Volkhovskiĭ Papers, Box 1, Folder 9: Breshko-Breshkovskaia, Ekaterina Konstantinovna, letter of Jan. 12, 1905; "Russkoe dvizhenie v Amerike," 15, 21.

[100] "Students Cheer Her: Mme. Breshkofskaya Lectures at Wellesley," *Boston Daily Globe*, Dec. 16, 1904, 2; "Sympathy For Russian People," unpag.; "Mrs. Breshkovskaya," *Woman's Journal* 36, no. 5 (Feb. 4, 1905): 17; Maxwell, *Narodniki*, 123.

[101] "Plea For Russian Freedom," *New York Times*, Dec. 23, 1904, 10.

[102] "Czar Has Few Followers in This Country. Russians in America Are All Extremists and Great Majority Oppose Present Ruling Class in Nation They Left," *St. Louis Post-Dispatch*, Jan. 24, 1905, 4.

[103] Maxwell, *Narodniki*, 124.

[104] "Welcome to a Russian Woman," 401, 404.

and political progress of her country to be able "to fill an honourable place among civilized nations." She presented a Manichean world view: the evil and despotic present of Tsarist Russia and the bright future of people's progress. Her rhetoric was imbued with biblical language and metaphors. She spoke of the readiness of her comrades "to offer their lives for the deliverance of their country."[105] The goal was emancipation from Tsarism to establish democracy and, ultimately, socialism.[106] Breshkovskaya finished her speech with a pathos-soaked appeal "to all the friends of freedom": "In the name of justice and of the general good, I entreat you, friends, to help us as you can and as much as you can, so that we may see our immense and beautiful country, with its kind-hearted and gifted people, free and civilized as soon as possible."[107]

Although Breshkovskaya criticized the American gender role model she was at the same time pleased with her outstanding relations with the Society of the Friends of Russian Freedom and other progressive intellectuals such as the economist Professor Richard T. Ely (1854–1943), who had taken a liking of the Russian anarchist Prince Petr Alekseevich Kropotkin (1842–1921). Breshkovskaya was aware that she and her party benefited from these privileged relations.[108] Moreover, Breshkovskaya established very close contacts with Mrs. Alice Stone Blackwell (1857–1950);[109] the socialist journalist and foreign correspondent for *Harper's Weekly*, *Collier's Weekly* and *The Outlook*, Arthur E. Bullard (1879–1929) and his comrades; and the so-called "gentlemen socialists," William English Walling (1877–1936), one of the founding members of the Intercollegiate Socialist

---

[105] For a similar expression, see "For Freedom: Meeting in Behalf of Russian People," 11. For the proximity of the SRs to biblical language and the aspect that their ideology could be seen as a secular religion, see Lutz Häfner, "'Gottesmutter', 'Rachegott' und 'Golgatha': Autokratie, Sozialrevolutionäre Partei und Legitimationsstrategien terroristischer Gewalt im Russländischen Reich an der Wende zum 20. Jahrhundert," in *Gewalterfahrung und Prophetie*, eds. Peter Burschel and Christoph Marx (Vienna: Böhlau, 2013), 183–208; Lutz Häfner, "'Nur im Kampf wirst Du Dein Recht erlangen!' Sozialrevolutionäre Maximalisten und Linke Sozialrevolutionäre in der Russischen Revolution 1917," in *Anarchismus und Russische Revolution*, ed. Philippe Kellermann (Berlin: Dietz, 2017), 108–110.

[106] Breschkovsky, "The Internal Condition of Russia," 34; Catherine Breschkovsky, "The Internal Condition of Russia," *The Independent* 58, no. 2927 (Jan. 15, 1905): 13. Breshkovskaya spoke about "the party of progress"; it is very likely that she used "progress" instead of "socialist" or "socialism." See "Welcome to a Russian Woman," 401; "For Freedom: Meeting in Behalf of Russian People," 11; "Russkoe dvizhenie v Amerike," 17.

[107] "Welcome to a Russian Woman," 404.

[108] Hoover Institution Archives, Felix Vladimirovich Volkhovskiï Papers, Box 1, Folder 9: Breshko-Breshkovskaia, Ekaterina Konstantinovna, letter of Jan. 12, 1905.

[109] Hoover Institution Archives, Felix Vladimirovich Volkhovskiï Papers, Box 1, Folder 9: Breshko-Breshkovskaia, Ekaterina Konstantinovna, letter of Jan. 12, 1905.

Society (now League for Industrial Democracy) and the Women's Trade Union League, the writer and social worker Kellogg Durland (1881–1911) and the writer and future foreign correspondent to Russia in 1917, Ernest Poole (1880–1950).[110]

Breshkovskaya's sojourn was a complete success. She was pleased with how she had been received not only by emigrants from Tsarist Russia but even more by U.S. Americans, especially feminists.[111] On her return to Europe in March 1905, she had become known more or less all over the United States. In many articles of U.S. newspapers she was affectionately portrayed as "Babushka,"[112] "Little Grandmother of the Russian Revolution," or even, and very intimately, "the dear little grandmother."[113] Her transformation from a well-known socialist into an above-class and nationwide-accepted celebrity with the best connections to U.S. high society was not only due to good luck and the chance of circumstances such as the defeats of Tsarist armed forces in the Russo-Japanese War, functioning as a harbinger of the fast-approaching Russian Revolution. "Bloody Sunday" gave her trip an additional boost. Given her previous revolutionary record, Breshkovskaya could offer first-hand expertise. Her hard work, personal charm and ability to conceal to a certain degree her preference for extreme political means contributed to her success story in the United States. Besides dissenting views uttered, for example, by the American suffragette Jane Addams,[114] it seems as if the American public either condoned Breshkovskaya's commitment to violence and terrorism or even went so far as to justify it, as the following quote by Alice Stone Blackwell shows: "Political assassination is rightly abhorred in America. But in Russia there is no possibility of obtaining justice by law."[115] In fact, Blackwell assumed the SRs' and Breshkovskaya's arguments: "We have no free speech or free press. … If violence is sometimes use[d] it is because it is the only method that can possibly prevail in restricted Russia."[116]

The SR party's investment in Breshkovskaya's fund-raising tour immediately amortized. Through entrance fees to her public speeches or offertories at their

---

[110] Hoover Institution Archives, Felix Vladimirovich Volkhovskiĭ Papers, Box 1, Folder 9: Breshko-Breshkovskaia, Ekaterina Konstantinovna, undated letter; see Foglesong, *Mission*, 38–39; Good and Jones, *Babushka*, 84.

[111] Hoover Institution Archives, Felix Vladimirovich Volkhovskiĭ Papers, Box 1, Folder 9: Breshko-Breshkovskaia, Ekaterina Konstantinovna, letter of Mar. 2, 1905.

[112] "Babushka Arrives Here: Noted Woman Socialist," 2; Poole, *Katharine Breshkovsky*, 3.

[113] Goldman, *Leben*, ii. 416; "Anarchist Poetess Quits Hospital to See Rally," 3.

[114] "Chicago Russians Show Sympathy: Cheer Mme. Breshkovsky and Give Liberally to Cause of Freedom," *Chicago Daily Tribune*, Jan. 23, 1905, 5.

[115] Stone Blackwell, *Little Grandmother*, 108.

[116] "Babushka Arrives Here: Noted Woman Socialist," 2; "Socialist Queen Is in New York," 3.

end,[117] the sale of postcards with her portrait[118] or of tickets to attend balls in her honor,[119] concerts[120] and last but not least donations from Russian, Jewish or Polish emigrants as well as liberal well-to-do U.S. Americans—quite often via the Society of Friends of Russian Freedom[121]—the SR Party solicited solid funds. It is not quite clear how much money Breshkovskaya collected for the party. Estimates vary between $10,000 and $50,000.[122] Moreover, during her U.S. trip, the SR's Central Committee received thousands of U.S. dollars directly,[123] and the flow of donations continued even after Breshkovskaya's return to Europe[124] and illegally to Russia in May 1905.[125]

[117] "Cheer and Pass Hat: Sing 'The Marseillaise.' Sympathizers Hail Uprising as Revolution—Pledge Support and Cash," *New-York Daily Tribune*, Jan. 24, 1905, 3; "Sympathy For Russian People," unpag.; "Mrs. Katherine Breshkovskaya," *Woman's Journal* 36, no. 5 (Feb. 4, 1905): 17.

[118] Hoover Institution Archives, Felix Vladimirovich Volkhovskiĭ Papers, Box 1, Folder 9: Breshko-Breshkovskaia, Ekaterina Konstantinovna, letter of Mar. 2, 1905.

[119] "Otchet kassy zagranichnago komiteta P. S. R. Aprel' 1905 g.," *Revoliutsionnaia Rossiia* 67 (May 1905): 24.

[120] "For Russian Freedom: Grand Concert in Aid of Oppressed," *Daily Morning Journal and Courier*, Nov. 30, 1904, 8.

[121] Hoover Institution Archives, Felix Vladimirovich Volkhovskiĭ Papers, Box 1, Folder 9: Breshko-Breshkovskaia, Ekaterina Konstantinovna, Boston, letter of Mar. 3, 1905.

[122] Egor Egorovich Lazarev, "Babushka Breshkovskaya," *Revoliutsionnaia Rossiia* 33–34 (Jan.–Feb. 1924): 33; Manfred Hildermeier, Die Sozialrevolutionäre Partei Russlands. Agrarsozialismus und Modernisierung im Zarenreich (1900–1914) (Cologne: Böhlau 1978), 273. The lowest figure is given in Columbia University, New York, Butler Library, Lillian D. Wald Collection, Box 93: Russia II, Folder: Breshkovsky, Catherine Notes, biographical, etc., Mscr. Anne K. Geddes, *The Little Grandmother of the Revolution* (1925); "Mme. Breshkowsky Dined," *The Sun*, Mar. 18, 1905, 5; Stone Blackwell, *Little Grandmother*, 132; Catherine Breshkovsky, *A Message to the American People*, with an introduction by George Kennan (New York: Russian Information Bureau in the U.S. Woolworth Building, 1919), 5; Good and Jones, *Babushka*, 88; Michels, *Fire*, 125–126; Schweigmann-Greve, *Zhitlowsky*, 180.

[123] In January and February 1905, the SR Party received about 4,800 francs from Chicago, more than 4,300 francs from Boston, and about 18,500 francs from New York, which, taken together, amounted to more than 27,600 francs (= $5,325 = 10,350 roubles). Some of these donations were appropriated to the Party's Fighting Organization [*Boevaia Organizatsiia*]; "Otchet kassy zagranichnago komiteta P. S. R. Ianvar' 1905 g., fevral' 1905 g.," *Revoliutsionnaia Rossiia* 60 (Mar. 1905): 24; see also "Russkoe dvizhenie v Amerike," 15, 22.

[124] In April 1905, the SRs received donations totaling 9,432 francs (= $1,820) from New York City, which amounted to 3,537 roubles. Cleveland contributed another 225 francs. "Otchet kassy zagranichnago komiteta P. S. R. Aprel' 1905 g.," 24; Jürgen Schneider, Oskar Schwarzer and Friedrich Zellfelder, eds., *Währungen der Welt I: Europäische und nordamerikanische Devisenkurse, 1777–1914* (Stuttgart: Franz Steiner, 1991), 468.

[125] Nikolai Dmitrievich Erofeev, "Breshko-Breshkovskaya Ekaterina Konstantinova," in *Politicheskie partii Rossii. Konets XIX—pervaia tret' XX veka. Entsiklopediia*, ed. Valentin Valentinovich Shelokhaev (Moscow: ROSSPEN 1996), 87.

In mid-1907, the SR Party's Central Organ disclosed the figure of 400,000 francs donated in cooperation with the Society of Friends of Russian Freedom by U.S. immigrants from Tsarist Russia to the party's coffers.[126] In 1906, the share of donations amounted to more than 50 percent of the party's revenue.[127]

Throughout the first Russian Revolution, the Society of Friends of Russian Freedom kept on working to focus American sympathy on the sufferers of the Tsarist regime and to provide them with material aid.[128] When Breshkovskaya and her comrade Nicholai Chaikovskii were arrested again in Russia in 1907 and consequently sentenced and exiled to Siberia, American citizens, the U.S. public and high-ranking politicians petitioned the Tsarist government to pardon her.[129] Breshkovskaya stayed in contact with some of her U.S. acquaintances, who became dear friends, well into the 1920s.[130] Moreover, she was extremely cordially received on her return to the United States via Japan in early 1919.[131] Lillian D. Wald summed up the essence of the longstanding and intimate relationship between her, her American friends and Breshkovskaya in a personal letter:

[126] "Amerikanskaia organizatsiia Partii Sotsialistov Revoliutsionerov," *Znamia Truda. Tsentral'nyi Organ Partii sotsialistov-revoliutsionerov*, no. 2 (July 1907): 24.

[127] The SR Party received 225,000 Roubles in 1906. See "Kratkii deneznhyi otchet Ts. K. P. S.-R. za 1906 g.," *Partiinyia Izvestiia* 6 (Mar. 1907): 4.

[128] "Campaign to Aid Russians," *Palestine Daily Herald*, Mar. 4, 1907, 2.

[129] Columbia University, New York, Butler Library, Lillian D. Wald Collection, Box 93: Russia II, Folder: Chaykovsky Nikolai V., Petition to the Russian ambassador Baron Alexander Rosen, Dec. 14, 1907; "Cable A Petition: Prominent Americans Ask Russia for Leniency to Two Prisoners," *Topeka State Journal*, Dec. 26, 1907, 1; "Cable Petition to Russia: Prominent Americans Ask Leniency for Alleged Revolutionists," *Bemidji Daily Pioneer*, Dec. 27, 1907, 4; "Leniency Is Urged: Prominent Americans Desire Pardon for Russian Revolutionists," *Salt Lake Herald*, Dec. 27, 1907, 3; "Prominent Americans Ask Russia to Be Lenient," *Evening Statesman* (Walla Walla, WA), Dec. 27, 1907, 2; Isabel Hayes Chapin Barrows, *A Sunny Life: The Biography of Samuel June Barrows* (Boston: Little, Brown & Co., 1913), 238–240; Stone Blackwell, *Little Grandmother*, 134–135; Alexander Kerensky, "Catherine Breshkovsky (1844–1934)," *Slavonic and Eastern European Review* 13 (1934–1935): 429; Maxwell, *Narodniki*, 153.

[130] Columbia University, New York, Butler Library, Lillian D. Wald Collection, Box 93: Russia II: Folder: Breshkovsky, Catherine Correspondence with her, letter of Lillian D. Wald to Louis Stoiber, Jan. 25, 1928; GARF, r-5975: Breshko-Breshkovskaya Ekaterina Konstantinova, op. 1, d. 137: Alice Stone Blackwell (1917); d. 688: Lillian Wald; Lillian D. Wald, *Windows on Henry Street* (Boston: Little, Brown & Co., 1934), 257–258.

[131] Columbia University, New York, Butler Library, Lillian D. Wald Collection, Box 93: Russia II, Folder: Breshkovsky, Catherine Printed—Clippings, Russian Heroine Sails For America; Folder: Breshkovsky, Catherine Notes, biographical, etc., Madame Breshkovsky's schedule Feb. 12–Mar. 10, 1919.

Beloved Babushka: Years ago when you came to America, almost the only friends you had were the Russian Revolutionists, almost all Russian Jews, members of your Revolutionary Society. The American friends you made then felt not only your personal greatness but also recognized the greatness of your cause and the lofty purpose for which you had sacrificed so much. We felt that in spite of all denunciations of you and your associates, all Americans should have a chance to know you and get your message. We did everything that was in our power to have your voice heard and your story known; for to us you symbolized the great struggle for freedom in Russia.[132]

The Price of Socialist-Revolutionary Terrorism

"Such assassinations as that of von Plehve cost money, and the Russian patriots lack the funds to carry on this work," uttered Bronislav Slavinsky, editor of the Polish socialist paper *Robotnik*, at a banquet in honor of Breshkovskaya at the Lessing Club in Chicago.[133] More or less every contemporary donator to the SR Party must have been aware of the fact that he probably subsidized terrorist assaults. The SRs' political endeavors were quite expensive. And this was in particular true for their terrorist activities. As for the assassination of Minister of the Interior Pleve in July 1904, the amount of money the Fighting Organization of the SR Party had to spend for it ran as high as $100,000.[134] According to other contradictory sources, however, the assassination of Pleve devoured between 30,000 and 75,000 roubles. Within four years, i.e., from January 1904 to December 1907, the SR Central Committee transferred 320,000 francs to the party's Fighting Organization.[135] It is not evident whether terrorism prevented solid

---

[132] Columbia University, New York, Butler Library, Lillian D. Wald Collection, Box 93: Russia II, Folder: Breshkovsky, Catherine—Correspondence with her, letter Lillian D. Wald to Breshkovskaia, Feb. 27, 1919.

[133] "Russian Patriots Lack Funds: Chicago Sympathizers Subscribe for Socialist Movement in Russia," *Evening Star*, Jan. 27, 1905, 2; "Russian Patriots Are in Need of Money: Editor Made Stirring Speech At Banquet For Russian Lady Exile," *Fairmont West Virginian*, Jan. 28, 1905, 2; *Los Angeles Herald*, Jan. 28, 1905, 2.

[134] "Terrorists Unhappy of Russia," *Bemidji Daily Pioneer*, Sept. 27, 1906, 4. See also *River Press* (Fort Benton, MT), Oct. 10, 1906, 6.

[135] Ekaterina Iosifovna Shcherbakova, ed., *Politicheskaia politsiia i politicheskii terrorizm v Rossii (vtoraia polovina XIX—nachalo XX vv.). Sbornik dokumentov* (Moscow: AIRO-XX, 2001), 170; Mikhail Ivanovich Leonov, "Partiia éserov: seredina 90-kh godov XIX veka—1907 god," in *Politicheskie partii v rossiiskikh revoliutsiiakh v nachale XX veka*, ed. Grigorii Nikolaevich Sevost'ianov (Moscow: ROSSPEN, 2005), 410; Dmitrii Borisovich Pavlov, "Iz istorii boevoi deiatel'nosti partii éserov nakanune i v gody revoliutsii 1905–1907 gg.," in *Neproletarskie partii Rossii v trekh revoliutsiiakh. Sbornik statei*, ed. Kirill Vladimirovich Gusev (Moscow: Nauka, 1989), 147, 151; L. Khefner [Häfner], "'Tovarishchi' ili 'nashi

and permanent party financing, as Christopher Rice claims. Without any empirical findings to substantiate his assumption, one is more likely to opt for the opposite: Viktor Chernov maintained that the party received lots of money because of its terrorist acts.[136] In this respect, Breshkovskaya's U.S. tour put it to the test.

Conclusion

In summing up, a reference to a quote from the French left-wing newspaper *L'Aurore* seems appropriate, as the newspaper—convinced of an existing iron law of human and political progress in the direction of democracy—explained: "History proves that the loyal establishment of a sincere *régime* of liberty is the safest means for closing the era of political crimes in a country."[137] Legal order and constitutional liberty were seen as the best devices when fighting terrorism. The Tsarist *ancien régime*, however, was adamant. Before the Revolution of 1905 it denied any concessions to its society, "shut every tap, screwed down every safety valve; and at last the world learns without surprise, that the boiler has burst."[138]

The United States did not differ from the European public. The U.S. tour of Breshkovskaya became a mass media spectacle. On the one hand, she was portrayed as a calm, mild, cordial and gentle woman, who looked younger than her sixty years.[139] On the other hand, however, she was not weak at all but rather a tough, resilient person and in the true sense of the word a strong freedom fighter [*borets za svobodu*].[140] Breshkovskaya was polyvalent and could be seen as a Russian martyr, an international heroine, a socialist-revolutionary living icon and a role model for the American suffragettes. The media coverage of Breshkovskaya was substantial not only

---

drugo-vragi?' Agrarnyi vopros, terrorizm i vzaimootnosheniia partii sotsialistov-revoliutsionerov s nemetskoi i rossiiskoi sotsial-demokraticheskimi partiiami v 1902–1914 gg." In *Sud'by demokraticheskogo sotsializma v Rossii: sbornik materialov konferentsii*, ed. Konstantin Nikolaevich Morozov (Moscow: Izd-vo im. Sabashnikovykh, 2014), 116.

[136] Viktor Mikhailovich Chernov, *V partii sotsialistov-revoliutsionerov: vospominaniia o vos'mi liderakh*, eds. Aleksandr Pavlovich Novikov and Karin Huser (St. Petersburg: Dmitrii Bulanin, 2007), 342; Shcherbakova, *Politicheskaia politsiia*, 472; Aleksandr Vasil'evich Gerasimov, "Na lezvii s terroristami," in *"Okhranka": Vospominaniia rukovoditelei politicheskogo syska*, vol. 1, ed. Zinaida Ivanovna Peregudova (Moscow: Novoe Literaturnoe Obozrenie, 2004), 196; Christopher Rice, *Russian Workers and the Socialist-Revolutionary Party through the Revolution of 1905–07* (New York: St. Martin's Press, 1988), 195.

[137] See *The Times*, June 21, 1904, 5.

[138] *The Times*, July 29, 1904, 7.

[139] "Socialist Queen Is in New York," 3.

[140] "Here to Oppose the Czar's Rule: Mme Breshkovsky, Who Saw Years of Captivity, Is Engaged in Her Life Work," *Chicago Daily Tribune*, Jan. 21, 1905, 2.

in opinion-forming and influential quality newspapers such as the *New York Times*, the *Boston Globe*, and the *Washington Post*, and thus in the bigger U.S. cities including those on the West Coast,[141] but also in the provincial backwaters, where we could occasionally find articles about Breshkovskaya, her past and present interests, and her future political aims.

During the Russian Revolution of 1905, terror became a ubiquitous phenomenon. However, its frequency as well as its mounting collateral damages delegitimized the terror. This weapon, which had been too much in use, became blunt. After years of upheaval, internecine war, punitive actions etc., the European public was all the more fed up with Russian interior politics. Prima facie, the autocracy made far-reaching concessions. A parliament had been granted as well as civil rights. The European public did not understand why the bombing still went on.

Even well-to-do American supporters, who hitherto had financed the terrorists, now felt deterred. After parliamentarianism had been established in Russia, liberal society began to reduce its funding of socialist parties such as the Socialist Revolutionaries more and more. Therefore, terror not only lost an important financial source[142] but also the support of the liberal mass media as a means of propaganda and—most importantly—of legitimacy.[143] As far as the financial aspect was concerned, increasing expropriations could be seen as compensation. However, they alienated the liberal society even more from their former brother in arms.

Indeed, public opinion on terrorism began to vacillate and its acceptance successively declined in Britain and the United States as well as in Russia. One could note the growing unease at the scale of societal violence. The expressed apology for bombs and dynamite, which had been totally accepted up to the October Manifesto of 1905 and partly right into 1906, turned into ambivalence. Still, the living conditions of the Russian people were regarded as odious in the extreme. However, salvation lay for liberals both in Russia as in Western countries not in terrorism but in democratic principles and the convocation of the State Duma. When terrorist acts and expropriations became ubiquitous, when bombs were thrown in crowded streets or establishments like the Café Libman in Odessa,[144] or when bystanders were killed as was

---

[141] "Says Patriots Lack Funds Needed to Carry on Assassinations," *Los Angeles Herald*, Jan. 28, 1905, 2.

[142] "'Liberal' v politicheskoi politsii: Zapiska nachal'nika Moskovskogo okhrannogo otdeleniia V. V. Ratko 1905 g.," *Istoricheskii Arkhiv*, no. 4 (2008): 74; Tyrkova-Vil'iams, *Na putiakh*, 70; Keep, "Terror," 32.

[143] "Dokumenty po istorii Partii S.-R.: Vopros o terrore na V. Sovete Partii," *Sotsialist-Revoliutsioner* 2 (1910), 41.

[144] *Narodnoe khoziaistvo. Ezhednevnaia gazeta*, Dec. 31, 1905, 5. See the leaflet of the Anarchist-Communist group of Odessa of mid-December 1905, "K vsem rabochim i

the case when Socialist Revolutionary Maximalists bombed the residence of Prime Minister Petr Arkad'evich Stolypin (1862–1911) on Aptekarskii Island in St. Petersburg in late August 1906, the public's sympathy for terrorists waned. Such terrorism was considered unjust and criminal.[145]

When Stolypin was finally assassinated in September 1911, *The Times* wrote: "All civilized men must feel horror at the crime by which he has perished."[146] What is more, although the Transatlantic Public discussed the death of Stolypin, they did so dispassionately and without any noticeable expression of regret. It praised, however, and this must be underlined, his energy in the struggle against terrorism.[147] It seemed as if sympathy for terrorism and its practitioners had never existed before.

Works Cited

Archival Sources
Columbia University, New York, Butler Library
Lillian D. Wald Collection, Box 93: Russia II
    Folder: Breshkovsky, Catherine Correspondence with her
    Folder: Chaykovsky Nikolai V.
    Folder: Friends of Russian Freedom

Gosudarstvennyi Arkhiv Rossiiskoi Federatsii (GARF), Moscow
r-5975: Breshko-Breshkovskaya Ekaterina Konstantinova, op. 1
d. 137: Alice Stone Blackwell (1917)
d. 688: Lillian Wald

International Institute of Social History, Amsterdam
Partija Socialistov-Revoljucionerov Archives, Folder 696: Letters received by Breškovskaja after her visit to the USA, of which two from A. Stone Blackwell. 1905

Stanford University, California, Hoover Institution Archives
Felix Vladimirovich Volkhovskiĭ Papers, Box 1, Folder 9: Breshko-Breshkovskaia, Ekaterina Konstantinovna, 1904–1905

---

rabotnitsam," in *Anarkhisty: Dokumenty i materialy 1883–1935 gg.*, vol. 1, *1883–1916 gg.*, ed. Valerii Vladimirovich Kriven'kii (Moscow: ROSSPEN, 1998), 167.

[145] Jane McDermid, "Mariya Spiridonova: Russian Martyr and British Heroine? The Portrayal of a Russian Female Terrorist in the British Press," in *Reinterpreting Revolutionary Russia: Essays in Honour of James D. White*, ed. Ian D. Thatcher (London: Palgrave Macmillan, 2006), 49.

[146] *The Times*, Sept. 19, 1911, 7.

[147] Cf. *The Times*, Sept. 20, 1911, 3.

Newspapers and Journals

Bemidji Daily Pioneer
Berliner Tageblatt
Boston Daily Globe
Caucasian (Shreveport, Los Angeles)
Chicago Daily Tribune
Daily Morning Journal and Courier (New Haven, Connecticut)
Daily Palladium (Richmond, Indiana)
Evening Star (Washington, D.C.)
Evening Statesman (Walla Walla, Washington)
Evening World (New York)
Fairmont West Virginian
Free Press (Hays, Kansas)
Hamburger Fremdenblatt
The Labor World. Devoted to the Industrial Welfare of the Head of the Lakes (Duluth, Minnesota)
Los Angeles Herald
Morning Astorian (Astoria, Oregon)
Münchner Neueste Nachrichten
Narodnoe khoziaistvo. Ezhednevnaia gazeta (St. Petersburg, 1905–1906)
New-York Daily Tribune
New York Times
Ocala Evening Star (Ocala, Florida)
Omaha Daily Bee
Osvobozhdenie (Stuttgart)
L'Ouest-Éclair (Rennes)
Palestine Daily Herald (Palestine, Texas)
Philadelphia Press
Providence Journal
River Press (Fort Benton, Montana)
St. Louis Post-Dispatch
St. Louis Republic
Salt Lake Herald
San Francisco Call
Social-Democratic Herald. Journal of the Coming Civilization (Chicago)
The Sun (New York)
The Times (London)
Topeka State Journal
The Virginia Enterprise (Virginia, Minnesota)
Vorwärts. Berliner Volksblatt. Zentralorgan der sozialdemokratischen Partei Deutschlands
Vossische Zeitung (Berlin)
Washington Post

Washington Times
Woman's Journal (Boston)

Published Primary Sources

"Amerikanskaia organizatsiia Partii Sotsialistov Revoliutsionerov." *Znamia Truda. Tsentral'nyi organ Partii sotsialistov-revoliutsionerov*, no. 2 (July 1907): 24.

Boevyia predpriiatiia sotsialistov-revoliutsionerov v osveshchenii okhranki. Moscow: Revoliutsionnyi sotsializm, 1918.

Breschkovsky, Catherine. "The Internal Condition of Russia." *The Independent* 58, no. 2927 (Jan. 15, 1905): 11–16.

——. "The Internal Condition of Russia: Catherine Breschkovsky in *New York Independent*." *The Comrade* 4, no. 2 (1905): 34–36.

——. "Iz istorii Partii S.-R. Pokazaniia V. M. Chernova po delu Azefa v sledstvennoi komissii Partii S.-R. 2 fevr. 1910 g." *Novyi Zhurnal* 101 (1970): 172–197.

——. *A Message to the American People*, with an introduction by George Kennan. New York: Russian Information Bureau in the U.S. Woolworth Building, 1919.

Chernov, Viktor Mikhailovich. *Pered bureĭ*. New York: Izd-vo im. Chekhova, 1953.

——. *V partii sotsialistov-revoliutsionerov: vospominaniia o vos'mi liderakh*, eds. Aleksandr Pavlovich Novikov and Karin Huser. St. Petersburg: Dmitriĭ Bulanin, 2007.

D. [Delbrück, Hans]. "Politische Korrespondenz: Der Königsberger Prozeß wegen Hochverrats gegen den Zaren. Der Krieg, Die Zukunft Rußlands." *Preußische Jahrbücher* 117, no. 1 (July–Sept. 1904): 374–383.

"Dokumenty po istorii Partii S.-R.: Vopros o terrore na V. Sovete Partii." *Sotsialist-Revoliutsioner* 2 (1910): 1–53.

Gerasimov, Aleksandr Vasil'evich. "Na lezvii s terroristami." In *"Okhranka": Vospominaniia rukovoditeleĭ politicheskogo syska*, vol. 1, ed. Zinaida Ivanovna Peregudova, 145–342. Moscow: Novoe Literaturnoe Obozrenie, 2004.

Goldman, Emma. *Gelebtes Leben*, 3 vols. Berlin: Karin Kramer, 1979.

Hayes Chapin Barrows, Isabel. *A Sunny Life: The Biography of Samuel June Barrows*. Boston: Little, Brown & Co., 1913.

"Here to Oppose the Czar's Rule: Mme Breshkovsky, Who Saw Years of Captivity, Is Engaged in Her Life Work." *Chicago Daily Tribune*, Jan. 21, 1905.

Kalinin, P. "Po povodu usilennoi okhrany." *Pravo* 48 (Nov. 11, 1904): 3304–3306.

Kennan, George. "A Ride Through the Trans-Baikal." *Century Magazine* 37 (May 1889): 69–83.

Kerensky, Alexander. "Catherine Breshkovsky (1844–1934)." *Slavonic and Eastern European Review* 13 (1934–1935): 428–431.

"Kratkii denezhnyi otchet Ts. K. P. S.-R. za 1906 g." *Partiinyia Izvestiia* 6 (Mar. 1907): 4.

Kriven'kii, Valerii Vladimirovich, ed. *Anarkhisty: Dokumenty i materialy 1883–1935 gg.*, vol. 1, *1883–1916 gg.* Moscow: Rosspen, 1998.

Lazarev, Egor Egorovich. "Babushka Breshkovskaia." *Revoliutsionnaia Rossiia* 33–34 (Jan.–Feb. 1924): 31–34.

"'Liberal' v politicheskoi politsii: Zapiska nachal'nika Moskovskogo okhrannogo otdeleniia V. V. Ratko 1905 g." *Istoricheskii Arkhiv* 4 (2008): 70–78.

Lipps, Theodor. *Die ethischen Grundfragen: Zehn Vorträge.* Hamburg: Voß, 1899.

Miliukov, Pavel Nikolaevich. "Pamiati E. K. Breshko-Breshkovskoi." *Posledniia Novosti*, Sept. 28, 1934.

"Mrs. Breshkovskaya's Farewell." *Woman's Journal* 36, no. 11 (Mar. 11, 1905): 41

"Mrs. Katherine Breshkovskaya." *Woman's Journal* 35, no. 51 (Dec. 17, 1904): 401.

"Mrs. Katherine Breshkovskaya." *Woman's Journal* 36, no. 5 (Feb. 4, 1905): 17.

"Otchet kassy zagranichnago komiteta P. S. R. Aprel' 1905 g." *Revoliutsionnaia Rossiia* 67 (May 1905): 24.

"Otchet kassy zagranichnago komiteta P. S. R. Ianvar' 1905 g., fevral' 1905 g." *Revoliutsionnaia Rossiia* 60 (Mar. 1905): 24.

Paléologue, Maurice. *Three Critical Years: 1904–05–06.* New York: Robert Speller, 1957.

Poole, Ernest. *The Bridge: My Own Story.* New York: Macmillan, 1940.

——. *Katharine Breshkovsky: For Russia's Freedom.* Chicago: Charles H. Kerr & Co., 1905.

"Russkoe dvizhenie v Amerike." *Revoliutsionnaia Rossiia* 60 (Mar. 5, 1905): 21–22; 61 (Mar. 15, 1905): 17–18; and 62 (Mar. 25, 1905): 15–16.

"Says Patriots Lack Funds Needed to Carry on Assassinations." *Los Angeles Herald*, Jan. 28, 1905.

Scudder, Vida Dutton. *On Journey.* New York: E. P. Dutton & Co., 1937.

Shcherbakova, Ekaterina Iosifovna, ed. *Politicheskaia politsiia i politicheskii terrorizm v Rossii (vtoraia polovina XIX–nachalo XX vv.). Sbornik dokumentov.* Moscow: AIRO-XX, 2001.

"Socialist Queen Is In New York: 'Grandma' Breshkovsky, Who Has Spent Twenty-two Years in Siberian Mines, Arrives Here from Russia." *Evening World* (New York), Nov. 12, 1904.

Stone Blackwell, Alice, ed. *The Little Grandmother of the Russian Revolution: Reminiscences and Letters of Catherine Breshkovsky.* Boston: Little, Brown & Co., 1919.

Tyrkova-Vil'iams, Ariadna. *Na putiakh k svobode.* Moscow: Moskovskaia shkola politicheskikh issledovanii, 2007.

Wald, Lillian D. *Windows on Henry Street.* Boston: Little, Brown & Co., 1934.

Weber, Max. *Zur Russischen Revolution von 1905: Schriften und Reden, 1905–1912*, eds. Wolfgang J. Mommsen and Dittmar Dahlmann. Tübingen: J. C. B. Mohr, 1996.

Weinberg, Chaim Leib. *Forty Years in Struggle: The Memories of a Jewish Anarchist*. Trans. Naomi Cohen; ed. Robert P. Helms. Duluth, MN: Litwin Books, 2001.

Secondary Works

Ascher, Abraham. *The Revolution of 1905*, vol. 1, *Russia in Disarray*. Stanford, CA: Hoover Institution Press, 1988.

Cassedy, Steven. *To the Other Shore: The Russian Jewish Intellectuals Who Came to America*. Princeton, N.J.: Princeton University Press, 1997.

Crenshaw, Martha. "The Causes of Terrorism." *Comparative Politics* 13 (1981): 379–399.

Daly, Jonathan W. "On the Significance of Emergency Legislation in Late Imperial Russia." *Slavic Review* 54, no. 3 (1995): 602–629.

Dietze, Carola. "Von Kornblumen, Heringen und Drohbriefen: Ereignis und Medienereignis am Beispiel der Attentate auf Wilhelm I." In *Medienereignisse der Moderne*, eds. Friedrich Lenger and Ansgar Nünning, 40–60. Darmstadt: Wissenschaftliche Buchgesellschaft, 2008.

Engelstein, Laura. "Weapon of the Weak (Apologies to James Scott): Violence in Russian History." *Kritika* 4, no. 3 (2003): 679–693.

Erofeev, Nikolai Dmitrievich. "Breshko-Breshkovskaya Ekaterina Konstantinova." In *Politicheskie partii Rossii. Konets XIX–pervaia tret' XX veka, Entsiklopediia*, ed. Valentin Valentinovich Shelokhaev, 86–88. Moscow: ROSSPEN, 1996.

——. "Zhitlovskii Khaim Osipovich." In *Politicheskie partii Rossii. Konets XIX–pervaia tret' XX veka, Entsiklopediia*, ed. Valentin Valentinovich Shelokhaev, 209. Moscow: ROSSPEN, 1996.

Foglesong, David S. *The American Mission and the "Evil Empire": The Crusade for a "Free Russia" since 1881*. New York: Cambridge University Press, 2007.

Good, Jane E. "America and the Revolutionary Movement, 1888–1905." *Russian Review* 41, no. 2 (1982): 273–287.

Good, Jane E. and David R. Jones. *Babushka: The Life of the Russian Revolutionary Ekaterina K. Breshko-Breshkovskaya (1844–1934)*. Newtonville, MA: Oriental Research Partners, 1991.

Grant, Ron. "The Society of Friends of Russian Freedom (1890–1917): A Case Study in Internationalism." *Journal of the Scottish Labour History Society* 3, no. 3 (1970): 3–24.

Häfner, Lutz. "'Die historischen Tage des 6.-8. November haben wie die Veče-Glocke die russische Gesellschaft aufgerüttelt': Zemcy und intelligenty als liberale Akteure der Russischen Revolution von 1905." In *Russland 1905: Perspektiven auf die erste Russische Revolution*, eds. Ludwig Steindorff and Martin Aust, 69–88. Frankfurt am Main: Peter Lang, 2007.

——. "'Gottesmutter', 'Rachegott' und 'Golgatha': Autokratie, Sozialrevolutionäre Partei und Legitimationsstrategien terroristischer Gewalt im Russländischen Reich an der Wende zum 20. Jahrhundert." In *Gewalterfahrung und Prophetie*, eds. Peter Burschel and Christoph Marx, 183–208. Vienna: Böhlau, 2013.

——. "'Nur im Kampf wirst Du Dein Recht erlangen!' Sozialrevolutionäre Maximalisten und Linke Sozialrevolutionäre in der Russischen Revolution 1917." In *Anarchismus und Russische Revolution*, ed. Philippe Kellermann, 100–127. Berlin: Dietz, 2017.

——. [Khefner, L.]. "'Tovarishchi' ili 'nashi drugo-vragi?' Agrarnyi vopros, terrorizm i vzaimootnosheniia partii sotsialistov-revoliutsionerov s nemetskoi i rossiiskoi sotsial-demokraticheskimi partiiami v 1902–1914 gg." In *Sud'by demokraticheskogo sotsializma v Rossii: sbornik materialov konferentsii*, ed. Konstantin Nikolaevich Morozov, 101–116. Moscow: Izd-vo im. Sabashnikovykh, 2014.

Hildermeier, Manfred. *Die Sozialrevolutionäre Partei Russlands: Agrarsozialismus und Modernisierung im Zarenreich (1900–1914)*. Cologne: Böhlau, 1978.

Keep, John L. H. "Terror in 1905." In *Reinterpreting Revolutionary Russia: Essays in Honour of James D. White*, ed. Ian D. Thatcher, 20–35. London: Palgrave Macmillan, 2006.

Leonov, Mikhail Ivanovich. "Partiia ėserov: seredina 90-kh godov XIX veka–1907 god." In *Politicheskie partii v rossiĭskikh revoliutsiiakh v nachale XX veka*, ed. Grigoriĭ Nikolaevich Sevost'ianov, 401–413. Moscow: ROSSPEN, 2005.

McDermid, Jane. "Mariya Spiridonova: Russian Martyr and British Heroine? The Portrayal of a Russian Female Terrorist in the British Press." In *Reinterpreting Revolutionary Russia: Essays in Honour of James D. White*, ed. Ian D. Thatcher, 36–54. London: Palgrave Macmillan, 2006.

Maxwell, Margaret. *Narodniki Women: Russian Women Who Sacrificed Themselves for the Dream of Freedom*. Elmsford, N.Y.: Pergamon Press, 1990.

Michels, Tony. *A Fire in Their Hearts: Yiddish Socialists in New York*. Cambridge, MA: Harvard University Press, 2005.

Pavlov, Dmitriĭ Borisovich. "Iz istorii boevoi deiatel'nosti partii ėserov nakanune i v gody revoliutsii 1905–1907 gg." In *Neproletarskie partii Rossii v trekh revoliutsiiakh: Sbornik statei*, ed. Kirill Vladimirovich, 144–151. Moscow: Nauka, 1989.

Pipes, Richard. *Russia under the Old Regime*. New York: Charles Scribner's Sons, 1974.

Requate, Jörg and Martin Schulze-Wessel. "Europäische Öffentlichkeit: Realität und Imagination einer appellativen Instanz." In *Europäische Öffentlichkeit: Transnationale Kommunikation seit dem 18. Jahrhundert*, eds. Jörg Requate and Martin Schulze-Wessel, 11–39. Frankfurt am Main: Campus, 2002.

Rice, Christopher. *Russian Workers and the Socialist-Revolutionary Party through the Revolution of 1905–07.* New York: St. Martin's Press, 1988.

Schneider, Jürgen, Oskar Schwarzer and Friedrich Zellfelder, eds. *Währungen der Welt I: Europäische und nordamerikanische Devisenkurse, 1777–1914.* Stuttgart: Franz Steiner, 1991.

Schweigmann-Greve, Kay. *Chaim Zhitlowsky: Philosoph, Sozialrevolutionär und Theoretiker einer säkularen nationaljüdischen Identität.* Hanover: Wehrhahn, 2012.

Thompson, Arthur William and Robert A. Hart. *The Uncertain Crusade: America and the Russian Revolution of 1905.* Amherst: University of Massachusetts Press, 1970.

Travis, Frederick F. *George Kennan and the American–Russian Relationships, 1865–1924.* Athens: Ohio University Press, 1990.

3

The Italian Anarchists' Network in São Paulo at the Beginning of the Twentieth Century

Carlo Romani and Bruno Corrêa de Sá e Benevides

It is impossible to investigate the early history of the Brazilian labor movement without taking a transnational approach to the networks established by leftist immigrants. Attention should be drawn not only to labor and leftist movement networks in immigrants' European countries of origin but also to networks among workers and leftist militants from neighboring countries in South America.[1] Thus, this study on the origins of the Brazilian labor movement aims to understand the transnational political practices of Italian and Iberian immigrants (the main groups) and the circulation of working-class and leftist ideas throughout Brazil, Argentina and Uruguay.

In the early years of the twentieth century, a strong labor movement emerged in São Paulo, the most important Brazilian industrial city. When we try to identify the left networks there, we discover that the support for Italian immigrants was essential for the town's development.[2] In fact, it is impossible to speak about the labor movement in São Paulo before the end of the nineteenth century, when most of the Italians that had emigrated to Brazil were moving from rural to urban areas. The huge influx of Italian immigrants to the state of São Paulo in the two last decades of the nineteenth century brought many anarchist and socialist ideas with them in their luggage, and they landed in a context marked by an almost

---

[1] With regard to Italian anarchism, such networks also existed in London or the United States. See, among other works, Pietro Di Paola, *The Knights Errant of Anarchy: London and the Italian Anarchist Diaspora (1880–1917)* (Liverpool: Liverpool University Press, 2013) and Kenyon Zimmer, *Immigrants against the State: Yiddish and Italian Anarchism in America* (Urbana: University of Illinois Press, 2015).

[2] Michael M. Hall, "Immigration and the Early São Paulo Working Class," *Jahrbuch für Geschichte Lateinamerikas* 12 (1975). For a comprehensive work, see Angelo Trento, *Là dove c'è la raccolta del caffè: L'emigrazione italiana in Brasile, 1875–1940* (Padua: Antenore, 1984).

complete lack of leftist ideas.[3] Therefore, the most visible actions were taken by anarchists and revolutionary socialist groups, whose militants were responsible for several newspapers printed from the middle of the 1890s and for most of the social circles that were founded at the beginning of the new century.[4] In this chapter, we will focus on the influence of Italian anarchism in São Paulo's early working-class organizations.

In order to study Italian anarchism, a transnational approach is not only an alternative but, according to Davide Turcato, a necessary and more effective way to evaluate its impact abroad.[5] When tracking the genealogy of Italian anarchism, we are usually directed to the first contacts within the International Workingmen's Association (IWA) and the falling-out between Karl Marx (1818–1883) and Carlo Cafiero (1846–1892), an Italian activist who followed Mikhail Bakunin's (1814–1876) ideas and the autonomous International that appeared after the end of the centralist one in 1872.[6] The main Italian activists in the IWA, especially Cafiero, Errico Malatesta (1853–1932) and Andrea Costa (1851–1910), became propagandists of non-authoritarian socialism (or anarchism) and builders of the IWA's sections in Italy during the 1870s.[7] The close relationship between

[3] For a general approach, see Timothy J. Hatton and Jeffrey G. Williamson, *The Age of Mass Migration: Causes and Economic Impact* (Oxford: Clarendon Press, 1998), 101 (Table 6.1 shows the impact of Italian migration in all parts of the world).

[4] Edilene Toledo and Luigi Biondi, "Constructing Syndicalism and Anarchism Globally: The Transnational Making of the Syndicalist Movement in São Paulo, Brazil, 1895–1935," in *Anarchism and Syndicalism in the Colonial and Postcolonial World, 1870–1940: The Praxis of National Liberation, Internationalism, and Social Revolution*, eds. Steven Hirsch and Lucien van der Walt (Leiden: Brill, 2010); Angelo Trento, "Wherever We Work, that Land is Ours: The Italian Anarchist Press and Working-Class Solidarity in São Paulo," in *Italian Workers of the World: Labor Migration and the Formation of Multiethnic States*, eds. Donna R. Gabaccia and Fraser M. Ottanelli (Urbana: University of Illinois Press, 2001).

[5] Davide Turcato, "Italian Anarchism as a Transnational Movement 1885–1915," *International Review of Social History* 52, no. 3 (2007): 407–444. For general information about Italian anarchism focusing since the IWA up to the fascist dictatorship, see Carl Levy, "Italian Anarchism, 1870–1926," in *For Anarchism: History, Theory and Practice*, ed. David Goodway (London, Routledge, 1989), 25–78.

[6] Pier Carlo Masini, *Cafiero* (Pisa: BFS ed., 2014).

[7] The standard study was done by Pier Carlo Masini, *Storia degli anarchici italiani da Bakunin a Malatesta (1862–1892)* (Milan: Rizzoli, 1974). For the Italian activists inside the IWA, see Gualtiero Marini, "Revolução, anarquia e comunismo: Às origens do socialismo internacionalista italiano (1871–1876)" (Ph.D. thesis, University of Campinas, 2017). After continual police persecution during the 1870s, with many arrests throughout Italy, Andrea Costa decided to change allegiances and became one of the most important leaders of the Italian Socialist Party. See Nunzio Pernicone, *Italian Anarchism, 1864–1892* (Princeton, N.J.: Princeton University Press, 1993), 166–178, chapter 8, "The Defection of Andrea Costa, 1879–1888."

the Italians and the many internationalist activists of the Jura Federation, based in the Swiss Confederation, shows the transnational characteristic of Italian anarchism from its origins. Furthermore, the relentless persecution of the Italian police against every internationalist activist of the IWA sections and, in the following years, against all the propagandists of anarchism, forced them to flee to foreign countries. The fugitive anarchists preferred to find refuge in neighboring countries, first of all in Switzerland, then France and Belgium soon thereafter. On the other hand, this later forced exiled individuals to become part of the Italian transatlantic diaspora in North and South American countries, who sometimes overcame their traditional ties but without ever forgetting their original practices.

As mentioned, the transnational networks built by anarchist activists at the end of the nineteenth and the beginning of the twentieth centuries are already well known in specialized historiography. Different kinds of studies have focused not only on North America but also on many Latin American countries, such as Mexico, Argentina, Uruguay and Brazil.[8] Of course, most of the works have focused on the labor movement, but there are also different views on cultural studies and libertarian education networks.[9] The Italian anarchists' emigration to South America was part of this transatlantic history, supporting unions, creating a workers' press and developing anarchist schools, and this has been studied in many of these and other works.[10] At the time of the great European migrations, Brazil was one of the

---

[8] The following provide overviews of Latin American anarchism. For Argentina, see Yacoov Oved, "The Uniqueness of Anarchism in Argentina," *E.I.A.L.* 8, no. 1 (1997): http://eial.tau.ac.il/index.php/eial/article/view/1126/1156; Juan Suriano, *Anarquistas: Cultura y política libertaria en Buenos Aires (1890–1910)* (Buenos Aires: Ediciones Manantial, 2001); Gonzalo Zaragoza Rivera, *Anarquismo Argentino (1876–1902)* (Madrid: Ed. de la Torre, 1996). For Brazil, see Silvia L. Magnani, *O movimento anarquista em São Paulo (1906–1917)* (São Paulo: Brasiliense, 1982); Sheldon L. Maram, *Anarquistas, imigrantes e o movimento operário brasileiro, 1890–1920* (Rio de Janeiro: Paz e Terra, 1979). For Mexico, see John M. Hart, *Anarchism and the Mexican Working Class, 1860–1931* (Austin: University of Texas Press, 1987); Colin MacLachlan, *Anarchism and the Mexican Revolution: The Political Trials of Ricardo Flores Magon in the United States* (Oakland: University of California Press, 1991). For Uruguay, see Carlos Zubillaga, *Pan y Trabajo* (Montevideo: Librería de la Facultad de Humanidades, 1996).

[9] A comparative study of Mexico and Argentina has been written by Martín Alberto Acri and María del Carmen Cácerez, *La educación libertaria en la Argentina y en México (1861–1945* (Buenos Aires: Libros de Anarres, 2011). For Brazilian and Argentinian education networks in early 1900, see Carlo Romani, "Le scuole libertarie in Brasile e Argentina nel primo Novecento: L'influenza degli emigrati italiani e iberici," *Officina della Storia* 15 (2016): www.officinadellastoria.eu/it/2016/07/06/le-scuole-libertarie-in-brasile-e-argentina-nel-primo-novecento-linfluenza-degli-emigrati-italiani-e-iberici-2/.

[10] Osvaldo Bayer, "La influencia de la inmigración italiana en el movimiento anarquista argentino," in *Los anarquistas expropiadores y otros ensayos* (Buenos Aires: Editorial Planeta,

most important receiving countries for Italian immigrants, including Italian anarchists. Those activists understood anarchism in different ways, based not only on concepts or ideas but also on kinds of anarchism that were strongly influenced by their class origins and their regional identities and culture. The encounters of many Italian anarchists in São Paulo allowed the creation of several affinity groups, which worked together and supported an important agenda for political propaganda.

One of these efforts resulted in their longest-lasting newspaper, *La Battaglia*, a very popular weekly periodical that was published uninterrupted for nine years after its first appearance in June 1904.[11] Luigi Biondi has focused on the ethnocentric vision or perception that the Italian anarchist group of *La Battaglia* had about their new country. We do not intend to contradict this interpretation but rather, using a different type of approach, to capture the regional identities of the anarchist network built overseas and how it interfered with that perception. Through biographical analyses of the anarchists who most often wrote in that newspaper, Oreste Ristori, Alessandro Cerchiai, Angelo Bandoni, Tobia Boni and Gigi Damiani (who initially called themselves "La Propaganda"), we intend to show that the affinity relationships, even in the transnational movement, were mediated by the original social identities of the activists. Like Bandoni, who was born in Corsica but spent most of his youth on the Peninsula, those men were born or grew up in central Italy. The first four came from Tuscany, something that made this group close-knit, and Damiani from Rome. Their trajectories paint a more or less similar picture. Everybody came from subaltern social classes, with few, if any, material resources. For instance, Ristori was a day laborer's son and Bandoni's father was an artisan. Everyone found anarchism very early in their youth on the streets and passed through the Kingdom's prisons in *domicilio coatto*,[12] where they got their political formation in contact with the masters of Italian anarchism. It is also possible to identify the common practice of individual actions, typical of the poorer classes, in their youth. In their more mature life, they changed their positions to anarchist-communist ideas, inspired by Errico Malatesta's thoughts,[13] but always preserved their rebel characteristic in facing all kinds of authority.

2003); Carlo Romani, *Oreste Ristori: Vita avventurosa di un anarchico tra Toscana e Sudamerica*, trans. Andrea Chersi (Pisa: BFS ed., 2015).

[11] Luigi Biondi, "Anarquistas italianos em São Paulo: O grupo do jornal anarquista 'La Battaglia' e a sua visão da sociedade brasileira: o embate entre imaginários libertários e etnocêntricos." *Cadernos AEL* 8/9 (1998): 117–147.

[12] *Domicilio coatto*, a prison category—Italian house arrest, usually on small islands near the coast, used frequently during the age of the International up until the twentieth century.

[13] Anarcho-communism, in Errico Malatesta, *Life and Ideas: The Anarchist Writings of Errico Malatesta*, trans. and ed. Vernon Richards (Oakland CA: PM Press, 2015), 27–30. For

Surprisingly, the heterodox group of *La Battaglia* has been diminished and classified pejoratively in recent years as insurrectionist or individualist by historians who are following Lucien van der Walt and Michael Schmidt's thesis.[14] This recent anarchist historiography, generalizing and so narrowly dividing global anarchism in two different ways, one anti-organizational and insurrectionist and the other organizational and syndicalist, strongly based on their own ideological positions, has not been able to highlight the singularity of each case that existed in different nations, movements and groups. On the contrary, following Turcato's interpretation of anarchism, we aim to stress that "a transnational analysis reveals new forms of integration, continuity, and organization, based on the mobility of militants, resources, and ideas across the Atlantic Ocean,"[15] suggesting also that a plural understanding of how Italian anarchism abroad was able to put together different practices of organization appropriate to each specific need is fundamental to its full understanding.

Italian Anarchism in Brazil

The idea of the exotic plant was an anecdotal thesis developed and diffused by Brazilian political elites at the beginning of the twentieth century to explain why it would be impossible for anarchism to grow in Brazilian tropical lands.[16] This was a great mistake, as in less than twenty years anarchist groups were operating inside and outside the unions, and the workers' movement organized several strikes, the main one being the general strike in São Paulo in July 1917.[17] Although many Italian immigrants had moved to South American countries since the middle of the nineteenth century, we can only talk about mass Italian emigration from the 1880s onwards. In fact, at first, most Italian immigrants moved to Argentina; it

---

a comprehensive study, see Errico Malatesta, *Complete Works of Malatesta*, vol. 3, *A Long and Patient Work: The Anarchist Socialism of L'Agitazione, 1897–1898*, ed. Davide Turcato (Chico, CA: AK Press, 2017).

[14] See Michael Schmidt and Lucien van der Walt, *Black Flame: The Revolutionary Class Politics of Anarchism and Syndicalism* (Chico: CA AK Press, 2009), 132. In Brazil, several works endorsing this interpretation have neglected or undervalued the rule of *La Battaglia*, the most important anarchist newspaper published in Brazil in the decade of the 1900s. See e.g. the work of Felipe Corrêa, "Anarquismo e Sindicalismo Revolucionário: uma Resenha Crítica do Livro de Edilene Toledo, a partir das Visões de Michael Schmidt, Lucien van der Walt e Alexandre Samis," in *Ideologia e Estratégia: anarquismo, movimentos sociais e poder popular,* ed. Felipe Corrêa (São Paulo: Faísca, 2011).

[15] Turcato, "Italian Anarchism," 407.

[16] Boris Fausto, *Trabalho urbano e conflito social: 1890–1920* (São Paulo: Difel, 1976), 67–68.

[17] Christina Lopreato, *O espírito da revolta: A greve geral anarquista de 1917* (Sao Paulo: Annablume, 2000).

was only a few years later that Brazil became a more important destination. In Brazil, they commonly settled in large coffee farms, but also in small family properties, especially in the south of the country. At the end of the century, the growing industrial towns began attracting another profile of immigrants. If in the first wave people from the north of Italy went in great numbers to Brazil, in the second wave they came from all over Italy. Between 1890 and 1920, the population of the city of São Paulo grew enormously, jumping from 65,000 inhabitants to 580,000, becoming an attractive industrial point for all the immigrants that traveled to South America.[18]

Traditional historiography points to the foundation of the Cecilia Colony in 1890, an experimental collectivist group established in Paraná State by Dr. Giovanni Rossi (1856–1943), as the initial moment in the emergence of anarchism in Brazil. The colony had initiatives of polyandrous relationships, free love (meaning the possibility of living together without official marriage) and cash from communal income. All these initiatives were very uncommon at that time, and this could perhaps partly explain the myths surrounding the Cecilia Colony.[19] The experiment lasted until 1894 when it closed because of internal conflicts, but, nevertheless, this unusual experience gained fame throughout the world and has been identified as the starting point of anarchism in Brazil and as being responsible for the diffusion of the "exotic plant" in other places in the country. After the end of the project, many of its members, such as Francesco Gattai and his family, and Arturo Compagnoli, remained in Brazil but moved to urban areas in Curitiba and São Paulo. Gigi Damiani, who could be added to this group, despite the fact that he did not belong to the original colony, had contact with some of its members during his stay in Curitiba after 1897. That singular experience happened in a moment of a large increase in Italian emigration to the country and the immigrants moving from rural to urban areas. On the other hand, the dissemination of anarchism in Brazil, credited to this "founding myth," has been contested by some historians, who consider that if the Cecilia Colony attracted anarchists to Brazil, its contribution was exaggerated. Work that has been done in the last thirty years, including the comprehensive research of Isabelle Felici,[20] has shown that important anarchist actions among Italian immigrants in São Paulo, Paraná and Rio

---

[18] "Prefeitura de São Paulo, "Histórico demográfico da Prefeitura de São Paulo," archived Mar. 28, 2012: www.webcitation.org/66VBsHm7i.

[19] Isabelle Felici, *La Cecilia: Histoire d'une communauté anarchiste et de son fondateur Giovanni Rossi* (Lyons: Atelier de création libertaire, 2001).

[20] Isabelle Felici, "Les Italiens dans le mouvement anarchiste au Brésil 1890–1920" (Ph.D. thesis, Université de la Sorbonne Nouvelle Paris 3, 1994).

Grande do Sul was organized by other militants who never got close to the rural area where the colony was installed.

Summarizing this story and approaching the organization of Italian workers in Brazil in more detail, we should return to 1892.[21] In that year, a group of Italian anarchists in São Paulo founded *Gli Schiavi Bianchi*, which could be considered the first libertarian newspaper printed in Brazil, whose editor, Galileo Botti, an anarchist propagandist, had arrived just two years earlier from Argentina. This periodical inaugurated a phase in which a series of Italian-language newspapers of a similar anarchist nature were published in São Paulo up to the end of the nineteenth century. The most prominent ones, *L'Operaio*, *L'Asino Umano* and *L'Avvenire* (all edited by Felici Vezzani), *Il Risveglio* (edited by Alfredo Mari and Gigi Damiani) had in common the persecution of the press by the police and the criminalization of their directors for the practice of "anarchism." After a meeting at the Centro Socialista Internacionalista in São Paulo, some fifteen militants were arrested and imprisoned for seven months in a federal prison in Rio de Janeiro.

The syndicalist Felice Vezzani may be considered the Italian activist who introduced the anarchist movement to the Paulista working class in the last decade of the century, before his expulsion to Buenos Aires in 1895.[22] Vezzani arrived in Brazil in 1893 from Bologna, where he had broken his links with the Italian Socialist Party and moved on to anarchist stances.[23]

---

[21] The problem of worker organization inside anarchist movements was one of the great polemics at the end of the nineteenth century, particularly in Italy where the debate between "associationism" and "non associationism" occupied several pages in anarchist papers until Malatesta's anarcho-communism position became the standard of Italian anarchism in the middle of the first decade of the twentieth century. This kind of anarchism defends the organization of the anarchists and their activities inside the unions, but at the same time it has serious divergences from revolutionary syndicalism, as revealed in the debate against Pierre Monatte (1881–1960) during the Amsterdam Congress of 1907. See https://robertgraham. wordpress.com/anarchy-and-organization-the-debate-at-the-1907-international-anarchist-congress/. In Brazil, anarchist activists had the same debate shortly after that in Italy. The positions of Italian anarchists in Brazil were well summarized by Isabelle Felici: "La polemica non verte sulla necessità dell'organizzazione poiché la maggior parte degli anarchici italiani di San Paolo non rifiuta l'organizzazione in sé. Quello che separa gli anarchici dai loro avversari è il metodo da usare, le basi su cui deve riposare questa organizzazione." [The controversy does not address the needs of the organization because most of the Italian anarchists in São Paulo did not reject the organization itself. What separates the anarchists from their opponents is the method they used and the foundations on which this organization rested.] Isabelle Felici, "Gli anarchici italiani di San Paolo e il problema dell'organizzazione operaia (1898–1917)," in *La Riscoperta delle Americhe*, eds. Vanni Blengino, Emilio Franzina and Adolfo Pepe (Milan: Teti ed., 1994), 326–338.

[22] "Paulista" is the name by which citizens of São Paulo are known.

[23] *Dizionario biografico degli anarchici italiani*, vol. 2., eds. Maurizio Antonioli, Giampiero Berti, Sante Fedele and P. Iuso (Pisa: BFS ed. 2004), s.v. "Vezzani, Felice." Colezioni Digitali

But he always occupied a singular position inside the movement, a kind of bipolar voice, due to his sympathy for individualist tendencies and his syndicalist positions at the beginning of the organization of the working class in São Paulo. In fact, until the beginning of the twentieth century, the Italian anarchist newspapers printed in São Paulo, such as *La Nuova Gente*, *Palestra Social* (edited by Tobia Boni) and *Germinal* (edited by Angelo Bandoni), were ready to defend the manual workers, but at the same time remained very defensive against the existing unions. In part, this can be explained because there was not a definitive organized labor movement in Brazil, but only charities and mutual aid societies strongly influenced by Freemasonry and linked or otherwise close to State institutions,[24] even inside the Italian circle of workers.[25] However, the strong increase in the Italian population among the workers forced a change in the discourse and practices of anarchist militants.

During the first decade of the 1900s, the socialist and anarchist movement in São Paulo, which was prevalent in the workers of the Italian colony, had to talk to these new kinds of urban workers and help them to organize themselves into unions where none had previously existed. At the beginning of this organization of the working class it is possible to identify a strong presence of socialism according to two different characteristic definitions. First, a revolutionary one, present in the syndicalist approach of Alceste De Ambris (who had founded the newspaper *Avanti!* in 1900, the homonymous edition of the Italian version), and, second, the reformist one of Antonio Piccarolo (who took over the editorship of *Avanti!* after De Ambris returned to Italy in 1903). In these early years, socialists and anarchists divided and disputed the leadership of the Italian-Brazilian labor movement in São Paulo almost until the celebration of the First Brazilian Labor Congress in 1906. From this moment onwards, the association between syndicalist revolutionary activists, such as Giulio Sorelli,[26] and anarchist-syndicalist positions inside the unions became hegemonic. Nevertheless, the anarchist groups always demonstrated significant vitality and diffusion, especially after the

---

Biblioteca Franco Serantini: http://bfscollezionidigitali.org/index.php/Detail/Object/Show/object_id/2259. Accessed May 15, 2019.

24 Claudio H. M. Batalha, "Cultura associativa no Rio de Janeiro da Primeira República," in *Culturas de Classe*, eds. Claudio Batalha, Fernando T. da Silva and Alexandre Fortes (Campinas: Ed. Unicamp, 2004), 95–119.

25 Luigi Biondi, "Mãos unidas, corações divididos: As sociedades italianas de socorro mútuo em São Paulo na Primeira República: sua formação, suas lutas, suas festas," *Tempo* 18. no. 33 (2012): 75–104.

26 For better understanding of the Italian syndicalism revolutionary practices of Alceste de Ambris and Giulio Sorelli, see Edilene Toledo, *Travessias revolucionárias: Idéias e militantes sindicalistas em São Paulo e na Itália, 1890–1945* (Campinas: Ed. Unicamp, 2004).

exit of De Ambris to Italy, which can be attested by several associations dedicated to propaganda and social activities and the constant presence of newspapers in circulation.

Meanwhile, in an attempt to broaden the target audience, there was an effort to circulate propaganda in Portuguese, but often still written by Italians, as was the case of *Germinal* in 1901–1903 (edited by Angelo Bandoni) and *O Amigo do Povo* in 1902–1905 (edited by the Portuguese anarchist syndicalist Neno Vasco), among others. Another important component for the spreading of anarchist propaganda and its simultaneous circumscription to an Italian audience was the arrival after 1900 of many militants who had already had contact with and experience of anarchism in Italy or Argentina. This second group of activists directly contributed to the spread of the anarchist movement in Brazil, as can be attested by the cases of Gigi Damiani, who only arrived in São Paulo in the year 1907 to help write *La Battaglia*, Alessandro Cerchiai from Lucca, who arrived in the city in 1901, Angelo Bandoni from Leghorn and Tobia Boni from Siena, who both arrived in 1900, and Oreste Ristori from Empoli, in the province of Florence, who entered in the country in 1904 after spending two years in Buenos Aires and Montevideo. Ristori became a target of the *La Battaglia* group and was the most important propagandist of anarchism in that first decade of the twentieth century.

The anarchist network had been connecting Italian activists based in Argentina and Brazil since the end of the previous century. We can exemplify that circulation by following the steps of Ristori through the Italian Public Security Police's individual dossiers.[27] As delegate Genovesi described to the Minister of the Interior of Italy, Ristori already knew about Vezzani's actions from the pages of *L'Avvenire*, published in Buenos Aires since 1895,[28] and he himself became a regular collaborator even before his arrival in Buenos Aires in August 1902: "The short time he has been here has been highlighted by tireless propaganda, with almost daily conferences and assiduous written collaborations with the periodical *L'Avvenire*."[29] After the Argentinian general strike of December 1902, Ristori, along with Pascual

---

[27] For studying anarchists' personal trajectories or biographies, one of the most important sources are the police registers, particularly dossiers and individual schedules, which sometimes follow the entire adult life of the militant. Of course, this source needs to be supplemented by newspapers and correspondence, but in most cases police sources allow the tracking of militants' movements.

[28] Zaragoza Rivera, *Anarquismo Argentino.*

[29] "Durante il breve tempo dacché è qui, si è messo in evidenza per una infatigabile propaganda, con la parola a mezzo di quasi quotidiane conferenze, con la penna merce la collaborazione assidua al periodico 'L'Avvenire.'" Direzione Generale della P. S. della Preffetura di Roma, Archivio Centrale dello Stato (ACS), Casellario Politico Centrale

Guaglianone, Felix Basterra and other Italian activists, was deported to Montevideo under the Residency Law, accused of being one of the leaders of the movement. In Uruguay he met up with other Italians who had been deported and who had also been registered in the same Genovesi report: "He sought to escape and managed to do so, fleeing along with several other sectarian leaders to Montevideo. With Scopetani and Serantoni, who had preceded him, he did everything to resume the publication of *L'Avvenire* in that city."[30]

According to the police sources, the Florentine Alessandro Scopetani was an activist of small learning but energetic character who arrived in Buenos Aires in 1898 and published the periodical *La Nuova Civiltà*.[31] Years before, in Italy, both Ristori and Scopetani were confined on Ventotene Island, where they met for the first time. Unlike Vezzani, Scopetani had an anti-organization profile—that is, he disliked activism inside the unions. On the other hand, Fortunato Serantoni, who had been living in Argentina since 1893, was one of the most important Italian anarchist booksellers and editors at the Libreria Sociologica, a specialized libertarian bookstore.[32] Since 1895, Serantoni was known in São Paulo as the editor of *La Questione Sociale*, published in Buenos Aires, and also for his renowned bookstore that remained open until 1901. The works he published were commonly sold in Brazil (books were also advertised in the pages of anarchist periodicals such as *Germinal*). The city of Montevideo in Uruguay, also called the South American Switzerland because of its libertarian characteristics, allowed deported people from Buenos Aires to stay there. In fact, the surveillance of Italian diplomatic forces never established the same kind of relationship with the Uruguayan police that they did with Argentinian and Brazilian police forces. In addition, Montevideo must be included as a strong column of support for the Italian anarchist network abroad, especially in the cultural sense. Talking about this in an autobiographical work, the novelist Manoel de Castro remembered the daily gatherings that he frequented at Café Polo Bamba, where he

---

(CPC), b. 4342, fasc. Ristori, Oreste. Reserved note to the Ministry of Interior, from Buenos Aires, Jan. 27, 1903.

[30] "Cercò e riuscì a mettersi in salvo, rifugiando insieme a parecchi altri caporioni della setta a Montevideo. Con lo Scopetani e il Serantoni che lo avevano preceduto colà, egli fece di tutto per poter riprendere in quella città le publicazioni dell'Avvenire." Ibid.

[31] *Dizionario biografico degli anarchici italiani*, ii. 530–531. Colezioni Digitali Biblioteca Franco Serantini: http://bfscollezionidigitali.org/index.php/Detail/Object/Show/object_id/2024. Accessed Apr. 25, 2019.

[32] Ibid., ii. 543–545. For further information about Serantoni, see Adriano P. Giordano, "L'Editore errante dell'anarchia: Appunti per una biografia di Fortunato Serantoni," *Rivista Storica dell'Anarchismo* 6, no. 1 (1999): 41–70.

could see, distributed in different tables but easily communicating with each other, a whole generation of poets, sociologists and literati, in the midst of activity and whose books were published by Orsini Bertani, an anarchist who had lived with Pietro Gori in Italy and with the revered Kropoktin in London, and whose bookstore, located in the heart of Sarandi Street, was at the same time another meeting place for intellectuals and propagandists. He was surrounded by other expatriate anarchists such as Guaglianoni, Felix Basterra, Ovidi, Gino Fabri and Ristori.[33]

Thus, the workers' struggle inside the factories and the rule of the unions organizing the general strike were tightly connected in cultural and social circles and supported by a very well-articulated network of syndicalists, propagandists, intellectuals and editors engaged in, as it was called, the Social Revolution. All these individuals that we have been writing about were looking for a libertarian socialist revolution. What we would like to reinforce here, referring back to our understanding of anarchism explained in the introduction, is that the strength of anarchism lies precisely on this premise, in its pluralistic character of organization and not in the division between pro- or anti-unionism, "mass organization" or "insurrectionists." Or other types of dual separations.

However, not all among the anarchist militants were good characters. Sometimes, differences overshadowed the wish to work together for a common cause. For instance, the strong persecution after the general strike of 1902 in Buenos Aires caused the anarchist movement to be divided over the strategies it should adopt. The group of Italians exiled in Montevideo, at the head of which was Ristori, attacked the syndicalist position of *La Protesta* with the argument of the "unconsciousness" of the masses to support a general strike. The discussion occupied many pages in the anarchists' and workers' presses in Buenos Aires and Montevideo during the year 1903 and was a determinant motivation for Ristori's move to São Paulo.[34] In fact, the increasing contacts between him and Italian-Paulista anarchists were quickly noticed by diplomatic surveillance:

Recently, we have noticed a close relation between him and many anarchists, notably with Vincenzo Sassi, also resident in S. Paolo and subject of my

---

[33] "Pude ver allí, distribuídos en distintas mesas, pero de fácil comunicación entre las mismas, a toda una generación de poetas, sociólogos y literatos, en plena actividad y cuyos libros publicaba Orsini Bertani, ácrata que había convivido con Pietro Gori en Italia y con el venerado Kropoktine en Londres y cuya librería, instalada en plena calle Sarandí, era a la vez, otro centro de reunión de intelectuales y propagandistas. Le rodeaban otros ácratas expatriados como Guaglianoni, Félix Basterra, Ovidi, Gino Fabri y Ristori." Manoel de Castro, *Oficio de vivir* (Montevideo: Banda Oriental, 1959), 271.

[34] Further information in Romani, *Oreste Ristori*, 83–106, 114–119.

recent report, with Ezio Bertolini, editor of a fanzine in Sanpierdarena, with Remo Borzachini [...] and finally with Enrico Travagllini, editor of *Grido della Folla* from Milan.[35]

Vincenzo Sassi was probably Attilio Sassi, an Italian anarchist worker at a manganese mine in the interior of Minas Gerais who had been living in São Paulo since 1904 after having been fired due to a strike. Deported from Italy, Sassi became an important syndicalist inside the anarchist movement.[36] On the opposite side, the *Grido della Folla*, from Milan, was a traditional stronghold of anti-organizationism, under the editorship of the blind Giovanni Gavilli, who had already met Ristori in the Ventotene Island prison. So, the anarchist network developing in São Paulo was not narrowly defined.

What the evidence shows is that Italian anarchists emigrated to South America, and right away, after establishing themselves in São Paulo, adopted different strategies of organization. But, overall, what they were clearly contrary to was the kind of organization of, for instance, the Anarchist Party in Italy that, at the beginning of the century, would have been absolutely irreconcilable with anarchist ideals, as Alessandro Cerchiai wrote in *Grido della Folla*.[37] Or there is the case of Gigi Damiani, who defended non-authoritarian socialism supporting a kind of organization that privileged the relationship between the individual and society, as explained by Maurizio Antonioli, at a moment in which the Italian Socialist Party, using syndicalism, was undermining the bases of Italian anarchism.[38] So, the network that was going to be organized in São Paulo in the 1900s assumed a complex form. Despite the fact that most of the anarchists had come from individualistic positions or had a negative

---

[35] "Si nota, da poco tempo, una più stretta relazione tra lui e varii anarchici, segnalatamente con Vincenzo Sassi, pure residente in S. Paolo oggetto di mio recente rapporto, con tal Bertolini Ezio redatore di un giornaletto anarchico in Sanpierdarena, col Borzachini Remo [...] e finalmente col Travagllini Enrico redattore del Grido della Folla di Milano." ACS, CPC, b. 4342, fasc. Ristori, Oreste. Correspondence of June 11, 1904, from Petrópolis, Legazione d'Italia alla Direzione Generale della PS a Roma. Protocol 12618.

[36] According to Attilio Sassi's biographers, he was probably the activist identified by the Italian diplomatic policy in São Paulo as Vincenzo. In fact, he passed by São Paulo during 1904 before his return to Italy. See Tomaso Marabini, Giorgio Sacchetti and Roberto Zani, *Attilio Sassi, detto Bestione: Autobiografia di un Sindacalista Libertario* (Milan: Zero in Condotta, 2008).

[37] Alessandro Cerchiai, "Cosa si Intende Anarchicamente per Organizzazione," *Il Grido della Folla*, Apr. 16, 1903; Fabrizio Giulietti, *Storia degli anarchici italiani in etá giolittiana* (Milan: Franco Angeli, 2012).

[38] Maurizio Antonioli and Pier Carlo Masini, *Il sol dell'avvenire: L'anarchismo in Italia dalle origini alla prima guerra mondiale (1871–1918)* (Pisa: BFS ed., 1999), 62–63.

position within syndicalism, they were able to talk to and move inside different organizations, establishing good relations with the *Amigo do Povo* group, or with Neno Vasco, Giulio Sorelli, Edgard Leuenroth and other syndicalist activists. Maybe it was exactly this ability to interchange ideas and actions that caused the close surveillance of the police, who were afraid that the propaganda could spread to different kinds of workers in São Paulo and other Brazilian places.

The Italian Public Security Police had an extensive reach abroad by using the secret service of Italian diplomacy in collaboration with foreign local police forces. Since the middle of the 1880s, there had been a close relationship between the Italian and Argentinian police, with the Italian consulate giving secret information to the Argentinian authorities about the arrival of anarchists, a group that was considered as a criminal category. The police network also started to involve Brazilian police in the following decade. In fact, correspondence exchanges between Buenos Aires, Montevideo, Rio de Janeiro and Santos port police monitoring Argentinian anarchists' deportations to Europe and the expulsion of foreign anarchists from Brazil show this interconnection. Anarchists deported by ship from Buenos Aires commonly got off in Rio de Janeiro and remained in South America.[39] The police information was the result of an effort by the Brazilian investigative authorities (in Rio de Janeiro, at that time the capital of the country) together with the police of some regions of Italy and Argentina, who were trying to stop this uncontrolled circulation. The implementation of measures of international cooperation to fight anarchism, considered at the time an evil that compromised the national security of the countries, became an end to be pursued in the new century.[40]

An example of this cooperation between the authorities of South American countries was the information collected by the Buenos Aires police in an exchange with the Brazilian police in 1902. Warned by the Italian police authorities that Angelo Bandoni, with his companion Gigi Damiani, were behind an anarchist plot in Brazil, and that both were making trips through the countryside of São Paulo and helping with the formation of anarchist centers,[41] the Argentinian police passed this information to their Brazilian counterparts. The interest of the Buenos Aires police in data about Bandoni (and Damiani) is possibly explained by the ephemeral circulation that his periodical—*Germinal*—had in the Argentinian capital (within the Italian

---

[39] Diego Galeano and Martín Albornoz, "Anarquistas y policías en el atlántico sudamericano: Una red transnacional, 1890–1910," *Boletín del Ravignani* 47 (2017): http://ppct.caicyt.gov.ar/index.php/ravignani/article/download/11080/9900.

[40] Ibid.

[41] ACS, CPC, Bandoni, Angelo, b. 305, f. 75150.

community established in the region), and that awakened the curiosity of the authorities, who wished to know more about its editor.[42] The richness of the police reports is notable, because on the one hand they make it possible to demonstrate the exchange of information by the police in an international data network of information, and on the other they allow us to visualize the penetration and the circulation of the periodicals published by the Italian anarchists in São Paulo within different countries of Latin America, especially Argentina and Uruguay.

An overview of Bandoni's biography may show us some interesting characteristics of transnationalism in Italian anarchism.[43] He was born in July 1868 in Bastia, Corsica, a territory that at the time already belonged to France. Bandoni had Italian roots through his parents, both of whom were from Leghorn. His father (Giovanni) was a skilled marble artisan, and the economic background of the family was therefore somewhat modest to humble. Bandoni lived in Corsica until the age of eighteen, when he migrated to Italy and settled in the city of La Spezia (in the region of Liguria) in 1886. By the time he arrived in Italy, the country's working mass was still predominantly agrarian and artisan, and it was experiencing great difficulties and growing misery. The process of industrialization in the northern region and the periodic economic crises generated a purge of unemployed proletarians, provoking a deep social inequality. These conditions favored the development of the anarchist movement, especially in the provinces of Tuscany—Florence, Prato, Leghorn, Massa, Carrara—and thereafter extended their radius of propagation throughout the peninsula until 1898, when it experienced a period of weakening because of intense repression.[44]

The young Bandoni passed through different parts of the northern Tyrrhenian coast. All these places were under great influence from anarchism.

---

[42] In his newspaper *Germinal*, which was short-lived, Bandoni published texts with articles where Buenos Aires readers wove considerations about the issues. Moreover, there are numerous published letters that praise the editor for the journal's existence. This fact allows us to conclude that *Germinal* certainly circulated among the Italian community established in that region.

[43] For further biographical information about Angelo Bandoni, see Bruno Corrêa de Sá e Benevides, "A Trajetória de Angelo Bandoni e o 'Individualismo' Anarquista no Brasil (1900–1920)," Seminar, I Congreso de Investigadorxs sobre anarquismo, 26–28 October 2016, Buenos Aires: http://congresoanarquismo.cedinci.org/wp-content/uploads/2017/04/Actas-Final.pdf. Accessed May 7, 2019. Bruno Corrêa de Sá e Benevides, "O anarquismo sem adjetivos: a trajetória libertária de angelo bandoni entre propaganda e educação," *Revista Semina* 15, no. 2 (2016): http://seer.upf.br/index.php/ph/article/view/6855. Accessed May 7, 2019.

[44] Carl Levy, *Gramsci and the Anarchists* (New York: Berg, 1999), 7.

It was in this context that, for the first time, he discovered libertarian ideas. After his first recorded appearance in La Spezia (1886), police records show that he was arrested in Lucca for smuggling (1887) and remained deprived of his freedom until the end of 1890. Having completed his sentence, Bandoni returned to La Spezia for a second time and then fled to Algeria, a colony administered by the State of France. There he was sentenced to five years in prison for theft, robbery and the use of false documents. In 1895, after leaving prison, he returned to La Spezia for a third time, where he was arrested and imprisoned again (for nine months) and then expelled from Italy indefinitely. In May 1898, a strong war of repression was waged against the anarchists as the forces of King Umberto I attacked the heart of the libertarian movement in an attempt to exile "subversives" from Italy.[45] A series of expulsions and arrests began all over the country. Moreover, to soften internal tensions, the Italian government found it expedient to encourage the proletarian mass to move to a more distant place. This was achieved by supporting mass emigration to America.[46] It was precisely in this conflicted context that Bandoni had his expulsion decreed, arriving in São Paulo in May 1900. In the forty years during which Bandoni lived in Brazil, he placed most emphasis on propaganda and information concerning the political organization of workers, writing for a number of periodicals including *Germinal*, *Guerra Sociale*, *Germinal!* and *Alba Rossa*, and raising issues that gained considerable notoriety. He also organized conferences, set up schools and even had time to write poetry.

The case of Angelo Bandoni allows us to view, as in the lives of other Italian libertarians, the transnational nature of Italian-Brazilian anarchism rooted in São Paulo during the first decades of the twentieth century, and, further, its regional characteristic that pertained to the movement in central Italy, especially in Tuscany. The anarchist transnationality can be perceived through two prisms: first, through the contact between militants who spread around the world through letters that were written and published in the anarchist press; and, second, by the intense displacement of activists to several regions of the world with the intention of making libertarian propaganda.[47] The anarchist newspapers also published numerous letters written by readers (the majority of whom were anarchists) from different regions of the country and the world. This correspondence was published

---

[45] The episode is known in Italian history as "i moti per il pane" [movements for bread]. See Louise Tilly, "I Fatti di Maggio: The Working Class of Milan and the Rebellion of 1898," in *Modern European Social History*, ed. Robert J. Bezucha (Lexington, MA: D.C. Heath, 1972), 124–160.

[46] Levy, *Gramsci and the Anarchist*, 6.

[47] Turcato, "Italian Anarchism."

in a specific section (generally named *Piccola Posta*,[48] or "Small Post"), establishing contact not only between libertarian companions in Brazil but also between those living in different parts of the world, including Italy (Siena, La Spezia and other places in Tuscany), Montevideo, Buenos Aires, Chicago, Paterson (a stronghold of Italian anarchism in the United States) and some regions of Europe, from Belgium to towns such as Marseilles, Paris and Barcelona. On the other hand, Bandoni's biographical trajectory is an example of an anarchist individual who moved from region to region, nationally and internationally, aiming to spread anarchism.

However, the transnational relationship was established not only through epistolary exchanges. Bandoni was also involved in the support (financial, for example) of his Italian companions abroad. In 1902, the periodical *Germinal* carried out a fundraising campaign on behalf of the anarchist Florentine Giovanni Gavilli and Ludovico Tavani, from Ravenna, in order to bring them to Brazil. Both were anarchists with extensive experience in propaganda, especially in the regions of Tuscany and Emilia-Romagna. The campaign, however, had a short life and was not a great success. Nevertheless, the companions in Brazil led by Bandoni managed to collect 268 lire. According to reports from the Italian police, which infiltrated anarchist groups in Paris (the informant was Enrico Insabato, an ex-anarchist who disguised himself under the pseudonym "Dante"), the money collected in São Paulo by Bandoni, Gaetano Sandri, his brother Pedro and other comrades was to reach Tavani through their partner, Pietro Mori.[49] The 2016 dissertation by Jorge Canales Urriola offers a comprehensive analysis of the transnational phenomenon of Italian anarchism and shows how the South American route, including the Brazilian ports of Santos and Rio de Janeiro, became the preferential gates for extradited Italian activists. But most of them, such as Mori, Sandri, Luigi Bezzi and many others, had the sole objective of collecting funds to support their comrades' struggles in Italy.

After Ristori's arrival, observing the actions of the group called La Propaganda, whose name made their main objective clear from the very beginning, we can see a changing attitude toward supporting the class struggle of Italian immigrants in the farms and in the factories.[50] Their

---

[48] "Piccola Posta," *Germinal* 1–11 (1902).

[49] ACS, CPC, b. 5049, fasc. Tavani Ludovico. See the report from Prefettura di Genova directed to Direction General of Public Security, DGPS, June 13, 1902. For more details, see Jorge Canales Urriola, "Le valigie dell'anarchia: Percorsi e ativismo degli anarchici emiliani e romagnoli in Argentina e Brasile nella avolta di fine Ottocento" (Ph.D. thesis, Università di Bologna, 2016), 411–413.

[50] "Il gruppo La Propaganda non è un gruppo permanente, né fisso; cioè la sua attività dipende da circonstanze di indole diversa, ad esempio la pubblicazione di un opusculo; l'aiuto materiale e morale ai rivoluzionari," calling for meeting in *La Battaglia* no. 35 (Mar. 19,

first step was the foundation of the weekly *La Battaglia*, in June 1904, a newspaper that became a kind of watershed in Italian-Brazilian anarchism. In less than six months, supported by a large network of distributors in São Paulo and inside the country, it printed up to five thousand copies and became the most widely read militant worker newspaper in Brazil, rising to more than eight thousand copies in some 1,908 editions.[51] The journal supported several campaigns in favor of Italian immigrant workers and also of the entire working class. The denunciation of crimes and the poor living conditions of settlers on farms, the exploitation of factory workers, investigations of Catholic priests' crimes, the promotion of factory boycotts, the disclosure of strikes, campaigns for the freedom of unjustly imprisoned men and many other forms of action by the press made the names of *La Battaglia* and Ristori known across large parts of the country. In fact, *La Battaglia* was distributed and sold in every Brazilian region. It had subscriptions in Belém, Manaus, Salvador and Recife in the north and north-east of the country, and it had a large diffusion in the whole of Minas Gerais State, Rio de Janeiro and in the southern states of the country, as well as Uruguay and Argentina.[52]

The great campaign carried out against Italian emigration to Brazil that started in 1906, which occupied several editions of *La Battaglia* throughout this year, can be used to illustrate the actions developed by the group. After the second edition, one of its most popular sections was a column of writings about the living conditions of coffee farms that settlers named "*Dalle Caienne Brasiliane*" (From Brazilian Cayenne). It published weekly denunciations about extortion, rapes, crimes and slavery on the coffee farms involving Italian settlers that they considered a real hell on *fazendas*. The La Propaganda group had the idea of exposing this situation abroad by publishing a thirty-page booklet in which different cases of settler exploitation would be shown. This booklet would be published in three languages (Italian, Spanish and Portuguese) and would be distributed in Italy, Argentina, Brazil, Spain and Portugal as a warning to potential immigrants to Brazil and to encourage them to give up their idea.[53] The subscription to collect funds to print the booklet went on for four months and did not reach its target, but it was possible to print ten thousand copies in Portuguese before the end of the year. *Contra a Immigração*, its title, was

---

1905). If the group had maintained these fluid characteristics after the foundation of *La Battaglia* as a permanent periodical, the operation of La Propaganda would have diminished considerably.

[51] Romani, *Oreste Ristori*, 140.

[52] Ibid., 133–140.

[53] Ibid., 151–159.

never printed in Spanish, and its distribution was limited to Brazil, with a few exemplars reaching Portugal in the following year.

The publication of the booklet had bad repercussions in the Italian embassy and with the *senhores* of the farms, who predicted economic losses. Oreste Ristori and Alessandro Cerchiai, the two editors of the booklet, were questioned by São Paulo State police. The case was considered a transgressive subversion against the Brazilian State and they were prosecuted under the Aliens Act for a crime against national security.[54] The Public Prosecution Office defended their expulsion, but in 1908 the trial was stopped, and they were allowed to remain in Brazil. It seems unlikely that a few pamphlets disseminated throughout the country could have been the principal cause of this persecution, but *La Battaglia* had in the meantime been publishing the same denunciations on a weekly basis. It is perhaps more probable that the complaint came from Italian diplomats. In fact, if the Portuguese print run had failed, the Italian one would have been successful. The first contact in Italy had happened with Gino Allari, who distributed *La Battaglia* in Florence and who always remained in contact with the regional anarchist network in Tuscany. Unfortunately, it was impossible to print it there but none other than Luigi Molinari, an important Italian anarchist involved in education programs, became interested in the denunciation and was responsible for its publication by Mantua's Università Popolare. It was only after the Italian printing and the continuing propaganda inside the country that the legal process against Ristori and Cerchiai was taken up again in Brazil.[55]

It was not our objective to show in detail how this specific case developed (the reader can consult the footnotes for a specialized bibliography). What we intended in using this example was better to characterize the Italian anarchist network that operated in São Paulo. It worked efficiently, established connections quickly with Italian activists, and circulated propaganda effectively among their regional groups in Tuscany. But it also communicated with anarchist groups in other regions of Italy and, surprisingly, despite having few people involved in the organization, the network was able to disrupt significant sectors of the Brazilian economy as well as the Italian emigration routes. This is not a small thing and helps to explain the reactions of the authorities.

Looking forward, the years from 1915 to 1919 saw a period of intense activity for the workers' movement in Brazil. The Russian Revolution of 1917 added a supplementary dose of enthusiasm to the workers. Many public

---

[54] National Archive of Rio de Janeiro, ANRJ, IJJ 7 179 (SPE-101).

[55] Detailed analyses of the booklet *Contra a Immigração* can be found in Luigi Biondi, "La stampa anarchica in Brasile" (Ph.D. thesis, Università La Sapienza, Rome, 1994), chapter 2, "La campagna contro l'immigrazione e l'opera di denuncia."

demonstrations supporting the Russian revolutionary process exposed the anarchist groups in the main cities of the country. In addition, the conjunction of World War I (1914–1918) and certain significant developments in the industrial sector helped to give the workers' demonstrations sometimes an insurrectionist character.[56] In this euphoria, for the Italian libertarians in São Paulo, the war that broke out in August 1914 was not of central concern among those who began to write for *La Propaganda Libertaria*, the voice of the militants that arose from the demise of *La Battaglia* in September 1912.

The attitude of these anarchists would only change when Italy entered the war in May 1915. Thus, in September of the same year, a new journal called *Guerra Sociale* was established by Bandoni, whose main focus, initially, was almost exclusively the war and other international conflicts.[57] The writers who collaborated in *Guerra Sociale* were almost all Italian, except the Spaniard Florentino de Carvalho, whose cooperation with the newspaper was frequent and of great importance. The journal was initially edited by Bandoni, and afterward, as had already happened with *La Battaglia* and *La Propaganda Libertaria*, Gigi Damiani took over its management. In the pages of the periodical, exchanges of information, correspondence and news from Argentina, Italy, France, Spain, the Netherlands, Russia and the United States were common.[58] Over the years, however, the journal began to follow the news of the social lives of the laborers of São Paulo more closely, leaving international news in the background. This was clear from the months of May and June 1917, when tension increased due to the context of emergency strikes throughout the city.

Thus, a landmark event in 1917 was the outbreak of a major strike in the city of São Paulo. The "General Strike of 1917," as it was known, had the fundamental participation of the anarchists at the head of several class associations, mainly gathered around the newspapers *Guerra Sociale* and *A Plebe*.[59] Need once again saw the anarchists and the socialists join forces and they gravitated toward the newspaper *Avanti!* The leftist militant ensemble decided to establish the Proletarian Defense Committee (CDP) in order to better organize the strikers and broker the negotiations. At the time, the famine had provoked a deep revolt among the workers, stimulating the spirits of the workers against the government. The second half of 1917

---

[56] Alexandre Samis, "Pavilhão negro sobre pátria oliva: Sindicalismo e anarquismo no Brasil," in *História do movimento operário revolucionário*, eds. Eduardo Colombo et al. (São Paulo: Imaginário, 2004), 132–147.

[57] *Guerra Sociale*, May 22, 1916. See also Felici, "Les Italiens dans le mouvement anarchiste."

[58] "Movimento Revolucionário Internacional," *Guerra Sociale*, June 23, 1917.

[59] One of the most important anarchist newspapers, under the direction of the militant Edgard Leuenroth, launched in the city of São Paulo in 1917 but which folded by 1951.

marked the end of the workers' belief in the promises made by politicians and businessmen. The high cost of living coupled with low pay had created a mix of revolutionary revolt and ecstasy. The strike ended with some advances for the working class of São Paulo, and, in this sense, an eight-hour day and increases in salaries were, undoubtedly, the greatest victories of the movement.[60] On 18 November 1918, in Rio de Janeiro, a movement started that became known as the Anarchist Insurrection, where workers from various factories throughout the city simply stopped work. But, once again, retaliatory repression was aimed at the anarchists in an attempt to dismantle the movement.[61]

The End of the Italian Transatlantic Network in Brazil

Despite some advances for the working class, such events made the Republican government, especially after 1919, determined to take firm control of certain class entities, specifically in the systematized repression of so-called "subversives." Among other measures, we should highlight the greater restrictions on the entry of foreigners "harmful to public order" and the summary expulsion of immigrant residents in Brazil under suspicion of involvement in "subversive actions," a practice that continued throughout the early years of the Republic.[62] At the same time, it should be made clear that some foreign workers were expelled or deported without due process of law or in total contradiction of the law, as was the case for Italian anarchists including Gigi Damiani, in 1919. Many simply disappeared from circulation, were stuck on the streets, or were thrown into detention in police cells, waiting for the first ship to leave the country.[63]

The beginning of the 1920s was also marked by the repeated establishment of "states of siege" by the Chief of the Federal Executive (the longest period lasted from 1924 to 1927). These provisions became common, especially from 1922 onwards, with the inauguration of President Arthur Bernardes (1875–1955). In addition to these actions, the creation in Rio de Janeiro of the political 4th Delegacia Auxiliar (Auxiliary Police Station) under Bernardes marked the height of repressive State action.[64] Following the creation of

---

[60] See Lopreato, *O Espírito da Revolta*.

[61] Carlos Addor, *A insurreição anarquista no Rio de Janeiro* (Rio de Janeiro: Dois pontos, 1986).

[62] The so-called Alien Expulsion Act or Adolpho Gordo Law, in reference to the politician who was involved in the making of this legal device.

[63] Lená M. de Menezes, *Os indesejáveis desclassificados da modernidade: Protesto, crime e expulsão na Capital Federal (1890–1930)* (Rio de Janeiro: EdUERJ, 1996).

[64] Carlo Romani, "Antecipando a era Vargas: A Revolução Paulista de 1924 e a efetivação das práticas de controle político e social," *Topoi* 12, no. 23 (2011): 161–178.

this police station, the political practice of the infiltration of police officers inside the unions and workers' associations increased dramatically, with the objective of controlling organized workers. If this was not enough, another measure used by the government was the deportation of undesirables to the agricultural colony in Clevelândia, in the state of Amapá, a region located in the far north of Brazil, far from the eyes of the two largest state capitals (Rio de Janeiro and São Paulo).[65]

The emergence of this period of greater repression in Brazil began in 1919, mainly because of the treatment of the foreigners involved in subversive actions and because of the criminalization of the practice of anarchism.[66] This might be considered the main factor that led to the break-up of the transnational network of communication between the Italian anarchists in São Paulo with other militants in Italy and other places around the world. Of course, the rise of Fascism in Italy after 1922 also has to be considered a strong cause of this break-up. After the 1917 strike, owing to his being considered a leader of the movement, Gigi Damiani ended up being expelled. He returned to Italy in 1919, but seven years later he needed to escape the country again.[67] The expulsion of Ristori would come later, in June 1936, on the aegis of a very authoritarian government in Brazil under the dictator Getúlio Vargas (1882–1954), who sent him into the arms of the Fascist government in Italy.[68] Angelo Bandoni, at the age of fifty-one, tried to provoke a reaction and established new newspapers in 1919 and 1921 (*Germinal!* and *Alba Rossa*), but he did not have much success. He remained in Brazil until his death in 1947. Alessandro Cerchiai remained in Brazil and published some papers such as *Quaderni della Libertà* with Nino Daniele in the early 1930s until his death in October 1936. The largest group of Tuscan anarchists who were fundamental to unleashing anarchism in Brazil and who had helped to stimulate the formation of massive workers' unions, such as the São Paulo Workers' Federation (FOSP), was definitively broken.

---

[65] Alexandre Samis, *Clevelândia: Anarquismo, sindicalismo e repressão política no Brasil* (São Paulo: Imaginário, 2002), 171.

[66] Anarchism was criminalized in Brazil in 1921 with federal law n. 4.269.

[67] After his expulsion, Damiani wrote a vehement leaflet entitled "I paesi nei quali non si deve emigrare: la questione sociale nel Brasile." [The Countries to Which We Should Not Emigrate: The Social Question in Brazil.]

[68] ANRJ, Fundo Tribunal de Segurança Nacional, TSN, MJNI, Ministério da Justiça e dos Negócios Internos (1933–1939), box 292.

Concluding Remarks

Anarchy: Once, in answer to a judge who had asked him to define his political ideal in a few words, an anarchist responded with a biblical spirit that, for him, anarchy was Noah's ark without Noah. But another anarchist immediately protested that it was reformism and that anarchy was the universal flood without the ark. In this clash of jokes, the two souls of anarchism faced each other, the optimistic and rational one, and the romantic and nihilistic one, *Le siècle des lumières* and the *Sturm und Drung.*[69]

With this joke, Masini, the greatest historian of Italian anarchism, starts his definition of anarchy. It is, of course, a provocative reference to the Bible for everybody, both Christians and anarchists. But, besides this tense and perhaps contradictory definition, what Masini intended to do by pointing to the opposition inside the movement itself was to reaffirm that characteristic as its strength. Since Bakunin, who continually alternated the passion on the barricades and in popular insurrections with the mass organization of the workers, and whose example was followed by his main Italian disciple Malatesta, many different understandings between these two extreme poles have been laid on the path of anarchy throughout history, even up to today. So, anarchism being divided into two rigid forms—insurrectionist or mass movement—is not only a mistake, because there was and still is large interconnections between them, but also a purely ideological position by the authors who defend it, and has nothing to do with serious and honest historiography.

What we have tried to show in these few pages is that the significance of the transatlantic Italian anarchist network across South America and Italy, France and other countries is not in its division but in the complementary actions promoted by activists who were moving themselves among different positions inside anarchism, from a more individualist defense of freedom to more coordinated organization inside the unions. Rather than an ideal position in the movement, most of the relationships were based on regional identities. In fact, if we observe the regions and provinces whence most of the activists came and where they maintained their preferential affairs, we

---

[69] "Anarchia: Una volta al giudice che gli chiedeva di definire in poche parole il suo ideale politico, una anarchico rispose con spirito biblico che per lui l'anarchia era l'arca di Noè senza Noè. Ma un altro anarchico subito protestò che quello era riformismo e che semmai l'anarchia era il diluvio universale e senza l'arca. In questo scontro di battute si fronteggiano le due anime dell'anarchismo, quella ottimista e razionale e quella romantica e nihilista (*Le siècle des lumières* e lo *Sturm und Drung*)." Pier Carlo Masini, "Anarchia," in *Le parole del Novecento* (Pisa: BFS ed., 2010), 47.

can identify Tuscany at the top followed by Emilia-Romagna, Liguria and Lazio, and provinces along the railway on the Tyrrhenian coast, regions in Italy where the anarchist federations had been very strong since the last decade of the nineteenth century. However, if in the early 1900s most of the relationships were still being established inside the Italian community abroad, we can also observe a significant change during the 1910s. The beginning of the Great War increased on the one hand the internationalism inside the anarchist movement and on the other the relationship with the national community of anarchist militants in Brazil supporting strong worker struggles.

With this short overview of the Italian anarchist network in Brazil at the beginning of the twentieth century, we hope to have introduced its transnational characteristic, which was of course influenced by the regional identities of the activists, but, principally, to have refuted the idea that there was any kind of rigidity or narrow division inside the movement. In our opinion, it was the openness and flexibility of the activists that allowed them to build a strong movement.

Works Cited

Acri, Martín Alberto and María del Carmen Cácerez. *La educación libertaria en la Argentina y en México (1861–1945)*. Buenos Aires: Libros de Anarres, 2011.

Addor, Carlos. *A insurreição anarquista no Rio de Janeiro.* Rio de Janeiro: Dois pontos, 1986.

Antonioli, Maurizio and Pier Carlo Masini. *Il sol dell'avvenire: L'anarchismo in Italia dalle origini alla prima guerra mondiale (1871–1918)*. Pisa: BFS ed., 1999.

Batalha, Claudio H. M. "Cultura associativa no Rio de Janeiro da Primeira República." In *Culturas de classe*, eds. Claudio Batalha, Fernando T. da Silva and Alexandre Fortes, 95–119. Campinas: Ed. Unicamp, 2004.

Bayer, Osvaldo. "La influencia de la inmigración italiana en el movimiento anarquista argentino." In *Los anarquistas expropiadores y otros ensayos*, 136–152. Buenos Aires: Editorial Planeta, 2003.

Benevides, Bruno Corrêa de Sá e. "A trajetória de Angelo Bandoni e o 'individualismo' anarquista no Brasil (1900–1920)." Seminar, I Congreso de Investigadorxs sobre anarquismo, Buenos Aires, Oct. 26–28, 2016. http://congresoanarquismo.cedinci.org/wp-content/uploads/2017/04/Actas-Final.pdf. Accessed May 15, 2019.

———. "O Anarquismo sem adjetivos: a trajetória libertária de Angelo Bandoni entre propaganda e educação." *Revista Semina* 15, no. 2 (2016): 76–95. http://seer.upf.br/index.php/ph/article/view/6855. Accessed May 15, 2019.

Biondi, Luigi. "Anarquistas italianos em São Paulo: O grupo do jornal anarquista 'La Battaglia' e a sua visão da sociedade brasileira: o embate entre imaginários libertários e etnocêntricos." *Cadernos AEL* 8/9 (1998): 117–147.

——. "Mãos unidas, corações divididos: As sociedades italianas de socorro mútuo em São Paulo na Primeira República: sua formação, suas lutas, suas festas." *Tempo* 18, no. 33 (2012): 75–104. https://dx.doi.org/10.1590/S1413-77042012000200004. Accessed May 15, 2019.

——. "La stampa anarchica in Brasile." Ph.D. thesis, Università La Sapienza, Rome, 1994.

Canales Urriola, Jorge. "Le valigie dell'anarchia: Percorsi e ativismo degli anarchici emiliani e romagnoli in Argentina e Brasile nella avolta di fine Ottocento." Ph.D. thesis, Università di Bologna, 2016.

Castro, Manoel de. *Ofício de vivir.* Montevideo: Banda Oriental, 1959.

Corrêa, Felipe. "Anarquismo e Sindicalismo Revolucionário: uma Resenha Crítica do Livro de Edilene Toledo, a partir das Visões de Michael Schmidt, Lucien van der Walt e Alexandre Samis." In *Ideologia e Estratégia: anarquismo, movimentos sociais e poder popular,* ed. Felipe Corrêa. São Paulo: Faísca, 2011.

Di Paola, Pietro. *The Knights Errant of Anarchy: London and the Italian Anarchist Diaspora (1880–1917).* Liverpool: Liverpool University Press, 2013.

Dizionario biografico degli anarchici italiani eds. Maurizio Antonioli, Giampiero Berti, Sante Fedele and P. Iuso, 2 vols. Pisa: BFS ed., 2004.

Fausto, Boris. *Trabalho urbano e conflito social: 1890–1920.* São Paulo: Difel, 1976.

Felici, Isabelle. *La Cecilia: Histoire d'une communauté anarchiste et de son fondateur Giovanni Rossi.* Lyons: Atelier de création libertaire, 2001.

——. "Gli anarchici italiani di San Paolo e il problema dell'organizzazione operaia (1898–1917)." In *La Riscoperta delle Americhe,* eds. Vanni Blengino, Emilio Franzina and Adolfo Pepe, 326–338. Milan: Teti ed., 1994.

——. "Les Italiens dans le mouvement anarchiste au Brésil, 1890–1920." Ph.D. thesis, Université de la Sorbonne Nouvelle Paris 3, 1994.

Galeano, Diego and Martín Albornoz. "Anarquistas y policías en el atlántico sudamericano: Una red transnacional, 1890–1910." *Boletín del Ravignani* 47 (2017): 101–134. http://ppct.caicyt.gov.ar/index.php/ravignani/article/download/11080/9900. Accessed Apr. 30, 2019.

Giordano, Adriano P. "L'Editore errante dell'anarchia: Appunti per una biografia di Fortunato Serantoni." *Rivista Storica dell'Anarchismo* 6, no. 1 (1999): 41–70.

Giulietti, Fabrizio. *Storia degli anarchici italiani in etá giolittiana.* Milan: Franco Angeli, 2012.

Hall, Michael M. "Immigration and the Early São Paulo Working Class." *Jahrbuch für Geschichte Lateinamerikas* 12 (1975): 393–407.

Hart, John M. *Anarchism and the Mexican Working Class, 1860–1931.* Austin: University of Texas Press, 1987.

Hatton, Timothy J. and Jeffrey G. Williamson. *The Age of Mass Migration: Causes and Economic Impact.* Oxford: Clarendon Press, 1998.

Levy, Carl. "Italian Anarchism, 1870–1926." In *For Anarchism: History, Theory and Practice*, ed. David Goodway, 25–78. London, Routledge, 1989.

———. *Gramsci and the Anarchists*. New York: Berg, 1999.

Lopreato, Christina. *O espírito da revolta: A greve geral anarquista de 1917.* São Paulo: Annablume, 2000.

MacLachlan, Colin. *Anarchism and the Mexican Revolution: The Political Trials of Ricardo Flores Magon in the United States.* Oakland: University of California Press, 1991.

Magnani, Silvia L. *O movimento anarquista em São Paulo (1906–1917).* São Paulo: Brasiliense, 1982.

Malatesta, Errico. *Complete Works of Malatesta*, vol. 3, *A Long and Patient Work: The Anarchist Socialism of L'Agitazione, 1897–1898*, ed. Davide Turcato. Chico, CA: AK Press, 2017.

———. *Life and Ideas: The Anarchist Writings of Errico Malatesta*, trans. and ed. Vernon Richards. Oakland, CA: PM Press, 2015.

Marabini, Tomaso, Giorgio Sacchetti and Roberto Zani. *Attilio Sassi, detto Bestione: Autobiografia di un sindacalista libertario.* Milan: Zero in Condotta, 2008.

Maram, Sheldon L. *Anarquistas, imigrantes e o movimento operário brasileiro, 1890–1920.* Rio de Janeiro: Paz e Terra, 1979.

Marini, Gualtiero. "Revolução, anarquia e comunismo: Às origens do socialismo internacionalista italiano (1871–1876)." Ph.D. thesis, University of Campinas, 2017.

Masini, Pier Carlo. *Cafiero.* Pisa: BFS ed., 2014.

———. *Storia degli anarchici italiani da Bakunin a Malatesta (1862–1892).* Milan: Rizzoli, 1974.

Menezes, Lená M. de. *Os indesejáveis desclassificados da modernidade: Protesto, crime e expulsão na Capital Federal (1890–1930).* Rio de Janeiro: EdUERJ, 1996.

Oved, Yacoov. "The Uniqueness of Anarchism in Argentina." *E.I.A.L.* 8, no. 1 (1997). http://eial.tau.ac.il/index.php/eial/article/view/1126/1156. Accessed May 15, 2019.

Pernicone, Nunzio. *Italian Anarchism, 1864–1892.* Princeton, N.J.: Princeton University Press, 1993.

Prefeitura de São Paulo. "Histórico demográfico da Prefeitura de São Paulo." Archived Mar. 28, 2012. www.webcitation.org/66VBsHm7i. Accessed May 15, 2019.

Romani. Carlo. "Antecipando a era Vargas: A Revolução Paulista de 1924 e a efetivação das práticas de controle político e social." *Topoi* 12, no. 23 (2011): 161–178. http://dx.doi.org/10.1590/2237-101X012023009. Accessed May 15, 2019.

———. *Oreste Ristori: Vita avventurosa di un anarchico tra Toscana e Sudamerica.* Trans. Andrea Chersi. Pisa: BFS ed., 2015.

——. "Le scuole libertarie in Brasile e Argentina nel primo Novecento: L'influenza degli emigrati italiani e iberici." *Officina della Storia* 15 (2016). www.officinadellastoria.eu/it/2016/07/06/le-scuole-libertarie-in-brasile-e-argentina-nel-primo-novecento-linfluenza-degli-emigrati-italiani-e-iberici-2/. Accessed May 15, 2019.

Samis, Alexandre. *Clevelândia: Anarquismo, sindicalismo e repressão política no Brasil*. São Paulo: Imaginário, 2002.

——. "Pavilhão negro sobre pátria oliva: Sindicalismo e anarquismo no Brasil." In *História do movimento operário revolucionário*, eds. Eduardo Colombo et al., 132–147. São Paulo: Imaginário, 2004.

Schmidt, Michael and Lucien van der Walt. *Black Flame: The Revolutionary Class Politics of Anarchism and Syndicalism*. Chico, CA: AK Press, 2009.

Suriano, Juan. *Anarquistas: Cultura y política libertaria en Buenos Aires (1890–1910)*. Buenos Aires: Ediciones Manantial, 2001.

Tilly, Louise. "I Fatti di Maggio: The Working Class of Milan and the Rebellion of 1898." In *Modern European Social History*, ed. Robert J. Bezucha, 124–160. Lexington, MA: D.C. Heath, 1972.

Toledo, Edilene. *Travessias revolucionárias: Idéias e militantes sindicalistas em São Paulo e na Itália, 1890–1945*. Campinas: Ed. Unicamp, 2004.

Toledo, Edilene and Luigi Biondi. "Constructing Syndicalism and Anarchism Globally: The Transnational Making of the Syndicalist Movement in São Paulo, Brazil, 1895–1935." In *Anarchism and Syndicalism in the Colonial and Postcolonial World, 1870–1940: The Praxis of National Liberation, Internationalism, and Social Revolution*, eds. Steven Hirsch and Lucien van der Walt, 363–393. Leiden: Brill, 2010.

Trento, Angelo. *Là dove c'è la raccolta del caffè: L'emigrazione italiana in Brasile, 1875–1940*. Padua: Antenore, 1984.

——. "Wherever We Work, that Land is Ours: The Italian Anarchist Press and Working-Class Solidarity in São Paulo." In *Italian Workers of the World: Labor Migration and the Formation of Multiethnic States*, eds. Donna R. Gabaccia and Fraser M. Ottanelli, 102–120. Urbana: University of Illinois Press, 2001.

Turcato, Davide. "Italian Anarchism as a Transnational Movement 1885–1915." *International Review of Social History* 52, no. 3 (2007): 407–444. https://doi.org/10.1017/S0020859007003057. Accessed May 15, 2019.

Zaragoza Rivera, Gonzalo. *Anarquismo Argentino (1876–1902)*. Madrid: Ed. de la Torre, 1996.

Zimmer, Kenyon. *Immigrants against the State: Yiddish and Italian Anarchism in America*. Urbana: University of Illinois Press, 2015.

Zubillaga, Carlos. *Pan y Trabajo*. Montevideo: Librería de la Facultad de Humanidades, 1996.

4

The Panama Papers

Anarchist Press Networks between Spain and the Canal Zone in the Early Twentieth Century

James Michael Yeoman

For a brief moment in the early twentieth century, Panama became one of the most important international locations in Spanish anarchist print culture. Between 1910 and 1915, notices to and from the region appeared 189 times in *Tierra y Libertad* (Barcelona)—the most important paper in the Hispanic anarchist world—making it the second highest area of correspondence outside Spain, behind only France (652), joint with the United States (189) and ahead of Argentina (182), Cuba (158) and the United Kingdom (96).[1] This correspondence came from Spanish migrant laborers working on the construction of the Panama Canal, who engaged in the movement's grassroots media to join the most pressing debates on the future of anarchism in Spain, and support solidarity and propaganda initiatives in the country they had left behind. Print was also a spur to coordinated activity in Panama, giving anarchists a shared purpose to create organizations dedicated to the distribution of propaganda, and inspiring them to create their own periodicals and pamphlets. This loose trans-Atlantic network soon fragmented following personal and ideological disputes and disappeared altogether as Spanish migrants left Panama upon the Canal's completion. Examining this network in detail reveals the centrality of print culture to the experience of radical migrants and the

---

[1] From data presented in Joan Zambrana, *El anarquismo organizado en los orígenes de la CNT: "Tierra y Libertad": 1910–1919* (Badalona: centre de documentació antiautoritari i llibertari, 2009), 915–935. The vast majority (82) of the letters to and from the U.K. were sent to and from the Spanish communities in Dowlais and Abercrave, both in South Wales. See James Michael Yeoman, *"Salud y anarquia desde Dowlais*: The Translocal Experience of Spanish Anarchists in South Wales, 1900–1915," *International Journal of Iberian Studies* 29, no. 3 (2016): 273–289. For a broader contextualization, see James Michael Yeoman, *Print Culture and the Formation of the Anarchist Movement in Spain, 1890–1915* (London: Routledge, 2020).

functioning and dysfunctioning of anarchist internationalism in the early twentieth century.[2]

Early Connections: *Tierra y Libertad,* 1910–1911

More than three million people emigrated from Spain over the turn of the twentieth century. Most crossed the Atlantic and settled into well-established migrant communities in Argentina, Uruguay, Brazil and Cuba, as well as areas of the United States, such as New York and Tampa (Florida).[3] Central America, in contrast, attracted relatively small numbers. The one exception was Panama, which became the destination for thousands of Spaniards between 1907 and 1914. They were drawn by the prospect of work on the construction of the Panama Canal, which had begun in 1904 after the United States gained control over 550 square miles of territory between the Atlantic and Pacific Oceans (the Canal Zone) in return for supporting Panamanian independence from Colombia.[4] This immense industrial project was administered by the U.S. Isthmian Canal Commission (I.C.C.), which facilitated a massive influx of unskilled migrant labor to undertake digging and construction work. The majority of these laborers were black Caribbeans, around 150,000 of whom traveled

---

[2] For similar studies of the role of the media in anarchist transnationalism, see Martha Acklesberg, "It Takes More Than a Village! Transnational Travels of Spanish Anarchism in Argentina and Cuba," *International Journal of Iberian Studies* 29, no. 3 (2016): 205–223; Constance Bantman, "Internationalism without an International? Cross-Channel Anarchist Networks, 1890–1914," *Revue belge de philologie et d'histoire* 84, no. 4 (2006): 961–981 and "The Militant Go-between: Émile Pouget's Transnational Propaganda (1880–1914)," *Labour History Review* 74, no. 3 (2009): 274–287; Kirwin Shaffer, "Havana Hub: Cuban Anarchism, Radical Media and the Trans-Caribbean Anarchist Network, 1902–1915," *Caribbean Studies* 37, no. 2 (2009): 45–81; Davide Turcato, "Italian Anarchism as a Transnational Movement, 1885–1915," *International Review of Social History* 52, no. 3 (2007): 407–444. See also James A. Baer, *Anarchist Immigrants in Spain and Argentina* (Urbana: University of Illinois Press, 2015); Tom Goyens, *Beer and Revolution: The German Anarchist Movement in New York City, 1880–1914* (Urbana: University of Illinois Press, 2007); Ilham Khuri-Makdisi, *The Eastern Mediterranean and the Making of Global Radicalism* (Berkeley: University of California Press, 2013); Pietro Di Paola, *The Knights Errant of Anarchy: London and the Italian Anarchist Diaspora (1880–1917)* (Liverpool: Liverpool University Press, 2013); Ampara Sánchez Cobos, *Sembrando ideales: Anarquistas españoles en Cuba (1902–1925)* (Seville: Consejo Superior de Investigaciones Científicas, 2008); Kenyon Zimmer, *Immigrants against the State: Yiddish and Italian Anarchism in America* (Urbana: University of Illinois Press, 2015).

[3] Blanca Sánchez-Alonso, "Those Who Left and Those Who Stayed Behind: Explaining Emigration from the Regions of Spain: 1880–1914," *Journal of Economic History* 60, no. 3 (2000): 730–731.

[4] David McCullough, *The Path between the Seas: The Creation of the Panama Canal, 1870–1914* (New York: Simon & Schuster, 1977), 361–402.

to the region over the period 1904–1914.[5] Yet the I.C.C. was unimpressed by what they saw as a "lack of energy" from this racially segregated and discriminated against workforce and began to encourage Spanish migration through its agents in Cuba and Europe. In 1907/8, around 8,000 Spaniards were commissioned to travel across the Atlantic to the Canal Zone, drawn by promises of regular work and good pay.[6]

Anarchists were part of this migration from the outset, despite attempts by the U.S. authorities to deny radical laborers entry to the region.[7] A significant part of the Spanish working class had identified with libertarian ideas and practices since the 1870s, making Spain one of the few European countries where anarchism could claim an equal, if not larger, influence amongst organized labor as democratic socialism. The anarchist movement dominated working-class politics in urban Catalonia and south-west Andalusia and claimed pockets of support in all of Spain's major cities, including the northern ports of Vigo, La Coruña, and Gijón, where many migrants to Panama originated. These migrants were generally not high-profile activists or propagandists, the "wandering proselytizers" so common to studies of anarchist transnationalism, nor political exiles or terrorists on the run from the law.[8] Rather, they were ordinary members of the movement, who, like their compatriots, had left Spain in search of material improvement.[9]

Communication from anarchists in Panama back to Spain was sparse in the first years of migration.[10] Sustained transatlantic exchange only began in mid-1910, when *Tierra y Libertad* began publishing a regular column, "Desde Panamá," from its new contact in the region, M. D. Rodríguez , known in the press by his pseudonym "Intransigente" (Intransigent). Rodríguez had left Spain for Argentina some years earlier, where he had been active in the workers' movement before being deported in 1907. He then moved to Cuba, before relocating to the Canal Zone in May 1910.[11] Rodríguez settled in

---

[5] Michael Conliff, *Black Labor on a White Canal: Panama, 1904–1981* (Pittsburgh, PA: University of Pittsburgh Press, 1985), 24–44; Julie Greene, *The Canal Builders: Making America's Empire at the Panama Canal* (New York: Penguin, 2009), 121–158.

[6] Greene, *The Canal Builders*, 160–163.

[7] Kirwin Shaffer, "Panama Red: Anarchist Politics and Transnational Networks in the Panama Canal Zone, 1904–1913," in *In Defiance of Boundaries: Anarchism in Latin American History*, eds. Geoffroy de Laforcade and Kirwin Shaffer (Gainesville: University Press of Florida, 2015), 52–54.

[8] See Bantman, "Internationalism," 961–981 for a sense of the distinction between "elite" internationalists and grassroots members of the French movement in exile.

[9] A comparable profile can be given to the Spanish anarchists who moved to South Wales in this period. See Yeoman, "*Salud y anarquía*," 284.

[10] Shaffer, "Panama," 53–54.

[11] Ibid., 54. See also M. D. Rodríguez, "¡Emigrante! ... presta atención," *Acción Libertaria*, Apr. 28, 1912, 4. If a cutting from an unspecified, undated paper bearing the handwritten

Gatún, a town of 8,000 built to support the construction of the largest lock system in the world, which bridged the Chagres River to form the Atlantic gateway of the Canal, raising ships 26.5 meters above sea level to the artificial Gatún Lake, from where they would pass on through the Isthmus.[12]

These vast industrial projects were hardly mentioned in Rodríguez's reports.[13] Instead, his column concentrated on the "infamies" of Panama, and attacking the international powers responsible for it: the Catholic Church and the I.C.C.[14] The Panamanian Church—which controlled the press and public services, and "persecuted those advocating advanced ideas"—was regarded as a "stooge" of the Vatican and the "Black International" [*sic*] of Jesuits, who aimed to "turn Panama into a land of the Pope."[15] This cultural oppression worked in tandem with the tyranny of American capital and imperialism, which, having "appropriated Louisiana, Texas, Florida, Hawaii, the Philippines, Cuba [and] Puerto Rico" had now turned to Panama.[16] American capital also extended its reach across the Atlantic, "importing" workers from Europe with the promise of a better life. These Spanish, Portuguese, Italian, Greek and French workers were a "dislocated people," lured from their homes by the liars and exploiters of the I.C.C.[17] When they arrived, they saw the realities of this "sarcastic joke": migrant workers were paid half of what had been agreed in Europe, their American employers "insult them, beat them, make them eat *bazofia* [pigswill]," gave them awful housing and filthy clothes, and forced them to work in waist-high water and mud.[18]

Rodríguez saw this oppression as racially motivated. From 1904, workers in the Canal Zone were segregated according to race. White, skilled, U.S.

---

label "Intransigente" in the collection of *El Único* at the International Institute of Social History does indeed refer to Rodríguez, his full name was Manuel Rodríguez Figueiredo, and he was originally from Orense (Galicia), became a "fugitive" in 1896, lived in Buenos Aires, Mexico and Havana and worked as a photographer. Only details verified by other sources have been kept in the above text.

12 McCullough, *Path*, 483–484, 550, 592–596; Greene, *Builders*, 56–57.

13 One of the few specific references to the Gatún locks was made in Rodríguez's first report to Spain. See Intransigente, "Desde Panamá: Campo Neutral: I," *Tierra y Libertad*, May 19, 1910, 3.

14 Intransigente, "Desde Panamá: Campo Neutral: II," *Tierra y Libertad*, June 8, 1910, 4.

15 M. D. Rodríguez, "Desde Panamá: Campo Neutral: Intercontinentales," *Tierra y Libertad*, Sept. 21, 1910, 3–4; Intransigente, "Desdé Panamá: Campo Neutral: Kaleidoscopio universal," *Tierra y Libertad*, Nov. 30, 1910, 3–4.

16 M. D. Rodríguez, "Desde Panamá," *Tierra y Libertad*, July 6, 1910, 4; Intransigente, "Desde...I," 3.

17 Intransigente, "Desde...II," 4.

18 Rodríguez, "Desde...II," 4; M. D. Rodríguez, "Desde Panamá: Campo Neutral: Intercontinentales," *Tierra y Libertad*, Oct. 5, 1910, 3–4; Intransigente, "Desde...I," 3.

citizens in Panama were paid on the "gold roll," receiving high wages and a range of benefits. Those on the "silver roll," which included almost all "colored employees," were paid far less, given substandard food and poor-quality housing.[19] Spaniards were placed within the latter categorization, regarded as "semi-white" and undeserving of the same pay and perks as "white" Americans, while receiving slightly better pay and conditions than black workers. This "liminal" status ascribed to Spanish workers was the source of resentment, not least for Rodríguez, who was angry at the treatment of those who did not "*spik inglés* [*sic*]." Yet Spanish complaints at racial segregation did not develop into a sense of common cause with Caribbean workers.[20] At best, Rodríguez demonstrated sympathy, not solidarity, across racial boundaries, acknowledging that Caribbean workers were paid even less than Spaniards and lived "in conditions much worse than Europeans."[21] At other times, he actively reinforced the idea of racial difference between Europeans and Caribbeans, stressing the latter's "natural" docility and abjection, which was a product of their love of nation, God and "every class of vice."[22] According to an I.C.C. informant, Rodríguez also invoked fears of blacks undercutting and replacing Spanish workers at a meeting held in 1911, and called upon his audience to "arise" if such a plan was implemented.[23]

Rodríguez was pessimistic about the revolutionary potential of Spanish migrant workers, labeling them "illiterates, brutes, troublemakers [and] drunks," who were "deeply fanaticized [i.e., Catholic]," timid in the face of abuses, and obsessed with money, gambling and the brothel. It was "disgraceful" to see "the proletariat of the twentieth century being humiliated so meekly," like "slaves in the middle ages."[24] He repeatedly advised his Spanish readers to stay where they were, fighting oppression where they lived, rather than "running around looking for someone to

---

[19] Greene, *Builders*, 62–69, at 63.

[20] This was in contrast to the Cuban anarchist movement and its press, which had incorporated antiracism into its ideology and practice since the late 1880s. See Joan Casanovas, *Bread, Or Bullets! Urban Labor and Spanish Colonialism in Cuba, 1850–1898* (Pittsburgh, PA: University of Pittsburgh Press, 1998), 194–195 and 217–218. On the waning of Cuban anarchism's antiracism, see Kirwin Shaffer, "Tropical Libertarians: Anarchist Movements in Networks in the Caribbean, Southern United States and Mexico, 1890s–1920s," in *Anarchism and Syndicalism in the Postcolonial World, 1870–1940: The Praxis of National Liberation, Internationalism and Social Revolution*, eds. Steven Hirsch and Lucien van der Walt (Leiden: Brill, 2010): 281–282.

[21] Rodríguez, "Desde Panamá," 4; M. D. Rodríguez, "Desde Panamá: Campo Neutral: Kaleidoscopio universal," *Tierra y Libertad*, Dec. 14, 1910, 3; Rodríguez, "Desde...II," 4.

[22] Rodríguez, "Desde...II," 4.

[23] Greene, *Builders*, 176.

[24] Rodríguez, "Desde...II," 4; Intransigente, "Desde...I," 3.

exploit them" like the thousands who had crossed the Atlantic.[25] This advice was common to Spanish anarchist papers in the early twentieth century, both from contributors based in areas of high emigration, such as Galicia, and from migrants advising comrades not to follow their example.[26] Rodríguez's only explanation for the continuing stream of migration to Panama was ignorance of the anarchist press: "do you not read *Tierra y Libertad*, workers? If you did you would not have to bear the misery that hounds you."[27]

Rodríguez also used his reports to comment on recent developments in the Spanish movement. In the first decade of the twentieth century, syndicalist ideas of worker organization had found support in anarchist movements on both sides of the Atlantic and led to the creation of a number of national confederations.[28] In Spain, these developments had first taken shape in Catalonia, where a regional syndicalist federation had formed in 1907/8, which then expanded in September 1910 into the *Confederación Nacional del Trabajo* (CNT). The CNT would go on to become the largest anarcho-syndicalist organization in the world, claiming the support of around 850,000 affiliates in 1919. Yet many within the movement were skeptical of both syndicalism and the CNT at its inception, and warned of the dangers of supporting a "conservative" organization that would "castrate" the independence of anarchist groups, while promoting unionist "mandarins and governors."[29]

Few in Spain, however, were as vociferous in their condemnation of syndicalism as Rodríguez, who saw it simply as a means to "establish a new state within the old … a new bureaucracy inside the current plutocracy."[30] Rodríguez adhered to an individualist interpretation of anarchism, which rejected of all forms of authority and union structures and saw no hope in organized collective action. This branch of anarchism had its roots in thinkers such as Max Stirner (1806–1856) and Friedrich Nietzsche

---

[25] Rodríguez, "Desde…Intercontinentales," 3–4; M. D. Rodríguez, "Desde Panamá: Campo Neutral: Kaleidoscopio universal," *Tierra y Libertad*, Dec. 21, 1910, 4; Rodríguez, "Desde…II," *Tierra y Libertad*, 4. See also Rodríguez, "¡Emigrante!" 4.

[26] "Actualidad: La emigración," *El Corsario*, May 28, 1893, 2; "La emigración," *Germinal*, July 22, 1905, 2. See also comments from F. Ramos in Yeoman, "*Salud y anarquía*," 282.

[27] Intransigente, "Desdé…Kaleidoscopio," 3–4.

[28] See the collections *Revolutionary Syndicalism: An International Perspective*, eds. Marcel van der Linden and Wayne Thorpe (Aldershot: Scolar Press, 1990) and Hirsch and van der Walt, *Anarchism and Syndicalism in the Postcolonial World*.

[29] José Sánchez Duque, "¿Una Confederación General de Trabajo en España?," *Solidaridad Obrera*, Apr. 16, 1910 and Nov. 26, 1910.

[30] Rodríguez, "Desde…Intercontinentales," 3–4; M. D. Rodríguez, "Desde Panamá: Campo Neutral," *Tierra y Libertad*, Jan. 25, 1911, 3–4.

(1844–1900), and was a minority position within the Spanish movement.[31] Only a handful of the hundreds of anarchist papers published over the turn of the century in Spain advocated similar ideas, all of which were short-lived.[32]

In early 1911, Rodríguez called for an essay competition [*concurso*] to be managed by *Tierra y Libertad*. The competition comprised of three questions, all of which were clear individualist provocations to the mainstream position of the movement. Reponses were to be judged by leading theorists and publishers, with the best in each category receiving 50 pesetas (pts). The second largest paper of the movement, *Acción Libertaria*, of Gijón, applauded this initiative, stating that it would stimulate discussion on "topics of the greatest importance to our ideals," while saving on the expenses incurred by a congress.[33] Thirty entries were sent to *Tierra y Libertad* over the following twenty-two issues, most of which were published on its front page. Contributions came from across Spain—from San Sebastian, Madrid, Seville, Valencia, Barcelona and Huelva—as well as Paris, New York and Argentina. Most entries rejected Rodríguez's positions, particularly the second, most contentious, question, which was to be judged by the editorial of *Tierra y Libertad*: "is worker organization, as proposed by syndicalists ... a means to perpetuate exploitation?"[34] One particularly strong response came from Joaquín Bueso (1878–1920)—a typographer with the CNT's periodical *Solidaridad Obrera*—who replied, "no, and a thousand times, no: syndicalism, to the contrary, is the genesis of our emancipation."[35] Another entry suggested that to deny the value of syndicalism was a "blunder" that went against "logic and reasoning."[36] Rodríguez himself joined in the debate with the piece, "I am an anti-syndicalist," which stated that syndicalists were "pseudoscientists" engaged in a distortion of anarchist principles, and called for revolution "without committees or shepherds."[37]

---

[31] Rodríguez, "Desde...Intercontinentales," 3–4. The most detailed study of this current of Spanish anarchism is Xavier Diez, *El anarquismo individualista en España (1923–1938)* (Barcelona: Virus, 2007). See 33–45 on Stirner and 79–108 on the turn of the century period.

[32] Papers of a Nietzschean influence include *Juventud* (Valencia, 1903: 26 issues), *Luz y Vida* (Santa Cruz de Tenerife: 17 issues) and *Anticristo* (La Línea de la Concepción, 1906: 2 issues). See Francisco José Fernández Andújar, "Anarquismo nietzcheano y el periódico *Anticristo*," *International Journal of Iberian Studies* 29, no. 3 (2016): 257–272 for a detailed study of the last.

[33] "Mesa revuelta: Iniciativa," *Acción Libertaria*, Mar. 17, 1911, 4.

[34] Los Egoistas, "Iniciativa," *Tierra y Libertad*, Feb. 22, 1911, 4.

[35] Joaquín Bueso, "El sindicalismo es necesario," *Tierra y Libertad*, July 12, 1911, 2.

[36] Danko, "Respuesta: ¡No!," *Tierra y Libertad*, June 14, 1911, 1–2.

[37] M. D. Rodríguez, "Soy antisindicalista," *Tierra y Libertad*, July 5, 1911, 2.

Selecting winners for the competition proved difficult. The pedagogue Federico Forcada, tasked with judging the third question on educational methods, was disappointed with the entries and refused to pick a winner.[38] Likewise, the publisher Leopoldo Bonafulla (?–*c*.1922/1925) neglected his role as judge of the first question, much to the annoyance of Rodríguez.[39] For the winner of the contentious second question, *Tierra y Libertad* selected M. Sánchez Romanista, whose piece had struck a balance between individualist and syndicalist positions, claiming that workers' organizations "will not *perpetuate*, but will *prolong* exploitation" unless guided by anarchist principles.[40] Sánchez Romanista was grateful for the recognition he received, and split his winnings into two donations, 25 pesetas to support anarchist prisoners and 25 to support *Tierra y Libertad*.[41]

Despite its limp conclusion, this competition demonstrates the reciprocal, bottom-up nature of ideological exchange that was sustained between anarchists in Spain and Panama. For over a year, Rodríguez had been given a platform in the most significant paper of the movement, which he used to inform readers of Spain of his views on religion, migration, imperialism, international capital and, more problematically, race, as well as more prosaic matters such as the food, housing and the weather in Panama. He also promoted his contentious interpretation of anarchist ideology, which provoked a heated debate about the future of the movement in its largest public forum. Soon, however, the network between Panama and Spain was being used not only to exchange words and paper—or "hot air," as one disillusioned reviewer of the *concurso* put it—but also to inspire action, and establish material support for anarchist initiatives on both sides of the Atlantic.[42]

Organizing for Print

Groups of anarchists began to form across the Canal Zone shortly after Rodríguez's connection to *Tierra y Libertad* was established. The first—"Los Egoistas" (The Egoists, in homage to Stirner's *The Ego and His Own*)—was formed in August 1910 by Rodríguez and around thirty others in Gatún. They were followed a month later by "The Invincibles" (another reference

---

[38] Federico Forcada, "Concurso científico-sociológico: Tema III," *Tierra y Libertad*, Aug. 16, 1911, 3.

[39] "Sobre el 1.ᵉʳ concurso," *Tierra y Libertad*, Dec. 20, 1911, 3.

[40] M. Sánchez Romanista, "El problema obrero," *Tierra y Libertad*, Aug. 2, 1911, 1–2. Winner announced in "Sobre el primer concurso," *Tierra y Libertad*, Nov. 29, 1911.

[41] "Sobre el 1.ᵉʳ concurso," 3.

[42] Federico Fructidor, "Después del concurso," *Tierra y Libertad*, Nov. 29, 1911, 2–3.

to Stirner), based at a work camp on the Culebra cut, a "long, devastating stretch that sliced through the Continental Divide" where workers were under constant threat of dynamite accidents and landslides.[43] By January 1911, groups had formed at work camps in Las Cascadas ("Ferrer," adopting the name of the martyred anarchist educator Francisco Ferrer (1859–1909)) and Gorgona ("Los Sin Nombre": Those Without Name); while "Los Sedientos" (The Thirsty) had been established in Balboa at the Pacific mouth of the Canal.[44]

The upsurge in activity in Panama fits a common pattern of anarchist geographical expansion. The arrival of a press correspondent embedded a locality into the geography of the movement, giving those that lived there the opportunity to read about their lives, experiences and struggles. Often this would spur the creation of an anarchist affinity group, where like-minded individuals would meet, discuss the latest reports on their area, write their own pieces for publication and collect money. In Spain, many such groups also acted as workers' societies, yet those in Panama avoided this kind of organization. Staying true to the "anti-syndicalist" individualism espoused by Rodríguez, their only function was to distribute propaganda, and they were held together only by the loose bonds of their shared ideals.[45]

This moment marked the beginning of a steady flow of money from Panama to Spain, which continued until the Canal's completion in 1914. Over the turn of the century, migrant communities were often amongst the most willing and generous backers of anarchist initiatives in Spain, and those in Panama were no exception.[46] Money was collected at the workplace and social events, sent to the nearest giro service—often via Rodríguez, who would use the bank in Colón—and wired over to Spain. Until mid-1911, almost all of the remittances from Panama to Spain were sent to the offices of *Tierra y Libertad*, who would then distribute it across the movement. Amongst the largest sums collected were passed on to anarchist prisoners and their families, as in March 1911, when 43 individuals in Gatún,

---

[43] McCullough, *Path*, 529–554; Greene, *Builders*, 44.

[44] "Maremagnum," *Tierra y Libertad*, Mar. 15, 1911, 4; "Maremagnum," *Tierra y Libertad*, Nov. 16, 1911, 4. On Ferrer's international martyr status, see Christoph De Spiegeleer, "'The Blood of Martyrs is the Seed of Progress': The Role of Martyrdom in Socialist Death Culture in Belgium and the Netherlands, 1880–1940," *Mortality* 19, no. 2 (2014): 194–195. Also see on Ferrer, among other works, Sol Ferrer, *Le Véritable Francisco Ferrer d'après des documents inédits* (Paris: L'Écran du monde, 1948).

[45] See the founding statements of "Ferrer" in "Maremagnum," *Tierra y Libertad*, Nov. 16, 1911, 4 and "Los Sedientos," in "Maremagnum," *Tierra y Libertad*, Jan. 22, 1911, 4.

[46] See Yeoman, "*Salud y anarquía*," 279.

Gorgona and Balboa collected 110 pts, which were then distributed to 32 prisoners in Albacete, Barcelona and Huelva.[47]

Money was also sent to support publishing activity. All anarchist papers in Spain operated at a loss and relied on donations in order to remain in print.[48] From September 1910 to November 1911, *Tierra y Libertad* had an income of over 17,500 pts, 12,220 (~ 70 percent) of which came from selling bulk packages across Spain, Europe and the Americas. A further 1,890 pts (~ 11 percent) came from copies sold in Barcelona, and 602 pts (~ 3 percent) from sales of books and pamphlets. The remainder, around 2,850 pts (16 percent) came from donations.[49] From 1910/11, the anarchist groups of Panama were the most substantial donators to the paper in the world, sending almost 900 pts (~ 31 percent of donations)—more than groups in Spain (~ 26 percent), the United States (~ 16 percent), Argentina (~ 7 percent), the United Kingdom (~ 6 percent), Cuba (~ 6 percent), Brazil (~ 5 percent) and France (~ 2 percent).[50]

The Panamanian groups also sent money via *Tierra y Libertad* to other publications in Spain, including *Acción Libertaria*, which helped it weather severe financial difficulties for several months. When the paper was finally forced to close in November 1911, it made a "special mention to the comrades of Panama who have always sent much more money than they owed," unlike its Spanish correspondents and distributors.[51] Money was also sent to anarchist papers around the world, above all to the Cuban publications *¡Tierra!* and *Via Libre* (which was financed primarily

---

[47] "Subscripción general," *Tierra y Libertad*, Mar. 22, 1911, 4.

[48] Francisco Madrid Santos, "La prensa anarquista y anarcosindicalista en España desde la I Internacional hasta el fin de la Guerra Civil" (Ph.D. thesis, Universidad Central de Barcelona, 1988–1989), 36–38.

[49] Data collected from balance columns published in *Tierra y Libertad*, Sept. 21, 1910 (no. 30)–Nov. 15, 1912 (no. 83), all 4. Total income (minus profits): 17,538.73 pts; from package sales: 12,220.85 pts; from individual sales: 1,886.40 pts; from sales of other print: 602 pts; from donations: 2849.48 pts. Some errors in accounting were published, thus figures cannot be treated as anything more than illustrative.

[50] Data collected from "Donativos" column published in *Tierra y Libertad*, Sept. 14, 1910 (no. 29)–82, Nov. 8, 1912 (no. 82) all 4. Exact totals as printed: donations from Panama: 892.18 pts (31.3 percent); Spain: 736.60 pts (25.9 percent); United States (almost all of which came from a single donation from Tampa, Florida): 468.06 pts (16.4 percent); Argentina: 202.50 pts (7.1 percent); United Kingdom: 173.75 pts (6.1 percent); Cuba: 169.90 pts (6 percent); Brazil: 136.70 pts (4.8 percent); France: 46.03 pts (1.6 percent); Morocco: 20 pts (0.7 percent); Switzerland: 1.07 pts (0.1 percent); Mexico: 1 pt. (< 0.1 percent); Portugal: 0.25 pts (< 0.1 percent). As above, figures are more illustrative than exact.

[51] Editorial, "Despedida," *Acción Libertaria*, Nov. 17, 1911, 1. See the section "Interiordades: Correspondencia administrativa," in *Acción Libertaria*, Nov. 18, 1910–Nov. 17, 1911 for money sent to the paper from Panama via *Tierra y Libertad*.

from Panama), much of which was directed via Barcelona.[52] This indirect movement of money, from Panama to Spain to Cuba, developed because *Tierra y Libertad* was the key hub through which countless connections across the world were managed.[53]

As well as donations, money was sent to buy print. Between them, the Panamanian groups subscribed to almost every Spanish anarchist periodical and requested hundreds of copies of pamphlets and books to distribute across the Canal Zone. Once again, *Tierra y Libertad* was pivotal in these exchanges, either carrying out the requests themselves, or contacting other publishers in Spain. In March 1911, for example, the paper called on editors to send one hundred copies of five pamphlets—*Anarquismo y terrorismo* by José Chueca, *Individualismo é* [*sic*] *individualismo* by Maximo Dubinsky (?–?), *Los crimenes de Dios* by Sebastián Faure (1858–1942), *Organización, agitación y revolución* by Ricardo Mella (1861–1925), *La peste religiosa* by the German-American anarchist Johann Most (1846–1906) and *Reacción y progreso* by the Spanish anarchist educator José Sánchez Rosa (1864–1936)— to J. V. Beverhoudet in Cristobál (Colón district).[54] Panama became so saturated with print that in September 1911 the Chief Medical Officer on the Canal stated that hospitalized Spanish workers almost always had anarchist literature in their possession.[55] Print was valuable not only for the ideas it contained but also for the sociability it encouraged. Reading was a collective experience, as educated activists would read papers to their illiterate and semi-literate comrades, and write up group responses and messages to be sent back to the papers.[56] Print also provided a key function

[52] Shaffer, "Panama," 55–56.

[53] One of many examples of this arrangement can be found in "Correspondencia administrativa," *Tierra y Libertad*, Mar. 15, 1911, 4, where Los Egoistas sent *Tierra y Libertad* 5 pts for *Tierra!* (Havana), 6 pts for *El Látigo* (Baracaldo) and 6 pts for *Acción Libertaria. Tierra!* played a similar role in the Caribbean region. See Shaffer, "Havana," 45–81 and "Panama," 50–51.

[54] "Maremagnum," *Tierra y Libertad*, Mar. 15, 1911, 4. First publications of these works in Spain: José Chueca, *Anarquismo y terrorismo* (Zaragoza: Tip. Nadal, 1910); Máximo Dubinsky, *Individualismo é* [*sic*] *Individualismo*, trans. José Prat (Barcelona: Salud y Fuerza, 1906); Sebastián Faure, *Los crímenes de Dios*, trans. José Prat (Barcelona: Juventud Libertaria, 1903); Ricardo Mella, *Organización, agitación y revolución* (first known standalone publication: Tarragona: Acracia, 1922), request may refer to an existing joint publication: Ricardo Mella, *Organización, agitación y revolución* and Soledad Gustavo, *El amor libre* (Montevideo: El Obrero, c.1890); Johann Most, *La peste religiosa*, trans. "Ross" (Barcelona: Juventud Libertaria, 1903); José Sánchez Rosa, *Las dos fuerzas: Reacción y progreso (diálogo)* (Los Barrios: José Sánchez Rosa, 1902).

[55] Cited in Greene, *Builders*, 175.

[56] Ángel Herrerín López, "Anarchist Sociability in Spain: In Times of Violence and Clandestinity," *Bulletin for Spanish and Portuguese Historical Studies* 38, no. 1 (2013): 163.

in anarchist social centers, which were often little more than spare rooms in the backs of taverns where a group's collection of periodicals and pamphlets could be stored.[57] When one such space opened in Gatún in late 1910, the main benefit offered to members was a monthly pamphlet and a weekly subscription to *Tierra y Libertad*.[58]

In March 1911, the five Panamanian groups formed the Federation of Free Groups and Individuals of the Isthmus of Panama (FAILP) to coordinate their propaganda activity.[59] As with its constituent groups, the FAILP was formed solely on loose ties of affinity, with no fixed regulations or *jefes* (bosses). Nevertheless, a clear set of informal elites were responsible for its operation, namely Rodríguez and his ally Antonio López in Gatún, Cirilo Ortega in Culebra, Cristobal Lorente in Balboa and Pedro Torres in Gorgona. These figures acted as "nodes" within the Panama network, responsible for writing reports, collecting money, receiving and distributing print, and arranging the FAILP's monthly meetings.[60] In the following months, the FAILP expanded to include groups in Punta Toro, Emperador, Corozal, Pedro Miguel, Miraflores, Colón, Panama City and Tabernilla: "in short, in almost every town where a significant number of Spaniards resided."[61] One U.S. observer claimed that over 800 belonged to "The Invincibles" alone by this point. Although almost certainly an exaggeration, subscription lists published in the anarchist press suggest that a figure of 800–1,000 may be estimated for the FAILP as a whole.[62]

Why so many Spaniards appeared to adhere to an individualist interpretation of anarchism in Panama can only be guessed. Rodríguez and his allies were certainly influential, as all were charismatic speakers and dynamic propagandists, who could assert their ideas in the small communities of the Canal workcamps. However, resting analysis on the activities of exceptional individuals—the archetypal "wandering proselytizer" so common to studies of anarchist transnationalism—only goes so far in explaining the spread of anarchist ideas. A more prosaic consideration may be that the ordinary members of the Federation did not fully engage with the ideological

---

[57] Ibid., 164; Madrid Santos, "La prensa anarquista," 50–51. This practice was common to anarchist groups in many areas. See Tom Goyens, "Social Space and the Practice of Anarchist History," *Rethinking History* 13, no. 4 (2009): 451–452.

[58] M. D. Rodríguez, "Desde Panamá: Campo neutral," *Tierra y Libertad*, Jan. 11, 1911, 4.

[59] FAILP founded in Gorgona, Mar. 19, 1911. See Bernardo Pérez, "Hacía la meta," *Acción Libertaria*, Apr. 21, 1911, 3.

[60] See the discussion of "imagineers" in decentered networks, in Andy Cumbers, Paul Routledge and Corinne Nativel, "The Entangled Geographies of Global Justice Networks," *Progress in Human Geography* 32, no. 2 (2008): 196.

[61] Greene, *Builders*, 175.

[62] Ibid.

posturing of its leaders, and simply joined the only workers' organization available to them. This may help to explain how the fractures that developed in the movement were healed so quickly after a number of the founding members of the FAILP left Panama (see below). Another consideration should be the context of Panama, where collective action was seen to have little scope for success. Large numbers of Spaniards had been present on the Canal Zone for three years, during which time only a few strikes or protests had taken place, none of which was particularly successful. Thus, in Panama, individualism may have made more sense than the collectivist, communist or syndicalist interpretations of anarchism that prevailed in Spain. It certainly appeared so to José Novo of the group "Libre Examen," who wrote to *Tierra y Libertad* to outline the "futility" of collective action for "imaginary gains" in Panama. Their employers knew that there were thousands of hungry mouths in Spain, Greece, Italy and England, which formed a desperate body of reserve labor that made strike action pointless.[63] Such attitudes may explain why anarchist correspondents to Spain made no reference to a wave of strikes that erupted in the Canal Zone in July 1911, which brought around 800 workers out in protest. While this was the biggest strike in the region during the Canal's construction, it was also small by the standards of Spanish labor militancy, and wholly unsuccessful in its aims.[64]

El Único: Mouthpiece of the Panamanian Federation, 1911/12

The FAILP had two major ambitions: the creation of its own periodical and the founding of an anarchist publishing house in Spain.[65] A new body, the International Individualist Federation (FII), was created to administer these projects, constituted from essentially the same groups as the FAILP, plus a handful of individuals in North America and Spain.[66] By the summer of 1911, the FAILP–FII had raised almost $500, enough to schedule the launch of its periodical, planned for the second anniversary of Francisco Ferrer's execution in Barcelona, 13 October 1911.[67] This paper was named *El Único*, after the Spanish title of Stirner's *The Ego and Its Own* (*El único y*

---

[63] José Novo, "Pasto de la dinamita," *Tierra y Libertad*, July 3, 1912, 2.

[64] Greene, *Builders*, 172–173; Shaffer, "Panama," 55.

[65] Intransigente, "Labor trascendental," *Acción Libertaria*, Sept. 6, 1911, 4.

[66] The FAILP–FII's North American contributors were based around Carlos Salamero (?–?), previously of Los Sedientos in Balboa. He had relocated from Panama, first to Seattle and then to Vancouver, where he opened a workers' center. See Carlos Salamero and Roque Lacoste, "Desde Seattle (USA)," *El Único*, Mar. 12, 1912, 95 and "Avisos y noticias: Para *El Único*," *El Libertario*, Aug. 17, 1912, 4.

[67] Intransigente, "Próxima aparición del periódico *El Único*: De todos y de nadie," *Acción Libertaria*, Sept. 13, 1911, 4 and "FII: Cuadro estadístico ...," *El Único*, Oct. 12, 1911, back

su propiedad), and declared on its masthead that it was prohibited reading for "clergy, politicians, exploiters, and governors."[68]

Fourteen issues and two supplements of *El Único* were produced over the next nine months, each with a print run of approximately 2,500 copies. The paper provided the FAILP–FII with a regular bulletin, which informed its members of upcoming meetings and the state of its funds. The relative size of these donations reveals the centrality of print culture to anarchist activity in Panama: of the roughly $2,750 dollars collected by the Federation by June 1912, 83 percent was spent on some form of publishing activity—with *El Único* receiving 42.5 percent alone—while only 12 percent went to prisoner relief funds and 5 percent on administration (stamps, transport costs and legal fees).[69] *El Único* was distributed across every work camp on the Canal Zone, where readers were advised to share copies with their friends and colleagues.[70] It was also sent to workers' centers, taverns, restaurants and barbers, who were threatened with boycotts if they did not make the paper available to customers: "every conscientious worker"—the paper declared in January 1912—"[should] not shave in barbers which do not stock *El Único*."[71] *El Único* was also distributed internationally by *Tierra y Libertad*, which was enthusiastic about the arrival of this "valiant defender of anarchism."[72] *Tierra y Libertad* continued to receive most of the money sent from Panama, managing the FAILP–FII's donations to Spanish prisoners and requests for print. This exchange was now reciprocal, as subscriptions for *El Único* were paid to *Tierra y Libertad* from across Spain and wired over to Panama.[73]

El Único was used to advocate a strident individualist interpretation of anarchism. Rodríguez dominated its pages, acting as the paper's editor and main contributor, often under a range of pseudonyms: Intransigente, Bernardo Pérez, M. D. Perez, Fray B. P. Pérez, E. Fraile, Zeugirdor

------

page b. In the event, the first issue of *El Único* appeared on 12 October. No explanation for this change was given in the paper.

[68] Masthead, *El Único*, Oct. 12, 1911, 1.

[69] Figures published in *El Único* for Oct. 1911–June 1912 show an income of $2766.34, distributed as follows: *El Único*—$1181.89 (~ 42.5 percent); printing house fund—$815.90 (~ 29.5 percent); prisoner and exile fund—$333.36 (~ 12 percent); assorted books and pamphlets—$136.10 (~ 5 percent); administration and other—$132.40 (~ 5 percent); assorted periodicals—$101.62 (3.5 percent); subscriptions for Rodríguez's pamphlet *Campo Neutral*—$65.07 (2.5 percent). As with all figures published in the anarchist press, this data should be treated as illustrative rather than precise account keeping.

[70] Notice printed in *El Único*, Dec. 12, 1911, 37.

[71] FII, "Biblioteca," *El Único*, Jan. 12, 1912, front page b; Shaffer, "Panama," 58.

[72] Editorial notice, "*El Único*: De todos y de nadie," *Tierra y Libertad*, Nov. 8, 1911, 3.

[73] Examples of requests published in "Maremagnum" column in *Tierra y Libertad*, Nov. 22, 1911, 4; Dec. 13, 1911, 4; Dec. 20, 1911, 4. See also Jan. 24, 1912, 4 for a request from Tigre (Argentina).

(Rodriguez backwards) and Etnegisnartni (Intransigente backwards).[74] Other contributors wrote in from across Panama supporting Rodríguez's line, including the aforementioned Aquilino López, Cristobal Lorente and Cirilo Ortega, as well as Sem Campo (?–?), J. P. Ferreira (?–?), J. R. Mares (?–?), Federico Melero "Amargo" Reyes (?–?) and Teofila Rebolo (?–?), the "first female comrade to spread the anarchist idea in Panama" and the only woman in the region to appear with any regularity in the anarchist press.[75]

To *El Único*, there was a simple and strict definition of anarchism: "no government."[76] Any other interpretation was an aberration, particularly any notion of class struggle and worker organization. Syndicalism—the paper claimed—was reliant on an economic reasoning and "excessive materialism," which belittled and gentrified men; it "perpetuates capitalism" and is "anti-intellectual"; it lays down rules and regulations that "sterilize activity."[77] Syndicalism was as much a doctrine as a religion, thus "the syndicalist, like the Catholic, cannot be an anarchist."[78] Jaime Vidal (1890–?), the secretary of the syndicalist Atlantic Sailors' Union, became a particular target of the paper: he was a "usurer," a fraud, "Judas"; he "kissed the shoes of any priest," while promoting "laws designed to guarantee placid workers for the state."[79] Rather than joining in union with this "false anarchist" the paper advised sailors to visit the FAILP–FII's social centers to "read libertarian sociology."[80]

---

[74] On Rodríguez's pseudonyms, see Shaffer, "Panama," 54 and 59, and "También en Panamá," *Tierra y Libertad*, Feb. 21, 1912, 4. Another example of this practice can be seen with the publisher Joan Montseny, editor of *La Revista Blanca*, in which he appeared as Federico Urales and eleven other pseudonyms.

[75] Rebolo had one article published in *El Único* and spoke at a number of FAILP–FII meetings, where she called upon women to reject the church, read sociology, educate their children and join the struggle for "bread, light, love and liberty." See Teofila Rebolo, "A las madres," *El Único*, Dec. 12, 1911, 42; Sin Dios, "Del Canal de Panamá," *Tierra y Libertad*, Feb. 7, 1912, 4; J. R. Mares, "Actitud politica," *El Único*, Feb. 12, 1912, front page b. According to the 1912 census, only 370 of the 4,012 Spaniards (~ 9.5 percent) in the Zone were women. See Greene, *Builders*, 398.

[76] M. D. Rodríguez, "Antídoto: A un comunista," *El Único*, Mar. 12, 1912, 89–90; Intransigente, "Refutación al más allá de la anarquía," *El Único*, May 31, 1912, 133.

[77] "Del peligro del sindicalismo," *El Único*, Oct. 2, 1911, 2–3; Eduardo G. Gillimon, "¿Materialismo ó determinismo?", *El Único*, Dec. 12, 1911, 36–37; A. Lorenzo, "La anarquía trifunfante," *El Único*, May 4, 1912, 120; Editorial note beneath masthead, *El Único*, May 10, 1912, 121.

[78] M. D. Rodríguez, "Concurso: De individuo á individuo," *El Único*, Dec. 12, 1911, 37–38.

[79] Brisas Libertarias, "Desde el mar Oceánico," *El Único*, Apr. 27, 1912, 115–116; Alma Roja, "A través del Océano," *El Único*, May 4, 1912, 119.

[80] Brisas Libertarias, "A los del mar," *El Único*, Feb. 12, 1912, 73; Brisas Libertarias, "A los obreros marítimos," *El Único*, Apr. 12, 1912, 102–103.

At times, *El Único* turned its critique from syndicalist leaders onto the workers themselves. In an article, "My Hatred," regular contributor "Amargo" outlined his loathing for the usual anarchist targets of the bourgeoisie, the government, the army and the clergy, before turning on "the masses": "th[e] shabby, filthy, riff-raff ... disgusting, putrid, prostituted, alcoholic and castrated."[81] Elsewhere, these "docile sheep" were reprimanded for failing to support the Federation and its propaganda, while spending their money on brothels, taverns, carnivals and the Church.[82] Such statements reflect the influence of Nietzsche on anarchist individualism, which rejected the "slave-mentality" of the working class in favor of the will of the individual. Nietzsche's influence in *El Único* can also be seen in references to "the whip of Zarathustra" being applied to "false anarchists," and a poem which contrasted "the rebel of Weimar" to Jesus: "the first taught to improve and know oneself, the second counselled castration."[83]

El Único was also used to attack the I.C.C. and the Catholic Church, who between them had made Panama a center of misery, vice and ignorance. While working conditions were discussed surprisingly little in the paper, commentators did make occasional remarks against I.C.C. foremen and the unhealthy diet of mangos, bananas and alcohol that Spanish workers were forced to subsist upon.[84] As in the previous year, international readers were advised against emigrating to areas dominated by American interests, such as Panama and the United Fruit Company's plantations in Guatemala.[85] These sites of misery demonstrated the need for international bodies like the FII, and the irrelevance of national bodies such as the CNT: "if our enemy, capital, has no *patria* ... why do we gracelessly insist on being divided by nations?"[86]

A great deal of space was given in *El Único* to attacking the Catholic Church and religion. The paper was full of stories about the sexual life of the clergy, such as priests who did not love their mothers, monks who kept nuns in a harem and rumors about a "lecherous sodomite" who had abused

---

81   F. M. Amargo, "¡Mi odio! ... ," *El Único*, Dec. 12, 1912, 43.

82   F. M. Amargo, "Integros ... del rebaño," *El Único*, Jan. 12, 1912, 55; Pedro Torres, "Trallazos carnavalescos," *El Único*, Apr. 12, 1912, 100–101.

83   F. M. Amargo, "¡Rémoras!," *El Único*, Mar. 12, 1912, 92–93; Mares, "Nietzsche y Jesús," *El Único*, May 25, 1912, 131.

84   El Acabose, "En la picota: Para la ICC," *El Único*, Dec. 12, 1911, 46–47; Sem Campo, "*La Estrella de Panamá*," *El Único*, Nov. 12, 1911, 30.

85   Amargo, "Polo a polo," *El Único*, May 18, 1912, 126; "Cable oficial," *El Único*, May 10, 1912, 123. See also Pantalcón García, "Desde Guatemala: En plena esclavitud," *El Libertario*, Oct. 12, 1912, 4.

86   Iquique, "Retrato y caricatura: Por Rene Riquelme," *El Único*, Nov. 12, 1911, 29–30.

young boys in a religious college.[87] The Church was also criticized for its grip on education, which prevented any intellectual or moral progress in Catholic countries, molding the brains of the youth with "the scholasticism of the Middle Ages."[88] The paper's regular column on education portrayed this schooling as "mental and physical violence" against the young, which fostered "mediocrity of the spirit" and obedience. What was needed was a rationalist, individualist school system, teaching "healthy" and "hygienic" science and committed to forging a "superior man."[89] No revolution would be possible without such a transformation, as the "intellectual," "cerebral" revolution had to precede any economic or political change.[90]

Another possible route to the revolution was violence. Support for "propaganda by the deed," or terrorism, had been largely absent from the Spanish anarchist press since the 1890s, yet *El Único* was keen to revive this aspect of the movement's history.[91] In March 1912, the paper reproduced the defense given by Italian anarchist Sante Caserio (1873–1894) at his trial for the murder of the French President Marie François Sadi Carnot (1837–1894) in 1894, and praised his declaration of "DEATH TO THE BOURGEOISIE!"[92] In the same issue, the paper printed an extract from Johann Most's article "Murder for Murder," which called upon readers to "save humanity with iron and with fire, with poison and dynamite!"[93] The paper also applauded contemporary authors of "propaganda by the deed," including Antonio d'Alba (1891–1953), who in March 1912 had "moved from theory to practice" in his attempt to assassinate Victor Immanuel III of Italy (1869–1947: reign 1900–1946).[94] For Rodríguez, direct, violent action was a legitimate revolutionary tactic, since "force is not repelled with

[87] Sergio A. Valenzuela, "Perjuicios de la religión," *El Único*, Oct. 12, 1911, 3–5; Francisco Gicca, "La virgen," *El Único*, Nov. 12, 1911, 28–29; O. F. El Cura, "Milagros," *El Único*, Mar. 12, 1912, 96.

[88] R. de la P., "Las ideas y los acontecimientos," *El Único*, Jan. 12, 1912, 52–53.

[89] "Fundamentos de la idea anarquista: Escuela individualista," *El Único*, Nov. 12, 1911, 26; Dec. 12, 1911, 35; Jan. 12, 1912, 56; Feb. 10, 1912, 71; Mar. 12, 1912, 87; Apr. 12, 1912, 104; May 4, 1912, 118.

[90] Aquilino López, "La revolución," *El Único*, Oct. 12, 1911, 10; Los Egoistas, "Federación individualista internacional," *El Único*, Oct. 12, 1911, 11.

[91] The most complete recent work on this subject is Ángel Herrerín López, *Anarquía, dinamita y revolución social: Violencia y represión en la España entre siglos (1868–1909)* (Madrid: Catarata, 2011).

[92] Sante Caserio, "Ante el tribunal," *El Único*, Mar. 12, 1912, 85.

[93] Juan [*sic*] Most, "Máximas anarquistas," *El Único*, Mar. 12, 1912, 85.

[94] Labor Libertaria, "Quitando obstáculos," *El Único*, Apr. 12, 1912, 105. See also the calls made by Pedro Torres to assassinate the leaders of Greece, Serbia and Montenegro at an FII meeting in Panama City in 1913, in Angel Blanco Juez, "La propaganda anarquista a través de Istmo de Panamá," *El Látigo*, May 31, 1913, 4.

litanies nor with pseudo-scientific fantasies, but with another force."[95] Despite calls to arrest Rodríguez and suppress the FAILP–FII from members of the Panamanian Church, this provocative propaganda activity was largely permitted to continue, as neither the Spanish Consul nor the I.C.C.'s Chief Engineer Goethals believed the anarchists of Panama to be a genuine threat.[96]

The belligerent stance of *El Único* attracted hostility both within Panama and in the wider international anarchist movement. Many early contributors broke relations with the paper in late 1911 and formed a group outside the Federation, in Culebra, named "Germinal."[97] Amongst these "defectors" and "serpents" was Aquilino López, who was routinely attacked in the paper, accused of freeloading, and starting fights.[98] When López left Panama for Bordeaux, the paper printed his description to forewarn their French comrades: "regular height; withered and pointed face; ossified, sunken mouth due to his few teeth … smallpox scars … a gambler, drunk, swindler, smoker and idler."[99] Around the same time, former contributor "Sem" Campos took Rodríguez to court for libel, in response to claims made in *El Único* that he was an abusive foreman of a Gatún work team.[100] Despite his "enviable, typical, unique calmness" on the stand, Rodríguez was required to pay a $15 fine and $35 court costs.[101] As with López, Campos received a fond farewell when he left Panama for the United States, with *El Único* labeling him a "Judas of propaganda … short, fat, [with a] contorted face [and] posture of a clown."[102] Another former colleague denounced by the paper was Teofila Rebolledo, who responded by labeling Rodríguez as "the persecutor of all the anarchists in Panama."[103] *El Único* also attacked international anarchist groups, such as the Havana periodical *¡Tierra!*, which it accused of defamation, theft, ideological bankruptcy, and collaboration with its enemies in Panama.[104] In response *¡Tierra!* ran several articles "exposing" Rodríguez as a former police informant and strike breaker.[105] Another target

---

[95] Intransigente: "La anarquía," *El Único*, Mar. 12, 1912, 81–82, "Partidarios y adversarios," *El Único*, Apr. 12, 1912, and "El atentado," *El Único*, May 4, 1912, 117.

[96] Greene, *Builders*, 176–177.

[97] La Federación, "Tartufos," *El Único*, Jan. 12, 1912, 64.

[98] Jose Roldan, "Paso libre," *El Único*, Apr. 12, 1912, 109; FAILP, "Un salibazo: Para *¡Tierra!*," *El Único*, Mar. 12, 1913, 94.

[99] "Internacionales," *El Único*, May 25, 1912, 130.

[100] "La picota: Para Geo W. Goethals," *El Único*, Jan. 12, 61–62; "La picota," *El Único: Suplemento al No.5*, Jan. 20, 1912, 1–2.

[101] Los Egoistas, "A dos pasos del Imperio Turco," *El Único*, Mar. 12, 1912, 94–95.

[102] "Alerta!," *El Único*, May 10, 1912, 124.

[103] "Permanente," *El Único*, Mar. 12, 1912, front page b; Shaffer, "Panama," 63.

[104] "La picota," *El Único*, Feb. 12, 1912, 77.

[105] "Biografía al galope," *El Único*, Mar. 12, 1912, 95–96 and Apr. 12, 1912, 109.

of Rodríguez's vitriol was *Regeneración*, the paper of the *Partido Liberal Mexicano* (PLM). The international movement had been largely supportive of this group in the early stages of the Mexican revolution, yet *El Único* was unceasing in its criticism of the PLM (which it regarded as a "political" movement that committed mass rapes and brutal violence in its areas of control) and its leader Ricardo Flores Magón (1873–1922).[106]

By the spring of 1912, *El Único*'s hostility to the PLM brought it into conflict with *Tierra y Libertad*, which was leading the international campaign to support Magón's cause. For *El Único*, this was hypocrisy, financing politicians, nationalists and warmongers, while diverting money from worthy causes such as the founding of rational schools, prisoner solidarity and propaganda. It attacked *Tierra y Libertad* for converting itself into a "standard-bearer of toads and venomous serpents" and believing the lies of "Trágon" ["Glutton," a play on Magón].[107] *El Único* also claimed that *Tierra y Libertad* had stolen thousands of pesetas from the FAILP–FII, and added its editor Tomás Herreros (1877–1937) to its list of "defectors and defamers."[108] Rodríguez then cancelled the Federation's subscription to *Tierra y Libertad* and removed it from its list of recommended reading. The two papers were now totally estranged, with the FAILP–FII calling for the "excommunication" of the paper it had once labeled the "dean" of anarchist publishing, claiming its editorial had been "working like Catholics" on a "filthy and despicable" campaign to destroy the Federation and *El Único*.[109] In response, *Tierra y Libertad* ceased publishing news from Rodríguez, the Federation and *El Único*, and turned instead to Braulio Hurtado of the rival Panamanian camp for its correspondence.[110]

Aquilino López placed the blame for the "chaotic and destructive" situation within the Panamanian movement squarely with Rodríguez. The optimism brought by the founding of the FAILP–FII and *El Único* had been trashed by his former colleague, who had turned both projects into vehicles for his abrasive understanding of anarchism. The result had been schism within

---

[106] "¡Oh, la de México!: La partida de Flores Tragón," *El Único*, Nov. 12, 1911, 28; José Gutierrez, "¡Oh, la de México!," *El Único*, Oct. 12, 1911, 13; Pedro Esteve "Así la de México," Nov. 12, 1911, 32; "Oh, la de México!: Museo de embaucadores," *El Único*, Dec. 12, 1912, 43. See Shaffer, "Panama," 60–64 on all of these disputes.

[107] "Oh, la de México!," *El Único*, Jan. 12, 1912, 58–59 and Feb. 12, 1912, 75.

[108] "Permanente," *El Único*, Apr. 12, 1912, 111.

[109] "Maremagnum," *Tierra y Libertad*, May 8, 1912, 4 and May 15, 1912, 4; "Revista de papel impreso," *El Único*, Feb. 12, 1912, front page b and Apr. 12, 1912, back page a; Heredero, "Noticia," *El Único*, May 4, 1912, 119; Notice in *El Único*, May 10, 1912, 124; FAILP, "Oficial," *El Único*, May 31, 1912, 134.

[110] For example, see Braulio Hurtado, "Un mitrado pernicioso," *Tierra y Libertad*, June 19, 1912, 3 and "Complicados," *Tierra y Libertad*, Dec. 4, 1912, 3–4. Shaffer, "Panama," 60.

the Federation, while *El Único* had become "a joke" to comrades in the Americas and Spain.[111] In June 1912, the paper folded. The exact reason for this development is unclear, although it can be assumed that *El Único* went bankrupt, which was the cause for the collapse of most anarchist periodicals. Growing controversies may have prompted a decline in sales of the paper, and from April 1912 it had attempted to move from a monthly to a weekly output, which may have put an unsustainable strain on its finances.[112] This did not, however, mark the end of the Federation, which soon turned back to Spain to reestablish its presence in the networks of anarchist print.

The Spanish Successors: *El Libertario* and *Acción Libertaria*, 1912-1914

In the summer of 1912, the FAILP–FII relocated its publishing activity to north-western Spain. The Federation contacted the former editors of *Acción Libertaria*—Ricardo Mella in Vigo and Eleuterio Quintanilla (1886–1966) and Pedro Sierra Álvarez (1888–1969) in Gijón—and gave them 140 pts to launch *El Libertario*, which would take over from *El Único* as the official organ of the Federation.[113] Rodríguez advised anyone wishing to contact the Federation to go through this paper, which he named (in a swipe at *Tierra y Libertad*) "the new leader of anarchist thought."[114] Money from Panama sustained this periodical from August 1912 to April 1913, when it was forced to relocate to Madrid and change its name to *Acción Libertaria*. This new publication maintained its links to the FAILP–FII until the end of the year, when it too was forced to close.[115] While these papers were backed by Panamanian money, neither bore much relation to *El Único* in terms of style or content; rather, they were part of a lineage of anarchist periodicals under the direction of Mella, which had begun in 1909 with *Tribuna Libre* and continued with the original *Acción Libertaria*. Although he was skeptical of syndicalism and the CNT, Mella was by no means an individualist, and was totally opposed to the positions taken by *El Único* on terrorism (which Mella saw as repugnant) and education (which he saw as indoctrination akin to Catholic education).[116]

---

[111] Scahaffer, "Panama," 63–64.

[112] Moves to increase output often led to the collapse of anarchist papers, as had happened in 1903 when *Tierra y Libertad* had attempted to publish a daily edition.

[113] "Avisos y noticias" and "Federación Internacional Individualista," *El Libertario*, Aug. 10, 1912, 4; Editorial note, *El Libertario*, Sept. 7, 1912, 2. See also Shaffer, "Panama," 64.

[114] Intransigente, "FII: Un llamiento," *El Libertario*, Aug. 31, 1912, 4.

[115] Editorial, "Explicación necesaria" and "En la brecha," *Acción Libertaria*, May 23, 1913, 1.

[116] Ricardo Mella, "El problema de la enseñanza: Ratificación," *Acción Libertaria*, Jan. 11, 1911, 1.

Both papers did, however, publish regular news of the FAILP–FII, which appeared to be functioning well, despite the schisms within the Panamanian movement. Collections for Spanish anarchist periodicals continued—although pointedly not for *Tierra y Libertad*—as did the fund for an anarchist publishing house. The Federation's monthly meetings and work in "encouraging the love of culture … by means of the free press, journals, books and pamphlets" were reportedly more successful than ever.[117] Yet there was also a striking absence from these reports. Rodríguez no longer appeared in collection lists, he had stepped down from his positions in the Federation, and at meetings he had been replaced by figures such as José Galabaldá (?–?), who reportedly gave such a passionate speech in Panama City in April 1913 that "if Intransigente were here today" he would be proud.[118] Although it was not explicitly stated, it appears that Rodríguez had left Panama to join the editorial board of *El Libertario* in Gijón. A "representative" of the Federation had arrived in Spain in September 1912, and for the next few months all administrative correspondence in the paper addressed to Panama was handled by "I." (almost certainly an abbreviation of Intransigente).[119] Even these vague hints at Rodríguez's location dried up in early 1913, when he disappeared from the anarchist press altogether. Neither his Spanish publishing contacts nor his former comrades in Panama knew where he had gone.[120]

Over the following eighteen months, several new groups affiliated to the FAILP–FII, and the flow of money and print between Panama and Spain remained strong. Jesús "Sin Díos" Loúzara took a leading role in the Federation in this period, affirming its individualist stance in his reports to Spain and speeches across Panama.[121] In early 1913, there were also signs that the rift within the Panamanian movement was healing, as formerly

[117] Sin Dios, "Movimiento social: Extranjero: Panamá," *El Libertario*, Sept. 28, 1912, 4.

[118] Blanco Juez, "Istmo," 4.

[119] Juan Blasco, "Asuntos varios," *El Porvenir del Obrero*, Sept. 7, 1912, 4. For example, see I., "Correspondencia: De redacción," *El Libertario*, Nov. 9, 1912, 4.

[120] "Entre nosotros," *Acción Libertaria*, June 27, 1913, 4; J. Lóuzara, "Federación de Agrupaciones," *Acción Libertaria*, Aug. 15, 1913, 4. Shaffer states that Rodríguez had disappeared with the Federation's printing house fund, which explains the angry and urgent tones of the above notices in *Acción Libertaria* asking for his whereabouts. "Panama," 65–66. However, these reports do not mention Rodríguez stealing any money, nor do any reports on the balance of the printing house fund, which was reportedly sent to *El Libertario* in November 1912 and then to *Acción Libertaria*. See C. Ortega, "FII: Desenmascarando á un farsante," *El Libertario*, Nov. 9, 1912, 4; El grupo editor de *El Libertario*, "FII: Pro-Imprenta," *Acción Libertaria*, May 23, 1913, 4; C. Ortega, "La necesidad de la imprenta," *Acción Libertaria*, June 20, 1913, 4; El grupo editor de *AL*, "Subscripción pro-imprenta," *Acción Libertaria*, June 27, 1913, 3; Aug. 29, 1913, 4; and Oct. 3, 1913, 4.

[121] Sin Dios, "FII: Labor que se impone," *El Libertario*, Jan. 18, 1913, 4.

antagonistic groups beginning to send money and reports to each other's papers.[122] Yet the Federation also suffered setbacks. In November 1912, "Amargo"—a founding member of both the Federation and *El Único*—stole \$266 of printing funds and fled Panama. The Federation alerted the Spanish movement of this "miserable wretch," who should be "hated by all for his hypocritical, farcical conduct," and shifted its funds to Gijón for safe keeping.[123] A year later, Ciliro Ortega, another key member of the Federation, left the movement to open a tavern. His former comrades in Panama were amazed that someone who had frequently denounced the "unconscious masses who occupy the drinking-dens" had now committed himself to "stupefying the working class with alcohol," and called for a boycott of his premises.[124]

By the end of 1913, the Federation was clearly winding down, as its members left Panama in droves as the Canal reached its completion.[125] As work camps were dismantled the Federation's propaganda groups dissolved and sent notices to the Spanish press to cancel their subscriptions.[126] Most Spanish workers did not stay in Panama, and either returned to Spain or moved on to the United States, Argentina or Brazil. Stripped of its membership, the FAILP–FII relocated out of the Canal Zone to Panama City, where it became a shell of an organization.[127] The final phase of the links between anarchists in Spain and Panama began in August 1914. As the Canal was officially opened, a new anarchist publisher arrived in Colón from Spain: José María Blázquez de Pedro (1875–1927), a poet, theorist and newspaper correspondent who had led a propaganda group in Béjar (Salamanca) for the previous decade. His reasons for traveling to Panama are unclear. If he had intended to join, or revive, the movement in the region, he was disappointed. Unlike Rodríguez, this traveling propagandist had

---

[122] Scahffer, "Panama," 65. Braulio Hurtado, "Crónicas internacionales: Panamá," *Acción Libertaria*, 13 June, 1913, 4.

[123] C. Ortega, "FII: Desenmascarando a un farsante," *El Libertario*, Nov. 9, 1912.

[124] C. Ortega, "Del Canal Panamá," *Tierra y Libertad*, Mar. 6, 1912, 3; Los Invencibles, "FII: ¡A la picota!," *Acción Libertaria*, Nov. 14, 1913, 4.

[125] See Greene, *Builders*, 334–366 and McCullough, *Path*, 604–610 on the final stages and opening of the Canal.

[126] See dissolution of "Los Sin Nombre" and work ceased in Gorgona: "Maremagnum," *Tierra y Libertad*, May 21, 1913, 4; relocation of "Los Iguales" as the Miraflores locks were completed: "FII: Aviso de importancia," *Acción Libertaria*, Sept. 26, 1913, 4; break-up of "Los Nada" and "Los Egoistas," as work ended in Pedro Miguel and Gatún: "FII: Suspensión de correspondencia," *Acción Libertaria*, Dec. 12, 1913, 4.

[127] J. Roldán, "FII: Cambio de residencia," *Acción Libertaria*, Oct. 17, 1913, 3–4. One of the few groups to continue after this point was "Los Sedientos," of Balboa. See Enrique Goñi, "Pensamientos," *Tierra y Libertad*, June 30, 1915, 1. Small groups also continued to send money to Cuba through 1914. See Shaffer, "Tropical Libertarians," 303.

no base of migrant labor to bring to the cause, and his reports to *Tierra y Libertad* over the following decade gave no impression that there was any movement worth noting in the region. In 1925, Blázquez de Pedro was deported to Cuba, where he died two years later, bringing to an end the transatlantic print network between Spain and Panama.[128]

Conclusion

The Canal Zone was an exceptional context—a slice of U.S. territory in Latin America where a colossal industrial project had drawn in labor from around the world throwing together people of different cultures, races, languages and political beliefs. Some of what took place in Panama regarding the anarchist movement was unique, befitting of this unique situation. But many of the developments in the Canal Zone were common to all anarchist movements, not least the deep connection that anarchists in Panama had with print, which meant much more to them than just paper and words.

Libertarian ideas had arrived in the area with the first Spanish migrants, but had only really taken hold when an idiosyncratic figure took it upon himself to engage with the movement's international press networks, above all with *Tierra y Libertad* of Barcelona. Rodríguez's activity gave impetus to action in the Canal Zone, encouraging radical workers to join together and raise remittances to support comrades and initiatives of the movement they had left behind. In exchange they received a wealth of print materials, which stimulated propaganda efforts and sociability. Supporting print was also the main objective of the next stage of the Panamanian movement: a Federation, which funded publishing activities in Spain and launched its own periodical. This high point was short-lived, however, as both the Federation and its paper were used by Rodríguez to advance an abrasive, minority view of anarchism, which was out of step with the prevailing trends within the international movement. The weaknesses of structuring activity around print culture and publishing elites was soon exposed, as groups in Panama, the Americas and Spain broke ties with Rodríguez, leaving the Federation isolated and assisting in the collapse of its mouthpiece. The situation was rescued only by handing over publishing concerns to a respected editing collective in Spain, relocating the Federation's affairs—and possibility Rodríguez—back across the Atlantic. While this move brought some stability to the Panamanian movement, it could not survive beyond the Canal's completion. The anarchists of Panama were there for work, and once this dried up, they moved on, leaving few records besides the reports of U.S.

---

[128] Hernando Franco Múñoz, *Blázquez de Pedro y los orígenes del sindicalismo panameño* (Panama: Movimientos Editores, 1986), 169–206; Shaffer, "Tropical Libertarians," 303.

agents and, above all, their contributions to the movement's print culture on both sides of the Atlantic.

Works Cited

Anarchist Periodicals

Acción Libertaria. Gijón, 1910–1911.

Acción Libertaria. Madrid, 1913.

El Corsario. La Coruña, 1890–1896.

Germinal. La Coruña, 1904–1905.

El Látigo. Baracaldo, 1912–1914.

El Libertario. Gijón, 1912–1913.

El Porvenir del Obrero. Mahón, 1912–1915.

Solidaridad Obrera. Gijón, 1909–1910.

Tierra y Libertad. IV Epoch. Barcelona, 1910–1919.

El Único. Colón, 1911–1912.

Anarchist Pamphlets

Cheuca, José. *Anarquismo y terrorismo*. Zaragoza: Tip. Nadal, 1910.

Dubinsky, Máximo. *Individualismo é [sic] Individualismo*, trans. José Prat. Barcelona: Salud y Fuerza, 1906.

Faure, Sebastián. *Los crímenes de Dios*, trans. José Prat. Barcelona: Juventud Libertaria, 1903.

Mella, Ricardo. *Organización, agitación y revolución*. Tarragona: Acracia, 1922.

Most, Johann. *La peste religiosa*, trans. "Ross." Barcelona: Juventud Libertaria, 1903.

Sánchez Rosa, José. *Las dos fuerzas: Reacción y progreso (diálogo)*. Los Barrios: José Sánchez Rosa, 1902.

Secondary Works

Acklesberg, Martha. "It Takes More Than a Village! Transnational Travels of Spanish Anarchism in Argentina and Cuba." *International Journal of Iberian Studies* 29, no. 3 (2016): 205–223.

Baer, James A. *Anarchist Immigrants in Spain and Argentina*. Urbana: University of Illinois Press, 2015.

Bantman, Constance. "Internationalism without an International? Cross-Channel Anarchist Networks, 1890–1914." *Revue belge de philologie et d'histoire* 84, no. 4 (2006): 961–981.

———. "The Militant Go-between: Émile Pouget's Transnational Propaganda (1880–1914)." *Labour History Review* 74, no. 3 (2009): 274–287.

Casanovas, Joan. *Bread, Or Bullets! Urban Labor and Spanish Colonialism in Cuba, 1850–1898*. Pittsburgh, PA: University of Pittsburgh Press, 1998.

Conliff, Michael. *Black Labor on a White Canal: Panama, 1904–1981*. Pittsburgh, PA: University of Pittsburgh Press, 1985.

Cumbers, Andy, Paul Routledge and Corinne Nativel. "The Entangled Geographies of Global Justice Networks." *Progress in Human Geography* 32, no. 2 (2008): 183–201.

De Spiegeleer, Cristoph. "'The Blood of Martyrs is the Seed of Progress': The Role of Martyrdom in Socialist Death Culture in Belgium and the Netherlands, 1880–1940." *Mortality* 19, no. 2 (2014): 184–205.

Di Paola, Pietro. *The Knights Errant of Anarchy: London and the Italian Anarchist Diaspora (1880–1917)*. Liverpool: Liverpool University Press, 2013.

Diez, Xavier. *El anarquismo individualista en España (1923–1938)*. Barcelona: Virus, 2007.

Fernández Andújar, Francisco José. "Anarquismo Nietzscheano y el periódico *Anticristo*." *International Journal of Iberian Studies* 29, no. 3 (2016): 257–272.

Ferrer, Sol. *Le Véritable Francisco Ferrer d'après des documents inédits*. Paris: L'Écran du monde, 1948.

Franco Múñoz, Hernando. *Blázquez de Pedro y los orígenes del sindicalismo panameño*. Panama: Movimientos Editores, 1986.

Goyens, Tom. *Beer and Revolution: The German Anarchist Movement in New York City, 1880–1914*. Urbana: University of Illinois Press, 2007.

——. "Social Space and the Practice of Anarchist History." *Rethinking History* 13, no. 4 (2009): 439–457.

Greene, Julie. *The Canal Builders: Making America's Empire at the Panama Canal*. New York: Penguin, 2009.

Herrerín López, Ángel. "Anarchist Sociability in Spain: In Times of Violence and Clandestinity." *Bulletin for Spanish and Portuguese Historical Studies* 38, no. 1 (2013): 155–174.

——. *Anarquía, dinamita y revolución social: Violencia y represión en la España entre siglos (1868–1909)*. Madrid: Catarata, 2011.

Khuri-Makdisi, Ilham. *The Eastern Mediterranean and the Making of Global Radicalism*. Berkeley: University of California Press, 2013.

McCullough, David. *The Path between the Seas: The Creation of the Panama Canal, 1870–1914*. New York: Simon & Schuster, 1977.

Madrid Santos, Francisco. "La prensa anarquista y anarcosindicalista en España desde la I Internacional hasta el fin de la Guerra Civil." Ph.D. thesis, Universidad Central de Barcelona, 1988–1989.

Sánchez Cobos, Ampara. *Sembrando ideales: Anarquistas españoles en Cuba (1902–1925)*. Seville: Consejo Superior de Investigaciones Científicas, 2008.

Sánchez-Alonso, Blanca. "Those Who Left and Those Who Stayed Behind: Explaining Emigration from the Regions of Spain: 1880–1914." *Journal of Economic History* 60, no. 3 (2000): 730–755.

Shaffer, Kirwin. "Havana Hub: Cuban Anarchism, Radical Media and the Trans-Caribbean Anarchist Network, 1902–1915." *Caribbean Studies* 37, no. 2 (2009): 45–81.

———. "Panama Red: Anarchist Politics and Transnational Networks in the Panama Canal Zone, 1904–1913." In *In Defiance of Boundaries: Anarchism in Latin American History*, eds. Geoffroy de Laforcade and Kirwin Shaffer, 48–71. Gainesville: University Press of Florida, 2015.

———. "Tropical Libertarians: Anarchist Movements in Networks in the Caribbean, Southern United States and Mexico, 1890s–1920s." In *Anarchism and Syndicalism in the Colonial and Postcolonial World, 1870–1940: The Praxis of National Liberation, Internationalism and Social Revolution*, eds. Steven Hirsch and Lucien van der Walt, 273–320. Leiden: Brill, 2010.

Turcato, Davide. "Italian Anarchism as a Transnational Movement, 1885–1915." *International Review of Social History* 52, no. 3 (2007): 407–444.

van der Linden, Marcel and Wayne Thorpe, eds. *Revolutionary Syndicalism: An International Perspective*. Aldershot: Scolar Press, 1990.

Yeoman, James Michael. *Print Culture and the Formation of the Anarchist Movement in Spain, 1890–1915*. London: Routledge, 2020.

———. "*Salud y anarquia desde Dowlais*: The Translocal Experience of Spanish Anarchists in South Wales, 1900–1915." *International Journal of Iberian Studies* 29 no. 3 (2016): 273–289.

Zambrana, Joan. *El anarquismo organizado en los orígenes de la CNT: "Tierra y Libertad": 1910–1919*. Badalona: Centre de documentació antiautoritari i llibertari, 2009.

Zimmer, Kenyon. *Immigrants against the State: Yiddish and Italian Anarchism in America*. Urbana: University of Illinois Press, 2015.

5

Man! and the International Group
Anti-Radicalism, Immigrant Solidarity and Depression-Era Transnational Anarchism

Hillary Lazar

In January 1940, Marcus (Shmuel) Graham (1893–1985), editor of *Man! A Journal of the Anarchist Ideal and Movement*, triumphantly declared in a note to the readers that despite six years of routine government harassment and political persecution "our journal has endured … our modest voice of truth … [has] carried on."[1] Graham had spoken too soon. Only three additional issues of *Man!* were to appear. After a seven-year run the periodical folded under the weight of repression and habitual debt.

Even so, throughout its duration, *Man!* served as a vital hub for American anarchism and was a central connector for a transnational anarchist network.[2] As the main organ of the "International Group"—an organization with chapters throughout the United States—*Man!* helped to link radical immigrant communities across America. Yet, even more than the creation of this U.S.-based network, the transnational nature of *Man!* is reflected in the far-reaching readership, which extended across multiple continents. It is also evident in the international solidarity movement, which grew in response to the several-year legal persecution and deportation trials of the editor Marcus Graham and his associates Vincenzo Ferrero (1885–1985) and Domenico Sallitto (1902–1991). In essence, then, the story of *Man!* and the International Group elucidates how American anarchism at this time (and since) must really be understood through a transnational lens. And, in particular, it highlights how anarchist print publications can act as critical avenues for inter-ethnic and transnational solidarity.

---

[1] Marcus Graham, "Our Eighth Year," *Man!*, Jan. 1940. Unless noted otherwise, all cited articles can be found in *Man! A Journal of the Anarchist Ideal and Movement* (New York: Greenwood Reprint Corporation, 1970).

[2] For an introductory survey of the journal, see Ernesto A. Longa, *Anarchist Periodicals in English Published in the United States (1833–1955): An Annotated Guide* (Lanham, MD: Scarecrow Press, 2010), 167–173.

The trials of Graham, Ferrero and Sallitto, and efforts to suppress *Man!* also provide an important window into mechanisms of State control by serving as a powerful example of the connections between emigration policy and political repression. As their cases show, deportation and the exclusion of certain populations is one of the tools used to quell dissent. Moreover, during periods of national crisis or instability, nativist fears often lead to intensified targeting of both immigrants and radicals. Yet, even so, in these moments, transnational activist networks such as those associated with *Man!* and the International Group can help to catalyze resistance efforts that transcend borders.

Man! and Anarchist Print Publications as Transnational Connectors

Until recently, the general consensus among historians and scholars of radicalism is that by the 1930s the American anarchist movement had petered out, becoming little more than a whisper of dissent and smattering of communitarian settlements until its resurgence in the 1960s. The argument was that by the 1920s, following the severe repression of the post-war era, the anarchist movement ceased to be a strong radical force in America. Classic texts such as Gerald Runkle's *Anarchism: Old and New* and George Woodcock's *Anarchism: A History of Libertarian Ideas and Movements* maintain that the negative perception of anarchists as violent foreigners—dating back to the Chicago Haymarket affair of 1886 and reinforced by the assassination of President William McKinley (1843–1901) by Leon Czolgosz (1873–1901) in 1903—paved the way for the persecution of anarchists and radical dissent in the post-war period.[3] This culminated in the Palmer Raids, which resulted in the rounding up and deportation of tens of thousands of suspected radicals in 1919 and 1920, including

---

[3] Gerald Runkle, *Anarchism: Old and New* (New York: Dell, 1972); George Woodcock's *Anarchism: A History of Libertarian Ideas and Movements* (New York: Meridian Press, 1962). In 1886, during a workers' protest for the eight-hour day gathered in the Haymarket Square in Chicago, a bomb exploded killing a police officer and injuring several others. Eight anarchists were accused of the bombing. Despite their innocence, four of the men were hanged on 11 November 1887 for their political convictions. For a full assessment of Haymarket, see Paul Avrich's *The Haymarket Tragedy* (Princeton, N.J.: Princeton University Press, 1984). On 6 September 1901, son of Polish immigrants Leon Czolgosz shot and killed President McKinley. Two years later, the 57th Congress passed an act known as the "Anarchist Act," excluding anyone "who disbelieves in or who is opposed to all organized government, or who is a member of or affiliated with any organization entertaining or teaching such disbelief in or opposition to all organized government." See "In Defense of Anarchy," *New York Times*, Dec. 5, 1903. For a discussion that contextualizes Czolgosz's attack on McKinley within progressivism, see Eric Rauchway's *Murdering McKinley: The Making of Theodore Roosevelt's America* (New York: Farrar, Straus and Giroux, 2004).

most of the "vibrant" figures such as Emma Goldman (1869–1940) and Alexander Berkman (1870–1936).[4] After this, the movement "settled down into self-contained inactivity," consisting of little more than "social and educational circles for the aging faithful" who "talked mainly to themselves."[5] By the 1930s, the once vibrant social network, with its "orchestras and theater groups ... debating clubs and literary societies involving hundreds if not thousands of participants ... concerts, picnics, dances, plays, and recitations" had effectively become "a mere shadow of what it had been only a decade or two earlier."[6]

As new accounts such as Kenyon Zimmer's *Immigrants against the State* and Andrew Cornell's *Unruly Equality* suggest, this narrative is not an entirely fair or accurate telling of what happened.[7] In fact, there is evidence that there was steady growth of the anarchist movement between 1920 and 1938, particularly within the Italian-American anarchist communities.[8] Anarchist print publications and, specifically, a number of journals coming out of urban immigrant enclaves were critical for helping to maintain the movement during this period. The circulation of these periodicals served not only as the lifeblood for the many anarchist communities across the United States, but also helped to forge inter-ethnic connections among these groups as well as with anarchist networks throughout the world. In so doing, the publications also promoted solidarity and a sense of common identity. As Benedict Anderson indicates in his treatise on nationalism, *Imagined Communities* (1991), print publications are essential for the creation of collective identity across geographic divides. For American anarchists at that time this was certainly the case—only instead of eliciting patriotic bonds it helped to form a transnational orientation and sense of shared struggle across communities and borders.[9] As Zimmer comments: "It would be difficult to overstate the functional importance of newspapers in the anarchist movement. The printed word created a transnational community of anarchists and transmitted the movement's ideology across space while sustaining collective identities across time."[10]

---

4 Woodcock, *Anarchism: A History*, 466.

5 Runkle, *Anarchism: Old and New*, 33; Woodcock, *Anarchism: A History*, 467.

6 Paul Avrich, *Anarchist Voices: An Oral History of Anarchism in America* (Oakland, CA: AK Press, 2005), 319.

7 Kenyon Zimmer, *Immigrants against the State: Yiddish and Italian Anarchism in America* (Urbana: University of Illinois Press, 2015); Andrew Cornell, *Unruly Equality: US Anarchism in the Twentieth Century* (Berkeley: University of California Press, 2016).

8 Zimmer, *Immigrants against the State*, 16.

9 Benedict Anderson, *Imagined Communities: Reflections on the Origins and Spread of Nationalism*, rev. ed. (New York: Verso Press, 1998 [1991]).

10 Zimmer, *Immigrants against the State*, 14–15.

Of these periodicals, *Man!* had some of the deepest transnational ties. Along with being one of the most widely distributed journals, with circulation reaching several continents, it was also published by the International Group, which was far more multi-ethnic in character than any other organizations in the U.S. anarchist network during this era.[11] From January 1933 to April 1940, *Man!* functioned as the International Group's primary organ and, by extension, was the central connector for a transnational community of anarchists. At the suggestion of Vincenzo Ferrero, former editor of the Italian-American anarchist periodical *L'Emancipazione*, Romanian-born Marcus Graham, né Shmuel Marcus, established *Man! A Journal of the Anarchist Ideal and Movement* as a successor to the earlier publication.[12] With the subheading, "man is the measurement of everything," the journal was intended to promote the more militant, individualist and insurrectionary form of Galleanist anarchism. In this vein, as Graham explained in the first issue, *Man!* was for "those who are willing to face the truth, and act for themselves" and enable "Man to regain confidence in himself, in his great power to achieve liberation from every form of slavery that now encircles him."[13] Furthermore, it would offer "no programs, platforms or palliatives on any of the social issues confronting mankind."[14]

Through articles and letters to the editor, the members of the International Group and other contributors also engaged in heated debates over political theory and strategy—often condemning more organized forms of resistance such as federative models and syndicalism.[15] The journal also frequently included articles that paid tribute to prominent anarchists

[11] The International Group was actually the informal name for the Road to Freedom Group, based in New York, that published the *Road to Freedom*, a journal edited by Hyppolite Havel from 1927 to 1931, which is considered by many to be the successor to Emma Goldman's periodical *Mother Earth* (1906–1917). Graham had actually been a member of the group in New York, and the International Group he later founded in San Francisco, which published *Man!*, was no doubt influenced by the former organization. Several of the oral histories in Avrich's *Anarchist Voices* refer to the Road to Freedom Group.

[12] Cornell, *Unruly Equality*, 114–120; Zimmer, *Immigrants against the State*, 178–218. For biographical information on Ferrero, aka "Johnny the Cook," see a brief oral history by him in Avrich's *Anarchist Voices*, 163–167. There are also scattered references to Graham in some of the historical testimonies. He also provides some additional commentary in his "Autobiographical Note" in the foreword to his anthology, *Man! An Anthology of Anarchist Ideas, Essays, Poetry and Commentaries* (London: Cienfuegos Press, 1974).

[13] "*Man!*," *Man!*, Jan. 1933. Interview with Dr. Barry Pateman, Oct. 15, 2002. Dr. Pateman is a historian of anarchism and former associate of Marcus Graham. For a discussion of Luigi Galleani and his theories of anarchism, see Robert Graham, *No Gods, No Masters: An Anthology of Anarchism* (San Francisco: AK Press, 1998).

[14] "*Man!*," *Man!*, Jan. 1933.

[15] See, for instance, articles in *Man!* including: "Onward-People of Spain," Aug.–Sept. 1936;

through biographical sketches on figures like Alexander Berkman, Voltairine De Cleyre (1866–1912) and Mikhail Bakunin (1814–1876). And it had an extensive "Arts and Literature" section, with visual work such as woodblock prints (now emblematic of radical graphic art) as well as poetry and fiction by "those in sympathy" with the aims of *Man!*.[16] Perhaps, above all, though, *Man!* functioned as a political watchdog. Reports like "Sparks (of Progress)" and "Under the Iron Heel of Government" provided readers with a running commentary on the current state of local, national and international developments, paying particular attention to labor issues or instances of political repression.[17]

In addition to keeping American readers abreast of international issues and linking U.S.-based struggles with those abroad—including the fight against fascism and the impact of the global depression on workers—the transnational elements of the journal were also apparent in its distribution, which linked anarchists across multiple continents. Although initially *Man!* was only available in California, within two years of its appearance, Graham was able to boast having readers in "every state in the union."[18] Eventually, *Man!*'s circulation even extended to locations as far spread as Cuba, the United Kingdom, Germany, Japan, New Zealand, Australia and Palestine.[19]

The multi-ethnic membership of the International Group and their orientation towards "internationalism" further informed the network's transnational dimensions. The vast majority of anarchists in America at this time were Jewish, Eastern and Southern European immigrants. And while maintaining ties to their respective cultural heritages was important to many of them, as Zimmer argues, most eschewed patriotic and nationalist identities in favor of a more universalist concept of "internationalism" or "global citizenry."[20] This was particularly the case for the members of the International Group, which intentionally sought to bring together members from San Francisco's many radical ethnic communities as a way to share

---

"Behind the Lines of Spain," Oct.–Nov. 1936; "They Shall Not Pass," Dec. 1936–Jan. 1937; and "Save Spain Save Yourselves," Feb.–Mar. 1937. Cornell, *Unruly Equality*, 114–118.

[16] "Errico Malatesta," *Man!*, Feb. 1933; "Alexander Berkman—Rebel Anarchist," *Man!*, July 1936; "Mikahil Alexandrovich Bakunin," *Man!*, May 1939. See, for instance, *Man!*, Feb. 1933.

[17] See, for instance, *Man!*, Feb. 1936.

[18] "Shall Man Continue to Exist?," *Man!*, Nov.–Dec. 1935; "Man is on Sale," *Man!*, Feb. 1937.

[19] "Man is on Sale," *Man!*, Feb. 1937; "An Appeal from Cuba," *Man!*, Feb. 1936; "A Letter from Japan," *Man!*, Mar. 1935; "By the Readers," *Man!*, Apr. 1933; "A Letter from New Zealand," *Man!*, Apr. 1935; "A Letter from Australia," *Man!*, Apr. 1939; "Two Letters from Palestine," *Man!*, Apr. 1938.

[20] Zimmer, *Immigrants against the State*, 17.

learning across their traditions and to forge a more cosmopolitan sense of interrelated struggle. True to its name, the International Group represented an impressive range of immigrant communities and was significantly more multi-ethnic in nature than other anarchist hubs at that time. For instance, the major anarchist communities in New York City or Patterson, New Jersey were largely Jewish and Italian. By contrast, the International Group also had large French- and Spanish-speaking contingents as well as members from Russian, Polish, Romanian, Chinese, Japanese, Korean and other ethnic radical circuits.[21] Necessarily, this reflects the demographic make-up of San Francisco and the Bay Area more generally. Yet the choice to adopt English as the lingua franca for the publication and to focus on sponsoring multicultural events reflects the transnational spirit of the paper and its network.

Within months of the periodical's launch party on 31 December 1932, it reported having chapters of the International Group around the country in cities like New York, Chicago, Detroit, Patterson and Philadelphia.[22] These local groups sponsored regular events—usually elaborate multi-ethnic affairs—with a focus on art and politics and almost always offering "eats aplenty."[23] Members and friends frequently gathered for picnics or dinners that offered cuisines ranging from Chinese to Russian, or Italian-American "Spaghetti-luncheons."[24] Lectures, forums and speaking-tours were also common and oftentimes co-sponsored with other immigrant organizations such as the Russian Progressive Club.[25] Mostly they involved talks related specifically to the U.S. movement, but sometimes they debated other radical topics about international issues like the rise of fascism.[26] The San Francisco chapter also held "monthly comraderies" at their "Freethought Library," where "[n]ewspapers, periodicals and other reading matter in various languages [were] available."[27]

Events and gatherings also served as a way to raise funds for *Man!*, which like the other gatherings sought to appeal to the different immigrant communities in the network. One typical benefit, for example, held on 22 April 1933 at the Equality Hall in San Francisco, presented a "three-act play in the Russian language," a piano recital, a reading, "songs in German

---

21　Ibid., 193–195.

22　"The Movement around Man," *Man!*, May–June 1933.

23　*Man!*, Oct. 1933. *Man!*, Nov. 1933. Although it seems likely that this was partly due to the cooperative ethic of the group as well as the central role of food in social gatherings for many cultures, undoubtedly, with breadlines and hunger a daily reality for many, this also reflected a pragmatic strategy for drawing larger crowds.

24　*Man!*, Mar. 1933. *Man!*, May–June, 1933; *Man!*, Jan. 1934.

25　*Man!*, Jan. 1933.

26　*Man!*, Mar. 1934.

27　"For an International Freethought Library," *Man!*, Mar. 1933.

and English," and ended with a dance and music by the "Popular Balalaika Orchestra." Admission was 25 cents.[28] The International Group helped fundraising for other radical causes as well. For instance, chapters gathered to support comrades in need like the "Italian and Spanish Political Prisoners," who received all proceeds from an evening of "Danc[ing] and Entertainment" accompanied by a speech by famous anarchist Rudolph Rocker (1873–1958). Other events supported "anarchist exiles in Russia" and went to the funding of *L'Adunta*, an Italian-language anarchist periodical.[29]

The Suppression of *Man!* and Solidarity across Borders

The international solidarity movement associated with the deportation trials of Graham, Ferrero and Sallitto speaks to another transnational dimension of *Man!* and its network. As an account of these trials and the defense efforts on the defendants' behalf shows, having a print publication to help disseminate news was critical in facilitating the growth of an international movement for immigrant political rights. Little more than a year following its debut, the local and federal governments began systematically to harass subscribers to the paper. In the May 1934 issue, Graham reported that readers were sending letters of complaint regarding visits from government agents. The officials had been detaining them at the local justice departments for questioning on their relationship with the periodical and demanding to know "why they read and lent material aid to an Anarchist journal such as *Man!*"[30] Sessions ended with threats of deportation against the foreign-born readers and criminal prosecution for those born in America. Meanwhile, a hold had been placed on the journal's mailing by the government, preventing the March issue from reaching many of the readers.[31] Despite the attempts to intimidate *Man!*'s followers and the members of the International Group, their commitment did not waiver. Letters continued to pour in, the gatherings went on, and every month individuals and organizations scraped together money to ensure that the next issue would appear. Yet, the governmental harassment of *Man!*'s readers and the delays in its distribution were just the beginning.

On 11 April 1934, emigration inspectors and local police led by E. C. Benson forcibly entered the restaurant owned and operated by Vincenzo Ferrero and Domenico Sallitto at 1000 Jefferson Street in Oakland, California and raided the small space they rented at the back of their business to Graham

---

[28] *Man!*, Apr. 1933.
[29] *Man!*, June 1939.
[30] "Government's Foul Conspiracy to Destroy *Man!*," *Man!*, May 1934.
[31] Ibid.

for use as the printing headquarters for *Man!*.[32] Although Ferrero had been the one initially to suggest that Graham start the paper, neither he nor Sallitto officially contributed to its publication. Both, however, were well known for their ties to the Italian-American anarchist communities in San Francisco and New York. Consequently, after the inspectors ransacked the backroom to obtain copies of the periodical and materials used for its production, they were both arrested on "telegraphic warrants from Washington to be seized for deportation."[33] Ferrero was then charged with "causing the publication of *Man!*" and Sallitto was picked up for chairing the debate on Marius Van der Lubbe the previous March, during which he purportedly advocated the violent overthrow of the government.[34] They were quickly released on a $1,000 bond apiece, but only nine days later a squad of detectives returned to Jefferson Street, allegedly in response to an attempted robbery of the restaurant, and raided the office for a second time. The two men were removed to Angel Island and it became clear that their charges were not going to be readily dropped.[35]

For a year, the cases of Ferrero and Sallitto remained at a standstill as they went in and out of custody, all the while working tirelessly with advocates from the International Group in concert with legal counsel from the American Committee for Protection of Foreign-Born, an affiliate of the American Civil Liberties Union (ACLU). Then, in June 1935, when their verdict did finally come in, they were dealt a crushing blow. Even though they were both legally resident in the United States—Ferrero, a thirty-year resident, and Sallitto, a fifteen-year resident and widowed father of a three-year-old daughter born to an American wife—the Immigration Bureau of the Labor Department ordered their deportation to Italy.[36] On 10 December 1935, the U.S. Labor Department issued a formal demand that Ferrero turn himself in to Ellis Island for the sailing of the S.S. *Conte di Savoia* to Italy two weeks later. He complied and arrived a day prior to his scheduled departure date. His attorney, however, managed to stay the deportation through a writ of habeas corpus.[37] Sallitto joined his comrade at Ellis Island

---

[32] Along with Ferrero's account, there is also a brief oral history by Sallitto in Avrich's *Anarchist Voices*, 166–167.

[33] "Government's Foul Conspiracy to Destroy *Man!*

[34] Ibid.

[35] Ibid.

[36] "Alleged Anarchist Fights Deportation," *San Francisco Chronicle*, Sept. 5, 1935; "Deportation Order Fought," *San Francisco Chronicle*, Dec. 29, 1935; "Resisting Attempt to Throttle Freedom of Thought," *Man!*, July–Aug. 1935; "Deportations Hysteria," *Man!*, Oct.–Nov. 1936.

[37] "The Struggle to Save Ferrero and Sallitto," *Man!*, Jan. 1936; "Deportation Order Fought."

shortly thereafter as he was scheduled to be deported on 11 January. Like Ferrero, he also secured a writ of habeas corpus, and after three months' detention both men were released. Even so, their legal persecution was still not over.[38]

Ultimately charged with "being a member of an organization advocating the overthrow of government by force and violence," Sallitto's ordeal persisted for two more years. It was not until January 1938, following four years of legal proceedings and several months of detention at both Ellis and Angel Islands (which meant prolonged periods of separation from his young daughter of whom he had sole custody), that his case was dismissed.[39] Ferrero did not fare so well. While the court never directly determined that he was involved with *Man!* in any official capacity, as the former editor of the Italian anarchist periodical *L'Emancipazione* he was charged with "writing or publishing printed material advocating the overthrow of government by force and violence."[40] And despite his claims that he qualified for political asylum as being sent back to Italy would condemn him to severe punishment for having "written and spoken violently against Mussolini for years," in February 1937 the Second District Court of Appeals denied his plea.[41] If he had not managed to evade the authorities by adopting the alias "Jonny the Cook" back in California, Ferrero would have been deported two years later, in November 1939.[42]

Throughout the years of Ferrero's and Sallitto's persecution, Graham faced similar tribulations. A few days prior to 11 June 1936, he received a notice from the Immigration Bureau upholding a mandate for his deportation issued seventeen years earlier. The nearly two-decades-old directive demanded his return to Canada, where he allegedly held citizenship, for the crime of possessing subversive anarchist literature.[43] Denied entry into Canada, and unable to ascertain Graham's nation of origin, the emigration officials allowed the expulsion to slip through the legal cracks. With pressure on the rise to shut down *Man!*, Graham felt threatened enough by the renewed interested

---

[38] "Bay Man Appeals Deportation Order," *San Francisco Chronicle*, Oct. 8, 1936; "The Ferrero and Sallitto Case," *Man!*, May 1936.

[39] "Anarchy on Trial in United States Court," *Man!*, Jan. 1938; "Deportations Hysteria," *Man!*, Oct.–Nov. 1936.

[40] "Deportations Hysteria"; "Another Refugee," *Man!*, Nov. 1939.

[41] "Deportations Hysteria."

[42] Ferrero Loses Deportation Plea," *San Francisco Chronicle*, Feb. 2, 1937; "Former Publisher Reported a Refugee," *San Francisco Chronicle*, Oct. 21, 1939; "Deportations Hysteria"; "Another Refugee." Interview with American anarchist, Audrey Goodfriend (1920–2013), Jan. 4, 2009.

[43] The controversial literature was a copy of *An Anthology of Revolutionary Poetry* (New York: The Active Press, 1929) that Graham had edited.

in his expulsion to go underground. And in the August–September 1936 issue he announced his termination as editor of *Man!*. He then temporarily entrusted its editorship to Ray Randall and Walter Brooks—pseudonyms for Sallitto and his partner Aurora Alleva (d. 1992)—although under Hippolyte Havel's name, and for a year the periodical was published out of New York.[44] The following July, Graham came out of hiding and reassumed his role as editor, relocating its headquarters to Los Angeles.[45]

Graham's return was short-lived. It was only two months before the authorities once again took action against him. On 6 October 1937, four plain clothes emigration officers raided the Los Angeles office and seized all materials relating to *Man!*. Graham was arrested on-site and incarcerated in the county jail for eight days.[46] Several months of hearings and appeals followed, and on 14 January 1938, Judge Leon R. Yankovich finally dismissed the seventeen-year-old edict. Nevertheless, Graham did not evade all legal repercussions. Judge Yankovich sentenced him to six months' imprisonment on the charge of "criminal contempt" for his persistent refusal to reveal his place of birth to emigration officials, making it impossible to deport him.[47] Again, he managed temporarily to elude punishment with additional legal appeals, although it was a Pyrrhic victory. By this point, sufficient enough damage had been done to the stability of *Man!*'s publication that it was now deeply in debt.[48] With the aid of contributions from supporters, *Man!* stayed afloat for another year and a half, but in April 1940 the U.S. District Attorney "advised" the journal's printer immediately to suspend the printing of the May issue. When Graham was unable to find an alternative publisher he was forced to end its publication.[49]

---

[44] Hippolyte Havel (1871–1950) is a famous Czech anarchist who lived in New York and was a close friend and biographer of Emma Goldman. Ray Randall and Walter Brooks were pennames and while their real names were never disclosed, their initials were "D.S." and "A.A.," standing for Domenico Sallitto and Aurora Alleva (d. 1992), his eventual life partner and secretary of the Ferrero and Sallitto Defense Conference in New York, who were both in New York at that time raising funds for his defense. Marcus Graham, "Autobiographical Note," in his *Man! An Anthology of Anarchist Ideas*, vii.

[45] "In Retrospect of Current Events: A Statement of Facts," *Man!*, Aug.-Sept. 1936; *Man!*, July–Aug 1937. Despite this, Graham did not remain overly silent or carefully hidden. Several times in late 1936, his name appears with "Bermuda" next to it in parentheses, as the author of articles in *Man!* This suggests that Graham went on the lam and sought refuge in Bermuda.

[46] "U.S. Government Raids '*Man!*' and Jails Editor Again," *Man!*, Oct. 1937; "Editor May Evade Deportation Charge," *San Francisco Chronicle*, Dec. 9, 1937.

[47] "Anarchy on Trial in United States Court."

[48] "Writers Assailed by Federal Judge," *New York Times*, June 27, 1939; "Marcus Graham Sentenced to Second Six Month Jail Term," *The Challenge*, July 22, 1939.

[49] Marcus Graham, "Autobiographical Note," xviii.

Two months later, he lost his appeal regarding the pending charge of contempt for refusing to cooperate with emigration officials, and was sentenced to serve out his time.[50]

Ironically, if the goal of Graham, Ferrero and Sallitto's persecution was to deter further radical agitation, it instead helped to unite the American Left—with important support from immigrant communities throughout the country as well as abroad—in one of the largest protest movements of the period. The ACLU, which had immediately taken on their cases, made sure to spread word on the issue to the wider public. In just over a year after the initial raid at 1000 Jefferson Street, hundreds of organizations and thousands of individuals joined the protests held throughout the country on their behalf. The first public gathering was held on 2 July 1935 at the San Francisco Labor College. Spokesmen at the event represented numerous labor and radical organizations including the ACLU; the Industrial Workers of the World; the International Group; the International Ladies Garment Workers Union; the Non-artisan Labor Defense; the Proletarian, Workers' and Socialist parties; and the Tom Mooney Molders' Defense Committee.[51] Soon thereafter, on 22 July, the Ferrero–Sallitto Defense Conference was established at the Stuyvesant Casino in New York and six days later the first mass demonstration outside of California was held at Union Square.[52]

Following this demonstration, numerous committees were formed across the country as part of the Ferrero–Sallitto Defense Conference to arrange local demonstrations and inundate Capitol Hill with letters of protest. Another rally held at Irving Plaza in New York City on 27 October 1935 had delegates from some 221 organizations, all of whom signed a declaration "that the traditional right of asylum in America for political and religious refugees from tyrannical governments be preserved."[53] Copies of the resolution were sent directly to President Roosevelt.[54] Within six months, in addition to New York and San Francisco, major protests were also held in Philadelphia, Chicago, Cleveland and Los Angeles.[55] Meanwhile, after Graham's arrest,

---

[50] "Silence About Birth Thwarts His Deportation," *San Francisco Chronicle*, June 7, 1940; "A 'Philosophical' Anarchist Gets 6 Months in Jug," *San Francisco Chronicle*, June 23, 1940.

[51] "Resisting Attempt to Throttle Freedom of Thought—First Public Protest," *Man!*, July–Aug. 1935; Albert Strong, "The Fight against Deportation of Ferrero and Sallitto," *Class Struggle*, Jan. 1936.

[52] Strong, "The Fight against Deportation of Ferrero and Sallitto."

[53] "On the Revolutionary Battlefront—In the Land We Live In," *Man!*, Nov.–Dec. 1935.

[54] Ibid.

[55] Strong, "The Fight against Deportation of Ferrero and Sallitto"; "Deportation Officials' Unlimited Perfidies," *Man!*, Feb. 1936.

separate defense committees were formed out of many of the same groups on his behalf.[56]

The movement to see justice for Ferrero, Sallitto and Graham continued to grow in size and intensity, catching the attention of numerous prominent citizens who joined the Defense Committees, often taking on coordinating roles for the protests and petitions. Multiple delegations of notable personalities, civil rights advocates and labor leaders even went so far as to travel to Washington to contest Secretary of Labor Perkins's sign-off on their deportation. On 23 December 1935, five members of the Conference met with Assistant Secretary of Labor Edward McGrady (1873–1960) to no avail. When that failed to work, another attempt to intercede on their behalf was made by "100 renown[ed] men and women in the realm of Art and Education."[57] Leading the group was the wife of former Secretary of Labor, Louis F. Post (1849–1928).[58] And by January 1938 upwards of forty thousand letters of protest representing five hundred thousand individuals were sent to Secretary of Labor Frances Perkins (1880–1965).[59] Several high-profile individuals including celebrated authors Sherwood Anderson (1876–1941), Jon Dos Passos (1896–1970), Sinclair Lewis (1885–1951) and Upton Sinclair (1878–1968); prominent socialists such as Max Eastman (1883–1969), Kate Crane-Gartz (1865–1949), Scott Nearing (1883–1983) and Norman Thomas (1884–1968); suffragist Alice Stone Blackwell (1857–1950); philosopher John Dewey (1859–1952); and founder of the ACLU, Roger Baldwin (1884–1981), were among them.[60]

Importantly, in terms of *Man!* and the International Group's transnational ties, it was not only the U.S. that saw a surge of solidarity on their behalf. Letters continued to pour in from abroad in support of their legal efforts. And along with the defense chapters established in the U.S., there was also defense support in France, Spain, Italy and Switzerland. Undoubtedly, it was the continued international distribution of *Man!* that helped to raise awareness about their legal proceedings. In effect, through the printed stories recounting the trials, the many appeals for help and the published letters of support,

---

[56] "U.S. Government Raids '*Man!*'"; "Editor May Evade Deportation Charge"; "Stop the Persecution of Graham and *Man!*," *Man!*, Mar. 1938.

[57] "Two Fight Deportation," *San Francisco Chronicle*, Oct. 7, 1937; "Anarchy on Trial in United States Court"; "Deportation of Sallitto Defeated," *Man!*, Jan. 1938.

[58] "Two Fight Deportation"; "Anarchy on Trial in United States Court"; "Deportation of Sallitto Defeated"; "Protesting Voices," *Man!*, Mar. 1938; Strong, "The Fight against Deportation of Ferrero and Sallitto."

[59] "Anarchy on Trial in United States Court."

[60] "America's Conscience Speaks Out," *Man!*, Oct. 1937; *Man!*, Dec. 1937; Strong, "The Fight against Deportation of Ferrero and Sallitto"; "Shall These Men and Women be Exiled," *Man!*, Dec. 1937; "Stop the Persecution of Graham and *Man!*"

Man! was able to serve as a vital mechanism for international PR about the case. This, in turn, translated to further momentum for the movement both in the U.S. and internationally. Nevertheless, despite the widespread international attention their trials received, with Ferrero still officially slated for deportation and Graham in jail for half a year, the protests had only met with partial success. The International Group simply could not withstand the weight of the persecution. *Man!* folded and the network disbanded.

Man! in the Bigger Picture: Immigration and Foreign Policy as State Control

Along with illustrating the transnational dimensions to the solidarity efforts on behalf of Ferrero and Sallitto and Graham, these trials also highlight the way emigration policy and deportation can be used as a tool to suppress radical dissent. The targeting of *Man!* reflects a combination of a long tradition of anti-immigrant and anti-anarchist policy in America and the ways in which they intersect. Throughout America's early history, laws such as the Alien and Sedition Act and the Indian Removal Act of 1830 were aimed at eliminating unwanted groups.[61] The Supreme Court decision in relation to *Fong Yue Ting* v. *The United States* in 1893, however, eliminated all constitutional safeguards against the expulsion of immigrants, opening the floodgates to the use of deportation as a tool of political repression and social control. It was in this case where deportation was determined to be an "administrative" process rather than a criminal matter and, hence, not subject to due process.

As the Bill of Rights only pertained to criminal cases, immigrants were now subject to expulsion based on star-chamber examinations and the arbitrary finding that they were somehow "inconsistent with public welfare."[62] There was also no longer a legal bar against lengthy incarcerations, repeated searches and seizures of their property, high bail and self-incrimination. Furthermore, the process was now, above all, to be based on expedience. This allowed for practices such as use of the telegraphic warrants, which effectively enabled emigration officers to round up aliens on the basis of "guilty until proven innocent."[63] It was this ruling, in hand

---

[61] Meant to free up land for white settlers, this Act did not actually forcibly remove native peoples from their homes but rather encouraged them to do so by offering provisions for the journey as an alternative to being unofficially pushed off the land by the encroaching settlements.

[62] William Preston, *Aliens and Dissenters: Federal Suppression of Radicals, 1903–1933* (Urbana: University of Illinois Press, 1994), 11.

[63] Preston offers a brilliant analysis of the "de-criminalization" of deportation making extradition of unwanted aliens a bureaucratic process rather than criminal and consequently not subject to due process and the legal safeguards of a right to trial by jury.

with the "Anarchist Act" of 1903, which made anarchists inadmissible for U.S. entry, as well as the hyper-patriotic Espionage and Sedition Acts of 1917 and 1918, that effectively shaped federal policy for alien radicals in the first decades of the twentieth century and paved the way for round ups of radicals like Ferrero, Sallitto and Graham.[64]

Immigration policy was also used to curtail potential "foreign threats" by proactively preventing entry of certain ethnic groups or immigrants with suspect political beliefs to the United States. In the decade just preceding the Depression, for example, amidst the post-World War I anti-alien hysteria and rise of white-supremacist nativism, the National Origins Act of 1924—designed to impede further emigration by Southern and Eastern Europeans and exclude Asians—put a 2 percent cap per country, based on their total population in the 1890 census. All Asians were barred. Then, during World War II (notably, overlapping timewise with Graham's trial and just shortly after the final verdicts came in for Ferrero and Sallitto), the government passed a barrage of anti-alien bills including the Foreign Agents Registration Act of 1938, which required all agents for foreign principles to register with the Secretary of State.[65] A few years later, in 1952, following the war, as anti-communist Cold War hysteria set-in, the United States passed the McCarran-Walter Act, which again seriously capped entry of Asians while establishing ideological criteria for expulsion—any immigrant or foreign-born resident could be expelled for "activities prejudicial to the public interest" or "subversive to national security."[66]

The political and economic instability of the Great Depression only added to the intensity of the xenophobic and anti-radical sentiment driving the efforts to deport Graham, Ferrero and Sallitto. Tensions ran particularly high in California where there was a deep history of conservative nativism and vigilantism. It was California, for instance, that served as the heart of

---

[64] The Espionage Act made it illegal to make any attempt to interfere with military operations, including recruitment, and the Sedition Act of 1918 forbade the use of any language aimed at criticizing the United States government, its flag or its armed forces. The act also allowed the Postmaster General to refuse to deliver mail that conveyed language deemed to meet these criteria.

[65] For a general discussion on American emigration, see Roger Daniels's *Guarding the Golden Door: American Immigration Policy and Immigrants since 1882* (New York: Hill and Wang, 2004). For an analysis of anti-alien and anti-radical legislation passed during World War II, see Margaret A. Blanchard, *Revolutionary Sparks: Freedom of Expression in Modern America* (Oxford: Oxford University Press, 1992), 159 and Robert Goldstein, *Political Repression in Modern America: 1870 to the Present* (Cambridge, MA: Schneckman Publishing, 1978), 245.

[66] From the foreword by Howard Zinn in Deepa Fernandes, *Targeted: Homeland Security and the Business of Immigration* (New York: Seven Stories Press, 2007), 15.

the anti-Chinese movement in the late nineteenth century that eventually led to the Chinese Exclusion Act of 1882. In 1916, anxieties over labor agitation allowed fear to trump justice when radical labor activist Tom Mooney (1882–1942), and his assistant Warren K. Billings (1893–1972), were incarcerated for twenty-three years for the bombing of the San Francisco Preparedness Day parade despite their obvious innocence.[67] And of thirty-three states to pass Criminal Syndicalist Acts in the wake of the Palmer Raids, California was one of the only ones actually to keep it on the books, rounding up some 504 members of the Industrial Workers of the World before it was repealed in 1924.[68]

By the 1930s, California served both as home to one of the most extensive and well-organized radical networks in the United States and had an economy that depended on immigrant labor. With agribusiness as the dominant industry, Mexican migrant laborers were in many ways the backbone of the state's financial well-being. Asian Americans, and more specifically Filipinos, were also a major source of labor-power for the farms. For this reason, the intersection of the radical presence with the large but virtually unorganized agricultural workforce gave rise to a powerful immigrant-based farm workers movement.[69] This growth in organized labor, coupled with the established pattern of scapegoating aliens and radicals during economic panics along with California's propensity for vigilantism, elicited an aggressive nativist and anti-radical response from the local elite. Hundreds of thousands of Mexicans were coerced or convinced into repatriating during the 1930s.[70] And, while not all faced deportation, many European ethnic radicals experienced political persecution and xenophobic harassment along the lines of the members of the International Group.[71]

It was the Longshoreman and Maritime Worker's General Strike of July 1934, though, that served as the immediate backdrop for the suppression of *Man!*. In May 1934, longshoremen had shut down every port along the west coast sparking bloody battles and rioting in several of the major cities including San Francisco. This came to a head following the killing of a striker and sympathizer during a clash with local police that led to a city-wide general strike. Although it only lasted four days, the National

---

[67] See Estolv E. Ward, *The Gentle Dynamiter* (Palo Alto, CA: Ramparts Press, 1983).

[68] Zechariah Chafee, *Freedom of Speech in the United States* (Cambridge, MA: Harvard University Press, 1941), 327.

[69] Goldstein, *Political Repression*, 221.

[70] No discussion of emigration and repression in 1930s California would be complete without an examination of Mexican repatriation. For an account of this, see Camille Guerin-Gonzales, *Mexican Workers and American Dreams: Immigration, Repatriation, and California Farm Labor, 1900–1939* (New Brunswick, N.J.: Rutgers University Press, 1994).

[71] Goldstein, *Political Repression*, 220–221.

Guard, local authorities and other vigilantes responded with an aggressive counteroffensive that targeted ethnic radical groups and, in particular, anarchists and communists. It comes as no surprise that only a month before the initial coast-wide walkout by the longshoremen local officials began rounding up suspected radical immigrants and tightening the rein on the distribution of pro-labor printed materials like *Man!*.[72] As foreign-born anarchists, the successful suppression of *Man!* and the vigorous efforts to deport these men represented a desperate attempt both to deter further labor agitation and to demonstrate the government and local authorities' abilities to reassert their control during a period of upheaval.

Conclusion: The Historical Significance of *Man!*

Despite *Man!*'s ultimate demise, for the better part of a decade, the periodical had been a vital channel for inter-ethnic and transnational movement building. During that time, it helped to connect thousands of radical immigrant communities throughout America with one another as well as with others across multiple continents. Moreover, the network itself was a vibrant hub for cross-cultural exchange and intentionally sought to encourage a cosmopolitan approach to internationalism. This serves as an instructive reminder that anarchist movements—including the struggle against fascism and political repression—have historically taken on transnational dimensions, including during the 1930s. It also illustrates how media (be it in print or nowadays digital form) can forge solidarity across borders and be a catalyst for on-the-ground defense work in shared struggles. It was through *Man!*'s circulation, in fact, that the International Group was able to mobilize an international solidarity movement on behalf of Ferrero, Sallitto and Graham by enabling activists across borders to share information and coordinate the defense committees.

Perhaps one of the most important elements to the story of *Man!*, however, is in its elucidation of State control through emigration policy. The trials of Ferrero, Sallitto and Graham typify a broader pattern of using deportation as a mechanism for quelling dissent and eliminating certain populations. Moreover, it points to the ways in which anti-radicalism has historically been bound to anti-immigrant, white-supremacist nativism. Furthermore, it underscores that these tendencies can become even more pronounced in periods of political or economic instability. Yet, that said, it is critical to note that an account of their persecution also suggests that while emigration

---

[72] For a full account of the strike, see Kevin Starr's chapter, "Bayonets on the Embarcadero: The San Francisco Waterfront and General Strike of 1934," in his *Endangered Dreams: The Great Depression in California* (Oxford: Oxford University Press, 1995), 84–120.

and foreign policy can function as a means of domestic repression, this repression, in turn, can spark vibrant, transnational resistance efforts.

Works Cited

Newspapers and other Periodicals
Challenge
Class Struggle
New York Times
San Francisco Chronicle

Secondary Works
Anderson, Benedict. *Imagined Communities: Reflections on the Origins and Spread of Nationalism*. New York: Verso Press, 1998.

Avrich, Paul. *Anarchist Voices: An Oral History of Anarchism in America*. Oakland, CA: AK Press, 2005.

Blanchard, Margaret A. *Revolutionary Sparks: Freedom of Expression in Modern America*. Oxford: Oxford University Press, 1992.

Chafee, Zechariah. *Freedom of Speech in the United States*. Cambridge, MA: Harvard University Press, 1941.

Cornell, Andrew. *Unruly Equality: US Anarchism in the Twentieth Century*. Berkeley: University of California Press, 2016.

Daniels, Roger. *Guarding the Golden Door: American Immigration Policy and Immigrants since 1882*. New York: Hill and Wang, 2004.

Fernandes, Deepa. *Targeted: Homeland Security and the Business of Immigration*. New York: Seven Stories Press, 2007.

Goldstein, Robert. *Political Repression in Modern America: 1870 to the Present*. Cambridge, MA: Schenkman Publishing, 1978.

Graham, Marcus, ed. *Man! An Anthology of Anarchist Ideas, Essays, Poetry and Commentaries*. London: Cienfuegos Press, 1974.

——. *Man! A Journal of the Anarchist Ideal and Movement*. New York: Greenwood Reprint Corporation, 1970.

Graham, Robert. *No Gods, No Masters: An Anthology of Anarchism*. San Francisco: AK Press, 1998.

Guerin-Gonzales, Camille. *Mexican Workers and American Dreams: Immigration, Repatriation, and California Farm Labor, 1900–1939*. New Brunswick, N.J.: Rutgers University Press, 1994.

Longa, Ernesto A. *Anarchist Periodicals in English Published in the United States (1833–1955): An Annotated Guide*. Lanham, MD: Scarecrow Press, 2010.

McElvaine, Robert. *The Great Depression: America 1929–1941*. New York: Three Rivers Press, 1993.

Preston, William. *Aliens and Dissenters: Federal Suppression of Radicals, 1903–1933*. Urbana: University of Illinois Press, 1994.

Rauchway, Eric. *Murdering McKinley: The Making of Theodore Roosevelt's America.* New York: Farrar, Straus and Giroux, 2004.

Runkle, Gerald. *Anarchism: Old and New.* New York: Dell, 1972.

Starr, Kevin. *Endangered Dreams: The Great Depression in California.* Oxford: Oxford University Press, 1995.

Ward, Estolv. E. *The Gentle Dynamiter.* Palo Alto, CA: Ramparts Press, 1983.

Woodcock, George. *Anarchism: A History of Libertarian Ideas and Movements.* New York: Meridian Press, 1962.

Zimmer, Kenyon. *Immigrants against the State: Yiddish and Italian Anarchism in America.* Urbana: University of Illinois, 2015.

Unpublished Interviews Cited

Goodfriend, Audrey. Hillary Lazar. Berkeley, California, Jan. 4, 2009.

Pateman, Barry. Hillary Lazar. Berkeley, California, Oct. 15, 2002.

II

Individual Perspectives

6

Global Master Workman

Terence Powderly (1849–1924), Transatlantic Radicalism and the Global History of the Knights of Labor, 1880–1900

Steven Parfitt

This is the story of a transnational figure who hardly ever crossed a national border in his career as labor leader. Terence Powderly (1849–1924) was born in Carbondale, Pennsylvania, in 1849, to Irish immigrants. He entered the labor force as a switchman for the Delaware and Hudson railroad at the age of thirteen, as the Civil War raged across the United States, and became a machinists' apprentice at the age of seventeen. He was marked out very early as a rising star in the American labor movement, rising quickly in the Machinists and Blacksmiths' Union after joining in 1871. In 1874, a year after the Panic of '73 brought economic depression to the United States and forced Powderly west to find work, he joined a relatively new, secret union that he would be associated with for the rest of his life: The Noble and Holy Order of the Knights of Labor.[1] Only five years later, at the age of only thirty, he became the Grand Master Workman of that Order. He stayed in that position for the next fourteen years, until 1893. During that time, the Knights became the first national movement of the American working class and attracted close to a million members in 1886, before their fortunes turned for the worse. As Grand (later renamed General) Master Workman, he became, in the words of Robert Weir, the first "labor superstar"—a figure looked up to by hundreds of thousands of American Knights, endlessly quoted and pressed for interviews by newspapers, and consulted (or impugned) by the most famous business leaders and politicians of the day.[2]

---

[1] For a detailed study, see Steven Parfitt, *Knights across the Atlantic: The Knights of Labor in Britain and Ireland* (Liverpool: Liverpool University Press, 2017).

[2] Robert Weir, *Knights Unhorsed: Internal Conflict in a Gilded Age Social Movement* (Detroit, MI: Wayne State University Press, 2000), 16.

Powderly divided opinion during his own life. As a labor celebrity he won the admiration of many Knights. His personal papers bulge with letters of praise from workers all over the United States; some of them named children after him, and in at least two cases, in Kentucky and Texas, named whole towns after him. But he attracted dislike as easily as admiration. His rivals inside and outside the Knights of Labor described him as vain, pompous, dictatorial in his leadership of the Order and responsible for numerous failed strikes and many other of the Order's woes besides. There can be no doubt that he was a prickly man, and that he often used his regular spot in the Order's newspaper, the *Journal of United Labor*, to blast his opponents and to mouth off in general. He actively courted the dislike of American socialists and anarchists when he refused to join calls for clemency for the famous Haymarket Martyrs, the anarchists accused of killing police with bombs at Haymarket Square in Chicago in 1886. When Friedrich Engels (1820–1895) surveyed the American scene in 1887 he dearly wished that the Knights would leave Powderly (and the economist Henry George (1839–1897)) "out in the cold with small sects of their own."[3] The President of the rival American Federation of Labor, Samuel Gompers (1850–1924)—a man who Powderly often accused in public of acting on "an excess … of intoxicants"— described the General Master Workman and the Order's leaders as "floating like a scum on the top of a part of the labor movement."[4]

Historians generally followed the critics. Norman Ware set the gold standard for scholarly criticism of Powderly early on when he described the General Master Workman as "a windbag whose place was on the street corner rousing the rabble to concert pitch and providing emotional compensation for dull lives."[5] Scholars well to the left, such as Philip S. Foner, castigated Powderly for his conservatism and unwillingness to support strikes—and blamed him for some of the more calamitous strike defeats in the Order's history, such as the debacles in the Chicago stockyards and on the Southwestern rail system in 1886.[6] Scholars further to the right, such as John Commons, Selig Perlman and Gerald Grob, cast Powderly instead as the spokesman of a dying utopian strain in the American labor movement— one that was bound to be superseded (and deservedly so) by the trade unions

---

[3] Friedrich Engels, "Preface to the American Edition," in *The Condition of the Working Class in England* (New York: s.n., 1887).

[4] Quoted in John Hollitz, *The Contenders*, vol. 2, *Since 1865* (Boston: Houghton Mifflin, 2003), 35.

[5] Norman Ware, *The Labor Movement in the United States, 1860–1895: A Study in Democracy*, 2nd ed. (New York: Vintage Books, 1964), xvi.

[6] See Philip S. Foner, *History of the Labor Movement in the United States*, vol. 2, 2nd ed. (New York: International Publishers, 1975).

of the American Federation of Labor.[7] Even after historians began to move away from the view that the Knights were nothing more than a gigantic anachronism, even after they began to consider the Knights instead as a viable and forward-looking response to the problems of the industrial age, they continued to see Powderly as one of the Order's least creditable features.

That picture has only slowly begun to change in recent decades. Richard Oestreicher and Craig Phelan have restored Powderly's reputation as a labor leader and put him back in his context as a representative of a longer, broader, working-class republican tradition in American labor history. Phelan especially has taken issue with the image of Powderly as a bumbling incompetent who wrecked strikes, spiked promising political campaigns and needlessly alienated many of his supporters. One man, after all, could not easily bring down a movement of nearly a million people. Nor is it fair to ascribe all the Order's successes to others and leave Powderly only with its failures. Phelan emphasizes Powderly's popularity among hundreds of thousands of American workers and claims that no other leader would have fared any better if confronted with the full weight of American capital and every level and branch of American government, as Powderly and the Knights were from at least 1886 onwards.[8]

Yet for all this criticism and revisionism, historians have approached Terence Powderly as a purely American figure, and judged him based on American events. That makes sense because until recently the Knights of Labor was generally seen only as an American movement, and sometimes as a Canadian one. We now know—something that Norman Ware alluded to but did not develop in his 1929 study of the Knights—that in the 1880s and the 1890s the Knights became one of the nineteenth century's largest global working-class movements. They established branches in Belgium, Britain, Ireland, France, Italy, New Zealand, Australia and South Africa, some of them large: well over thirty thousand Knights in Belgium, and at least ten thousand each in Britain and New Zealand.[9] Powderly was not

---

[7] John R. Commons et al., *History of Labour in the United States*, vol. 2, *1860–1896* (New York: Macmillan, 1936); Gerald Grob, *Workers and Utopia: A Study of Ideological Change in the American Labor Movement, 1865–1900* (Chicago: Quadrangle, 1969); Selig Perlman, *A Theory of the Labor Movement* (New York: Macmillan, 1928).

[8] Richard Oestreicher, "Terence V. Powderly, the Knights of Labor, and Artisanal Republicanism," in *Labor Leaders in America*, eds. Melvyn Dubofsky and Warren van Tine (Urbana: University of Illinois Press, 1987), 30–61; Craig Phelan, *Grand Master Workman: Terence Powderly and the Knights of Labor* (Westport, CT: Greenwood Press, 2000).

[9] See Steven Parfitt, "The First-and-a-Half International: The Knights of Labor and the History of International Labour Organizations in the Nineteenth Century," *Labour History Review* 80, no. 2 (2015): 135–167; Robert Weir, *Knights Down Under: The Knights of Labor in New Zealand* (Newcastle upon Tyne: Cambridge Scholars Press, 2009).

just the General Master Workman of the Knights of Labor: he was also its Global Master Workman.

This chapter examines his work as leader of a global movement. By looking at Terence Powderly through this transnational lens we can better understand his strengths and weaknesses, and the nature of transatlantic radical networks in the late nineteenth century. It will focus on transatlantic networks between workers in the United States and those in three other countries: Britain, Ireland and France. To promote the growth of the Knights of Labor abroad, Powderly drew on these networks and his own connections with leading figures in the Irish independence movement and the British trade union movement, and with enthusiasts for the Knights within the fledgling French labor movement. His work did not always end in triumph. Connections with French trade unionists, as we will see, ended in abject failure and pointed to some of Powderly's weaknesses as a leader. On the other hand, through his ties with leading radicals such as Michael Davitt (1846–1906) and Thomas Burt (1837–1922), he made it possible for the Knights to set up the first of their assemblies in England, and then to grow to over ten thousand members by 1890. The image that emerges of Powderly as an international leader, not just as a national one, is rather different from the one drawn by his critics.

The Irish Cause

Terence Powderly never failed to talk up his credentials as an American patriot. His enthusiasm for flag-waving and meditations on American greatness led some of his radical opponents to accuse him and the Knights of "Yankee-doodleism" and "spread-eagleism."[10] In the final chapter of his memoirs he made it clear that his keenly developed sense of American nationalism was not antithetical to his internationalism but was instead the basis for it. Yet Powderly's patriotism was confined not just to the land of his birth but to the land of his parents as well. He later wrote, that in 1866, at the age of seventeen, he attended by chance a meeting of the Irish Republican Brotherhood in Carbondale and was so enthused by what was said that he ran home, took $5 from his savings, and invested the money in bonds of the Irish Republic—redeemable when the Brotherhood freed Ireland from British rule.[11] From then until the end, Powderly remained a staunch defender of Irish independence. Through this cause, he

<hr>

10   Leon Fink, *Workingmen's Democracy: The Knights of Labor and American Politics* (Urbana: University of Illinois Press, 1983), 13.

11   Terence V. Powderly, *The Path I Trod: The Autobiography of Terence V. Powderly* (New York: Columbia University Press, 1940), 175.

became part of one of the largest and most powerful radical networks that spanned the Atlantic in the nineteenth and twentieth centuries—between the United States and Ireland—based on emigration and the desire for Irish independence or Home Rule.

Historians have always recognized the importance of Irish immigrants in American labor history. Millions of Irish moved across the Atlantic during the nineteenth century, whether fleeing famine and poverty or simply in search of a better life, and many of them and their descendants soon became a large fraction of the membership of American unions. As late as World War I, Irish-Americans were among the loudest opponents of American entry into that conflict, insisting that they would not give their lives to defend British imperial interests. Along with German-Americans, Irish-Americans in the labor movement nearly forced the American Federation of Labor either to oppose the war or at least to adopt a more neutral stance.[12]

Ties between Irish immigrants and the Knights of Labor became especially close, but not by the original design of its founders. Uriah Stephens (1821–1882), the first Grand Master Workman of the Knights and the writer of its early ritual and constitutional documents, had trained for the Baptist ministry, and retained, like many other American-born Protestants of the period, more than a trace of anti-Catholic (and therefore, to some extent, anti-Irish) bigotry. Nor was it due to the friendliness of Catholic prelates to the Order. From the early 1880s, when Jesuits in Quebec refused the sacraments to local Knights on the basis that the Order was a masonic, and hence anti-Catholic, organization, Powderly and others spent a great deal of time convincing bishops and cardinals that the Knights did not contravene the teachings or practices of the Church. They eventually succeeded in convincing the Vatican not to ban Catholics from joining the Order, but at the price of convincing many American Protestants that the Order, and Powderly himself, was in some way the tool of Rome.

Despite these religious problems, Irish immigrants joined the Knights in such large numbers that the Order was at least in part an Irish organization. Powderly, of course, symbolized this association, and he certainly made it clear in his memoirs that he always saw his work for the Knights and his advocacy of Irish independence as very closely related. As

---

[12] See, for instance, Kevin Kenny, "Labor and Labor Organisations," in *Making the Irish American: History and Heritage of the Irish in the United States*, eds. John Lee and Marion Casey (New York: New York University Press, 2006), 354–363; Joseph McCartin, *Labor's Great War: The Struggle for Industrial Democracy and the Origins of Modern American Industrial Relations, 1912–1921* (Chapel Hill: University of North Carolina Press, 1997); or David Montgomery, *The Fall of the House of Labor: The Workplace, the State, and American Labor Activism, 1865–1925* (Cambridge: Cambridge University Press, 1989).

Grand (General) Master Workman from 1879, and Mayor of Scranton, Pennsylvania from 1878, Powderly combined his official duties with work on behalf of what became the American section of the Irish National Land League. Given that the Knights practiced strict secrecy until the early 1880s, he followed open meetings for the League with secret ones of Knights all over the United States. "In this way," he later wrote, "I was of use to both organizations."[13]

If the story stopped there, with an American labor leader of Irish stock calling for Irish independence, it would hardly be considered exceptional. Yet Powderly went much further than that. During the 1880s, he tapped into this Irish-American radical network to make the Knights of Labor the first, and largest, American working-class movement to operate all over the world. The key figure in this process, apart from Powderly himself, was Michael Davitt. Davitt, born in Ireland in 1846, had been taken to England by his mother at the height of the Great Famine and grew up in industrial Lancashire. Like Powderly, Davitt was drawn to the Irish Republican Brotherhood (IRB) in his teens; unlike Powderly, he spent more than seven years in prison for his work on behalf of the IRB. In the late 1870s and early 1880s, Davitt became, along with the MP Charles Stuart Parnell, one of the leaders of the Irish Land League, set up to demand fairer rents, guaranteed tenure and free sale for Irish tenant farmers. Both Davitt and Parnell traveled more than once to the United States to rally support for the League, and that is where the paths of Powderly and Davitt finally crossed.

There is no precise date for when the two men first met, or when Powderly conceived of the idea that Davitt might speak on the Order's behalf in Britain and Ireland. The seed had certainly been planted by 1886, when the labor newspaper *John Swinton's Paper* published a letter from an English socialist inquiring about the possibility of starting an assembly in London (as we will see later, assemblies in Britain, if not in London itself, did in fact already exist). In the next issue, the prominent socialist and Knight from Chicago, George Schilling, moved that "MICHAEL DAVITT be called upon to accept a commission as Organizer of the K. of L. on the other side of the Atlantic, and espouse the cause of our Holy Order."[14] Schilling's motion was seconded by others from all over the country.[15]

In 1887, Davitt appeared at the General Assembly of the Knights of Labor. Delegates passed strong resolutions in favor of Irish Home Rule, and they mobbed Davitt after his speech. More importantly, it is about this time that Powderly initiated Davitt as a Knight of Labor. Newspapers speculated

---

13 Powderly, *The Path I Trod*, 159.
14 *John Swinton's Paper*, Feb. 28, and Mar. 7, 1886.
15 *John Swinton's Paper*, Mar. 14, 1886.

that Davitt would merge the Land League into the Order, work for the Knights in Britain and Ireland, and Powderly would join him in agitation on the other side of the Atlantic. Powderly made private promises to English and Belgian Knights on that last point.[16] These speculations caused consternation among many well-to-do people in Britain: at this point, after all, the Knights had earned worldwide fame as a labor organization embroiled in vast strikes across the United States, and with a strong connection to the Chicago anarchists recently convicted of throwing bombs at police during a rally in the city's Haymarket Square. Davitt denied them.

He did, however, accept an organizers' commission from Powderly before he returned to Ireland. In the following year, he had cause to use it: he accepted an invitation from the leaders of the Order's first English District Assembly, No. 208, to address a public meeting in Smethwick, a suburb of Birmingham. "The Knights of Labor is not an American society, or an Irish society or an English society," Davitt claimed: "It is a society of all of these and more. By its aid here in England we are enabled to meet on common ground for the first time and to each of us is given the great privilege of taking a member by the hand and calling him brother regardless of his country, creed, or condition in life."[17] Davitt's speech, widely reported and reprinted in the British press, played a crucial role in the growth of the Knights in Birmingham and the surrounding Black Country, one of Britain's most important industrial regions.

Powderly then secured the services in 1889 of another Irish-American Knight, James P. Archibald of New York, to continue Davitt's work. After an exhaustive series of lectures, from Birmingham to Liverpool and Glasgow, Archibald contributed to the substantial growth of the Order's British assemblies in the late 1880s, up to around ten thousand members by the decade's end. The officials of District Assembly 208 proved so grateful for Archibald's work all over Britain on their behalf that they presented him with a gold pocket watch during a farewell dinner at Smethwick in September 1889.[18]

There is, however, an irony here. It was precisely because Powderly made use of Davitt's services in Britain that the Knights only established the barest foothold in Ireland itself. Davitt refused to agitate for the Order there, saying in 1887 that he "would not countenance the establishment of any society that might become opposed to the National League," and

---

[16] *Chicago Daily Tribune*, Sept. 3, 1887; Alberte Delwarte to Hayes, May 20, 1889, Washington, D.C., Catholic University of America Archives, Terence V. Powderly Papers (TPP), Box 54; Powderly to Jesse Chapman, Feb. 8, 1889, TPP, Box 99.

[17] *Freemen's Journal*, May 9, 1888.

[18] *Journal of United Labor*, Nov. 14, 1889.

Knights did not press the point.[19] It took the former Master Workman of an assembly in Columbus, Georgia to open the first Irish assembly, in Belfast, in 1888. Only a handful of other assemblies in Belfast and Derry joined that one over the course of the Order's history. Davitt did speak at a meeting of Derry's LA1601 at the start of 1890, stating his "pride that the son of an Irish workingman should become the head of the greatest labor organization of the world," but it was due to Davitt's desire to promote the Land League above all else that the Order never achieved critical mass in the birthplace of Powderly's parents.[20]

Close ties between Powderly and the cause of Irish independence did occasionally land the General Master Workman in trouble. In 1887, in London, *The Times* accused Charles Parnell of various crimes, including the murder of two British officials in Ireland in 1882.[21] One of the witnesses against Parnell at an ensuing commission investigating *The Times*'s allegations in 1889, a certain Major Henri Le Caron—actually a British spy, Thomas Beach, who had infiltrated Irish revolutionary movements for twenty-five years—claimed that Powderly, among other prominent Irish-Americans, had supported a secret organization, Clan na Gael, which advocated Irish independence by violent means. Powderly recounted in his memoirs that "Le Caron" had urged Powderly to make liberal use of dynamite during the Great Southwest rail strike of 1886, only for the General Master Workman to assume that the "Major" was an agent provocateur in the pay of the railroad companies. He would find out three years later how right he was.[22]

Beach's charges against Powderly were overblown. Nor should they obscure the tremendous debt that the Knights of Labor owed to Irish-American radical networks and to Powderly's ability to make use of those networks to further the Order's ends. His association with Davitt might have delayed its growth in Ireland, but this was more than made up for by Davitt's and then Archibald's successful promotion of the Knights in Britain. Indeed, few American labor leaders could claim to have made more of the Irish-American connection than Powderly or to have used it to greater effect. Powderly's name might not come as readily to mind as the central figure in Irish-American labor and radical history, the socialist, Scottish-born, Irish rebel James Connolly, who spent formative years as a labor leader in the United States before returning to Ireland, only to be executed by the British after the Easter Rising of 1916. Like Connolly, however, Powderly also tapped into another, related radical network: the one between British

---

[19] *Birmingham Daily Post*, Oct. 21, 1887
[20] *Journal of United Labor*, Feb. 13, 1890.
[21] *The Times*, Mar. 7, 1887.
[22] Powderly, *The Path I Trod*, 185–186.

and American trade unionists, equally important and longstanding as the one between Americans and the Irish.

Knights of Labor and the British Trade Unions

Fraternal ties between the British and American labor movements went back to the years before the American Revolution and the earliest unions in Philadelphia and New York. British-born figures such as Tom Paine became closely associated with the plebeian discontent of the Revolutionary period. The Welsh factory manager turned utopian socialist Robert Owen achieved as much popularity in the United States as in Britain after several tours to the New World in the 1820s, and many Americans went west to turn his plans and principles into a model community in what they thought was virgin wilderness. When the Chartist movement went into decline at the end of the 1840s, many of its members streamed across the Atlantic to find safe haven in America.[23] Lancashire mill workers became the most consistent British supporters of the northern cause during the Civil War, even though they faced unemployment due to the interruption of cotton from southern plantations to North England mills. Their determination partly stemmed from their hatred of slavery. It also arose from the deep attachment that many British radicals felt towards the democratic and republican institutions of the United States. The ties between British and American labor movements followed this general trend throughout the nineteenth century—emigrating British workers greatly influenced the early development of the American labor movement, while many of those who stayed in Britain looked to the United States as an exemplar of the democratic Republic they wished they could build at home.[24]

Terence Powderly became a key figure in this wider story. He came of age in the 1870s, a decade punctuated in the United States by economic crisis, political counter revolution and spontaneous uprisings. Having learned his trade as a machinist, he was thrown out of work after the Panic of '73 led to a grinding economic depression across the country (and much of the world). Powderly traveled west, carting snow, vainly looking for permanent work, finding as he did so that his name often appeared on a blacklist of suspected union activists. In the same decade, two major events thrust industrial

---

[23] Ray Boston, *British Chartists in America, 1939–1900* (Manchester: Manchester University Press, 1971).

[24] See, for instance, Henry Pelling, *America and the British Left, from Bright to Bevan* (London: Adam and Charles Black, 1956) and Clifton Yearley, *Britons in American Labor: A History of the Influence of the United Kingdom Immigrants on American Labor, 1820–1914* (Baltimore, MD: Johns Hopkins University Press, 1957).

problems and class conflict to the center of American politics. The first was a political counterrevolution, namely the withdrawal of Northern soldiers from the southern states in 1876 and the end of Reconstruction.[25] African Americans were left to face the old slave-owning class and their allies alone, who moved in to restore their former social, economic and political power.

The second event was an uprising of workers across the United States in 1877. It began with a nationwide railroad strike, but in some cities, as state militia moved in to confront the pickets, the strike became a general assault on the railroad companies and even on property itself. For a time, the respectable classes of the United States feared a repeat of the Paris Commune in St. Louis, Chicago and other industrial centers and railroad hubs. Their fears were eventually unfounded. The strikes ended in failure and the defeated strikers dispersed throughout the United States in search of work. For the moment, the prospects for racial equality faded into the background. Class conflict on a national scale seemed to replace it as the most pressing social question in the United States.

Powderly and many other younger activists were greatly affected by these developments. As young men and women they had grown up in an era defined by the abolitionist movement and the fight to preserve the Union against secessionist slave-owners, and they had absorbed a general commitment to racial equality, in a formal if not in a real sense. Their experiences of unemployment, blacklisting and the wholesale destruction of trade unions in the economic depression of the 1870s had convinced them that narrow sectional trade unionism, concerned only with the affairs of a single trade, could not resist big capital. And the failure of the 1877 Uprising convinced Powderly, and some others, that strikes would not bring about the improvements that workers needed, and could not succeed against corporations allied with local, state and federal governments.

They needed to look elsewhere for support. Powderly followed in the train of trade unionists who had attempted to forge transatlantic alliances with British unions throughout the 1860s and 1870s. William Sylvis (1828–1869), the President of the National Labor Union from 1868 until his early death the following year, had seen the solution to the suffering of workers in the Old and New Worlds as "the united and fraternal agency of our organs of labor."[26] He had sent A. C. Cameron, editor of the Chicago labor paper,

---

[25] See Kenneth M. Stamp, *The Era of Reconstruction, 1865–1877* (New York: Vintage, 1965) and Donna L. Dickerson, *The Reconstruction Era: Primary Documents on Events from 1865 to 1877* (Westport, CT: Greenwood Press, 2003) for a still readable introduction and some of the main sources related to that era of U.S. history.

[26] William H. Sylvis, *The Life, Speeches, Labors and Essays of William H. Sylvis* (Philadelphia: Claxton, Remsen & Haffelfinger, 1872), 455–456.

Workingmen's Advocate, to the Basle Conference of the First International in 1869 to create some kind of "closer union" between American and European workers and to encourage European unions to regulate if possible the flow of migrants from Europe to the United States. These connections led nowhere, and both the First International and the National Labor Union fell apart several years after the Conference took place, but transatlantic connections between individual British and American unions continued in the 1870s.[27]

First, several British unions established branches in the United States. The Amalgamated Engineers and the Amalgamated Carpenters and Joiners opened the most American branches. These were started by British emigrants who wanted to maintain their connection to the death, medical and other benefit systems operated by their union. In the twentieth century, these unions merged with their American equivalents—the Amalgamated Engineers, for instance, were absorbed into the International Association of Machinists—but they remained distinct throughout the late nineteenth century. Second, these and other British unions established close working arrangements with their American counterparts. Boilermakers, shipbuilders, cigar makers and ironworkers came to agreements regarding the mutual exchange of union cards, the exchange of information in their respective union journals and the exchange of delegates between their respective conventions. The Machinists and Blacksmiths' Union, where Powderly first made his name as a labor agitator, was one of the organizations involved.[28] As Powderly gravitated towards the Knights of Labor, and especially when he became its second Grand Master Workman in 1879, he immediately made plans to build on these earlier connections and, if possible, to surpass them.

His first step was to write in 1879 to Alexander MacDonald (1821–1881), the Scottish Lib.–Lab. MP, coal miners' leader and an admirer of American labor politics since a trip to the United States in 1868, to see about the prospects for a closer bond between organized labor in Britain and the United States.[29] Their correspondence did not lead to a practical outcome, but it did serve as a guide to Powderly's intentions. In 1880, at the annual conference of the Knights of Labor, the General Assembly, he told the delegates of his contact with MacDonald and how he "learned that the idea of adopting some means of cooperating with the workingmen of America was an agreeable one." Powderly urged the delegates to "do something

[27] A. T. Lane, *Solidarity or Survival? American Labor and European Immigrants, 1830–1924* (Westport, CT: Greenwood Press, 1987), 49.

[28] Yearley, *Britons in American Labor*, 58–62.

[29] W. H. Marwick, *A Short History of Labour in Scotland* (Edinburgh: W. & R. Chambers, 1967), 75.

whereby the benefits of a union between the workingmen of America and Europe may become so plain that a connecting link may be forged, binding them closely together."[30]

He was even more cryptic at the next General Assembly in 1881. "I believe the hour is ripe for planting the Order in Europe," he claimed, and "correspondence has been had with members of the Order who have crossed the ocean in the interest of one of our branches, giving very encouraging news of the possibilities for organization in England especially. A request was made that the necessary material be sent over to these brothers by which they could commence work." The only problem, he continued, was "how to convey the private work of the Order to these brothers and avoid the governmental scrutiny which would surely be directed against any effort we could make." Unfortunately for us, Powderly hinted at a suggestion to overcome this difficulty but went on to claim that "it would be manifestly indiscreet to publish this plan in the proceedings," and preferred instead to consider it in secret session.[31]

The branch he referred to was almost certainly Local Assembly 300, Window Glass Workers of America. The window glass workers of LA300, a national organization covering almost every skilled worker in their industry, were amongst the best-paid wage earners in the country, with a closed shop and guaranteed holidays in the summer. Yet they feared that technological change in European glassworks would leave many European craftsmen unemployed, and willing to come to America in search of work. If they migrated to the United States in sufficient numbers the Assembly might be overwhelmed, its closed shop broken and the high living standards of its members reduced to lower European levels.[32]

To meet this danger, LA300 sent two officials to Europe in 1880 to gauge the prospects for a formal organization spanning the Atlantic that would regulate the flow of window glass workers from Europe to America and ensure that those who did arrive in the New World would join the union and maintain the closed shop. Moves towards this international organization were interrupted by a series of strikes in 1882 and 1883, as window-glass manufacturers tried in vain to break the union and its closed shop. In 1884, with the strikes won, LA300 sent two more officials, Isaac Cline and Henry Burtt, across to Europe to resume the work broken off in 1880. Their tour

---

[30] Knights of Labor, *Proceedings of the General Assembly of the Knights of Labor* (Philadelphia: s.n., 1880), 175.

[31] Ibid., 175–176.

[32] Ken Fones-Wolf, "Immigrants, Labor and Capital in a Transnational Context: Belgian Glass Workers in America, 1880–1925," *Journal of American Ethnic History* 21, no. 2 (2002): 61–63.

around Britain, France, Belgium, Italy and Germany bore fruit with the creation of an International Federation of Window-Glass Workers, which held its first convention at St. Helens, England, in the same year.[33]

Powderly's help proved critical at every stage in this process. Many Knights resented the calls that the Knights' leaders made for financial assistance to help the glass workers win their strikes. Rural Knights especially disliked sacrificing their modest earnings to the support of the best-paid workers in the country. Powderly made sure that these resentments did not prevent assistance from the Order at large from continuing to flow to LA300. Self-interest played a role here. LA300 possessed immense financial reserves, and one of the most intriguing aspects of the financial history of the Knights of Labor is the fact that several thousand glass workers subsidized a movement of tens and then hundreds of thousands of members for the rest of the 1880s and 1890s. Powderly's firm support for the glass workers in their time of need made that subsidy possible. He also established correspondence with important figures in the British labor movement, such as the miners' leader and Liberal MP Thomas Burt, so that when the representatives of LA300 arrived in Britain they were seen as allies and not as unwelcome interlopers.

Powderly further made sure that the new International Federation worked to the advantage of the Order at large. After the first convention of the Federation, LA300 sent another organizer, A. G. Denny, to complete the work and place the Federation on as solid a basis as possible. Powderly arranged for Denny to meet several prominent British trade union leaders, including Burt.[34] The connections between Powderly and his counterparts across the Atlantic, forged first with Alexander MacDonald in 1879, finally appeared to be moving beyond words and into practice. The General Master Workman further made sure that Denny voyaged to Europe with the authority to initiate all willing workers into the Knights. For their part, the leaders of LA300 appreciated Powderly's support during their strikes and gave Denny free rein to work on behalf of the Order at large. Denny arrived in England, and then in continental Europe, financed in part by the General Assembly and in part by LA300.

Few Knights could have foreseen the importance of Denny's mission. In 1884 and 1885, he brought English and Belgian window glass workers into the Knights of Labor. In England, the Knights remained restricted to workers in that trade for two more years; in Belgium, they quickly spread among the coal and iron workers of the Charleroi Basin, and from there

[33] Henry Pelling, "The Knights of Labor in Britain, 1880–1901," *Economic History Review* 9 (1956): 315.

[34] A. G. Denny to Powderly, Dec. 29, 1884, TPP, Box 12.

to the luxury trades of Brussels.[35] Even at that early stage, the number of Belgian Knights reached into the thousands. Powderly had helped to transform what might have been a narrow federation of workers in a single trade into the start of the global expansion of the Knights of Labor.

He continued to assist the British assemblies until they began to decline and then fall apart between 1890 and 1894. Through Michael Davitt and James P. Archibald, Powderly brought together Irish-American and British-American radical networks to further the Order's cause in Europe. He maintained steady correspondence with the British assemblies until they began to decline and fall apart in 1893 and 1894 and allowed British Knights to make minor tweaks to the Order's ritual and methods of operation where necessary. He became, in short, key to the Order's introduction and expansion into Britain, and succeeded where few Americans have done before or since: setting up branches of American unions in the home of trade unionism itself.

Powderly and the Paris Exposition

By 1886, when the Knights of Labor reached the height of their strength and mustered nearly a million American members, Terence Powderly had become a figure of national importance. Reporters pressed him for comment on the events of the day. Sacks full of letters arrived daily from all parts of the country. Newspapers and politicians mused on what the rise of the Knights would mean for the future of the United States. Powderly and the Knights also attracted the attention of commentators far beyond North America. Leaf through his personal papers and you find mail from all over the world, whether admirers who wished to form branches of the Knights of Labor in their own countries, or scholars interested in the rise of such a powerful labor organization seemingly out of nowhere, or the merely curious. The Knights became a staple of the international pages of newspapers all over the world, especially when they engaged in the rash of strikes, boycotts and political campaigns of 1885–1887, the Great Upheaval, and Powderly occupied an outsized place in these reports as the Order's leading spokesman. He became the United States' first "labor superstar," as Weir describes him; he became one of the first internationally known labor leaders as well. His picture hung in union halls from Finland to Australia, a fact that doubtless gave him enormous pleasure.

As the Knights extended from their North American home to Britain and Belgium, then to Italy, Ireland, Australia and New Zealand in 1888,

---

[35] Leon Watillon, *The Knights of Labor in Belgium* (Los Angeles: University of California Press, 1959), 21–34.

and South Africa in 1890, Powderly was in most cases the first point of contact for would-be foreign initiates, and despite the enormous pressures of his post he seems to have stayed in regular and close contact with them until he was deposed as General Master Workman in 1894. While his American opponents often denounced him as a tyrant who kept his position by manipulating its conventions and administrative machinery and expelling his rivals, he proved more than willing to let foreign Knights run their own affairs. Inflexible at home and flexible abroad, Powderly seems to have succeeded as the leader of an international movement much more than at the head of a national one.

He proved his worth when drawing on Irish-American and British-American radical networks to grow the Knights in Europe. Yet he also showed his limitations when it came to dealing with trade unionists in another country across the Atlantic: France.[36] Radicals there were still recovering from the aftermath of the Paris Commune in 1870. Trade unions were banned in the early years of the Third Republic, and only legalized in 1884. Whether Marxists, anarchists, radical Republicans or trade unionists of no settled political opinion, they all welcomed the rise of the Knights of Labor and saw it as a potential model for the weak French labor movement. Jules Guesde (1845–1922), one of the main French socialists of the period, saw the Knights and American workers in 1886 as sounding "the tocsin for the social revolution [...] in all the civilized world."[37] A bookbinder in Annonay was so impressed by what he read of the Knights that he wrote to Powderly asking if he could be initiated as an individual member. The General Master Workman made sure that the Belgian assemblies fulfilled that request.[38]

Two French labor activists, F. Veyssier and Abel Davaud (1828–1898), were particularly impressed with the Knights and with Powderly himself. They edited a Parisian trade union journal, the *Moniteur des syndicats ouvriers*, with ties to the so-called "Opportunist" liberal republican government that legalized unions in 1884. Veyssier and Davaud began to reprint speeches from Belgian Knights in 1887. As they later told the *Journal of United Labor*, they saw the Order as a way to unite French workers, then divided

---

[36] For a broader treatment of the Knights in France, see Maurice Dommanget, *La Chevalerie du travail française, 1893–1911: contribution à l'histoire du socialisme et du mouvement ouvrier* (Lausanne: Mulhouse, 1967) and Steven Parfitt, "Powderly Will Go to Paris: The Paris Exposition and the Knights of Labor," *International Labor and Working-Class History* 92 (2017): 183–212.

[37] Quoted in John Laslett, "Haymarket, Henry George, and the Labor Upsurge in Britain and America during the Late 1880s," *International Labor and Working-Class History* 29 (1986): 69.

[38] Maurice to Powderly, Oct. 30, 1888, TPP, Box 48.

between many competing socialist, anarchist and republican tendencies, under one banner.[39] In 1888, they wrote to Charles Lichtman, then the Order's General Secretary, asking for more information about the Knights, and soon developed an elaborate plan to promote the Order across France at one of the great international events of the nineteenth century: the Paris Exposition of 1889.

The Paris Exposition remains famous for the opening of the Eiffel Tower, then considered a temporary building and now the city's outstanding symbol. Yet it also introduced another innovation unknown in previous exhibitions: the Section on Social Economy, showcasing attempts all over the world at social reform, from model housing and sanitation to cooperatives and trade unions. Veyssier and Davaud wanted the Knights to send an exhibit to Paris and advertise themselves to the millions of French and foreign visitors, while they laid the groundwork for the Order's first assembly in Paris and overcame a final legal hurdle, namely a law aimed at the International Workingmen's Association just after the Commune, which banned the affiliation of labor groups with international bodies.[40] Powderly and Lichtman agreed; and they and the latter's successor as General Secretary, John Hayes, promoted the exhibit and collected banners, flags and other memorabilia from assemblies across the United States to send for inclusion in the Order's exhibit at the Paris Exposition.[41]

Powderly went one step further. Since 1887, newspapers in the United States and other countries had reported that the General Master Workman intended to visit Europe sometime in the near future.[42] Some reports suggested he would agitate in Ireland for Home Rule and independence, others that he would visit Britain, France and a number of other countries to promote the Knights and international labor cooperation. Powderly never denied these rumors. The Order's General Assembly upped the ante in 1888 when it voted that he attend the Paris Exposition itself. Through the French translator at headquarters, B. Maurice, Powderly then informed Veyssier and Davaud that he was in the advanced stages of planning his trip across the Atlantic to visit them. The two French activists could not contain their excitement and redoubled their efforts to open the first French assembly before the General Master Workman arrived in country. They also oversaw the shipping of the

---

[39] *Journal of United Labor*, Oct. 25, 1888.

[40] *Journal of United Labor*, Sept. 6, 1888. The Section on Social Economy also was involved in the founding of the Musée Social. See Janet Horne, *Le Musée social, aux origines de l'État providence* (Paris: Belin, 2004).

[41] *Journal of United Labor*, Feb. 28, 1889.

[42] Examples include *Sheffield and Rotherham Independent*, Sept. 9, 1887; *Newcastle Weekly Courant*, Apr. 15, 1887; *Chicago Daily Tribune*, Sept. 3, 1887; *Los Angeles Daily Herald*, Oct. 15, 1887; *Reynolds's Newspaper*, 2 Oct. 1887.

objects destined for the Order's exhibit from the coast to Paris and put it all together as the Section for Social Economy took shape in early 1889.

It seemed as if the General Master Workman stood on the verge of another personal triumph. Having made use of ties with British and Irish radicals to promote the Order's growth in Britain, he would now appear as the representative of American labor on the world stage and extend the Knights of Labor into France. Yet where Powderly's dealings with Davitt, Archibald, Burt and MacDonald had emphasized his strengths, and the strength of the radical networks they represented, his dealings with his French admirers brought his failings into sharp relief. In June 1889, the same month that Veyssier and Davaud opened Local Assembly 489, the Order's first branch in France, Powderly began to backtrack from his earlier promises to visit Paris. He complained to Maurice that nobody had told him when he should arrive at the Exposition, and in July he wrote a long letter to Veyssier explaining why he was now unable to make it across the Atlantic.[43] He claimed to have long suffered from an extreme form of seasickness, along with several other internal ailments, and his doctor had told him that this combination could prove fatal on a long ocean voyage.[44] Powderly never explained why this longstanding problem had not stopped him making rash promises to foreign friends over the last few years.

Veyssier and Davaud received this unwelcome news at the same time as two other leading Knights, Hugh Cavanagh, a Powderly friend and loyalist, and Leonora Barry (1849–1923), the Order's leading woman member and Investigator for Women's Work, were due to arrive at the Exposition, as members of a delegation of American workers organized by the Scripps Newspaper League. Powderly made no effort to put Cavanagh and Barry in touch with Veyssier and Davaud; to make matters worse, when the French Knights hunted down their American visitors at a lunch, and made arrangements for them to meet with their new Parisian assembly, Cavanagh and Barry failed to show.[45] To put the final seal on this shambles, neither Powderly nor General Secretary-Treasurer Hayes responded to Veyssier's and Davaud's requests that they be repaid for the costs of shipping the Order's exhibit to and from Le Havre, except for a perfunctory letter from Hayes in October demanding that the Order's property be returned to the United States at once. Spurned, let down and out of pocket, Veyssier, Davaud and the other founding members of Local Assembly 489 soon abandoned the Knights and went their own way.[46]

---

43 Powderly to Maurice, June 1, 1889, TPP, Box 42.
44 Powderly to F. Veyssier, July 15, 1889, TPP, Box 54.
45 F. Veyssier to Powderly, Sept. 20, 1889, TPP, Box 56.
46 F. Veyssier to Powderly, Feb. 28, 1890, TPP, Box 59.

Having wrested defeat from the jaws of victory, the General Master Workman reverted to what his scholarly detractors would regard as typical Powderly style. He blamed Maurice for supposed miscommunications, did not seem to have bothered to have replied to Veyssier's last, desperate appeals for assistance, and then absolved himself of all blame at the next General Assembly in 1889.[47] "To cross over and visit the Exposition would be very pleasant," he told the delegates, leaving out the original objectives and high hopes that led him to promise to the Order's French admirers his presence in Paris, "but it would leave whoever went open to the charge of going on a junketing tour, and there are those who would be uncharitable to make such remarks." To the unspoken question as to why he failed to honor the commitments made by the General Assembly in 1888, which voted that he visit the Exposition, he now claimed, disingenuously, that "I could not see that any gain would accrue to the Order on either side of the Atlantic from such a step."[48]

In the end, the Knights of Labor did establish assemblies in France several years later. They owed little to Powderly, and in fact owed a great deal to the very forces within the Knights that he always distrusted: Marxists in the Socialist Labor Party. In 1893, Chicago held its own Columbian Exposition and, like the gathering in Paris in 1889, hosted meetings and exhibits of trade unionists, cooperators and social reformers in general. A group of French socialists visiting the Exposition met Lucien Sanial (1835–1927), a French-born member of the SLP and former editor of its English-language journal *The People*, about the possibility of forming assemblies in France. Sanial got them in touch with Knights in Belgium, still going strong even though, by this time, the Knights were rapidly dwindling into insignificance in the United States. The French assemblies survived as small, secret organizations into the twentieth century, proof if nothing else of the potential power of transatlantic ties between workers in Europe and the United States.[49]

Conclusion: Global Master Workman

Terence Powderly may have been, at various times, a "windbag," a poor leader, conceited and unwilling to brook even the mildest opposition to his rule as General Master Workman. There are plenty of examples in the American history of the Knights of Labor where Powderly made a bad situation worse, even if the fault was not his alone—from strikes on the

---

[47] Powderly to F. Veyssier, Aug. 27, 1889, TPP, Box 101.

[48] Knights of Labor, *Proceedings of the General Assembly* (1889), 9.

[49] A. F. Parmentier to Powderly, Feb. 2, 1894, TPP, Box 84; Dommanget, *La Chevalerie*.

Southwestern rail system and the Chicago stockyards in 1886 to a succession of damaging splits and public rows within the Order and between the Knights and rival trade unions. He proved much more successful on an international stage. His commitment to the cause of Irish independence brought him into contact with some of the most famous Irish radicals of the day, and his friendship with Michael Davitt made possible the expansion of the Knights' British assemblies. He went much further than any previous American labor leaders, and most future ones, in establishing meaningful ties with British trade unionists, making the British Knights of Labor possible in the first place.

Powderly made a better Global Master Workman than a General Master Workman. He was able to tap into British-American and Irish-American radical networks to make the Knights of Labor the first and the largest American labor movement to organize on a global scale—larger in numbers even than the Industrial Workers of the World, the other radical American working-class movement to organize on an international scale, and the subject of much recent scholarly attention.[50] He still showed, it is true, traces of the qualities that landed him and the Knights of Labor in so much trouble in the United States. By overpromising, under-delivering, and blaming everything in a petulant way on his aides, he ruined a golden opportunity for the Knights to break new ground in France at a time when all the news at home was bad. Yet his successes in Britain and Ireland more than made up for that failure, and illustrated other of his qualities that his detractors usually glanced over: patience, passion for causes outside himself, flexibility and perseverance with the key people who enabled the British assemblies to grow.

This evaluation of Powderly's successes and failures is, like all previous ones, only a provisional verdict. Further research into his dealings with the many admirers who never joined the Knights, but corresponded with him or enlisted him for some cause or other all over the world, will add to our understanding of the General Master Workman as an international figure. The Knights were more than just a transatlantic movement, and although outside the scope of this book it would be useful to delve more deeply into Powderly's connections to radicals and trade unionists around the Pacific basin, whether or not they joined the Knights, as some did. This research will shed more light on the nature and scale of transatlantic, transpacific and global radical networks, and on the Knights of Labor, one of the forgotten international working-class movements to rise and fall in the last decades of the nineteenth century. We can say, however, that Terence Powderly became a crucial, if often unacknowledged, transatlantic radical figure, and that he

---

[50] Peter Cole, David Struthers and Kenyon Zimmer, eds., *Wobblies of the World: A Global History of the IWW* (London: Pluto, 2017).

was very much a part of several key networks that spanned the Atlantic. That alone should be enough to rescue him from being labelled only as a windbag, a bumbler and someone to be remembered solely for his mistakes and the arrogant way in which he made them.

Works Cited

Archival Sources
Washington, D.C., Catholic University of America Archives
Powderly Papers

Secondary Works
Boston, Ray. *British Chartists in America, 1939–1900.* Manchester: Manchester University Press, 1971.

Cole, Peter, David Struthers and Kenyon Zimmer, eds. *Wobblies of the World: A Global History of the IWW.* London: Pluto, 2017.

Commons, John R., et al. *History of Labour in the United States*, vol. 2, *1860–1896.* New York: Macmillan, 1936.

Dickerson, Donna L. *The Reconstruction Era: Primary Documents on Events from 1865 to 1877.* Westport, CT: Greenwood Press, 2003.

Dommanget, Maurice. *La Chevalerie du travail française, 1893–1911: Contribution à l'histoire du socialisme et du mouvement ouvrier.* Lausanne: Mulhouse, 1967.

Engels, Friedrich. "Preface to the American Edition." In *The Condition of the Working Class in England.* New York: s.n., 1887. www.marxists.org/archive/marx/works/1886/02/25.htm. Accessed Oct. 20, 2020.

Fink, Leon. *Workingmen's Democracy: The Knights of Labor and American Politics.* Urbana: University of Illinois Press, 1983.

Foner, Philip S. *History of the Labor Movement in the United States*, vol. 2, 2nd ed. New York: International Publishers, 1975.

Fones-Wolf, Ken. "Immigrants, Labor and Capital in a Transnational Context: Belgian Glass Workers in America, 1880–1925." *Journal of American Ethnic History* 21, no. 2 (2002): 59–80.

Grob, Gerald. *Workers and Utopia: A Study of Ideological Change in the American Labor Movement, 1865–1900.* Chicago: Quadrangle, 1969.

Hollitz, John. *The Contenders*, vol. 2, *Since 1865.* Boston: Houghton Mifflin, 2003.

Horne, Janet. *Le Musée social, aux origines de l'État-providence.* Paris: Belin, 2004.

Kenny, Kevin. "Labor and Labor Organisations." In *Making the Irish American: History and Heritage of the Irish in the United States*, eds. John Lee and Marion Casey, 354–363. New York: New York University Press, 2006.

Lane, A. T. *Solidarity or Survival? American Labor and European Immigrants, 1830–1924.* Westport, CT: Greenwood Press, 1987.

Laslett, John. "Haymarket, Henry George, and the Labor Upsurge in Britain and America during the Late 1880s." *International Labor and Working-Class History* 29 (1986): 68–82.

McCartin, Joseph. *Labor's Great War: The Struggle for Industrial Democracy and the Origins of Modern American Industrial Relations, 1912–1921.* Chapel Hill: University of North Carolina Press, 1997.

Marwick, W. H. *A Short History of Labour in Scotland.* Edinburgh: W. & R. Chambers, 1967.

Montgomery, David. *The Fall of the House of Labor: The Workplace, the State, and American Labor Activism, 1865–1925.* Cambridge: Cambridge University Press, 1989.

Oestreicher, Richard. "Terence V. Powderly, the Knights of Labor, and Artisanal Republicanism." In *Labor Leaders in America*, eds. Melvyn Dubofsky and Warren van Tine, 30–61. Urbana: University of Illinois Press, 1987.

Parfitt, Steven. "The First-and-a-Half International: The Knights of Labor and the History of International Labour Organizations in the Nineteenth Century." *Labour History Review* 80, no. 2 (2015): 135–167.

——. *Knights across the Atlantic: The Knights of Labor in Britain and Ireland.* Liverpool: Liverpool University Press, 2017.

——. "Powderly Will Go to Paris: The Paris Exposition and the Knights of Labor." *International Labor and Working-Class History* 92 (2017): 183–212.

Pelling, Henry. *America and the British Left, from Bright to Bevan.* London: Adam and Charles Black, 1956.

——. "The Knights of Labor in Britain, 1880–1901." *Economic History Review* 9 (1956): 313–331.

Perlman, Selig. *A Theory of the Labor Movement.* New York: Macmillan, 1928.

Phelan, Craig. *Grand Master Workman: Terence Powderly and the Knights of Labor.* Westport, CT: Greenwood Press, 2000.

Powderly, Terence V. *The Path I Trod: The Autobiography of Terence V. Powderly.* New York: Columbia University Press, 1940.

Stamp, Kenneth M. *The Era of Reconstruction, 1865–1877.* New York: Vintage, 1965.

Sylvis, William H. *The Life, Speeches, Labors and Essays of William H. Sylvis.* Philadelphia: Claxton, Remsen & Haffelfinger, 1872.

Ware, Norman. *The Labor Movement in the United States, 1860–1895: A Study in Democracy*, 2nd ed. New York: Vintage Books, 1964.

Watillon, Leon. *The Knights of Labor in Belgium.* Los Angeles: University of California Press, 1959.

Weir, Robert. *Knights Down Under: The Knights of Labor in New Zealand.* Newcastle upon Tyne: Cambridge Scholars Press, 2009.

———. *Knights Unhorsed: Internal Conflict in a Gilded Age Social Movement.* Detroit, MI: Wayne State University Press, 2000.

Yearley, Clifton. *Britons in American Labor: A History of the Influence of the United Kingdom Immigrants on American Labor, 1820–1914.* Baltimore, MD: Johns Hopkins University Press, 1957.

7

Transatlantic Workers' Solidarity
The Kuzbas Autonomous Industrial Colony (1920–1926)

Frank Jacob

[H]ad Lenin remained at the head of the Kuzbas program, relying on the world's class-conscious workmen and engineers brought to the Soviet Union, we would have developed such industrial power by our production that the Second World War would have been impossible.

Herbert S. Calvert (1973)[1]

Herbert S. Calvert (1889–1981) truly believed in the idea of the Kuzbas Autonomous Industrial Colony, which was designed to help post-revolutionary Soviet Russia to build up its industrial capacities with the help of workers and specialists from the United States, who were supposed to settle in Siberia.[2] However, Calvert's idea was utopian, and the realities of the Kuzbas colony would soon disprove it. The discrepancy between the hopes and dreams related to the future of industrial production in Siberia and the actual realities related to Soviet rule and the New Economic Policy (NEP)[3] made the success of the idea, in the form that Calvert shared it with others from the beginning in 1921, impossible.[4]

---

[1] Herbert S. Calvert and Mellie M. Calvert, "The Kuzbas Story: History of the Autonomous Industrial Colony Kuzbas." Wayne State University, Detroit, Michigan, Walter P. Reuther Library, Archives of Labor and Urban Affairs, Mellie and Herbert S. Calvert Papers, LP000778, Box 1, Folders 3–14 (cited henceforth as CKS). Here Folder 3, 88.

[2] Julia L. Mickenberg, *American Girls in Red Russia: Chasing the Soviet Dream* (Chicago: University of Chicago Press, 2017), 129–162 provides an insight into the women's perspective, who were eager to settle in Siberia.

[3] For an introduction that provides a historical survey from Tsarist Russia to the later NEP, see Robert W. Davis, ed., *From Tsarism to the New Economic Policy: Continuity and Change in the Economy of the USSR* (Ithaca, N.Y.: Cornell University Press, 1991).

[4] Many American radicals, who were initially enthusiastic about the Russian Revolution, should be frustrated about the Bolshevist realities. For a detailed case study, see Frank

The Kuzbas (short for the Kuznetsk Basin, in Western Siberia) was the largest coal-mining region and one of the most important industrial centers in the Soviet Union.[5] However, when the Kuzbas initially started to be exploited by Vladimir Lenin's (1870–1924) post-revolutionary government in the 1920s, there were not sufficient skilled workers and engineers available.[6] The level of the coal and steel industry, which would not start to flourish before the late 1920s, therefore provided an opportunity in the early period of the Soviet Union, when Kuzbas became a dream of international workers collaborating to build their own future, far away from Western capitalism, a radical dream that would also challenge the official U.S. position towards the Soviet Union.[7] An Autonomous Industrial Colony (AIC) was established and attracted around a hundred of the first foreign workers of Soviet Russia, who came to Siberia to experience true communism and the free and unexploited life of a working class that would no longer be exploited by capitalist oligarchs.[8] As British geographer Kenneth Warren emphasized, from "1920 onwards the new Soviet government, while struggling with the day-to-day problems of a ravaged economy, began to give form to the thesis of a planned economy by elaborating a regional planning framework appropriate to the immensity of the state which they had inherited"[9] and

---

Jacob, *Emma Goldman and the Russian Revolution: From Admiration to Frustration* (Berlin: De Gruyter, 2020).

[5] Julia Franziska Landau, *"Wir bauen den großen Kuzbass!" Bergarbeiteralltag im Stalinismus, 1921–1941* (Stuttgart: Franz Steiner Verlag, 2012), 11.

[6] Kuzbas was only one example for the Bolshevist corruption of utopian revolutionary ideas, as they had been expressed in February 1917. On the moral corruption process between February and October 1917, see Frank Jacob, *1917: Die korrumpierte Revolution* (Marburg: Büchner, 2020).

[7] The United States had, together with other Allied Powers, like Japan, sent intervention troops to Russia to suppress the spread of the Russian Revolution. For a detailed study of the U.S. intervention see Peter G. Boyle, *American–Soviet Relations: From the Russian Revolution to the Fall of Communism* (London: Routledge, 1993), chapter 1 and Ilya Somin, *Stillborn Crusade: The Tragic Failure of Western Intervention in the Russian Civil War, 1918–1920* (London: Routledge, 2018). For a survey of the U.S. diplomacy and the role of Woodrow Wilson with regard to United States–Russian and United States–Soviet relations in the 1910s and 1920s, see Donald E. Davis and Eugene P. Trani, *The First Cold War: The Legacy of Woodrow Wilson in U.S.–Soviet Relations* (Columbia: University of Missouri Press, 2002).

[8] Between 1917 and 1939, approximately 70,000 to 80,000 foreign workers arrived in the Soviet Union. Andrea Graziosi, "Foreign Workers in Soviet Russia, 1920–40: Their Experience and Their Legacy," *International Labor and Working-Class History* 33 (1988): 38. Graziosi mentions 566 foreign workers in the AIC (p. 39).

[9] K. Warren, "Industrial Complexes in the Development of Siberia," *Geography* 63, no. 3 (1978): 170.

consequently developed plans for the Kuzbas as well. While technical assistance would become a new feature of the unofficial U.S.–Soviet relations, especially in the later 1920s,[10] the AIC was more than that. The German-born American mathematician, electrical engineer and socialist Charles P. Steinmetz (1865–1923) commented in the *Llano Colonist*, the newspaper of the socialist colony at New Llano, California, that existed between 1917 and 1937, in September 1923:

> I wish I could go to Kuzbas ... that is the place for the working class movement to concentrate its activities. America, as I see it, will not be ready for any radical change for many years. We have an advanced industrial science. We have developed a technique of production which in many ways is superior to that of any other country. American workers have learned to work at a terrific rate. In Siberia, I am told, the slow-moving Russians are amazed at this display of energy and refer to the immigrant workers as the "mad Americans." But ... we are not sufficiently advanced socially, politically, psychologically, to permit those changes in our economic system which are most necessary to the development of the race.[11]

Steinmetz therefore expressed the hopes that many American socialists had in mind when talking about Kuzbas.[12] Since "Big Bill" Haywood (1869–1928), one of the founding members of the Industrial Workers of the World (1905), was involved in the AIC's establishment, support for the initiative in the United States would not be that easy, as will be shown in more detail later. Haywood had been convicted for conspiring to organize strikes against World War I on U.S. soil and skipped bail while out on appeal, fleeing to Soviet Russia in 1918, where he was supposed to support the international revolutionary movement. Haywood, however, who had chosen exile in the Soviet Union over prison in the United States, might have really intended, as the New Yorker labor historian Melvyn Dubofsky emphasized, "to make a contribution to building the new Soviet society."[13]

In the present chapter, I will focus on the American perspectives on Kuzbas as a real chance to build a workers' utopia and discuss what had been promised as achievable in Siberia. In the second part, the voices of those who worked and later returned from Siberia will be compared with the

---

[10] Wladimir Naleszkiewicz, "Technical Assistance of the American Enterprises to the Growth of the Soviet Union, 1929–1933," *Russian Review* 25, no. 1 (1966): 55.

[11] "What Steinmetz Said," *Llano Colonist*, Sept. 23, 1922, 6.

[12] Steinmetz had also sent a letter to Lenin on 16 February 1922 offering his help with problems related to electrical engineering. Mellie M. Calvert, "The American Organization Committe[e] Kuzbas," CKS, Folder 4, 18.

[13] Melvyn Dubofsky, *"Big Bill" Haywood* (Manchester: Manchester University Press, 1987), 136.

arguments of those who did not believe the terrible reports that were brought back from the Soviet Union, the place where a worker could eventually be freed from the harrowing chains of capitalism.

Siberian Promises

In February 1921, Herbert S. Calvert left his "employment as a unit foreman in the forge department at the Ford automobile plant in Highland Park, a suburb of Detroit," inspired by the idea to provide "technical aid to the Russian Revolution."[14] In Moscow, which at this time was a center of international radicalism, with delegates from all around the world meeting for the Third International Congress of the Communist International or the First Trade Union International Congress, many different ideas were discussed among those who had come to see the center of communist utopia.[15] As Calvert points out, "Most of the foreigners who came to Moscow were interested in seeing Russia and attending the tremendous demonstrations and conventions that were being held. Everyone's head was more or less turned by the glamour and romance of Moscow, for this was the capital of the world's proletariat!"[16] Calvert got in contact with Mikhail Borodin (1884–1951), a Comintern agent with close ties to Lenin, and persuaded him about some ideas related to the industrial development of Soviet Russia:

> It is not possible to escape immediately the existing vicious circle of no food, no factory production—no factory production, no food. It is not easy to teach millions how to work. But if it is possible to employ the returning Russian-Americans as *shock troops* of the industrial army of production and transplant to Soviet Russia in a *given region* a complete *industrial unit* of that modern economy for which America is famous. This unit [is] to become the hub around which communist economy will be most quickly developed.[17]

According to Calvert, the idea was also promoted by Sebald J. Rutgers (1879–1961),[18] a Dutch Marxist who would later be involved in the AIC. Borodin eventually sent the proposal to Lenin, who agreed: "A good

---

[14] Calvert and Calvert, "Kuzbas Story," 1.

[15] Different utopian ideas were related to the post-revolutionary order (e.g., women's liberation). See Richard Stites, *The Women's Liberation Movement in Russia: Feminism, Nihilism, and Bolshevism, 1860–1930*, rev. ed. (Princeton, N.J.: Princeton University Press, 1990), 392–415.

[16] Calvert and Calvert, "Kuzbas Story," 7.

[17] Ibid., 8–9 (emphasis in original).

[18] For a biography, see the Dutch work G. C. Trincher and K. Trincher, *Rutgers: Zijn leven en streven in Holland, Indonesië, Amerika en Rusland* (Moscow: Uitg. Progres, 1974).

idea. Give us something definite."[19] Consequently, an inspection of the Kuzbas region was arranged and Calvert was all for the possibilities in the region, which was visited during the summer season:

> I already knew that Kuzbas might be the place, and never a doubt arose as further facts unfolded to fit the proposal and plan. Imagine the Kemerovo coal veins on barge and railroad! Five years of development work had been done! A chemical plant was almost completed! A sawmill! Housing for several hundred people! A big university at Tomsk! Virgin black-earth meadows and timber up river! Food surplus! Surplus peasant labor![20]

Lenin also eventually agreed to the project on 22 June 1921, but demanded that the American workers bring their own provisions and clothing with them.[21] The Council of Labor and Defense was also willing "[t]o pronounce desirable the development of certain industrial enterprises by way of turning them over to groups of American workers, or industrially developed peasants, on conditions which will guarantee to them a certain degree of economic autonomy."[22]

Regardless of the euphoria over the project, the first problems had already been identified when foreign industrial specialists had visited the Kolchugino coal mines at Kemerovo:

> In this vein we encountered some 18 miners who had had experience in England, being Russians who had returned in the first days of the Revolution. The working day underground was eight hours, but the 18 who had mined in England were producing 50% more coal than the others, so they worked only four or five hours a day in order not to produce more than the others. The mine was operated on the basis of a certain task and a bonus and these skilled workers did not wish to arouse the antagonism of the other Russian workers so they thought it best to produce a rather restricted amount.[23]

Kemerovo itself was deemed to be ideal for the developmental plans, since it was perceived as a "grand little industrial city, like Gary, Indiana, in the heart of Siberia."[24] The Siberian Revolutionary Committee, whose members were also consulted during the summer trip to south-western Siberia, were also "unanimously in favor of our proposition to mine coal and develop the industries of the Kuznetsk Basin with the use of foreign labor."[25]

---

19 Calvert and Calvert, "Kuzbas Story," 12.
20 Ibid., 17–18.
21 Ibid., 22.
22 Ibid., 25.
23 Ibid., 41.
24 Ibid., 44.
25 Ibid., 51.

When Calvert and the members of the inspectional trip returned to Moscow, other delegates of the Communist International and the trade unions got interested in the project:

> Tom Barker, an English I.W.W., who had been an outstanding labor leader both in Australia and South America;
> Jack Beyer, an American Indian, who was a strong supporter of industrial freedom and the Soviet Union;
> William D. Haywood, an internationally known I.W.W.;
> Tom Mann, leader of the Trade Union Council in England;
> and Nat Watkins, a leader of English mine workers.[26]

Together with Calvert, they argued on behalf of the Kuzbas idea, and Lenin met Calvert, Rutgers and Haywood to talk about the "bold plan"[27] on 19 September 1921.[28] It was eventually agreed that an organization committee was to be formed in the United States to organize the workers' transport to Soviet Russia. It was assumed that around 2,800 industrial workers were necessary.

Regardless of Calvert's enthusiasm for the idea of the AIC, there were multiple problems on American soil that required resolution before the first workers could leave for Kemerovo. The I.W.W. General Executive Board was not willing to support the Kuzbas plan, especially since Haywood was involved, "a man who deliberately ran away and left his friends who put up bail suffer possible losses."[29] In addition, the board was not willing to cooperate closely with the communists. The latter were also not willing to officially support the project, because they feared a negative impact for the AIC as an aftermath of the Palmer Raids.[30] Furthermore, the communists argued that the possible failure of the Kuzbas project would damage the reputation of the Communist Party in the United States. Consequently, the "polemics of the leaders of the I.W.W. and the Communist Party had effectively blocked plans for recruiting," because Calvert and his supporters were unable to use the I.W.W. and the CPUSA's organizational structures and publications actively to recruit settlers to be sent to Soviet Russia.

---

[26] Ibid., 68.

[27] Joseph P. Morray, *Project Kuzbas: American Workers in Siberia (1921–1926)* (New York: International Publishers, 1983), 3.

[28] Calvert and Calvert, "Kuzbas Story," 70.

[29] Calvert, "The American Organization Committe[e] Kuzbas," CKS, Folder 4, 5.

[30] On the raids, named after U.S. Attorney General A. Mitchell Palmer (1872–1936), see the older but still recommended Robert K. Murray, *Red Scare: A Study in National Hysteria, 1919–1920* (Minneapolis: University of Minnesota Press, 1955). See also with a broader perspective on the American mind, David M. Kennedy, *Over Here: The First World War and American Society*, 25th anniversary edition (New York: Oxford University Press, 2004), 45–92.

Nevertheless, an organization committee was eventually formed, and it consisted of the following members:

> Roger Baldwin, President of the American Civil Liberties Union,
> Tom Barker, journalist and seaman,
> Herbert S. Calvert, autoworker,
> P. Pascal Cosgrove, labor organizer,
> Claire Killen, electrician,
> Matti Mulari, auto mechanic,
> Edgar Owens, Labor Defense Committee,
> Tom Reese, sheet metal worker, and
> Mont Schuyler, management engineer.[31]

With three communists (Cosgrove, Mulari and Owens), three I.W.W. members (Barker, Calvert and Killen) and three liberals (Baldwin, Reese and Schuyler), it represented itself as a balanced body that would take care of the workers' interests during the "Kuzbas adventure." On 20 May 1922, the organization committee published the first issue of the *Kuzbas Bulletin*, a monthly journal that was supposed to inform U.S. industrial workers about the possibilities for a new life in Soviet Russia. The funding of the publication was secured by a $500 donation by Bishop William Montgomery Brown (1855–1937), author of *Communism and Christianism* (1920).[32] Rutgers declared in the first issue of *Kuzbas: A Bulletin Devoted to the Affairs of the Industrial Colony Kuzbas* that the workers of the United States had now received a chance actively to support the survival of the ideas and ideals related to the Russian Revolution and Soviet Russia alike:

> [A]ll friends of Soviet Russia must be the natural friends of Kuzbas, and all friends of Kuzbas must see in their efforts the most efficient support of Soviet Russia in its struggle for existence, in its struggle against hunger and disorganization. Soviet Russia needs foreign engineers and workers with their skill, tools and machinery. Here is an opportunity for only those who are willing to support in PERSON by THEIR LABOR Soviet Russia.[33]

Further articles of the *Kuzbas Bulletin* were also supposed to inform about the progress of the settlement project in Siberia.[34] According to Mellie M. Calvert, who was very engaged in the New York Kuzbas office's work,

---

[31] Calvert, "The American Organization Committe[e] Kuzbas," CKS, Folder 4, 14–15.

[32] William Montgomery Brown, *Communism and Christianism* (Galion, OH: Bradford Brown Educational Co., 1920).

[33] Sebald J. Rutgers, "Kuzbas: An Effort to Strengthen Soviet Russia," *Kuzbas: A Bulletin Devoted to the Affairs of the Industrial Colony Kuzbas* 1, no. 1 (May 20, 1922): 1.

[34] For example, Frank Kennell, "What is Kuzbas," *Kuzbas: A Bulletin Devoted to the Affairs of the Industrial Colony Kuzbas* 2, no. 3 (Aug. 30, 1923): 9.

the bulletin was a success, as many workers responded to the articles and the announcements.[35] The office recruited the following numbers of workers and sent them to Soviet Russia in 1922, along with tools that were partly funded by the settlers themselves and partly through the New York Kuzbas office by Moscow (see Table 7.1).[36]

Table 7.1 Workers and their families sent to Soviet Russia, 1922

Group	Departure Date	Number of Workers	Number of Wives	Number of Children
1	6 April 1922	60	9	1
2	13 May 1922	66	17	18
3	17 June 1922	66	17	20
4	22 July 1922	79	25	23
5	31 August 1922	31	17	9

The target of the Kuzbas settlers was Kemerov, a small Siberian town that fewer than 3,000 people called their home in 1920.[37] Regardless of the Soviet plans and American assumptions about the region, most of the small towns in Siberia lacked basic infrastructure, including water pipes and sewers. Only 3.3 percent of Siberian houses had a functioning water supply, and only large cities like Omsk or Novosibirsk could offer such a "luxury."[38] Regardless of such shortcomings, however, initially the mood of the settlers in 1922 was not too bad. Frank Krutsky-Novak described his feelings when he arrived in Soviet Russia in a letter published by the *Kuzbas Bulletin* on 20 August 1922:

> At last we have set foot upon Russian soil. I cannot describe the feeling of all of us, as on the morning of our disembarkation we saw battalion after battalion of the Red Army ... Each battalion carried its red battle colors with gold letters proclaiming its deeds. We disembarked to the music of the International and lined up before the red regiments. As we did so they placed one foot forward and thrust their bayonets forward as if to attack.

---

[35] Considering the real numbers, this evaluation must be rather taken as a euphemism or a very optimistic perception.

[36] Calvert, "The American Organization Committe[e] Kuzbas," CKS, Folder 4, 20.

[37] Julia Franziska Landau, "Wir bauen den großen Kuzbass! Der Aufbau des Bergbaus in der sibirischen Provinz und seine Folgen für die lokale Gesellschaft," *Akkumulation: Informationen des Arbeitskreises für kritische Unternehmens- und Industriegeschichte* 22 (2005), 22 states the number as 2,828.

[38] Ibid., 24.

There was a look of determination upon their faces such as a man only sees once in a lifetime.[39]

The euphoria of Russian soil, however, would not last very long.

The expansion of mining and steel production in the Kuzbas region, far away from the political center of Soviet Russia, was based on multiple considerations. While the Donbass Basin was closer to the industrial centers of European Russia, could provide sufficient skilled workers, did not need new railway tracks to connect the region with other industries and was therefore cheaper to develop, the new Soviet leaders demanded a Siberian project, not only since the region might be easier to defend in the future but also for ideological reasons: in Soviet Russia everything was possible.[40] "Big Bill" needed a job, and the Russians needed skilled workers for the project, which is why "Big Bill" became a willing servant of Soviet progress. Haywood, to quote his biographer Dubofsky again, "promised to recruit thousands of American engineers and skilled workers, who would develop a modern steel plant at Kuzbas and open coal mines in the Kuznetz Basin."[41] To achieve this aim, the American I.W.W. leader helped to publish an anonymous prospectus to attract American industrial workers for the Siberian venture, who needed to register for the journey in the New York Kuzbas office at 110 West, 40th Street.[42] It was stated that: "The group of foreign workers will produce for use and the extension of its enterprises without the limitations of capitalist industry—rent, interest and profit"[43]—a fact that made Kuzbas "a great experiment to create a big machine industry that will not feed a parasitic society, but will return to the worker the full product of his labor. Many difficulties must be overcome, but it is a milestone along the road of human progress that such resources and opportunities are now available for such an experiment."[44] Kuzbas would provide the American engineer with the "opportunity to build what heretofore only a few have dared dream—a co-ordinated industry that will serve mankind."[45] All in all, Kuzbas was described as an "immense industrial project" that was able to change the world, especially since the American volunteers would "develop it for the benefit of humanity, and not for a horde of hungry, profit-seeking concessionaries."[46] The whole venture was described as an incredible

---

[39] Cited in "Off to Siberia," CKS, Folder 5, 10.

[40] Landau, "Wir bauen den großen Kuzbass!," 14.

[41] Dubofsky, *"Big Bill" Haywood*, 136.

[42] *Kuzbas: An Opportunity for Engineers and Workers* (New York: Kuzbas, 1922), 1.

[43] Ibid.

[44] Ibid.

[45] Ibid.

[46] Ibid., 2.

dream and the worker who decided to participate in it would find a plan that will stimulate the imagination of men of industrial vision, a plan for the first industrial colony in the world, where engineers will find freedom to work out experiments they cannot attempt under the profit system, and where workers will find that self-government, that sense of social creativeness, that solidarity and equality they have never found anywhere in the history of the world until this present hour.[47]

Soviet Russia, it was stated, lacked sufficient skilled workers for the project and therefore "Proletarians should occupy and use the factories and resources of Russia, which the Russian workers cannot adequately use."[48] It was the Russian Revolution that "gave ... the factories to the working man"[49] and only those who dared to leave their home would find the benefit of working without the boundaries of a capitalist system. Six thousand American workers were supposedly needed in the first year of the program, which would transform the Kuzbas into one of the most thriving industrial centers in Russia.

The prospectus also provided a detailed description of Kemerovo, the town that would be "taken over" by the American workers.[50] The new Siberian home was described in detail, and the prospectus named a lot of things that would be provided for the settlers:

> The town is well laid out, with broad streets and attractive double log bungalows of three or four rooms, with fenced yards. The houses are lighted with electricity and many have running water.
> A well built hospital, situated in the forest of pine that comes down to the edge of the city, now employing a medical staff of 61, including two doctors, a surgeon, two dentists and two midwives.
> A hotel dining room accommodating 250 and employing ten persons.
> Three bath houses, one for miners.
> A shoe repair shop with 22 shoe-makers.[51]

In addition, a cinema, a theater, a school for 500 children and many more things were awaiting the American workers. The Siberian weather was also described as being rather pleasant with a "very cold, but dry" winter, but

> Spring comes in Kuzbas suddenly the latter part of April. One day the frozen river will carry the weight of horse and cart—three days later the river is free of ice. Surplus water runs off quickly as the snow melts.

---

47 Ibid.
48 Ibid., 3.
49 Ibid.
50 Ibid., 7.
51 Ibid., 8.

In addition, "The summers are delightful with the greenest possible meadows."[52]

While just a small number of women and children were supposed to be part of the first groups to reach the colony, the prospectus declared that "strong, healthy women who are accustomed to outdoor life can be taken care of by the organization. Some women and children are desirable to maintain the proper home life and home atmosphere."[53] The information that "Single women will also be considered, providing they are also industrially qualified, physically fit and politically reliable"[54] might also have been important for the miners. Each worker only needed to provide $300 for this dream: $100 for travel costs, $100 for food and $100 for small tools.[55] The money for the food would

> provide sugar, coffee, chocolate, tea, dried fruits, rice, beans and such food as is not available in Russia for mass distribution. The Russian government will supply the food as to other industries on the basis of production, i.e. in exchange for coal. This will ensure meat and grain. Kuzbas will manufacture articles of wood and metal and exchange with peasantry for food.[56]

There were supposed be no real wages, but the workers would, in relation to their production rates, be provided with "a satisfactory standard of living, which will include a yearly bonus."[57]

The Kuzbas project was a radical idea, but it seemed to offer the fulfillment of any worker's dream and it was obviously not long until volunteers signed up, although the above-mentioned groups did not provide the 2,800 workers that had been initially discussed in 1921. One female worker that was particularly celebrated was Ruth Kennell from San Francisco, whose decision (and image) was reported in many U.S. newspapers: "[She] will have charge of the 20,000-volume library in the Kuzbas colony, Russia, a settlement backed by Americans where money will be unknown and 'hours of service' will be the medium of exchange."[58] However, there were also

---

[52] Ibid., 20–21.

[53] Ibid., 22.

[54] Ibid.

[55] Ibid., 24.

[56] Ibid., 23.

[57] Ibid. The prospectus also stated: "What is meant by a satisfactory standard of living will be determined by the board of managers, who are responsible both to the workers and to the Soviet Government" (p. 25).

[58] "Librarian to Kuzbas," *The Rock Island Argus and Daily Union*, July 15, 1922, 20. The news and her image were also published in *South Bend News Times*, July 8, 1922, 16 (South Bend, IA); *The Bismarck Tribune*, July 12, 1922, 3 (Bismarck, ND); *Bisbee Daily Review*,

critical voices. In the *New York Tribune*, W. A. Davenport asked on 9 July 1922:

> "Why, just why," demand the fierce reconstructionists, "are thousands of industrial workers clamoring at the doors of the Kuzbas organization, the Society for Technical Aid for Russia and the nascent Russian-American Industrial Corporation, begging to be sent to Soviet Russia that they might expend the well known sweat of their honest brows in cooperative, community and even subsidized mines, farms and factories?"

He critically added, with regard to the capitalist system of the United States: "Is there any defense of a system that cannot offer sufficient inducement to industrial workers to discourage them from wanting to work in Soviet Russia?"[59] Davenport, like many others, simply could not believe why somebody would voluntarily leave the United States to work and live in Soviet Russia, the home of Bolshevist terror and suppression of individual freedom.

Davenport wanted to provide an explanation, and he quotes some of the workers. One said "he is tired of working for the bosses and, inasmuch as he has not made a spectacular success of working for himself here in America, he desires to join the forthcoming Kuzbas pilgrimage in order that his individualistic tendencies may not be hampered by business competition." Another one emphasized:

> We are the pilgrim fathers in this great industrial movement. Slowly at first, brother, but later in a torrent that will sweep everything before it the workers of America will swarm to the great Soviet Republic and there produce wealth for themselves—wealth that will not go into the pockets of Wall Street jackals and political blackguards.[60]

A lumberjack, called Smith, had an even easier explanation:

> I don't know anything about the politics of Soviet Russia and I don't give a damn. Bill Haywood says it's a good graft and I'm taking a chance. Like a lot of guys I ain't got the hundred bucks that goes into food, but some rich guy that's with us puts up that for me and I'm going.[61]

Davenport, in the end, found his own explanation for the phenomenon, because he got "the impression that these men would not fit into nor be

---

Aug. 25, 1922, 6 (Bisbee, AZ); *The Seattle Star*, July 20, 1922, 2 (Seattle, WA); *The Ogden Standard Examiner*, July 30, 1922, 10 (Ogden, UT).

[59] W. A. Davenport, "Why Mr. Pujo Was Not Americanized," *New York Herald*, July 9, 1922, 5.

[60] Ibid.

[61] Ibid.

happy in America unless it was conducted on a plan drawn up by themselves. And there is no visible suggestion that they would be satisfied with that [for] very long."[62] Eventually, he would be proved right.

Siberian Realities

Regardless of the workers' enthusiasm, the Kuzbas dream, however, would not last for long. When Ruth Kennell arrived in Kemerovo and met Haywood for the first time, she was probably as shocked as the workers, who realized that the place was even less promising than the I.W.W. icon's appearance: "Bill Haywood was a shock to me. I knew he was that big but didn't know he was fat. He has a real corporation front, one eye is gone, and he was wearing a loose, gray Russian blouse."[63] That said, the first letters from the Siberian settlers emphasized that the reality was much harsher than what was promised: "The mines are very wet in places, and that is why the miners need rubber boots and coats. They are very necessary. But there are some good places in the mines."[64] The problems with the mines seemed not to be too discouraging, and the tone of the writer is still full of hope even with regard to the actual housing situation: "All of the houses on the same side of the river as the Chemical Plant do not have running water, and very few have sewers. But between every street there are pipes where we can get water, although they have not been connected with the houses."[65] However, what clearly uncovered the lies within the above-quoted prospectus is the comment of the settler that "There is no shoemaker's shop and no machinery for one."[66] While this might not have been the last shoe factory in the Soviet Union that only existed on paper, the eyewitness was not willing to leave yet, as some of his fellow workers obviously already had. The report, however, does have one serious complaint: "One fact is true—a new system cannot be installed so long as the Russians are in control; for they do not like to change from the old methods they are accustomed to."[67]

In November 1922, further news reached the United States, and the headline of the *Great Falls Tribune* in Montana on 30 November reads: "Americans Trapped by 'Reds' in Siberian Get-Rich-Quick Scheme."[68] Joseph Krajewski and Otto Nemitz, two "naturalized Americans," reported:

---

[62] Ibid.

[63] "Off to Siberia," CKS, Folder 5, 31.

[64] "Kusbas Colony," *Llano Colonist*, Nov. 11, 1922, 7.

[65] Ibid.

[66] Ibid.

[67] Ibid.

[68] "Americans Trapped by 'Reds' in Siberian Get-Rich-Quick Scheme: Two Escape to Riga," *Great Falls Tribune*, Nov. 30, 1922, 1 (Great Falls, MT).

> The experiment was a terrible failure ... There were no profits to divide. The colony, consisting of 400 persons, half of whom were women and children, was in a deplorable situation. Its members all lacked the money with which to return to the United States. Sanitary conditions were described as awful. Food was short and there was much sickness. More than half the men and a majority of the women and children were incapacitated. One American woman committed suicide because of despair.

The report also stated that "The illness of members of the colony, which included scurvy, w[ere] attributed to malnutrition. The colonists receive three meals daily, consisting of black bread and mush." The situation must have been desperate, and, in the end, the colonial project failed. On 12 August 1923, the Washington *Evening Star* reported that:

> "Big Bill" Haywood's dream of an American communist colony in Soviet Russia has exploded. ... [The settlers] had visions of a fair land of promise, where man should work, but not for money; where free homes with running water would house the contented proletariat, and where each should be granted rein to follow his chosen calling according to his own free will and for the good of all.[69]

Eventually, "the sweet Utopia of vision has become a vile failure in fact" and "[i]nstead of the four-room cottages with running water they were promised they were confronted with filthy barracks and houses alive with vermin." The *Bourbon News* of Paris, Kentucky, had already published an obliterative comment on the Kuzbas project on 15 December 1922: "Seemingly the American colony of Kuzbas in Siberia would be a model of its kind if somebody should run a wall around it, put a roof over it, and let the label 'Lunatic Asylum' tell."[70]

It was, however, not only the press that discussed the case. On 5 January 1925, the famous American anarchist Emma Goldman (1869–1940), who was born in Tsarist Russia herself, was politically radicalized in the New Yorker anarchist milieu[71] and spent almost two years in Soviet Russia after her deportation from the United States in December 1919, in a letter from London to Roger Baldwin (1884–1981), the first executive director of the American Civil Liberties Union (ACLU), Kuzbas advocate and member

---

[69] "American Colony Fails Under Russian Control," *Evening Star*, Aug. 12, 1923, 4.

[70] "Editorial Flings," *Bourbon News*, Dec. 15, 1922, 2 (Paris, KY).

[71] Johann Most (1846–1906) was one of the influential figures with regard to Goldman's radicalization and early career as an anarchist activist. On the New Yorker German–American anarchist milieu around Most, see Tom Goyens, *Beer and Revolution: The German Anarchist Movement in New York City, 1880–1914* (Urbana: University of Illinois Press, 2014).

of the organization committee for the AIC,[72] made it clear that "Kuzbas, like every other venture in Russia, is primarily for propaganda purposes ... no matter how many lives are sacrificed and how discredited the idealist becomes."[73] The anarchist continues her argument by mentioning that "the scheme [Kuzbas] was a means of Communist propaganda for the United States and for no other purpose," and that "Bill Haywood is disintegrating at a very fast pace and ... he would give anything in the world now if he could get out of Russia and go back to America." Baldwin, however, did not share Goldman's view, regardless of the fact that the colony had failed some years before. He rather argues to be careful with anti-Soviet sentiments:

> Of course the main obstacle that you run into in all this business concerning Russia is the outstanding fact that it is a dictatorship in the interest of workers and the peasants, however much it may be actually deceiving the ultimate interests of workers and peasants. Attacked by all the capitalist governments of the world and issue[s] in their internal as well as external affairs, it is natural that labor and radicals should on the whole be cautious about attacking that which is also attacked by their bitterest enemies.

He continued to argue that, at least for those workers who remained in Siberia, a brighter perspective would eventually be reached and that the settlement had never been a political venture:

> Kuzbas is succeeding insofar as some degree of autonomy, of participation and of cooperation is accorded to the individual units making up its industrial complex. You are wrong about Kuzbas. I have had close and intimate connections with it ever since it started, and I know personally many of the men and women who went there. Most of them are not Communists and have not become Communists. And yet over two-thirds of them have stuck. The Kuzbas enterprise was not used for Communist propaganda in the United States. The committee here was controlled by non-Communists.[74]

Of course, Baldwin is right with regard to his description of the communist involvement in the scheme of Kuzbas, but he is misinterpreting the situation of the workers in Kemerovo, many of whom were just not able to return to the United States. The initial idea of the AIC was soon to be "Sovieticized"

---

[72] Robert C. Cottrell, *Roger Nash Baldwin and the American Civil Liberties Union* (New York: Columbia University Press, 2000), 169–182 describes the role of Roger N. Baldwin and the ACLU in the organization of the settlement.

[73] Emma Goldman to Roger Baldwin, London, Jan. 5, 1925, 4, in New York Public Library, Emma Goldman Papers, ZL-386, Reel 1.

[74] Roger Baldwin to Emma Goldman, Mar. 27, 1925, unpag. Emma Goldman Papers, ZL-386, Reel 1.

and "[i]n Moscow Rutgers also found that the New Economic Policy made it very difficult for the Kuzbas organization to proceed as planned."[75] It was eventually the real necessities of Soviet Russia that defined the shape of economic developments in Siberia and not the idea of some radical workers who had once met in Moscow and were able to persuade Lenin to grant them support. One also has to admit that, in 1925, one year after Lenin's death, which Calvert saw as being partly responsible for the failure of the AIC, the discussion about the success or failure of Kuzbas must rather be considered an intellectual "Glass Bead Game." The American historian Frank Costigliola summed up the whole story very simply as follows:

> Once the Americans arrived at Kuzbas in 1922, however, the Soviets rejected as anarchic and inefficient the Wobblies' insistence on worker control and equal pay. Protesting what they termed Communist authoritarianism and wage slavery, many of the Wobblies struck. When the other American colonists refused to support the strike, some of the Wobblies left and the others accepted differential wages and supervision of a government appointed Dutch engineer. Kuzbas was a failed labor experiment, but an industrial success.[76]

The radical ideas did not become realities at Kuzbas, but were prevented from doing so by the actual demands of a government that needed to mine coal instead of discussing a utopian workers' wonderland.

Conclusion

The image of the Bolsheviks and the Soviet Union in the United States had not been a positive one since the days of the Russian Revolution in 1917. Kuzbas, however, further destroyed the hopes and dreams that the working class had attached to the Soviet utopia. It was the unexpected hardships in the Siberian environment, and the non-existent dream that so many had left their homes for, that filled the workers' minds with bitterness towards a political system that supposedly promised a better future for all of them. Like many other disappointed Americans, in 1922, Haywood, to quote Dubofsky's judgment,

> [was] a 53-year old man suffering from ulcers, diabetes and plagued by a drinking problem ... [and] found the Kuzbas region of Siberia too inhospitable to endure. After only a few months at the site, the winter cold, the primitive living conditions, the scarcity of fresh foods and production supplies and the spread of disease among the "colonists"

---

[75] Resistance encountered by S. J. Rutgers en route to Kemerovo, CKS, Folder 6, 2.

[76] Frank Costigliola, *Awkward Dominion: American Political, Economic, and Cultural Relations with Europe, 1919–1933* (Ithaca, N.Y.: Cornell University Press, 1984), 161.

depressed Haywood. As few Americans responded to his call for their labour and many of those who did left disenchanted, Haywood also packed up and departed.

The initial visit by Calvert and his fellow radicals was a summer trip to Siberia, and one might have overrated the possibilities, without knowing the winter conditions of the region. It seems, nevertheless, interesting that so many of the American settlers were surprised by the hardships of the Siberian environment, although it had been quite well known to a large number of U.S. readers since the late 1860s, and I would therefore like to conclude with an interesting anecdote about this region and its climate. The settlers might have been unfamiliar with the writings of George Kennan the Elder (1845–1924), who had traveled throughout Siberia in the 1860s and 1890s and wrote about it extensively. He, a well-read author of the late nineteenth century, in a letter to his mother in December 1866, described the natural hardships of the Siberian winter, in the same way that it might have been experienced by the Kuzbas workers:

> The nights were around twenty hours in length. To try my hardest I couldn't sleep more than twelve, so every evening I was compelled to sit on the snow around the camp fire for six to eight hours. I don't care how fertile a man's mind is in ideal, he can't sit and think eight hours every night for forty nights without exhausting all the subjects for thought which a Siberian steppe affords.[77]

The early Soviet "everything is possible" mentality might have made a successful Kuzbas possible in the late 1920s and 1930s—by using a lot of forced labor, of course—but it could not change the Siberian environment, including its depressing climate, to create the utopia that American workers were dreaming of. It is ironic that the weather conditions eventually seemed to be more radical than those who had arrived in Siberia to change the workers' world forever.

Works Cited

Archival Sources
New York Public Library, Manuscripts and Archives Division
Emma Goldman Papers, Astor, Lenox, and Tilden Foundations. ZL-386, Reel 1
George Kennan Papers, Astor, Lenox, and Tilden Foundations. Box I, Series
    I. Correspondence, 1866–1924, 1.1

---

[77] George Kennan to his mother, Ghijiga. Dec. 14–26, 1866. New York Public Library, George Kennan Papers, Astor, Lenox, and Tilden Foundations. Box I, Series I. Correspondence, 1866–1924, 1.1.

Wayne State University, Detroit, Michigan, Walter P. Reuther Library, Archives of Labor and Urban Affairs

Herbert S. Calvert and Mellie M. Calvert, "The Kuzbas Story: History of the Autonomous Industrial Colony Kuzbas," Mellie and Herbert S. Calvert Papers, LP000778, Box 1, Folders 3–14

Newspapers and Periodicals

Bisbee Daily Review
The Bismarck Tribune
The Bourbon News
Evening Star
Great Falls Tribune
Kuzbas: A Bulletin Devoted to the Affairs of the Industrial Colony Kuzbas
The Llano Colonist
The New York Herald
The Ogden Standard Examiner
The Rock Island Argus and Daily Union
The Seattle Star
South Bend News Times

Secondary Works

Boyle, Peter G. *American–Soviet Relations: From the Russian Revolution to the Fall of Communism.* London: Routledge, 1993.

Brown, William Montgomery. *Communism and Christianism.* Galion, OH: Bradford Brown Educational Co., 1920.

Costigliola, Frank. *Awkward Dominion: American Political, Economic, and Cultural Relations with Europe, 1919–1933.* Ithaca, N.Y.: Cornell University Press, 1984.

Cottrell, Robert C. *Roger Nash Baldwin and the American Civil Liberties Union.* New York: Columbia University Press, 2000.

Davis, Donald E. and Eugene P. Trani. *The First Cold War: The Legacy of Woodrow Wilson in U.S.–Soviet Relations.* Columbia: University of Missouri Press, 2002.

Davis, Robert W., ed. *From Tsarism to the New Economic Policy: Continuity and Change in the Economy of the USSR.* Ithaca, N.Y.: Cornell University Press, 1991.

Dubofsky, Melvyn. *"Big Bill" Haywood.* Manchester: Manchester University Press, 1987.

Goyens, Tom. *Beer and Revolution: The German Anarchist Movement in New York City, 1880–1914.* Urbana: University of Illinois Press, 2014.

Graziosi, Andrea. "Foreign Workers in Soviet Russia, 1920–40: Their Experience and Their Legacy." *International Labor and Working-Class History* 33 (1988): 38–59.

Jacob, Frank. *1917: Die korrumpierte Revolution*. Marburg: Büchner, 2020.

——. *Emma Goldman and the Russian Revolution: From Admiration to Frustration*. Berlin: De Gruyter, 2020.

Kennedy, David M. *Over Here: The First World War and American Society*, 25th anniversary edition. New York: Oxford University Press, 2004.

Kuzbas: An Opportunity for Engineers and Workers. New York: Kuzbas, 1922.

Landau, Julia Franziska. "Wir bauen den großen Kuzbass! Der Aufbau des Bergbaus in der sibirischen Provinz und seine Folgen für die lokale Gesellschaft." *Akkumulation: Informationen des Arbeitskreises für kritische Unternehmens- und Industriegeschichte* 22 (2005): 9–29.

——. *"Wir bauen den großen Kuzbass!" Bergarbeiteralltag im Stalinismus, 1921–1941*. Stuttgart: Franz Steiner Verlag, 2012.

Mickenberg, Julia L. *American Girls in Red Russia: Chasing the Soviet Dream*. Chicago: University of Chicago Press, 2017.

Morray, Joseph P. *Project Kuzbas: American Workers in Siberia (1921–1926)*. New York: International Publishers, 1983.

Murray, Robert K. *Red Scare: A Study in National Hysteria, 1919–1920*. Minneapolis: University of Minnesota Press, 1955.

Naleszkiewicz, Wladimir. "Technical Assistance of the American Enterprises to the Growth of the Soviet Union, 1929–1933." *Russian Review* 25, no. 1 (1966): 54–76.

Somin, Ilya. *Stillborn Crusade: The Tragic Failure of Western Intervention in the Russian Civil War, 1918–1920*. London: Routledge, 2018.

Stites, Richard. *The Women's Liberation Movement in Russia: Feminism, Nihilism, and Bolshevism, 1860–1930*, rev. ed., 392–415. Princeton, N.J.: Princeton University Press, 1990.

Trincher, G. C. and K. Trincher. *Rutgers: Zijn leven en streven in Holland, Indonesië, Amerika en Rusland*. Moscow: Uitg. Progres, 1974.

Warren, K. "Industrial Complexes in the Development of Siberia." *Geography* 63, no. 3 (1978): 167–178.

8

"Alles z'Unterobsi"

Hannes Meyer and German Communist Exiles in Mexico

Georg Leidenberger

During the course of 1940 and 1941, as German forces occupied northern France and pressured the southern Vichy government to hand over members of the resistance, thousands of militants were confined in the concentration camp of Le Vernet and hoped to obtain an entry visa to a country across the Atlantic. A contingent of about sixty leaders of the German Communist Party (KPD) was among them. Many of them wished to emigrate to the United States, yet their political stance rendered their chances of going there slim. Their chances were better with that country's southern neighbor, Mexico, for they had found a patron who promoted their arrival with Mexico's Exterior Ministry: the influential labor leader, head of the Confederación de Trabajadores de México (CTM), Vicente Lombardo Toledano. Besides his sympathies with Soviet communism, Lombardo was also a cultural Germanophile, and he knew many artists and intellectuals among the group of German communists in Marseilles.[1] As a result of Lombardo's lobbying and the engagement of the Mexican consul in France, Gilberto Bosques, some 300 German-speaking communists had managed to travel by ship to Mexico, the final contingent arriving on the ship *Serpa Pinto* in December 1941 at the harbor city of Veracruz.[2] Many of these exiles—some of whom

---

[1] Heidi Zogbaum, "Vicente Lombardo Toledano and the German Communist Exile in Mexico, 1940–1947," *Journal of Iberian and Latin American Research* 11, no. 2 (2012): 1–28, esp. 1, 3–4. Another of Lombardo's interests in granting exile to the German communist was staffing his recently founded Universidad Obrera (Workers' University) in Mexico City. Ibid., 4; Andrea Acle-Kreysing, "Antifascismo: un espacio de encuentro entre el exilio y la política nacional. El caso de Vicente Lombardo Toledano en México (1936–1945)," *Revista de Indias* 76, no. 267 (2016): 573–609. For a critical view on Bosques's handling of the exile situation, see Daniela Gleizer, "Gilberto Bosques y el consulado de México en Marsella (1940–1942): La burocracia en tiempos de guerra," *Estudios de Historia Moderna y Contemporánea de México* 49 (2015): 54–76; Acle-Kreysing, "Antifascismo," 575, 580–581, 600.

[2] Lizette Jacinto, "Desde la otra orilla: Alice Rühle-Gerstel y Otto Rühle: La experiencia

also arrived in Mexico via the United States—were writers, journalists and artists; for example, the Czech reporter Egon Kisch, the Swiss anthropologist Gertrude Duby, the German writers Anna Seghers, Bodo Uhse and Gustav Regler, the Bukovinian (Romanian) journalist and activist Leo Katz.[3] Others were dedicated KPD leaders, such as Paul Merker, Alexander Abusch and Georg Stibi, or spies, such as the legendary Otto Katz, alias André Simone. They came to stay in Mexico for the remainder of World War II, where they joined other German exiles who had arrived during the previous decade.[4]

The present chapter will detail one of these exile's situation in Mexico and, in particular, his interactions with German-speaking communists in Mexico. The case of the Swiss architect Hannes Meyer (1889–1945) both underscores the general picture and differs from the general picture of left-wing exile. Meyer's case confirms the precariousness of exile in both economic and political terms; it also illustrates communists' strong, often uncritical, embrace of the Soviet Union. Meyer's engagements in Mexico reveal the forming of an intricate network of personal and organizational relationships that kept the exile community together. At the same time, Meyer, like so many exiles, was not aloof from the intense conflict that reigned within the exile community: disputes and permanent ruptures were caused by differences in ideology and politics.[5] Meyer's case also contrasts with the

---

del exilio político de izquierda en México 1935–1943," *Historia Mexicana* 64, no. 1 (2014): 159–242, esp. 175, 185, 206, 216; Helga Prignitz-Poda, *El Taller de Gráfica Popular en México, 1937–1977* (Mexico City: INBA/CENIDIAP, 1992).

[3] "Leo (Lieb) Katz," *Diario Judío México.* http://diariojudio.com/opinion/personalidades/leo-lieb-katz-intelectual-politico-y-escritor-padre-de-friedrich-katz/23428/. Accessed Feb. 9, 2018. On Kisch, see Friedhelm Schmidt, "Los descubrimientos en México de Egon Erwin," in *México, el exilio bien temperado*, eds. Renata von Hanffstengel and Cecilia Tercero (Mexico City, UNAM, Instituto Goethe, 1995).

[4] Jacinto, "Desde la otra orilla," 182–183; Acle-Kreysing, "Antifascismo," 591–592. The two monographs on the German exiles in Germany are Wolfgang Kießling, *Alemania Libre in Mexiko* (Berlin: Akademie Verlag, 1974) and Fritz Pohle, *Das mexikanische Exil: Ein Beitrag zur Geschichte der politisch-kulturellen Emigration aus Deutschland (1937–1946)* (Stuttgart: Metzler, 1986). For a collection of articles on the subject, see Renata von Hanffstengel and Cecilia Tercero, eds., *México, el exilio bien temperado* (Mexico City: UNAM, Instituto Goethe, 1995). Another important study on German exiles in Mexico that places emphasis on its spatial dimension in Mexico City is Aribert Reimann, "Espacios del Exilio: La experiencia transnacional en la Ciudad de México, 1934–60," in Entre espacios: La historia latinoamericana en el contexto global. *Actas del XVII Congreso Internacional de AHILA* (Berlin, 2016), 2950–2970.

[5] On Meyer in Mexico, see also Georg Leidenberger, "'Todo aquí es vulkanisch': El arquitecto Hannes Meyer en México, 1938 a 1949," in *México a la luz de sus revoluciones*, vol. 2, eds. Laura Rojas and Susan Deeds (Mexico City: El Colegio de México, 2014); Werner Kleinerüschkamp, "Exilarchitektur: Hannes Meyer in Mexiko," in *Hannes Meyer*

communist exile experience. Unlike most exiles, he arrived in Mexico as a professional immigrant and as such he was more prone to integrate into his host country. As an architect and urban planner, he worked closely with Mexican colleagues and professional institutions, and as an activist and artist politically committed to the cause of communism, he worked closely with Mexican labor leaders and political activists, government officials as well as the country's artistic community. Moreover, as a (German-speaking) Swiss citizen, Meyer entertained an uneasy relationship with German communists, a fact that would also lead him to step out of the latter's enclave and associate with exiles from other nationalities: the Swiss one, naturally, as well as the Italian one.

German Communists in Mexico

The fact that German communists would receive favorable treatment by Mexico reflected not only the influence of trade-union leader Lombardo Toledano but also the recent Mexican policy of receiving political refugees from Europe. Under President Lázaro Cárdenas (1934–1940), political sympathies with the cause of Spanish republicans led the country to admit about twenty thousand refugees from the Civil War in 1939.[6] Among these were also numerous German communists who had fought in the war's International Brigades, such as the writer Ludwig Renn as well as Merker, Stibi and Regler. Two years earlier, Cárdenas had granted asylum to Leon Trotsky, who had become the pariah of pro-Soviet communists and had been escaping persecution by Joseph Stalin's secret services all across Europe. The practice of welcoming left-wing immigrants and particularly professional ones escaping German Nazism and Italian Fascism was continued, albeit on a smaller scale, during President Manuel Ávila Camacho's government (1940–1946).[7] As a result, by the early 1940s, Mexico hosted an ethnically diverse group of the European Left, with contingents from countries such as Italy, France, Austria, Switzerland, Czechoslovakia and Romania.

Escaping from political persecution by the Nazis and/or "racial" persecution as Jews (in the case of Seghers and Leo Katz, for example),

---

1889–1954 Architekt Urbanist Lehrer: Catalogue/Exposition of the Bauhaus Archive Berlin and the Deutsches Architekturmuseum, ed. Klaus-Jürgen Winkler (Frankfurt am Main: Ernst und Sohn, 1989); Patricia Rivadeneyra, "Hannes Meyer en México (1938–1949)," in *Apuntes para la historia y crítica de la arquitectura mexicana del siglo XX: 1900–1980* (Mexico City: SEP/ INBA, 1982); Susanne C. Dussel Peters, "La arquitectura de Hannes Meyer y Max Cetto: De la modernidad alemana a la mexicana," in von Hanffstengel and Tercero, *México.*

6 Friedrich Katz, "Mexico, Gilberto Bosques and the Refugees," *The Americas* 57, no. 1 (2000): 1–12, esp. 3–9.

7 Zogbaum, "Vicente Lombardo Toledano," 2; Jacinto, "Desde la otra orilla," 182.

and dedicated to spreading communism, many of these new arrivals had been on the move for years, and to them Mexico signified only another temporary stopping point.[8] Their cases represent historian Silvia Pappe's general observation of the identity of the political exiles, who "conceive and plan their lives in terms of their own world, not with regard to the foreign country where they have come to rest involuntarily. To be an exile means *to see oneself obligated* to leave, it stands for the desire to return; only rarely does it mean having arrived."[9]

Exiles' living conditions in Mexico further contributed to their sense of dislocation. Notwithstanding Mexico's openness to the politically persecuted, the country was also passing through a nationalist period, one that had ensued since the Revolution of 1910. At least in part, Presidents Cárdenas's and Ávila Camacho's decision to receive European exiles reflected national interests, such as the wish to obtain well-trained professionals and to further *mestizaje* (racial intermixing) between indigenous and European bloods.[10] Exiles in Mexico might well face a nationalist, and even xenophobic, climate. They could not obtain work permits and, like all foreign nationals, were prohibited from engaging in political activity, as stipulated by Article 33 of the 1917 Constitution. Furthermore, the Ávila Camacho government, whether due to its political conservatism or to the obligations it felt to its northern neighbor, permitted U.S. intelligence to spy on the communist arrivals.[11]

Conscious of the temporary and precarious nature of their stay, political exiles tended to associate among themselves, orienting their activities toward the exile community in the host country by setting up organizations of their own, as well as to comrades, friends and family who lived dispersed across the globe and with whom they maintained constant written correspondence; as historian Acle-Kreysing noted, "correspondence played a cathartic role."[12]

---

[8] Two key centers of the German left's exile were Paris and Prague. From there, many would join the Spanish Civil War, then escape to southern France. Others, especially those of the KPD cadre, had stints in the Soviet Union (such as Stibi) or in the United States (Merker and Otto Katz).

[9] Silvia Pappe, "De tantas llegadas, una: Cinco fragmentos acerca de la llegada de Getrude Duby a México," in von Hanffstengel and Tercero, *México*, 173 (my translation).

[10] Daniela Gleizer, *El exilio incómodo: México y los refugiados judíos, 1933–1945* (Mexico City: El Colegio de México/ UAM Cuajimalpa, 2011).

[11] Alexander Stephan, "El FBI y los exiliados germanoparlantes en México," in von Hanffstengel and Tercero, *México*; W. Dirk Raat, "Intelligence Services during the Second World War: Part 2," *Journal of Contemporary History* 22, no. 4 (1987): 615–638, esp. 630–631; Acle-Kreysing, "Antifascismo," 600; Zogbaum, "Vicente Lombardo Toledano," 1.

[12] Andrea Acle-Kreysing, "Shattered Dreams of Anti-Fascist Unity: German-Speaking Exiles in Mexico, Argentina and Bolivia, 1937–1945," *Contemporary European History* 25, no. 4 (2016): 667–686, esp. 670.

They also worked to obtain visas for those still in danger in Europe by petitioning the Mexican government and by working with international, often U.S.-based, relief organizations. If being a political exile proved conducive to leading a more or less insular life, being a communist one furthered that condition. Most communist exiles held fervent loyalties to the Soviet Union, and in Mexico they spent most of their time promoting, defending and supporting their "flagship"; as foot soldiers of that distant land, they cared little about their host country.

The first key organization of German exiles in Mexico was the Liga Pro-Cultura Alemana (League for German Culture), founded in 1938 mainly by German émigrés from the Spanish Civil War. Its purpose was to aid exiles in settling down in Mexico and to promote German-language culture in literature, the fine arts, history and music. In doing so, the Liga explicitly sought to provide a counterpart to the cultural promotions of Nazis, both those abroad and the numerous ones living in Mexico.[13] The Liga's first director was Enrique Guttman, followed by the Marxist economist Alfons Goldschmidt, and, upon the latter's death in 1940, Ludwig Renn.[14] The Liga reflected a broad spectrum of the left and was explicitly non-partisan.

Upon their arrival in 1940, the cadre of German communists joined the Liga and, in fact, two of them assumed its leadership: Renn as director and Stibi as administrative secretary.[15] Yet they came to disdain—or were told to do so by the Soviet government—working with the non-communist left and in late 1941 abandoned the Liga in order to form their own association: the Bewegung Freies Deutschland, or Alemania Libre, in Spanish.[16] Closely allied to the Communist International, Freies Deutschland was directed by Merker and it included, among others, Uhse, Kisch and Renn. Seghers led the organization's Heinrich Heine Club, which held lecture series on German as well as Mexican culture.[17] Above all, Freies Deutschland dedicated itself to denouncing Nazi Germany to aid the war effort of the Soviet Union. It set up the publishing press El Libro Libre (The Free Book), the journal *Freies Deutschland* and a modest library, Biblion. It managed widely to disseminate its publications in Mexico and in several other Latin American countries.[18]

---

[13] Mexican artists and writers, such as Leopoldo Méndez, the head of the print workshop Taller de Gráfica Popular and the composer Silvestre Revueltas also counted among its members. Acle-Kreysing, "Antifascismo," 594.

[14] Prignitz, *El Taller de Gráfica Popular*, 81; Acle-Kreysing, "Shattered Dreams," 670.

[15] Acle-Kreysing, "Shattered Dreams," 670.

[16] Acle-Kreysing, "Antifascismo," 593.

[17] Jacinto, "Desde la otra orilla," 201; Acle-Kreysing, "Shattered Dreams," 672. After the war, Renn returned to the Soviet-occupied zone of Germany and eventually published a travel report on his years in Mexico. Ludwig Renn, *In Mexiko* (Berlin: Aufbau Verlag, 1979).

[18] The journal first appeared in November 1941. Prignitz, "Taller de Gráfica Popular," 83.

In doing so, Freies Deutschland formed part of an anti-fascist front,[19] which was backed by key Mexican organizations, including the CTM trade union federation, and by the Mexican government, especially after Mexico declared war on Germany in May 1942.[20] German communists in Mexico thus collaborated with their Mexican hosts, yet they did so from the vantage point of their own organizations and in pursuit of interests essentially shaped by international developments.

Having sketched a general picture of communist exiles' life in Mexico, I now zoom in on the experience of a single man and his family: the Swiss architect and communist Hannes Meyer.

Hannes Meyer in Mexico

Whereas most communist exiles' stay in Mexico lasted for the duration of the war, the Meyers arrived earlier and stayed for longer. Hannes Meyer first came to Mexico in the summer of 1938, and after three months returned to Switzerland, to then return to the Central American country a year later, in June 1939, with his wife Lena Meyer-Bergner and his daughter Lilo. The Meyer-Bergner family, whose size extended with the birth of Mario-Pierre in 1944, stayed in Mexico for ten years and then returned to live in the (Italian-speaking) Tessin region of Switzerland in August of 1949.

Meyer's main reason for setting out for Mexico was his hope to find work. His last permanent employment had been as an urban planner and professor in the Soviet Union, where he and Lena Meyer-Bergner had lived from 1930 to 1936.[21] Back in Geneva, and notwithstanding his reputation of being at the vanguard of architectural modernism and as the second director of the German Bauhaus, Meyer found himself without work (Lena fared better as she was able to sell her tapestries).[22] As a card-carrying member of the

[19] Acle-Kreysing, "Antifascismo," 573–609.

[20] Ibid., 600. In May 1943, *Freies Deutschland* organized the first national Anti-Fascist Congress. Acle-Kreysing, "Shattered Dreams," 679.

[21] There Meyer taught in architectural schools in Moscow and he drafted plans for a number of new industrial cities in the far east of the Soviet Union. Leidenberger, "Architect Hannes Meyer."

[22] Meyer became known in Switzerland upon the completion of a housing complex for the Swiss Co-operative movement in Freidorf, near his native Basle. He also frequently contributed as author to the journal of the Swiss Werkbund, the country's leading association of design and architecture. In 1927, architect Walter Gropius invited him to join the new Architecture Division of the Bauhaus, where a year later he replaced Gropius as director. Upon returning from the Soviet Union, he did obtain one assignment to construct a youth recreational center for the Swiss co-operative movement, in the town of Mümliswil. Leidenberger, "Architect Hannes Meyer."

Kommunistische Partei der Schweiz (Swiss Communist Party) and as a public promoter of the Soviet Union, Meyer found it impossible to obtain a position either within the Swiss public sector or in the private sector, which he generally disdained in any event.[23]

The occasion for his trip across the Atlantic was an upcoming congress, to be held in the summer of 1938 in Mexico City, on behalf of the International Federation for Housing and Town Planning (IFHP), a well-known British-based organization of planners. At the congress, Meyer got to know a group of young architects who had formed the Unión de Arquitectos Socialistas (Association of Socialist Architects) as well as the renowned Mexican urban planner José Luis Cuevas Pietrasanta, who was in search of a leader for a new institute on planning.[24] Meyer also met Lombardo Toledano with whom he shared mutual friends and contacts, among them the economist Goldschmidt, who, alongside other German exiles, was teaching at Lombardo's Universidad Obrera (Workers' University). Lombardo Toledano also invited Meyer to teach there once he settled in Mexico. For now, he asked him to attend the First Congress of the Confederación de Trabajadores de América Latina (Latin American Workers' Confederation), which the Mexican labor leader was about to inaugurate. Through his encounters with the Unión de Arquitectos Socialistas, Cuevas and Lombardo, Meyer made himself known among Mexico's architects and among key figures of the left. Most importantly, when Meyer sailed back to Europe in the fall, his briefcase contained a contract appointing him as the director of the new Instituto de Planeación y Urbanismo (Institute of Planning and Urbanism), to be housed by the country's leading public university of engineering, the Instituto Politécnico Nacional (National Polytechnic Institute).

Yet, as the profiles of Meyer's contacts in Mexico City suggest, his interest in Mexico was of both a professional and a political nature. Like many exiles, he had eyed the country out of its revolutionary reputation: there, as an architect, as a planner *and* as a communist, he could contribute to a State-led project of social and cultural reform. Two persons had conveyed the image of a "progressive" Mexico to Meyer previous to his journey. First, there was Goldschmidt, whom he probably met by way of

[23] Accused because of his leanings toward the Communist Party, Meyer was dismissed as Bauhaus director in the summer of 1930, upon which he followed an invitation to work in the Soviet Union. While still residing in the Soviet Union, Meyer undertook conference tours across Europe (including Switzerland) in order to promote the regime. Leidenberger, "Architect Hannes Meyer."

[24] Georg Leidenberger, "Los orígenes de la educación urbanística en México: El Instituto de Planificación y Urbanismo dirigido por el arquitecto Hannes Meyer (1938–1941)," *Espacialidades* 8, no. 1 (2018): 24–38.

their mutual friend, the political theorist Hermann Duncker, also founder
of and teacher at the Marxist Workers' School of Berlin (Berliner Marxis-
tische Arbeiterschule). Most likely through Goldschmidt, he had become
acquainted with the political scientist (and fellow Swiss) Fritz Sulzbacher,
who now, together with Goldschmidt, served as first liaison to Mexico.[25]
Hannes and Lena were not political exiles as such, for, unlike the German
communists who two years later would be awaiting exit visas in southern
France, they proved safe from Nazi persecution in Geneva. Nonetheless,
their decision to leave Hannes's home country (and Lena's adopted one)
reflected political reasons: the anti-communist climate that extended
from Nazi Germany across the Alps that prevented him from obtaining
employment.[26]

Having settled in Mexico, in June 1939, the Meyers' lives resembled a
typical exile existence. Early on, they became involved with the German-
speaking exile community, which was then represented by the Liga. Meyer
had brought with him books for the Liga, which Erwin Friedeberg had
requested be purchased for him in Paris.[27] A few months after the Meyers'
arrival, World War II commenced, leading Meyer to lobby the Mexican
authorities for visas for friends and comrades who lay stranded in Europe.
For example, he sought to obtain an entry visa for Duncker, who had been
interned in a camp in southern France for two years.[28] Together with Liga
member Bodo Uhse, Meyer asked the New York-based League of American

[25] When Goldschmidt died in January 1940, Meyer stated that he had lost a friend and
a key contact who had facilitated his dealings with government officials. Hannes Meyer
(HM) to Thildy Fraenkel, Jan. 11, 1940. Archiv Hannes Meyer, Deutsches Architekturmuseum, Frankfurt am Main (cited henceforth as Meyer, DAM Archiv). It has been
claimed that Meyer traveled to the United States in search of employment in that country
and that it was in New York City where Meyer met Goldschmidt, who then suggested to
Meyer that he look for work in Mexico. In fact, Meyer intended from the outset of his
journey to travel to Mexico City, in order to attend the IFPH's Congress (even though
he was not a registered speaker there) and to find employment. His stay in New York was
planned as a stopover only and, after three days, he continued his travels, by train, to the
Mexican capital.

[26] The case of Getrude Duby, a compatriot of Meyer, provides a similar, somewhat
ambiguous profile of the political exile. As a communist, Duby was persecuted by the Nazis
and she was arrested in France sometime between 1939 and 1940. After the intervention of
the Swiss government she was released and returned to live in Switzerland. Yet, "she did not
find peace in the (relatively) pacific Switzerland" and chose to emigrate, first to the United
States and shortly thereafter to Mexico. Pappe, "De tantas llegadas," 175.

[27] HM to Erwin Friedeberg, Nov. 11, 1939, Meyer, DAM Archiv. On Meyer's collaboration with the Liga, see Prignitz, *El Taller de Gráfica Popular*, 81.

[28] HM and Francisco Frole to Secretary of Labor, July 16, 1942; HM to Käte Duncker,
May 12, 1940 and Aug. 8, 1940, Meyer, DAM Archiv.

Writers to sponsor this and other cases and then proceeded to pressure the Mexican authorities. Meyer also helped with the logistics of travel and the obtaining of start-up funds for arriving exiles. Partly due to his efforts, communists such as Otto Katz, Leo Katz, Seghers and Regler managed to obtain entry into the Central American country.

Meyer's Mexican Experience with German Communists

Meyer was certainly aware of the difficulties exiles faced in their host country. In letters to friends and colleagues, he reported of exiles being unemployed and poor, facing health problems due to the elevated location of Mexico City (7,350 feet) as well as their psychological crises.[29] For these reasons, Meyer occasionally advised his correspondents to reconsider their decision to move to Mexico. The most dramatic incident Meyer faced in that regard was the suicide of his neighbors on Villalongin Street, the Rühles. Meyer wrote to a friend that the couple had jumped out of their apartment.[30] The actual facts were slightly different yet no less disheartening. On 24 June 1943, Otto Rühle, a German communist, died of heart failure in his apartment, and, two hours later, his wife, the psychologist and translator Alice Rühle-Gerstel, took her life in the way described by Meyer. Like so many exiles, the couple faced economic difficulties. Furthermore, they had fallen into the cracks of the intensive ideological disputes among the left and as a result had lived politically and socially isolated.[31]

Hannes and Lena Meyer associated closely with the German communists, especially with regard to the group's cultural work and social life.[32] At Seghers's Heinrich Heine Club, Meyer gave lectures on Mexican urbanism and he designed covers and published an article—on the war-caused destruction of Soviet cities—in *Freies Deutschland*. The Meyers formed part of the exiles' wide social network, their apartment, located in the central neighborhood of Colonia Cuauhtémoc, being the site of a "three-times weekly lunch table of emigrant friends."[33] Among those who circulated

---

[29] For example, Meyer recommended that his friend Käte remain in Vienna for as long as she could earn money. "It is difficult for foreigners to move to a lower terrain outside of Mexico City, given the isolation and frequent xenofobia [*sic*] they face." HM to Käte Duncker, May 12, 1940, DAM Archiv.

[30] HM to Paul Artaria, Mar. 23, 1947; HM to Käte Duncker, May 12, 1940, DAM Archiv.

[31] Jacinto, "Desde la otra orilla," 175, 206, 216; Acle-Kreysing, "Shattered Dreams," 672.

[32] HM to Hans Stark, Aug. 14, 1949, DAM Archiv.

[33] HM to Käte Duncker, Nov. 16, 1940, DAM Archiv. In 1943, 18 of the 654 members of Freies Deutschland reported their residence in the Colonia Cauhtémoc. Reimann, "Espacios del Exilio," 14.

at 46 Villalongin Street were the late Goldschmidt, Renn,[34] Friedeberg, Kisch[35] and his wife Duby, Leo Katz with his wife and son, and even the infamous Otto Katz and his wife.[36] Another frequent guest was the Italian photographer and communist Tina Modotti, who belonged to the Italian group of communist exiles, the Alianza Internacional Giuseppe Garibaldi. In fact, Modotti would spend the last evening of her life at the Meyers' apartment, for that night, on 5 January 1942, upon leaving for her home, she boarded a taxicab in which she suddenly died from heart failure.[37]

Meyer was a communist and he unwaveringly celebrated life in the Soviet Union. During his first stay in Mexico in the summer of 1938, Meyer received the honor of addressing the Sociedad de Arquitectos de México (Association of Mexican Architects), the country's most prestigious organization of the profession, at the colonial Academia de San Carlos, then the main school of architecture. He dedicated one of the conferences to the "Life of the Soviet Architect," presenting an extensive and enthusiastic take on the subject matter.[38] Meyer was fully committed to the Soviet Union and did not address Stalinist terror, even when people close to him became its victims. The case of Wolfgang Duncker illustrates that point. As part of his efforts to obtain a visa for Hermann in Mexico, Meyer was in correspondence with Käte, who was exiled in the United States. In a letter, Käte expressed her worries to Meyer about her son Wolfgang, who for two years had been a prisoner in a Soviet camp. In response, Meyer assured her that he believed in her son's innocence and that he would surely be released shortly. Meyer advised her against trying to get Wolf out of the country, stating: "To me it is simply a grotesque idea that you want to get Wolf out of the USSR."[39] As to the prisoner camps, the Gulags, they had "no sad aspect about them," and as to the country, it was simply the best place to be for a communist: "Don't you see that finally there is only one country that will hold on until

[34] Meyer helped Renn obtain a teaching position at the Universidad de Morelia in Morelia, Michoacán, where the latter began to work in April 1940. Prignitz, *El Taller de Gráfica Popular*, 81.

[35] HM to Katja von Gunten, Jan. 1, 1941, DAM Archiv.

[36] Prignitz, *El Taller de Gráfica Popular*, 81.

[37] Leidenberger, "Architect Hannes Meyer."

[38] In his talk, Meyer praised architects' work in collectives, the fact that they did not need to compete with private architectural bureaus and the fact that they could design projects without having to confront capitalist speculation on ground rents. Three years later, Meyer presented the article "The Soviet Architect" in a Mexican professional journal. Hannes Meyer, "El arquitecto soviético," *Arquitectura México* 9 (1942). An English version of the article was published by Harvard Graduate School of Design in February 1943 in *TASK: A Magazine for the Younger Generation in Architecture*.

[39] HM to Käte Duncker, May 12, 1940, DAM Archive.

the end of the race?" Meyer thus subsumed the uncertain fate of his friend's son to his belief in a regime and the utopia it stood for. At that time, though unbeknownst to Meyer, his former lover Margarete Mengel had also been arrested. She would die in a camp, and her son Peter, who was Meyer's son, was placed in an orphanage.[40] Meyer should have known better about the situation in the Soviet Union, for he and Lena themselves had been forced to leave the country, in 1936, in the wave of Stalinist xenophobia. As to Wolfgang Duncker, he died two years after Meyer and Käte Duncker's exchange, at age forty-two, in the Gulag.

Yet Meyer was not a Communist Party activist as such, as he once forcefully stated to his friend Käte Duncker: "He who tries to identify my driving forces in areas other than those of my basic professional ones, will always be mistaken. I can only serve the socialistic ideal by means of my profession."[41] Moreover, Meyer disapproved of the German communist exiles' lack of integration in Mexican affairs. A little over a year after his arrival, in October 1940, Meyer made the following comment to an émigré friend in the United States:

> some "prominent" emigrants [from Germany] ... always think that because they were members of the Reichstag, they will be once again of use in the *heimat*. Instead of making themselves useful here. I think that it is not *us* who will be needed for the reconstruction over there ... our place is *here*, where we can accomplish a lot for the cause. So I am quite willing to be a NEO-MEXICAN ...[42]

Meyer's willingness "to be a NEO-MEXICAN" represented his deep involvement in the country's professional life. He was publicly recognized as director of the innovative research center on urban and rural development, the Institute of Planning and Urbanism (IPU), as an author of publications on architecture and urbanism and as a teacher at Lombardo's Universidad Obrera. As such, his situation differed considerably from most communist exiles who lacked formal employment and who operated from within their exile enclave. It was in that sense, and under the optimism of the moment, that Meyer criticized comrades with an eye on returning to Europe. Meyer admired the country, and, like many foreigners, was fascinated by its exotic features: indigenous peoples, volcanos and snakes.[43]

---

[40] Leidenberger, "Architect Hannes Meyer."

[41] Hannes Meyer to Käte Duncker, Feb. 5, 1941, DAM Archiv. Meyer considered himself a socialist architect (as well as teacher, administrator and urban planner) by the time he came to direct the German Bauhaus in the late 1920s, where he became involved in communist politics. Leidenberger, "Architect Hannes Meyer."

[42] HM to Käte Duncker, Oct. 22, 1940, DAM Archiv.

[43] Leidenberger, "Architect Hannes Meyer."

Yet while he stood on the margins of Communist Party politics, he did not escape the ideologically polarized climate of the Mexican Left, which centered on those who approved of Trotsky's presence in Mexico and those who opposed it, those who distanced themselves from the Stalinist regime and those who backed it.[44] Without ever expressing himself on the former leader of the Red Army, Meyer clearly belonged to the latter group: his friend Lombardo Toledano had been an outspoken critic of President Cárdenas's decision to grant asylum to Trotsky; most German communist exiles in Mexico openly attacked Trotsky's presence in Mexico. People who knew of Meyer's ties to Lombardo, of his favorable coverage of life in the Soviet Union and of his German communist friends proved quick to label him as a "Stalinist," a pigeonholing that affected Meyer's professional standing. One of his colleagues at the IPU was the architect Juan O'Gorman; a declared Trotskyist and close friend of Trotsky's hosts Diego Rivera and Frida Kahlo, O'Gorman refused to collaborate with Meyer and possibly worked to have him dismissed altogether.[45]

The conflict around Trotsky greatly intensified when Trotsky was murdered in August 1940 by a Soviet agent in his house in Coyoacán, Mexico City. Rivera—whom Meyer always referred to as "der Dicke" (the fat one)—publicly accused a group of pro-Soviet communists of the crime, Meyer included, an accusation that would cost the Swiss architect his job and would deeply affect his public standing. In the summer of 1941, Meyer was dismissed as director of the IPU.[46] "Here [in Mexico] everything is z'Unterobsi [heads to tails], as we say in Switzerland," he wrote to his friend Käte Duncker shortly after Trotsky's assassination.[47] Once he found himself dismissed as the IPU's director, his own life would be "z'Unterobsi" as well; from then he received only temporary work assignments, faced economic uncertainty and clearly lost the initial prestige he had been enjoying in the country.

Henceforth, Meyer's stay in Mexico, which was to last for another eight years, resembled that of the German exiles. Like them, he now stood at the margins of the nation's professional life and also lived under precarious economic conditions. And he spoke ever more frequently of returning to

---

[44] Acle-Kreysing, "Antifascismo," 581–582.

[45] O'Gorman had built a house and studio for the painter couple.

[46] Meyer applied to the Swiss legation to cleanse his name from Rivera's charges. HM to Dr. E. Grosheintz, Jan. 19, 1940, DAM Archiv. Meyer attributed his dismissal from the IPU to these accusations. HM to Paul Artaria, Mar. 23, 1947, DAM Archiv. The historian of U.S. secret service operations in wartime Mexico, Dirk Raat, noted the large number of false allegations made by Rivera. Raat, "Intelligence Services," 629.

[47] HM to Käte Duncker, Aug. 27, 1940, DAM Archiv.

Europe after the war; like most exiles, he now marked an imaginary end to his and his family's stay.[48]

At least verbally, Meyer partook intensively in the hostile strife among the communist exile community. Trotskyists, such as the "fat one," were of course first on the list of undesirables. Meyer might have felt empathy with his neighbors, the Rühles, upon learning of their tragic deaths, yet he had most likely never engaged in a single conversation with them, for they were known as "Trotskyists" and he as a "Stalinist."[49] Never mind that the Rühles, who were outspoken critics of Stalinism, had also marked their distance from Trotsky, and thus, until their sudden death, had been social and political outcasts.[50] Moreover, Meyer had been well acquainted with the Rühles's son-in-law, the already mentioned Fritz Sulzbacher, but likewise the latter's turn toward Trotskyism left the two estranged.[51]

Meyer's breaking with Sulzbacher illustrates the way ideological warfare among the left generated deep rifts among people who otherwise shared similar fates or shared common interests and outlooks. Sulzbacher and Meyer, for example, held a remarkable set of affinities. They were born in Basle, they were friends with Goldschmidt, and, in their respective professional work—Meyer in architecture and planning, Sulzbacher in political economy—they adapted the statistical and graphical methods of Otto Neurath, a member of the so-called Vienna Circle of scientists.[52] The same held true for the architects Meyer and O'Gorman. The former stood at the forefront of a socially oriented functionalist architecture in Europe, the latter, in Mexico, yet as bitter enemies on the political front they never engaged in any professional exchange.[53] Finally, there was the case of

---

[48] Meyer's difficulties also resulted from a general political shift in Mexico after the end of Cardenas's presidency in 1940 as his successor Manuel Avila Camacho steered away from the former's pro-labor and nationalist radicalism toward a policy of industrial modernization in cooperation with U.S. capital—a policy fomented by the war alliance of the two countries against the Axis powers. Acle-Kreysing, "Shattered Dreams," 672.

[49] Like Meyer, Otto Rühle had worked for Mexican state agencies and on the planning of rural schools. Also, both of them applied a wide range of disciplines to their work as planners. Like Meyer, the Rühles were also fascinated by certain "exotic" features. Alice Rühle-Gerstel wrote an article on the phenomenon of "jealousy in Mexican marriages." Jacinto, "Desde la otra orilla," 178, 196, 216; Leidenberger, "Architect Hannes Meyer."

[50] Jacinto, "Desde la otra orilla," 187–190.

[51] It was Sulzbacher, alongside Rivera, who was behind the accusations on the Trotsky murder raised against Meyer. HM to Paul Artaria, Mar. 23, 1947, DAM Archiv.

[52] Jacinto, "Desde la otra orilla," 175; HM to Federico Bach, Jan. 11 and Mar. 13, 1939, DAM Archiv.

[53] On the professional affinities between Meyer and O'Gorman, see Antonio Toca Fernández, "Héroes y herejes: Juan O'Gorman y Hannes Meyer," *Casa del Tiempo* 3, no. 32 (2010): 18–23.

Meyer's neighbor on Villalongin Street, Otto Rühle. Both held prominent positions in Mexico's public sector, and yet both found themselves ousted from them for political reasons. Note the similarities in their reactions to being fired:

> I have become the object of Stalinist hatred, [of those] who label me a Trotskyist, in order to fire me from my post at the SEP [Secretaría de Educación Pública, Ministry of Education].[54]—Rühle

> Everything is done to provoke my leaving [the country], problems are being fabricated, they prohibit people from paying me, they fire me (without notice) … hostility directed against one of us: a FOREIGNER, and even a RED-PINK one, a speaker of GERMAN, and a CARDENAS man …[55]—Meyer

Both, as outraged as they were, were helpless; both perceived themselves to be victims of stereotyping, one fired for being a "Trotskyist," the other for being a "RED-PINK" Stalinist. Both lived side by side yet refused to speak to each other. Historian Lizette Jacinto aptly generalizes on such ideological fallouts among the Mexican exile community: "A distancing and polemics emerged among culturally similar intellectuals, who far from forming a unified group attacked and denounced each other in public."[56]

A rule seemed to apply where the greater the similarities among a group, the greater the perceived differences and tensions. Thus, Meyer saved his most virulent attacks (and sarcasm) for pro-Soviet communists with whom he differed. It was the German CP leader Paul Merker, who in Mexico assumed the leadership of Freies Deutschland, whom Meyer frequently despised in his letters—for example, labeling him and his followers as an "extended and tricky gang of ruffians" ("*verzweigte und verzwickte Strolchenbande*").[57]

Such a polarized coexistence of left-wing exiles can only in part be accounted for by the ideological clashes provoked by the global context:

---

[54] Rühle to Erich Fromm, Apr. 1937, quoted in Jacinto, "Desde la otra orilla," 193. Rühle and his wife were fired from their jobs a year later, in the summer of 1938. Ibid.

[55] HM to Paul Artaria, Sept. 8, 1941, DAM Archiv.

[56] Jacinto, "Desde la otra orilla," 190 (my translation). Historian Aribert Reimann observed that "urban geography brought exile communities into proximity with their opponents." Reimann, "Espacios del Exilio," 5.

[57] HM to Hans Stark, Oct. 13, 1950, DAM Archiv. After his return to Europe, Merker held a leading party post in the East German occupied zone and later German Democratic Republic. Because of his favorable stance toward Israel and being susceptible to the last Stalinist post-war purges due to his trajectory as an emigrant communist who had returned from the West, Merker was charged as a traitor and imprisoned in the early 1950s. HM to Hans Stark, Oct. 13, 1950, DAM Archiv; Matthew Stibbe, "Jürgen Kuczynski and the Search for a (Non-Existent) Western Spy Ring in the East German Communist Party in 1953," *Contemporary European History* 20, no. 1 (2011): 61–79.

Stalin's terrorizing push for orthodoxy or the challenges of fascism against the left. It also reflected the condition of being in exile. As Pappe stated in her reflections on the situation of another Swiss exile and communist in Mexico, the anthropologist Gertrude Duby:

> when, at given moments, reality loses consistency and breaks apart, one would have to consider the [subject's] manifold possibilities of clinging to life by means of finding security in political theories, of maintaining one's discipline through life in the party, [as part of] an ongoing dream amidst (both personal and collective) utopias.[58]

Escaping political persecution and war and subject to the vagaries of Stalin's alliances—his popular front against fascism, then the alliance and finally a state of war with Hitler—communist exiles, more than other exiles, perhaps, lived indeed on unstable ground and thus clung firmly to their ideology and strategies.

Notwithstanding his "official" label, Meyer did not integrate plainly into the German communist exile community. In fact, he soon broke with it, because he opposed their leader Merker's strategy of forming a cell outside the Mexican Communist Party. The Swiss resented what he perceived as a certain pan-German attitude among that country's communist exiles. When *Freies Deutschland* published an open letter addressed to the USSR that referred to "Our [Germans'] responsibility [for the war]" and included Meyer's name among the signatories, Meyer drafted a letter to the editors, in which he vehemently denied assuming such a burden.[59] For Meyer, it was one thing to join German exiles in the anti-fascist campaign, which he certainly did, but it was another to assume any responsibility for the acts of their fatherland. Meyer's Swiss nationality was directly tied to his status as a professional, as opposed to political, exile. Unlike the German communists, he could theoretically return to live in the neutral Alpine country at any time. Yet this was "theory," for the military situation rendered travel to Europe nearly impossible and hardly desirable. In fact, Meyer feared that Switzerland could be invaded by the Axis powers.[60]

Although the "internationalist" Meyer had held an ambivalent relationship toward his native country ever since he left it at the age of twenty, he did have ties to the Swiss community in Mexico City. In political terms, after his break with Merker and the German exile group, Meyer found a home with the group of Italian communist exiles, who centered on the infamous

---

[58] Pappe, "De tantas llegadas," 174 (my translation).

[59] Meyer to Paul Merker, Alexander Abusch and Bruno Frei, Nov. 6, 1946. DAM Archiv.

[60] In fact, Meyer feared that Switzerland could be invaded by the Axis powers.

Vittorio Vidali alias Carlos Contreras, who also collaborated with Lombardo Toledano.[61] Besides the already mentioned Modotti, he became close friends with Italian CP leader Mario Montagnano, and he also gave talks at the Italian communists' cultural club, the Alianza Internacional Giuseppe Garibaldi.[62]

Meyer's rift with the German communist exile community also reflected differences in how to face the economic and political marginalization of an exile. Meyer confronted that condition, which was exacerbated with the closing of the IPU, by immersing himself in the community of Mexican artist-activists—that is, he opted for a strategy of *integration* into Mexican life, rather than clinging to the exiles' enclave. His new home became the Taller de Graphical Popular (TGP—Workshop of Popular Print Art), led by Leopoldo Méndez from its founding in 1934.

Meyer had known the print artist Méndez for some time, as the latter had collaborated with the Liga and with Freies Deutschland. Méndez had also been teaching at the Workers' University and, like Meyer, did work for the progressive Teatro de las Artes (Theater of the Arts) led by the Japanese director Seki Sano.[63] It was the anti-fascist campaign that led to Meyer's first contact with Méndez's TGP. When asked by Freies Deutschland to design the edition of *El libro negro del terror nazi* [Black Book on Nazi Terror] (1943), Meyer worked closely with several of the TGP's artist members who provided prints for the book. (This included Méndez's impressive depiction of German train transports of prisoners headed toward their execution.[64]) Fascinated by the possibility of applying his skills toward the dissemination of the political and social realist art of the TGP, and also attracted by its cosmopolitan membership—which

[61] Vidali was a leading figure of the Italian CP (before and after World War II). His notoriety stemmed from his apparent implication in the murder of the Cuban communist Julio Antonio Mella, who was killed in Mexico in 1929 for his declared sympathies for Trotsky. Tina Modotti was also accused of participating in the killing. Pino Cacucci, "¿Un complot internacional de mentirosos?," *La Jornada*, June 21, 2017; Claudio Albertani, "Vittorio Vidali, Tina Modotti, el stalinismo y la revolución," *Servicio Informativo, Ecuménico y Popular El Salvador*, Apr. 8, 2014; Antonio Elorza, "El hombre tapado por Tina," *Letras Libres*, Apr. 23, 2014. Vidali, alias Carlos Contreras, was also accused, and briefly imprisoned, for the murder of Trotsky. HM to Paul Artaria, Mar. 23, 1947, DAM Archiv; Vicente Lombardo Toledano to Vidali, Jan. 26, 1947, DAM Archiv.

[62] HM to Mario Montagnano, undated [1949], DAM Archiv. Meyer addressed the Italian Left community with a conference on his personal exposures to Italian urbanism. See "Spaziergang als Städtebauer durch Italien," in Hannes Meyer, *Bauen und Gesellschaft. Schriften, Briefe, Projekte*, ed. Lena Meyer-Bergner (Dresden: VEB Verlag der Kunst, 1980).

[63] Acle-Kreysing, "Antifascismo," 594; Prignitz, *El Taller de Gráfica Popular*, 81.

[64] Acle-Kreysing, "Antifascismo," 597–598. The book was sponsored by the Mexican government of President Ávila Camacho. Acle-Kreysing, "Shattered Dreams," 680.

included U.S. artists such as Pablo O'Higgins and Marianna Yampolsky as well as the Italian graphic designer Albe Steiner—Meyer eventually became the business administrator of the collective and also edited several of its other publications.[65]

Conclusions

A tracing of Hannes Meyer's life amidst the German-speaking communist exile community in Mexico illustrates the multivalence of the exile experience of the European Left.[66] This begins with the conditions that prompted his exile, or so-called push-factors, which stood somewhere in between economic and political considerations. His situation also changed from that of being a professional immigrant, once he had lost his post as director of the IPU, to that of a political exile and all that came with it: uncertainty as to employment, economic insecurity and a mindset centered on an eventual return "home."

While Meyer engaged in extensive social and work-related ties to the German-speaking communist exile community, he was eventually pulled away from it. Unlike most German communist exiles who held tight to their own kind and who also engaged in intensive internecine strife, Meyer oriented his skills to Mexican groups and public sector institutions, working as a curator of exhibitions, graphic designer, editor and writer as well as administrator.[67] Like many communist exiles, Meyer held a "trans-Atlantic" identity, yet, notwithstanding his relatively advanced age at his time of arrival (he was aged fifty then), he developed partial roots in Mexico. While he followed exiled communists' well-trodden path of return to Europe in 1949, from his home in Tessin, Switzerland, he would promote Mexican architecture and art in Switzerland, Italy and (West) Germany.[68]

Meyer's political engagement was inextricably tied to his architectural profession as well as to his other skills in art, administration and "publicity," and it was in these areas that he contributed to the causes of anti-fascism and the left as well as to national institutions in education, health and

---

[65] Prignitz, *El Taller de Gráfica Popular*, 81–83. Meyer shared with the members of the TGP the conviction that art's main purpose was to propagate socially and politically relevant messages and therefore had to be undertaken in a realist style. Leidenberger, "Architect Hannes Meyer." When Meyer left as administrator of the TGP in late 1942, he handed the post to the German communist Georg Stibi. Stibi had served as administrative secretary of *Freies Deutschland* until he was fired by its head Paul Merker. Ibid., 87; Acle-Kreysing, "Antifascismo," 577.

[66] Jacinto, "Desde la otra orilla," 159.

[67] Leidenberger, "'Todo aquí es vulkanisch.'"

[68] Leidenberger, "Architect Hannes Meyer."

housing and finally to the artists' workshop TGP. As such, he could move beyond the spaces of engagement of most German communist exiles, whose political identity as communists and standard-bearers of the Soviet Union predominated in their doings and in how they related to Mexico. While Meyer certainly suffered from serious setbacks, such as when he was dismissed from the IPU, he managed to transcend an exile condition that most German communists saw as a temporary interlude in their lives and one marked, above all else, by their origin and world view.

Works Cited

Acle-Kreysing, Andrea. "Antifascismo: un espacio de encuentro entre el exilio y la política nacional. El caso de Vicente Lombardo Toledano en México (1936–1945)." *Revista de Indias* 76, no. 267 (2016): 573–609.

——. "Shattered Dreams of Anti-Fascist Unity: German-Speaking Exiles in Mexico, Argentina and Bolivia, 1937–1945." *Contemporary European History* 25, no. 4 (2016): 667–686.

Albertani, Claudio. "Vittorio Vidali, Tina Modotti, el stalinismo y la revolución." *Servicio Informativo, Ecuménico y Popular El Salvador.* Apr. 8, 2014. https://ecumenico.org/?s=Albertani. Accessed June 1, 2017.

Cacucci, Pino. "¿Un complot internacional de mentirosos?" *La Jornada*, June 21, 2017.

Dussel Peters, Susanne C. "La arquitectura de Hannes Meyer y Max Cetto: De la modernidad alemana a la mexicana." In *México, el exilio bien temperado*, eds. Renata von Hanffstengel and Cecilia Tercero. Mexico City: UNAM, Instituto Goethe, 1995.

Elorza, Antonio. "El hombre tapado por Tina Modotti." *Letras Libres*, Apr. 23, 2014. www.letraslibres.com/mexico-espana/el-hombre-tapado-por-tina-modotti. Accessed Feb. 14, 2018.

Gleizer, Daniela. *El exilio incómodo: México y los refugiados judíos, 1933–1945.* Mexico City: El Colegio de México/UAM Cuajimalpa, 2011.

——. "Gilberto Bosques y el consulado de México en Marsella (1940–1942): La burocracia en tiempos de guerra." *Estudios de Historia Moderna y Contemporánea de México* 49 (2015): 54–76.

Hanffstengel, Renata von and Cecilia Tercero, eds. *México, el exilio bien temperado.* Mexico City: UNAM, Instituto Goethe, 1995.

Jacinto, Lizette. "Desde la otra orilla: Alice Rühle-Gerstel y Otto Rühle: La experiencia del exilio político de izquierda en México 1935–1943." *Historia Mexicana* 64, no. 1 (2014): 159–242.

Katz, Friedrich. "Mexico, Gilberto Bosques and the Refugees." *The Americas* 57, no. 1 (2000): 1–12.

Kießling, Wolfgang. *Alemania Libre in Mexiko.* Berlin: Akademie Verlag, 1974.

Kleinerüschkamp, Werner. "Exilarchitektur: Hannes Meyer in Mexiko." In *Hannes Meyer 1889–1954 Architekt Urbanist Lehrer: Catalogue/Exposition of the Bauhaus Archive Berlin and the Deutsches Architekturmuseum*, ed. Klaus-Jürgen Winkler, 316–353. Frankfurt am Main: Ernst und Sohn, 1989.

Leidenberger, Georg. *Architect Hannes Meyer: Globetrotting Modernist and Socialist in a Tumultuous World, 1889–1954*. Forthcoming.

——. "Los orígenes de la educación urbanística en México: El Instituto de Planificación y Urbanismo dirigido por el arquitecto Hannes Meyer (1938–1941)." *Espacialidades* 8, no. 1 (2018).

——. "'Todo aquí es vulkanisch': El arquitecto Hannes Meyer en México, 1938 a 1949." In *México a la luz de sus revoluciones*, vol. 2, eds. Laura Rojas and Susan Deeds. Mexico City: El Colegio de México, 2014.

Meyer, Hannes. "El arquitecto soviético." *Arquitectura México* 9 (1942).

——. *Bauen und Gesellschaft. Schriften, Briefe, Projekte*, ed. Lena Meyer-Bergner. Dresden: VEB Verlag der Kunst, 1980.

Pappe, Silvia. "De tantas llegadas, una: Cinco fragmentos acerca de la llegada de Getrude Duby a México." In *México, el exilio bien temperado*, eds. Renata von Hanffstengel and Cecilia Tercero. Mexico City: UNAM, Instituto Goethe, 1995.

Pohle, Fritz. *Das mexikanische Exil: Ein Beitrag zur Geschichte der politisch-kulturellen Emigration aus Deutschland (1937–1946)*. Stuttgart: Metzler, 1986.

Prignitz-Poda, Helga. *El Taller de Gráfica Popular en México, 1937–1977*. Mexico City: INBA/CENIDIAP, 1992.

Raat, W. Dirk. "Intelligence Services during the Second World War: Part 2." *Journal of Contemporary History* 22, no. 4 (1987): 615–638.

Reimann, Aribert. "Espacios del Exilio: La experiencia transnacional en la Ciudad de México, 1934–60." In *Entre espacios: La historia latinoamericana en el contexto global. Actas del XVII Congreso Internacional de AHILA, Berlín 9–13 de septiembre de 2014*. Berlin, 2016: 2950–2970.

Renn, Ludwig. *In Mexiko*. Berlin: Aufbau Verlag, 1979.

Rivadeneyra, Patricia. "Hannes Meyer en México (1938–1949)." In *Apuntes para la historia y crítica de la arquitectura mexicana del siglo XX: 1900–1980*. Mexico City: SEP/INBA, 1982.

Schmidt, Friedhelm. "Los descubrimientos en México de Egon Erwin." In *México, el exilio bien temperado*, eds. Renata von Hanffstengel and Cecilia Tercero. Mexico City: UNAM, Instituto Goethe, 1995.

Stephan, Alexander. "El FBI y los exiliados germanoparlantes en México." In *México, el exilio bien temperado*, eds. Renata von Hanffstengel and Cecilia Tercero. Mexico City: UNAM, Instituto Goethe, 1995.

Stibbe, Matthew. "Jürgen Kuczynski and the Search for a (Non-Existent) Western Spy Ring in the East German Communist Party in 1953." *Contemporary European History* 20, no. 1 (2011): 61–79.

Toca Fernández, Antonio. "Héroes y herejes: Juan O'Gorman y Hannes Meyer."
    Casa del Tiempo 3, no. 32 (2010): 18–23.
Zogbaum, Heidi. "Vicente Lombardo Toledano and the German Communist
    Exile in Mexico, 1940–1947." *Journal of Iberian and Latin American Research*
    11, no. 2 (2012): 1–28.

9

Damned to Do Nothing

The Transnational Network of Rosi Wolfstein and Paul Frölich in American Exile (1941–1950)

Riccardo Altieri

Who were Rosi Wolfstein (1888–1987) and Paul Frölich (1884–1953)? In short, they were socialists who radicalized themselves in a classical way in the context of World War I and the German post-war conditions—they went from being German Social Democrats to the more radical and internationalist Communist Party of Germany. They also represent biographies that were very typical for German radicals of the interwar period, who eventually had to leave Germany and make a living in exile. There, they were also forced to rebuild their radical networks, as many friends and colleagues were simultaneously forced to leave their homes in Germany, and with the continuing German success in war, other parts of Europe as well. A study of these two radical lives can.[1]

At the beginning of this chapter, a brief presentation of the biographies of these two important members of the German labor movement will be given. First, we will talk about Rosi Wolfstein's formative years until the mid-1920s, after which the subject will switch to Paul Frölich's biography. Afterwards, a few words will follow about the couple's time in Germany and their European exile before their emigration to the United States in 1941, where "New Freedom" as well as "Forced Integration" took place. The couple lived there for almost a decade, made new friends, and used or renewed old contacts. It was historically one of the most eventful decades of human history—the demise of the Nazi empire, World War II, the Holocaust and its consequences, as well as Stalin's reign of terror, all of which shaped the image of the "Age of Extremes," as Eric Hobsbawm

Special thanks to John Stern (Louisville, Kentucky) for his proofreading and editing service.

[1] Riccardo Altieri, "Paul Frölich, American Exile, and Communist Discourse about the Russian Revolution," *American Communist History* 17, no. 2 (2018): 220–231 provides a first biographical study of Frölich. Some elements of this work could have been used in this chapter as well, especially with regard to the part on him.

called it.[2] How did Wolfstein and Frölich, who had married in New York in 1948,[3] experience these events? Who were they in contact with and who were they avoiding, consciously or unconsciously? What role did both play in the reconstruction of a left-wing, post-war alternative to the Social Democratic Party of Germany (SPD) and the Communist Party of Germany (KPD), and how did they relate to the developments in the Federal Republic of Germany (FRG) and the German Democratic Republic (GDR)?

In order to map the Wolfstein/Frölich network, which is necessary to answer these questions, letters to and from Wolfstein and Frölich will be used.[4] A second source are letters from direct acquaintances of the two protagonists to third parties, in which Wolfstein and Frölich are mentioned. The relevant material for this work came primarily from the Berlin Federal Archives or was already available in an edited form, as for example in the case of Käte and Hermann Duncker.[5] With the help of the method of "reconstructivism," relationships of a third kind which could not be substantiated by correspondence can be established. Here, references are primarily made to surveillance files of the CIA,[6] which partially monitored former German Communists in American exile. The entire exile period for the two protagonists was characterized by a transnational relationship network, which will be presented in this chapter in its most important components. But, as was said at the beginning, some biographical information is needed,

---

[2] Eric Hobsbawm, *The Age of Extremes: The Short Twentieth Century, 1914–1991* (New York: Vintage Books, 1994). This book is the fourth part of a tetralogy with similar titles. See Eric Hobwbawm, *The Age of Revolution: Europe 1789–1848* (New York: World Publishing, 1962); *The Age of Capital: 1848–1875* (New York: Vintage Books, 1975); *The Age of Empire: 1875–1914* (London: Weidenfeld & Nicolson, 1987).

[3] Specifically, on 25 October 1948. See Institute for City History of Frankfurt am Main, Civil registry records, death record of Paul Frölich, No. 437/V (1953), 3/21/1953.

[4] Bernd Klemm has already published six of these letters from the private estate of Paul Frölich, which were left to him by Rosi Frölich. See Bernd Klemm, "Paul Frölich (1884–1953). Politische Orientierung und theoretische Reflexionen von Linkssozialisten nach dem Zweiten Weltkrieg: Sechs Briefe Paul Frölichs aus der Emigration (1946–1949) an ehemalige KPO/SAP-Mitglieder in Berlin, Duisburg, Offenbach, Wesel, La Habana/Cuba und Stuttgart," *Internationale wissenschaftliche Korrespondenz* 2 (1983): 186–229.

[5] Käte Duncker and Hermann Duncker, *Ein Tagebuch in Briefen*, ed. Heinz Deutschland (Berlin: Dietz, 2016). See also Klemm, "Paul Frölich." The archival material comes primarily from the estates of Käte and Herrmann Duncker or Jacob and Hertha Walcher. See Foundation of the Archives of Parties and Mass Organizations of the GDR in the Berlin Federal Archives (SAPMO), NY 4087, 54–57 (Walcher) and NY 4445, 171, 250, and 262 (Duncker). SAPMO will be henceforth abbreviated as: Berlin Federal Archives.

[6] For example, information about new publications by Paul Frölich were sent to the CIA at irregular intervals. See Information Report from June 29, 1948, "sanitized" copy of CIA-RDP93-00415R003200030003-9.

first about Rosi Wolfstein and then about Paul Frölich, all of which comes from a still relatively small amount of research;[7] a comprehensive narrative is therefore still missing.[8]

Brief Biographies

Alma Rosalie, known as Rosi, Wolfstein was born on 27 May 1888 in Witten in the south-east of the Ruhr region (Figure 9.1). Her paternal family originally came from East Westphalia, more precisely from Körbecke in the district of Warburg.[9] Wolfstein's parents were businessman Samuel

[7] Frank Ahland, *Rosi Wolfstein in Witten* (Witten: self published, 2007); "Alma Rosali (genannt Rosi) Wolfstein," in *"…vergessen kann man das nicht": Wittener Jüdinnen und Juden unter dem Nationalsozialismus*, eds. Martina Kliner-Lintzen and Siegfried Pape (Bochum: Winklerverlag, 1991), 293–294; "Frölich, Paul (*1884–†1953)," in *Deutsche Kommunisten: Biographisches Handbuch 1918 bis 1945*, eds. Herrmann Weber and Andreas Herbst (Berlin: Dietz, 2008), 271–272; "Frölich, Paul," in *Biographisches Handbuch der deutschsprachigen Emigration nach 1933*, Institut für Zeitgeschichte (Munich)/Research Foundation for Jewish Immigration (New York) (Munich: De Gruyter, 1980), 203; "Frölich, Paul," in *Biographisches Staatshandbuch: Lexikon der Politik, Presse und Publizistik*, vol. 1, ed. Wilhelm Kosch (Berne: Francke, 1963), 363; "Frölich, Rose," in *Biographisches Handbuch der deutschsprachigen Emigration nach 1933*, Institut für Zeitgeschichte (Munich)/Research Foundation for Jewish Immigration (New York) (Munich: De Gruyter, 1980), 203–204; Helga Grebing, *Lehrstücke in Solidarität: Briefe und Biographien deutscher Sozialisten* (Stuttgart: DVA, 1983), 330–331; Ludger Heid, "Wolfstein-Frölich, Rosi (Rose). Partei- und Gewerkschaftspolitikerin," in *Jüdische Frauen im 19. und 20. Jahrhundert: Lexikon zu Leben und Werk*, eds. Jutta Dick and Marina Sassenberg (Hamburg: Rowohlt, 1993), 403–406; Klaus Kinner, "Paul Frölich," in *Demokratische Wege: Deutsche Lebensläufe aus fünf Jahrhunderten*, eds. Manfred Asendorf and Rolf von Bockel (Stuttgart: Springer, 1997), 196–197; Bernd Klemm, "Paul Frölich (1884–1953)"; Ottokar Luban, "Rosi Wolfsteins antimilitaristische Aktivitäten 1916/17: Neue Quellenfunde," *Mitteilungsblatt des Instituts für soziale Bewegung* 44 (2010): 123–133; Ernst Massmann, "Frölich, Paul," in *Geschichte der deutschen Arbeiterbewegung: Biographisches Lexikon*, eds. Rudolf Grau et al. (Berlin: Dietz, 1970), 145–146; "Paul Frölich," in *Lexikon Linker Leitfiguren*, ed. Karljosef Kreter (Frankfurt am Main: Büchergilde Gutenberg, 1988), 132–134; Christian Steinacker, "Rosi Wolfstein—Ein Leben in der Arbeiterbewegung," *StadtMagazin Witten* 88 (Dec. 2013–Jan. 2014): 7; Klaus-Dieter Vinschen, "Rosi Wolfstein-Frölich," in *Juden und deutsche Arbeiterbewegung bis 1933: Soziale Utopie und religiös-kulturelle Traditionen*, eds. Ludger Heid and Arnold Paucker (Tübingen: Mohr Siebeck, 1992), 165–176; Herrmann Weber, "Rosi Wolfstein: Eine zweite Rosa Luxemburg," in *Wittener Biografische Porträts*, eds. Frank Ahland and Matthias Dudde (Witten: Ruhrstadt-Verlag, 2000), 119–124; "Wolfstein (Frölich), Rosi," in Weber and Herbst, *Deutsche Kommunisten*, 1043–1044 and all papers in *"Sie wollte und konnte nie etwas Halbes tun": Die Sozialistin Rosi Wolfstein-Frölich 1914 bis 1924*, eds. Frank Ahland and Beate Brunner (Witten: Rosi-Wolfstein-Gesellschaft e.V., 1995).

[8] The author is currently working on double biography, which has been submitted as a doctoral thesis at the University of Potsdam.

[9] Ahland, *Rosi Wolfstein*, 6.

Wolfstein and Klara, née Adler.[10] The parental home was liberal, civic and deeply religious. Rosi Wolfstein had two sisters and one brother. Together they lived at Poststraße 12, before the father could finance his own house at Nordstraße 12, in Witten, in 1891.[11] There was certainly little sympathy for the working class in the house of the self-made man, who worked at the stock market.[12] Samuel and Klara Wolfstein were devout believers who were engaged in their local community. Samuel even ran for the synagogue council in Witten (though unsuccessfully). Frank Ahland wrote: "[The] Wolfsteins were Jewish, but reformed. They were German, loyal to the emperor and liberal."[13] After Rosi's father committed suicide because of his gambling when she was aged only thirteen, there was no other choice but to work in order to pay the school tuition fees for herself and her younger sister Berta Wolfstein (b. 1891).[14]

Four years later, in 1905, Rosi Wolfstein finished her training as a salesperson. She received her first job in Hagen at a furniture factory.[15]

---

[10] Beate Brunner, "'Alles kritisch nachprüfen…' Rosi Wolfstein—eine der bedeutendsten Frauen der Arbeiterbewegung," in *Wittener Frauengeschichte(n): Dokumentation anläßlich einer frauengeschichtlichen Stadtrundfahrt*, ed. Arbeitskreis Frauengeschichte Witten (Witten: Laube, 1992), 39–41, here 39. Beate Brunner writes about Klara Wolfstein, née Warburg, who died in 1931. Ludger Heid identified Klara with a born Adler (1851–1938), see Heid, *Wolfstein-Frölich*, 403.

[11] Steinacker, "Rosi Wolfstein," 79.

[12] Esther Dischereit, "'…eigentlich könnte es doch viel besser und anders sein,'" in Ahland and Brunner,"*Sie wollte und konnte nie etwas Halbes tun*," 22–28, here 23.

[13] Ahland, *Rosi Wolfstein*, 8.

[14] Ibid., 12; Luban, *Rosi Wolfstein*, 124. Both her sisters, Berta and Wilhelmine Gisela (b. 1886) were murdered by the Nazis between 1942 and 1945. Wilhelmine Gisela Wolfstein was deported to the Auschwitz extermination camp on 29 January 1943 and was either murdered there immediately because she was too old to work or lived in the camp for no longer than a few months. Berta Wolfstein was married to Hermann Steinberg (b. 1877) and was deported to the Ghetto Warsaw on 31 March 1942, where she was murdered in April or May 1943, as a result of the Warsaw Ghetto "uprising." However, when exactly the sisters died has not been determined. Hermann Steinberg was arrested during the November Pogrom, kidnapped to Buchenwald and held there for two weeks. On 26 November 1938, he died in Paderborn under the Nazi persecution. See the online memorial, Berlin Federal Archives, "Gedenkbuch für die Opfer der Verfolgung der Juden unter der nationalsozialistischen Gewaltherrschaft in Deutschland 1933–1945," www.bundesarchiv.de/gedenkbuch/de974228; www.bundesarchiv.de/gedenkbuch/de1183519; www.bundesarchiv.de/gedenkbuch/de296712. See also "Steinberg, Helene," in *Jüdische Familien in Münster 1918–1945*, vol. 1, *Biographisches Lexikon*, eds. Gisela Möllenhoff and Rita Schlautmann-Overmeyer (Münster: Westfälisches Dampfboot, 2001), 429. Her brother Paul (b. 1884) died during World War I. Thomas Föhl, Record of Paul Wolfstein at www.geni.com/people/Paul-Wolfstein/6000000050839443417.

[15] Ahland, *Rosi Wolfstein*, 14.

9.1 Rosi Wolfstein, 1921, Berlin,
in the Minute Book of the
Prussian Landtag
© Salomon-Ludwig-Steinheim
Institute, Essen, Gidal Photo
Archive 3875

Following a dispute between her boss and the local workers regarding a raise of a few pennies, Wolfstein quit and became a housekeeper. In her new position, she often talked with the bourgeois family for whom she worked, which had greater sympathies with regards to Social Democracy.[16] In 1907, she became a member of a women's and worker's association in Hagen, and one year later she also became a member of the SPD.[17]

It was in 1910 that she first met Rosa Luxemburg (1871–1919), and they later became friends.[18] After the election campaign in 1912, where Wolfstein made thirty-five speeches for the SPD, Luxemburg managed to get her into the party school in Berlin.[19] Here, Wolfstein wrote some 150 pages on what she had learned from Luxemburg's lessons.[20] When she had any problems with male party members, her teacher would cheer her up with

[16] Ibid., 15.

[17] Weber, "Rosi Wolfstein," 119.

[18] Vinschen, "Rosi Wolfstein-Frölich," 165.

[19] Wladislaw Hedeler, "Vier Bemerkungen zu einem Lebenslauf," in Ahland and Brunner, *"Sie wollte und konnte nie etwas Halbes tun,"* 19–21, here 19.

[20] They were published by Annelies Laschitza in 2017. See Rosa Luxemburg, *Gesammelte Werke*, vol. 7/1, *1907 to 1918*, eds. Annelies Laschitza and Eckard Müller (Berlin: Dietz, 2017), 409–564.

sentences like: "Do not be discouraged by the agitation of a certain side. Make it like me: whistle for the wretchedness and continue your journey."[21] And Wolfstein did just that.

During World War I, Wolfstein became increasingly radicalized, going from the SPD to the Independent Social Democratic Party (USPD) and the left-wing Spartakusbund. In that period, she was arrested three times for a total of a few months.[22] She was a warrior against the war, not as a pacifist, as she confirmed many times, but as an anti-militarist and anti-imperialist.[23] Her soon-to-be-husband Paul Frölich was not convinced at that time, although he criticized the Spartakusbund,[24] especially after the conferences at Zimmerwald and Kienthal.[25] He was a member of the left-wing radicals in Bremen. In Kienthal, he even criticized Lenin (1870–1924) and the Bolsheviks, a fact that provoked Angelica Balabanova (1878–1965) so much that she stopped translating his speeches for the Russians.[26] At the end of 1918, Rosi Wolfstein and Paul Frölich became members of the new Communist Party (KPD). At this time, Frölich was still married to Clara, née Hartung, with whom he had three sons: Wolfgang (b. 1909), Hans (b. 1910) and Karl (b. 1913).[27] In 1923, he had a fourth child, his daughter Edda, but this time with another woman, Maria Louise Hoppe (b. 1891).[28] Frölich and Wolfstein became a couple shortly after this period, probably in the summer of 1924.[29] A look back at the first years of Paul Frölich's life

[21] Quoted from Weber, "Rosi Wolfstein," 120. Copies of the original letters can be found in Berlin Federal Archives, SAPMO, NY 4002, 48, letter from Rosa Luxemburg to Rosi Wolfstein, no location, undated, papers 18h–18k, here 18i.

[22] Luban, "Rosi Wolfstein," 124–127; Dischereit, "'…eigentlich könnte es doch viel besser und anders sein,'" 27.

[23] Ottokar Luban integrated this nuance into his essay title. See Luban, "Rosi Wolfstein."

[24] *Die Gründung der KPD: Protokoll und Materialien des Gründungsparteitages der Kommunistischen Partei Deutschlands 1918/1919*, ed. Hermann Weber (Berlin: Dietz, 1993), 152–154. See also the references in Paul Frölich's autobiography *Im radikalen Lager: Politische Autobiographie 1890–1921*, ed. Reiner Tosstorff (Berlin: BasisDruck, 2013), 129.

[25] Bernard Degen and Julia Richers, eds., *Zimmerwald und Kiental: Weltgeschichte auf dem Dorfe* (Zurich: Chronos Verlag, 2015).

[26] Frölich, *Im radikalen Lager*, 122.

[27] Leipzig City Archive, Birth Record No. 460/1884, Register Office Volkmarsdorf. Concerning Karl Frölich, who was born in Altona, so far there is no record of his death available. He died at the age of about 27 of a lung disease from which he suffered his entire life and because of which he lived for many months in health resorts in Switzerland. Telephone information from the half-sister Edda Tasiemka, June 28, 2017.

[28] Information from Edda Tasiemka.

[29] Letter No. 2233, from Hermann to Käte Duncker, Kislowodsk, Aug. 7, 1924, in Duncker, *Tagebuch*, 3930–3933, here 3931. Edda Tasiemka confirmed this assumption. She knows that her father left her mother soon after Edda's birth, but of course she did not know the exact date.

is now necessary, before moving onto their time together in the Weimar Republic, in the Nazi era and in exile.

Frölich was the second of eleven children, born in 1884 in Neuseller-hausen (Saxony), not far from the workers' stronghold in Leipzig.[30] Unlike Rosi Wolfstein, Frölich's parents, Minna, née Munkwitz (b. 1860) and Max Albin Frölich (b. 1858), worked as a factory worker and locksmith for many years. They were excited advocates of social democracy and the young Paul lived in a rather cramped apartment under the watchful eyes of Karl Marx and Ferdinand Lassalle, whose portraits hung in the living room.[31] Paul also had to help earn income for the household, and as a young child he had to walk for two to three hours each day delivering the party newspaper *Wähler*, and later also the *Leipziger Volkszeitung*.[32]

From 1904 to 1905, Paul Frölich lived for a short time in Dresden and then in Neustadt, near Poznań. He then stayed in Leipzig until 1906, before being drafted into the military in the same year. Until 1907, he served in the 179th Infantry Regiment in Wurzen, the region from which his paternal grandparents came. From 1907 to 1910 he lived once again in Leipzig before he "emigrated" to Hamburg to take up the offer of a job.[33] In 1912, he applied for Prussian citizenship.[34] After a short intermission as editor-in-chief of the *Altenburger Volkszeitung*, Frölich took up his job as a reporter for the *Hamburger Echo*. For a long time, however, he did not stand out in the highly reserved editorial department. Apart from his own articles, which focused primarily on Altona's policy, where he was active as a town councilor, the newspaper was bland and uninspiring—he had never really been able to sympathize with the chief editor.[35] In 1913, after three and a half years in Altona, he moved to Bremen.

Here, at last, he was free to develop politically. His criticism of the SPD grew. "The party worked according to old rules without any initiative, and was restricted from above,"[36] he wrote in his autobiography. But he took advantage of the opportunity to speak politically, as well as from his new job at the *Bremer Bürgerzeitung*, especially in light of the July Crisis and World

---

[30] Leipzig City Archive, Civil Registration of Volkmarsdorf, 1885–1888, A–G, PoA No. 1039, F, cont. No. 184. Also see the Civil Registration of Neusellerhausen, 1882–1891, A–L, PoA No. 785, F, cont. No. 40. Eight years later, on 1 January 1892, the suburb Neusellerhausen was incorporated into Leipzig. Information from Olaf Hillert (Leipzig City Archive); mail from June 7, 2017 to the author.

[31] Frölich, *Im radikalen Lager*, 20.

[32] Ibid., 31–32.

[33] Leipzig City Archive, F 2535, Questionnaire, p. 3.

[34] Leipzig City Archive, birth record.

[35] Frölich, *Im radikalen Lager*, 80–82; Weber and Herbst, *Deutsche Kommunisten*, 271.

[36] Frölich, *Im radikalen Lager*, 104.

War I, at which time the SPD began to split with the "party truce policy" (*Burgfriedenspolitik*).[37] Both Frölich and his then best friend Johann Knief (1880–1919) were drafted shortly after the beginning of the war.[38] It was during the various engagements with the enemy and dangerous adventures in the field, in which Corporal Frölich gained impressions of the growing unwillingness of the German soldiers for the loss-making war, that he was severely injured, treated in a hospital and after a short time released from his service.[39] What followed was the founding of the newspaper *Arbeiterpolitik*, which would later become the heart of the Bremen left-wing radicals and which he edited with Knief.[40] At the end of 1916, he was recalled and transferred to the Eastern Front. For him, the motto was, "Why the whole muck? That was the constant question?"[41] He now communicated his criticism of the war and the backers involved with the soldiers and other socialist comrades, which led to his arrest and internment in a health care institution in Kiel in the middle of 1918. He was liberated from this political imprisonment only after the coup d'état in November 1918, when a paramedic freed him.[42] That same day he took over the editorial office of the occupied *Hamburger Echo*, which became the *Rote Fahne*.[43]

After the war, both Wolfstein and Frölich became active politicians for the KPD. From 1921 to 1924, he was a member of the German Reichstag while she was part of the Prussian Landtag.[44] After Lenin's death and the Stalinization of the KPD shortly thereafter, Frölich and Wolfstein, now in a serious relationship, were suppressed by the new party leadership. In the following years, both worked in private, Frölich as an author and journalist, Wolfstein as a lecturer for the Berlin publishing house Malik.[45] In 1928, Frölich was elected again and represented the KPD-Opposition (KPO) in

---

[37] Weber and Herbst, *Deutsche Kommunisten*, 271.

[38] Frölich, *Im radikalen Lager*, 102–105. For more information on the relationship between Knief and Frölich, see Gerhard Engel, *Johann Knief—ein unvollendetes Leben* (Berlin: Dietz, 2011), 182, 199, 227–330.

[39] See also Russian State Archive of Socio-Political History, Fond 340, Opis 4, Folder 271, war letter from Paul Frölich to Karl Radek, Bailly, Dec. 3, 1914, fols. 6–8.

[40] Weber and Herbst, *Deutsche Kommunisten*, 271.

[41] Frölich, *Im radikalen Lager*, 110.

[42] Ibid., 144–145.

[43] Volker Ulrich, "Weltkrieg und Novemberrevolution: die Hamburger Arbeiterbewegung 1914 bis 1918." In *Hamburg im ersten Viertel des 20. Jahrhunderts: die Zeit des Politikers Otto Stolten. Sieben Abhandlungen*, ed. Heinrich Erdmann (Hamburg: Landeszentrale für politische Bildung, 2000), 118–194; here 121. See also Christiane Teetz, *Otto Stolten und die Sozialdemokratie in Hamburg bis zum Ende der Kaiserzeit* (Münster: Lit-Verlag, 2004), 159–160.

[44] Weber and Herbst, *Deutsche Kommunisten*, 272, 1044.

[45] Ibid.

9.2 Paul Frölich, 1921, Berlin, in the Minute Book of the German Reichstag © Bureau of the Reichstag, 1924 (638)

the Reichstag. He remained part of the parliament, even after the departure of the party, until 1930.[46] It was then that they both became members of the Socialist Workers Party of Germany (SAPD). After Hitler came to power in 1933, the illegal party convention in Dresden decided to send Frölich to Norway, where he was meant to be the head of the German foreigners in the SAPD.[47] His exile had begun (Figure 9.2).

Exile in Europe and America

Rosi Wolfstein, too, had to flee the Nazi thugs. In 1933, when the Gestapo inspected their apartment in Berlin, they found neither Wolfstein nor Frölich. She had emigrated on foot to Brussels after crossing the German border near Aachen.[48] She lived there for two and a half years without her partner, save for his later visits. Frölich, who was brought to Lübeck, started

---

[46] Ibid., 272.

[47] Gertrud Lenz, "Gertrud Meyer: Eine politische Biographie" (Ph.D. thesis, Universität Flensburg, 2010), 54, 72, 75–76.

[48] Institute for the City History of Frankfurt am Main, Estate Althart/S1/452, No. 8: Statutory declaration of Rosi Frölich, born Wolfstein, Frankfurt am Main, Mar. 18, 1955.

his emigration on a boat heading to Oslo. There he received help from Herbert Frahm, a young cabin boy aged twenty who later became famous under his SAPD codename, Willy Brandt (1913–1992). Unfortunately, the ship got caught in a storm and was forced to land on Fehmarn Island. Not surprisingly, the local Nazis suspected Frölich of being a communist, arrested him and brought him to a prison in Kiel.[49] Later, Frölich was deported to the concentration camp at Lichtenburg (part of the Prussian province of Saxony), where he was imprisoned for four to five months. He was erroneously released in the 1933 Christmas amnesty and fled to Czechoslovakia.[50] After he reached Paris, his desired destination, he began his work in exile for the SAPD. Wolfstein was already part of the exiled party, and both resisted Nazi Germany in the following years. However, the beginning of World War II resulted in all German "enemies" living in France being imprisoned.[51] Again, Rosi and Paul were separated, because the prisons were split into male and female camps.

In 1940, the German Wehrmacht conquered the area where Frölich's prison stood, which caused the camp warden to release the prisoners. Paul and some others were on a list of prisoners who were to remain interned until the end of the war. However, the indulgent French guards did not notice the "escape" of the special prisoners. The spectacular flight and the subsequent weeks in France were described by Henry Jacoby in his report on the emigration.[52] "Jacky," as Paul called him, was one of those who later formed the transatlantic network along with Paul Frölich and Rosi Wolfstein in New York.[53] A few months later, Frölich and Wolfstein got the chance to emigrate to New York from Marseilles. The Jewish Labor Committee in New York arranged the essentials.[54]

---

[49] Lenz, *Gertrud Meyer*, 75–76. See also Reinhard Jacobs, *Terror unterm Hakenkreuz—Ort des Erinnerns in Niedersachsen und Sachsen-Anhalt* (Berlin: Otto-Brenner-Stiftung, 2001), 44–45; no author, "Brandt—Nr. F 2019," *Der Spiegel* 36 (1976): 76–79, here 78–79.

[50] Information from Edda Tasiemka.

[51] For this whole period see e.g. Ursula Langkau-Alex, *Deutsche Volksfront 1932–1939: Zwischen Berlin, Paris, Prag und Moskau*, 3 vols. (Berlin: Akademie-Verlag, 2004–2005). For the imprisonments, see Weber and Herbst, *Deutsche Kommunisten*, 272, 1044.

[52] Henry Jacoby, *Davongekommen: 10 Jahre Exil 1936–1946. Prag, Paris, Montauban, New York, Washington: Erlebnisse und Begegnungen* (Frankfurt am Main: Sendler-Verlag, [1982]), 82–89.

[53] Henry Jacoby, "Begegnung mit Paul Frölich," in *Internationale wissenschaftliche Korrespondenz* 2 (1983): 181–186, here 183.

[54] Columbia University, New York, Butler Library, Varian Fry Collection I 1D. See "Frölich, Paul," and "Frölich, Rose (Rosi)," *Biographisches Handbuch*, 203–204; Peter Y. Medding, ed., *Values, Interests and Identity: Jews and Politics in a Changing World*, Studies in Contemporary Jewry, 11 (New York: Oxford University Press, 1996), 271.

New York, 1941–1950

Because of the pervasive anti-communism in the United States, it was almost impossible for Paul Frölich and Rosi Wolfstein to appear politically during the time of their exile. They attended public lectures and events, drove to congress meetings in Canada and maintained their personal network, but active policies or even interference in American acts were prohibited. Thus, Frölich retired into private life, mainly as an author, either continuing work on his important books or writing them anew. He rewrote the treatises on the French Revolution that had been stolen by the Gestapo from his apartment in Paris in 1940.[55] The Rosa Luxemburg biography, *Thought and Action*, was also written in exile, published in 1939 for the twentieth anniversary of Luxemburg's death.[56] Wolfstein, on the other hand, earned a large part of the household income by working for a Jewish refugee committee, coordinating the emigration of those persecuted by the Nazi regime,[57] or again as a housekeeper and nanny.[58] In 1948, under a little pressure from new American friends, the couple finally married in New York, and Rosi, aged sixty, took the surname Frölich.[59] They shared an apartment in Kew Gardens, in Queens, for financial reasons with a friendly couple, Ilya and Lisa Laub.[60]

Their network was built up under various circumstances (Figure 9.3). Shortly after their arrival in New York, the couple came into conflict with their old friends Jacob and Herta Walcher. The main reason for the quarrels was the fact that Wolfstein and Frölich had withdrawn from the political roundtables that took place at irregular intervals. The group of about twenty people in New York (all of them former SAPD members) met again and again to assess the political situation in Europe. Early on, their first proposals were about a transformation of the German power structure "after Hitler." Frölich had also commented on this in a futuristic way a few

---

[55] Institute for the City History of Frankfurt am Main, Estate Alfhart/S1/452, No. 8: Request of Indemnity, Paul Frölich, Kew Gardens, Apr. 11, 1949. See also Paul Frölich, *1789—Die große Zeitenwende. Von der Bürokratie des Absolutismus zum Parlament der Revolution* (Frankfurt am Main: Europäische Verlagsanstalt, 1957).

[56] Paul Frölich, *Rosa Luxemburg: Gedanke und Tat* (Paris: Éditions nouvelles internationales, 1939).

[57] Brunner, "Rosi Wolfstein," 41.

[58] Berlin Federal Archives, SAPMO, 4445, 250 (Estate Duncker), letter from Paul Frölich to Kaete Duncker, July 18, 1943.

[59] Institute for the City History of Frankfurt am Main, death records 1953, No. 437/V.

[60] Ilya or Elias Laub was formerly the owner of a social democratic publishing bookstore in Berlin, which was named after him. See Klemm, "Paul Frölich," 220 n. 2.

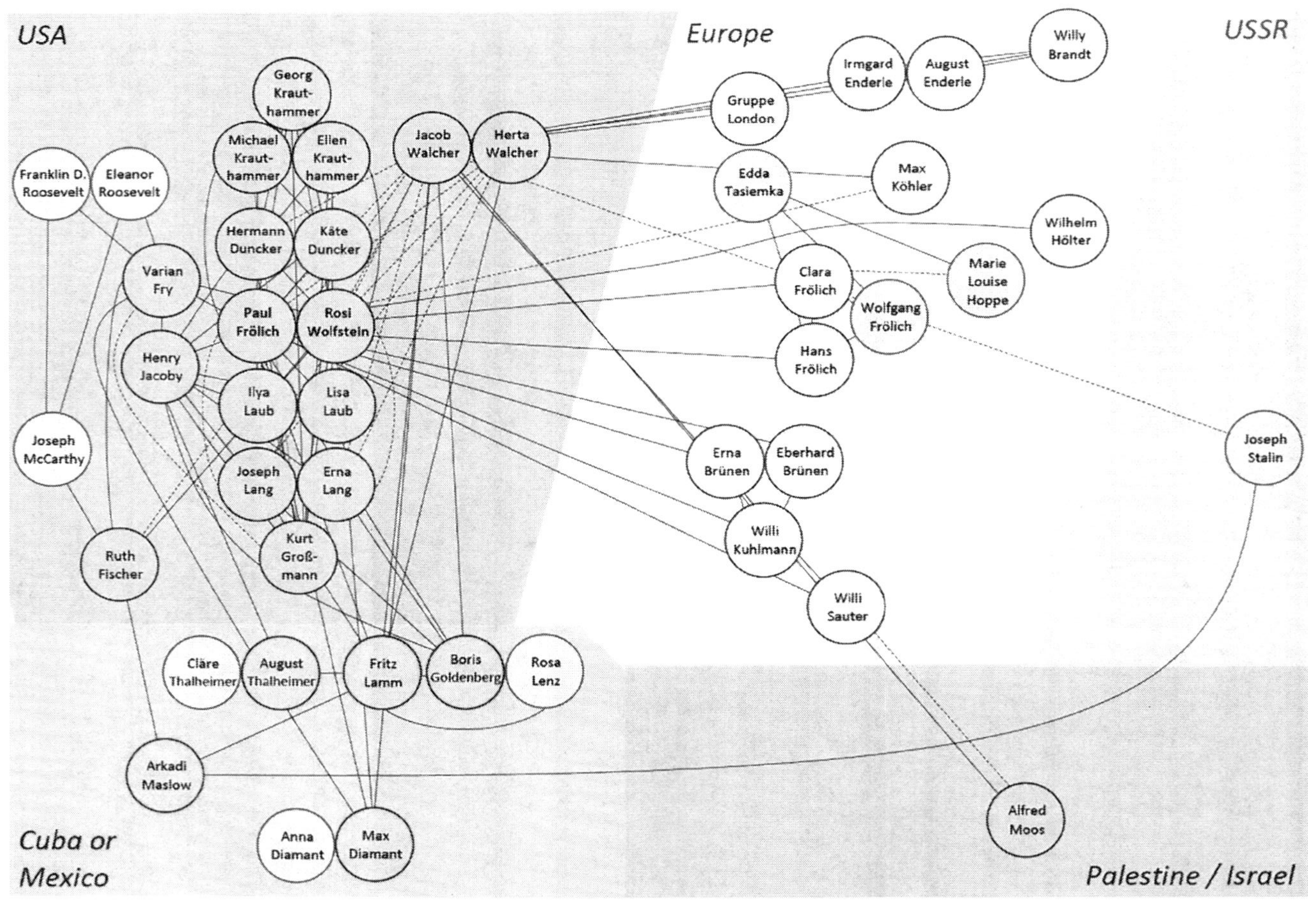

9.3 The Transnational Wolfstein/Frölich Network between 1941 and 1950 © R. Altieri

years before.[61] Hardly a conversation turned to the past; it was probably very rarely that they talked about their own times in prison. Even the atrocities of the concentration camp system did not become part of the discussions, although they certainly knew about them—they had to have known. Varian Fry had already reported on one of the first reports of the atrocities inside the concentration camps in 1942,[62] albeit without encountering any understanding or interest from the Roosevelt administration.[63]

Of course, the former SAPD members did not need any scientific support for their own empirically experienced fates. To top it all off, Marseilles's hero, Varian Fry, was not immune—the Roosevelt government was excessively anti-communist, and some of its members at first even sympathized with Hitler and the National Socialists.[64] What followed after 1945 was the Second Red Scare and, after 1950, the McCarthy trials. And in those years before, when surveillance was still subtle and secret, several former German Communists met in the Queens district or in the Bronx, where the Walchers lived, to discuss critical issues. It is no wonder that, after a few sessions, Frölich and Wolfstein decided to retire because they did not feel comfortable in the general atmosphere.[65] Any conversation about critical content could potentially be monitored; they never knew how or when they would be spied upon. And so, together with Joseph (1902–1973) and Erna Lang (1892–1983), independently they decided that they would retire.[66]

This contributed to the demise of the old social circle, which for the most part had already existed in Paris, Montauban and Marseilles. Jacob Walcher, who had repeatedly quarreled with Frölich in the years prior

---

[61] [Paul Frölich], *Was kommt nach Hitler? Probleme der deutschen Revolution*, ed. the SAPD (Brussels: WUYTS, 1937).

[62] Varian Fry, "The Massacre of Jews in Europe," *New Republic*, Dec. 21, 1942: 816–820.

[63] "President Roosevelt could and should speak out again against these monstrous events. A stern warning from him will have no effect on Hitler, but it may impress some Germans like the officer who helped the Jews from Brussels to escape." Ibid., 818. Contrary to the views of the president, who sometimes tolerated anti-Semitic views within his inner circle, his wife Eleanor Roosevelt (1884–1962) had been an advocate for more African American rights since 1934, was actively urging Washington to accept Jewish refugees in the United States and criticized Senator Joseph McCarthy (1908–1957) for his communist hunt, whose inherent mistrust she found profoundly un-American. See Angelika Meyer, "'Gesucht von der Gestapo': Varian Fry und die amerikanische Fluchthilfeorganisation 'Emergency Rescue Committee,'" in *Ohne zu zögern. Varian Fry: Berlin—Marseille—New York*, ed. Aktives Museum Faschismus und Widerstand, Berlin (Leipzig: Messedruck, 2008), 126–149, here 134.

[64] Peter von Becker, "Der amerikanische Engel—Fluchthelfer Varian Fry: eine Erinnerung zum 100.," *Der Tagesspiegel* (online), Oct. 14, 2007.

[65] Berlin Federal Archives, SAPMO, NY 4087, 54 (Estate Walcher), letter from Jacob Walcher to Fritz Altwein, July 15, 1946, 1.

[66] Ibid.

to emigrating,[67] regarded the couple's decision as an irrefutable betrayal. Walcher did not give them any sympathy, and called Wolfstein and Frölich "cowards" and "chicken shit" in later letters.[68] He did not understand why the two were afraid to face the war between Russia and Hitler's Germany, taking the side of Joseph Stalin (1878–1953). Apart from the fact that they had always rejected the dictator's policy, they also had a thorn in their flesh, which everyone else seemed to completely ignore.

In the 1920s, Frölich and Wolfstein had been excluded from the KPD as so-called "right-dissenters." This was mainly due to the leader of the German party, Ernst Thälmann (1886–1944). But the problems with the KPD were even older: both had differences with Arkadij Maslow (1891–1941) and Ruth Fischer (1895–1961), and also with Stalin himself. Fischer and Maslow were initially loyal to Stalin and demanded a new direction for the party after Lenin's death.[69] Those who opposed them were defamed as part of the party's "right wing."[70] After internal disputes and problems with Moscow, which could not be solved at this point,[71] Maslow and Fischer had to end their careers in the KPD in 1926. From 1933 to 1940 they also lived in French exile, after which they fled to Spain and Portugal. While Fischer was granted an entry visa to the United States, Maslow had some bad luck after

---

[67] Ibid.

[68] Ibid.; Max Diamant to Jacob Walcher, Mexico City, Sept. 21, 1942; Jacob Walcher to August and Irmgard Enderle, [New York], Oct. 9, 1945, 2. Berlin Federal Archives, SAPMO, NY 4087, 55 (Estate Walcher), Boris Goldenberg to Jacob "Jim" Walcher, Havana, Dec. 15, 1942, 2; Boris Goldenberg to Jim [Jacob Walcher] and Hexe [Herta Walcher], Havana, Dec. 22, 1945, 2; Jacob Walcher to Boris Goldenberg, [New York], Feb. 28, 1946, 1–2; Max Köhler to Jacob Walcher, [Copenhagen], Aug. 23, 1944; Jacob Walcher to Max and "Lieschen" Köhler, New York, Aug. 19, 1945, 1–2. Berlin Federal Archives, SAPMO, NY 4087, 56 (Estate Walcher), Herta Walcher to "Lämmchen" [Fritz Lamm], New York, Oct. 13, 1944; Fritz Lamm to Jacob Walcher, Havana, Oct. 17, 1944, 1–2; Fritz Lamm to Jacob Walcher, Havana, Sept. 17, 1945, 2; Jacob Walcher to "Liebe Freunde" ["dear friends" in London], New York, Jan. 10, 1944; Jacob Walcher to "Liebe Freunde" ["dear friends" in London], [New York], Dec. 1945, 1. SAPMO, NY 4087, 57 (Estate Walcher), Jacob Walcher to Alfred Moos, [New York], Aug. 10, 1945, 1; Jacob Walcher to Willi Sauter, [New York], Aug. 19, 1946, 2; Willi Sauter to Jacob Walcher, Ulm, Oct. 9, 1946, 2.

[69] For their biography, see Mario Keßler, *Ruth Fischer: Ein Leben mit und gegen Kommunisten (1895–1961)* (Cologne: Böhlau, 2013) and Mario Keßler, *A Political Biography of Arkadij Maslow, 1891–1941: Dissident Against His Will* (London: Palgrave Macmillan, 2020).

[70] For the so-called "right-wing" Communism, see Bernd Dieter Fritz, *Die Kommunistische Arbeitsgemeinschaft (KAG) im Vergleich mit der KPO und SAP: Eine Studie zur politischen Ideologie des deutschen "Rechts"-Kommunismus in der Zeit der Weimarer Republik* (Ph.D. thesis, Bonn, s.n., 1966). See also: Theodor Bergmann, *"Gegen den Strom": Die Geschichte der KPD (Opposition)*, 2nd ed. (Hamburg: VSA-Verlag, 2001).

[71] See Keßler, *Ruth Fischer*, 219–268.

traveling to Cuba in 1941.[72] His unconscious body was found in the streets of Havana, and a few hours later he died of a cerebral hemorrhage.[73] But Fischer suspected the NKVD (People's Commissariat for Internal Affairs) of murdering her companion with some kind of poison. While I generally agree with the murder hypothesis of Fischer's biographer Mario Keßler,[74] clear evidence is missing, and the truth might never be fully discovered. Hurt by hatred, Fischer became an anti-communist, and later acted as an informant for the FBI and as a researcher of the history of communism for Harvard University.[75] Without reason or proof, she accused a multitude of German emigrants of being agents of Stalin. This brought her former comrades into life-threatening situations.[76]

Paul Frölich's far-sightedness, not pursuing any obviously left-wing activities in America, where even old friends could now be spies, is therefore only too understandable. In this poisoned atmosphere, which Frölich judged far better than, for example, Jacob Walcher, the old network of German socialists in American exile broke apart. In the following years, Frölich sat down at his desk each day and read old books again, began to recognize connections and considered his judgment against Lenin one last time.[77]

Thereafter, the Walchers ended their friendship with Frölich and Wolfstein, stopped all contact and retired to work.[78] It is striking how rarely Paul Frölich spoke about this incident in his correspondence with third parties, whereas Jacob and Käte Walcher told almost all their conversational partners that their relationship with Frölich and Wolfstein had broken off.[79] Some of them—both on the side of the Walchers as well as on the part of the Frölichs and Wolfstein—referred to these lost connections in future communications. Others, like Fritz ("Lämmchen") Lamm (1911–1977), for example, kept in touch with both sides throughout their years of exile and did not want to know about the quarrels.[80]

---

[72] Ibid., 372.

[73] Ibid., 386–387.

[74] Ibid., 390.

[75] Ibid., 415, 417–423, 467–491.

[76] See e.g. the chapter "Ruth Fischer vor dem Ausschuss für Unamerikanische Tätigkeit," ibid., 629–648.

[77] Jacoby, "Begegnung," 183. See also Altieri, "Paul Frölich," 220–231.

[78] SAPMO, NY 4087, 56 (Estate Walcher), Jacob Walcher to "Liebe Freunde" ["dear friends" in London], New York, Jan. 10, 1944.

[79] See n. 68, above.

[80] SAPMO, NY 4087, 56 (Estate Walcher), Fritz "Lämmchen" Lamm to Jacob "Jim" Walcher, Havana, Oct. 3, 1944, 2. For his biography, see Michael Benz, *Der unbequeme Streiter Fritz Lamm. Jude, Linkssozialist, Emigrant 1911–1977: Eine politische Biographie* (Essen: Klartext, 2007).

Interestingly enough, copies in the CIA's archive give rise to the suspicion that Paul Frölich and Rosi Wolfstein had acted very wisely.[81] There is other material, albeit little of it, that suggests that surveillance began very early.[82] However, Wolfstein went about her day's work, and Frölich was mainly concerned with writing. Considering additionally what role Ruth Fischer played at this time and how she had repeatedly tried to establish contact with Frölich and Wolfstein,[83] the impression that the two had done very well to leave the former SAPD network during their New York exile is further strengthened.[84]

Until 1945, the main themes in the letters between the Frölichs and their old friends in Europe and America were the war, how it could be stopped and what had happened to their old friends who remained in Nazi Germany. After 1945, the main themes were the East–West conflict, the building of a new third party between KPD and SPD, the dealings with the Soviet Union under its leader Stalin, the last splinter of the German working-class movement. In the following, excerpts from five letters written or received by Paul Frölich and Rosi Wolfstein will be presented. The first letter will show the emotional part of the exile, the aspects of friendship, hope and the will to fix everything that had gone wrong in the Nazi era. The second letter shows Frölich as a worried Marxist who had changed his mind on the topic of the October Revolution, on his old comrade Lenin and on the benefits of Bolshevism. The third letter from an old friend to Frölich shows the worries and hardships, the moment of getting back old contacts and the conscious decision to re-enter the SPD, which definitely influenced Frölich and Wolfstein in their own decisions. The fourth letter, from Wolfstein to Hermann and Käte Duncker, shows how few problems the couple had with having friends who disagreed with their own opinions. While the Dunckers, like the Walchers, deliberately opted for the Socialist Unity Party of Germany (SED), and the Frölichs for the SPD, their friendship did not break, while the one with the Walchers

---

[81] See Information Report from June 29, 1948, "sanitized" copy of CIA-RDP93-00415R003200030003-9.

[82] However, it seems almost certain that Ruth Fischer had not monitored Paul Frölich and Rosi Wolfstein. She was rather connected with the FBI than with the CIA, and in the FBI archives there are currently no documents on Frölich and Wolfstein—maybe because they withdrew early from the conspiratorial meetings.

[83] Letter No. 125: Ruth Fischer to Rose Frölich-Wolfstein, New York, Mar. 28, 1953, in *Abtrünnig wider Willen: Aus Briefen und Manuskripten des Exils*, ed. Peter Lübbe (Munich: Oldenbourg, 1990), 298.

[84] Ruth Fischer, for example, gave information to the OSS about the "Council of a Democratic Germany," a group that also included Jacob Walcher. See Keßler, *Ruth Fischer*, 421, especially n. 97.

broke through sophistry. The fifth and last letter provides insight into Frölich's inner thoughts during the exile and after his return. While his long-time friend Fritz Lamm expressed himself several times in a manner that Frölich was reluctant to condone, he did not just end the friendship. Not least because of that, Frölich became a friend of Lamm, with whom he could argue about all theoretical questions without the friendship ever being broken.

Letter 1 Paul Frölich [and Rosi Wolfstein] to Wilhelm Hölter (Berlin), Kew Gardens, 31 July 1946

> You cannot imagine what each word from home means to us. It is always a building block for the reconstruction of the reality there. We read the letters over and over, we weigh every sentence and look behind the lines for the man to sense how he has come out of this catastrophic year, whether he has not suffered too heavily, how he now bears the time and how he feels and thinks. We are very grateful when he not only talks about the past, but also expresses his opinion on present things. There is nothing more important to us. … Too many stones are missing from the mosaic we have to put together. What we hear from friends and alike is often quite contradictory, as it cannot be otherwise. … We heard of serious, judgmental returnees, and we found in letters again and again confirmation that events which have an immeasurably deep impression on us, which practically formed our opinions, which caused an inner crisis, and, in some cases, changed our character—that you know these events only superficially and cannot estimate their significance.[85]

The sluggish flow of information, both from Europe to the Americas and vice versa, is characteristic of the war years and the first post-war years. Although only a few sporadic SAPD groups had been connected across the world in recent years, only very sporadic information arrived at the target addresses.[86] The dissolving SAPD camp at the end of the war (including the return to the SPD) contributed to the deterioration of communication.[87] And so the exile symbolizes their damnation: the actors were damned to do "nothing."[88]

---

[85] Paul Frölich to Wilhelm Hölter (Berlin), [New York], July 31, 1946, in Klemm, "Paul Frölich," 202–205.

[86] Ibid.

[87] See the letters in n. 68, above.

[88] Of course, they did "things," as we can see in this chapter, but they weren't able actively to participate in political events, either in the United States or in Europe.

Letter 2 Paul Frölich [and Rosi Wolfstein] to Eberhard and Erna Brünen and Willi Kuhlmann (Duisburg), Kew Gardens, 24 August 1946

> We have managed the legacy of Marxism poorly. After Rosa's and Lenin's death, hardly any progress has been made. Trotsky, who had the means to do it, showed that he was too exhausted. Bukharin has tackled many problems and has given important suggestions. But the fact that he is forgotten is due only to the fact that he was silenced, as planned, there [in Moscow]. Reformism has not happened. Hilferding is always slumped, even in emigration. … Thalheimer can formulate well theoretically, but … looks after the powerful and therefore makes excuses. If I mention the epigones, I can speak of myself. In my field of history, I have something to say, and in part it is laid down: history and yet actuality.[89]

Thus, Frölich set himself the goal of finding answers to National Socialism in his biography of Rosa Luxemburg,[90] among other things, without drifting off into the dangerous field of anachronism. Even between the French Revolution and the Russian Revolution of 1917, Frölich always saw parallels, forming his own revolutionary model and always trying to relate the answers of history to questions of the present.[91] The relationship with August Thalheimer (1884–1948), who died two years after this letter and with whom Frölich was closely associated in KPO times, is only sporadically hinted at, and is comparable to his relationship with Jacob Walcher, though it was not so violent and emotional, as it were, and did not end so dramatically.[92]

Letter 3 Willi Sauter to Paul Frölich, Ulm, 16 April 1947

> Even if we no longer talk of an organizational link or that we work mostly in the SPD, it is from the point of view that we want to do everything, to give our world of ideas a breakthrough to a greater extent than presently, in a separate group. Whether we will be successful remains to be seen. We would be very pleased if we were able to support our comrades who are still abroad, that we would be provided with the necessary material through the theoretical discussions and the events, especially among those comrades who have the basic idea of the events of each day, there is a great lack of relevant literature, since our comrades are those who have lost them either by confiscation of the Gestapo or by the results of the bombing war.[93]

---

[89] Paul Frölich [and Rosi Wolfstein] to Eberhard and Erna Brünen and Willi Kuhlmann (Duisburg), Kew Gardens, Aug. 24, 1946, in Klemm, "Paul Frölich," 206–211.

[90] Thanks to Julia Killet (Rosa Luxemburg Foundation) for this point of view.

[91] Frölich, *Rosa Luxemburg*, 145.

[92] Weber and Herbst, *Deutsche Kommunisten*, 930.

[93] Doc. No. 20: Willi Sauter to Paul Frölich (New York), Ulm, 16 Apr. 1947, in *Entscheidung für die SPD: Briefe Aufzeichnungen linker Sozialisten*, ed. Helga Grebing (Munich: Oldenbourg, 1984), 86.

In fact, theoretical texts of the pre-war and inter-war periods circulated very far in those days. Especially people like Fritz Lamm, who was sitting in Cuba in direct proximity to theorists like August Thalheimer, found it extremely difficult to obtain valuable literature.[94] The directional conflict implied here, as it should proceed in the context of democratization, is paradigmatic for the socialists in exile. Wolfstein and Frölich had made a clear decision here: the KPD was excluded, not necessarily because of political radicalism, but because of its cadre structure and orientation towards Moscow. Moreover, after the "Stalinist purges," only Stalinists remained in the party, and the anti-Stalinists Frölich and Wolfstein no longer wanted to have anything to do with them.[95] The looming SED, which at least embodied one of the earlier goals of the united front policy of the SAPD in its name, was also not an option due to its ties to Moscow.[96] Finally, there was the option of founding a third party between the SPD and the KPD in West Germany, but Frölich and Wolfstein no longer saw any prospects for the future. First, there would be a lack of a mass base, which was an absolute necessity for actively shaping politics. The Weimar Republic had already shown what could happen if the left-wing camp split too far. Thus, as a last resort, the motto was: back to the SPD. And that after more than 30 years![97]

Letter 4 Rosi Wolfstein [and Paul Frölich] to Käte Duncker, Kew Gardens, 8 February 1948

> My dear Kaethe(!), at first: a week ago, the package with the suit fabric went off. We, Lisa [Laub] and the Krauthammers,[98] have added a little packet each. Michael [Krauthammer] got the fabric, really beautiful and

---

[94] The same happened, for example, to Max Diamant (1908–1992) or Boris Goldenberg (1905–1980). In letters, the friends often asked each other for new publications or theoretical classics, because even those were not available. See Berlin Federal Archives, SAPMO, NY 4087, 54 (Estate Walcher), letter from Max Diamant to Jacob Walcher, Mexico City, Sept. 5, 1942, 2; Berlin Federal Archives, SAPMO, NY 4087, 55 (Estate Walcher), letter from Boris Goldenberg to [Jacob and Herta] Walcher and [Joseph and Erna] Lang, Havana, May 29, 1944.

[95] See Paul Frölich, *Zur Stalin-Legende* (Munich: E. W. Schumm, [1949]).

[96] Letter No. 6: Paul Frölich to Fritz Lamm, New York, Oct. 1, 1949, in Klemm, "Paul Frölich," 225–229, here 229.

[97] Ibid., 228–229.

[98] Dr. Georg Krauthammer, Ellen Krauthammer and Michael Krauthammer were close American friends of the Frölichs and the Dunckers and later settled in the GDR. Georg Krauthammer gave an interview about his time with Hermann and Käte Duncker in New York. See Berlin Federal Archives, SAPMO, DY 79 (Duncker Archive), 1611, also 1613. See also Berlin Federal Archives, SAPMO, NY 4445, 184.

very fine material, Hermann will outshine any other professor in this costume.[99] …

We are still well supplied with ice and snow. How often do we say that if Hermann were to flap around here this year, how many times would he fall? It is always black ice and you have to be able to balance quite well to stay on your feet. At the same time, we ask ourselves then: but how can he only flap around like that? Well, he is able to do it, luckily, and we wish him on to it: break a leg (so one must indeed wish it?[100]), so that he doesn't slip on the black ice![101]

The old friendship between the Frölichs and the Dunckers would last until their deaths. Of course, the Iron Curtain made all communication much more complex, but except for a short time in the 1920s, when Paul Frölich was part of the left-wing radicals, the four were friends for their whole lives. The earliest contact between Frölich and Hermann Duncker had to be before 1905. Therefore, the earliest letter is known, but its content shows that they knew each other well before that letter was written.[102]

Letter 5 Paul Frölich to Fritz Lamm, Kuhgarten [Kew Gardens],[103] 12 July 1947

But the problems! Yes, maybe we are quite united, we are only concerned with emphasis, on the circumstances in which we are debating. And, of course, you have to sprinkle the necessary grain of salt on whatever you

---

[99] Hermann Duncker was a professor teaching the history of social movements and Dean of the Faculty of Social Sciences at Rostock University from September 1947. See *Deutsche Kommunisten: Biographisches Handbuch 1918 bis 1945*, eds. Herrmann Weber and Andreas Herbst (Berlin: Dietz, 2008), 202–203. For his biography, see Mario Keßler and Heinz Deutschland, *Hermann Duncker: Sozialdemokratischer "Wanderprediger," Spartakist, Gewerkschaftslehrer* (Hamburg: VSA-Verlag, 2001).

[100] The German "Hals- und Beinbruch" means, literally, "neck and leg fracture." It doesn't appear to make any sense because it is a translation of a Yiddish phrase, "hazlóche un bróche," which means "good fortune" and "blessing." Several German writers used the apparently nonsensical phrase "Hals und Beinbruch" in poems or novels—for example, Hans Jakob Christoffel (1668), Hermann Lön (1911) and Karl Bleibtreu (1915). See Christoph Gutknecht, "Viel Glück und viel Segen: Wie aus der hebräischen Redewendung 'Hazloche und Broche' 'Hals- und Beinbruch' wurde," *Jüdische Allgemeine* (online). July 20, 2015. www.juedische-allgemeine.de/article/view/id/22853.

[101] Rosi Wolfstein [and Paul Frölich] to Käte Duncker, Kew Gardens, Feb. 8, 1948, Berlin Federal Archives, SAPMO, NY 4445, 262. Rosi Wolfstein really used the blinking emoticon with an exclamation mark. But this is a phenomenon that has been known in Germany since the late nineteenth century. See "Telegraphische Zeichenkunst," *Deutsche Postzeitung* VII (Nov. 16, 1896), No. 22: 497.

[102] Letter No. 0461 Hermann to Käte Duncker, Dresden, Aug. 14, 1905, in Duncker, *Tagebuch*, 936.

[103] This German word means "cow garden." It is unclear why Paul Frölich chose this word instead of Kew Gardens.

say. A fair amount of salt is needed if you set up something like a principle that requires you to shoot defensively [*to the Soviet Union*, R.A.]. This is not quite understandable and it will be less so if you continue: Who shoots at the Soviet Union, shoots offensively. Well, I think shooting is necessary, and that's more than just criticizing. If what the SU represents, what determines all political action, tramples down the working class of any country, then it means shooting. One might say that one is on the defensive, but the shot is directed against the nature of the regime. It is not necessary to put this regime on the right path, but to overcome it. Therefore, the crucial question is from which front one shoots. If I hear about the people who call themselves socialists and sit in the editorial office of the local *New Leader*, who can't have the war against Russia fast enough and greedily swallow everything that serves this noble purpose, then I sit down at the table of the "hard-tested." This Russophobic species is indeed spreading in a frightening way. One recently sent me a confession: 1. Restoration of the teachings of Marx, 2. Fundamental rejection of any kind of planned economy (e.g. also of the English), 3. Alliance with the conservative forces in the world, which alone are effective in fighting fascism and forming a wall against it! ... Of course, it must be clearly stated that such "Marxist" anti-Soviet hysterics are not part of our neighborhood.[104]

In the 1933 exile in Prague, which Lämmchen and Frölich had to live through together (which was not easy for either of them[105]), both the anti-Stalinists looked with a smile and a crying eye toward Moscow and founded the "Union of the hard-tested friends of the Soviet Union" as a joke. In the context of a letter from Lämmchen to Frölich on 6 June 1947, which, in spite of all criticism, did not cause any real scandal, but rather resulted in the reply letter presented here in excerpts, Lämmchen reminded his friend of the principles of this association for a while to offer the Soviet Union a chance to make amends.[106]

The fact that Lämmchen, as already suggested, had a good relationship with Jacob Walcher for all these years was certainly not the reason for the occasional discord between him and Frölich. On the contrary, the letter was too polite to hold more decisive criticism from Frölich if he did not agree with him on a theoretical level.[107] This was especially in the magazine

---

[104] Paul Frölich to Fritz "Lämmchen" Lamm, Kuhgarten (!) [Kew Gardens], July 12, 1947, in Klemm, "Paul Frölich," 220–221.

[105] See, for example, the International Institute of Social History, Amsterdam, Fritz Brupbacher Papers/61: Frölich, Paul, letter from Paul Frölich to Fritz Brupbacher, Prague, Feb. 7, 1934.

[106] Klemm, "Paul Frölich," 221 n. 4.

[107] Gregor Kritidis, *Linkssozialistische Opposition in der Ära Adenauer: Ein Beitrag zur Frühgeschichte der Bundesrepublik Deutschland* (Hanover: Offizin, 2008), 63, 72.

Funke: Aussprachehefte für internationale sozialistische Politik,[108] the journal that Lämmchen edited after his return to Germany. Frölich and Henry "Jacky" Jacoby both wrote for this journal. In this same magazine, in the eleventh issue, of April 1953, there was a moving obituary for "Jacky's" old friend, Paul Frölich, who had gone through hell and high water with him and whose friendship survived to the last, notwithstanding all the transnational problems. The obituary says:

> But we loved you not only because of your experience and your knowledge, as much as these pleased us and as masterfully you could dress them in words. We loved you because we felt that everything was real on you because we knew you would never succumb to the bureaucratic spirit, because you were a living person, because you could sympathize with all human suffering, because everything about you was clean and clear.[109]

Conclusion

As we can see, Paul Frölich and Rosi Wolfstein-Frölich were one part of a much bigger exile network in the United States, which was connected to many emigrants not only in the transatlantic world but also back home in Europe. Some of their old friends were murdered by Hitler or Stalin, and some family members too, like Wolfstein's two sisters. Frölich's son Hans was forced into a concentration camp as early as his father but survived the Nazi era.[110] The transatlantic network was based on the exchange of letters. The communication of the participants was always detailed, concerned about the fate of the German post-war landscape and characterized by the insufficient transmission of information through the media from one part of the network to another.

The period of the American exile was shaped by combat against Social Democratic reformism and Stalin's conformism, and by the reestablishment of a post-1945 line for a Marx-oriented new-line Socialism in Germany (and Europe). Some of the friendships, such as those between Paul Frölich and Fritz Lamm, fell apart owing to the disagreement over developments

---

[108] "Sparks. Pamphlets for international socialist policy."

[109] Sebastian Franck [= Henry Jacoby], "Paul Frölich ist tot," in *Funken. Aussprachehefte für internationale sozialistische Politik* 3 (Apr. 1953) No. 11: 1. The alias Sebastian Franck refers to the theologian, writer and publicist who began his career as a Catholic priest, then converted to Martin Luther's reformed Christian church and ultimately took a radical reformist and anti-authoritarian path. For his biography, see Patrick Hayden-Roy, *The Inner World and the Outer World: A Biography of Sebastian Franck* (New York: Peter Lang, 1994).

[110] *Information from Edda Tasiemka.* See also State Archives Hamburg, Reparation Office, 47133, letter from Hans Frölich to the Hamburg Reparation Office, Hamburg-Altona, May 18, 1961.

9.4 Willy Brandt, Rosi Frölich and Max Diamant in the AWO retirement home,
Frankfurt am Main
© Max Mannheimer (Frank Ahland)

in Germany after 1945. Others, such as Ruth Fischer, show that old discrepancies from the time before the Nazi rule were only due to shared suffering, such as involuntary exile. Fischer regretted this fact and wrote to Wolfstein in 1953, after Frölich's death, that she would have liked to have been reconciled with him.[111] Sadly, it did not happen. Before Frölich passed away, the two would never see each other again—even during the entire length of their exile.

Wolfstein, who survived her husband by many years, kept in touch with friends from all phases of her volatile life. A picture can speak more than a multitude of words at this point to symbolize how important the personal component of the Wolfstein/Frölich network was throughout the years (Figure 9.4). In the photograph, Rosi Frölich sits in her Arbeiterwohlfahrt (AWO) retirement home in Frankfurt am Main. On her right, sits Willy Brandt, ex-Chancellor of the Federal Republic of Germany, an SPD party comrade and her friend since their time in exile in Paris.[112] On Rosi's left sits

---

[111] Letter No. 125: Ruth Fischer to Rose Frölich-Wolfstein, New York, Mar. 28, 1953, in *Abtrünnig wider Willen*, 298.

[112] The connection between Paul Frölich and Willy Brandt was mentioned at the beginning of this chapter.

Max Diamant (1908–1992), also an SPD party member, and, since her time in the Prussian state parliament, a friend of Wolfstein. She advised Diamant, who was also a member of the KPD, at that time after an educational trip to Russia, as she gained a very early idea about what was happening there with young people in party schools, but without success.[113] The photograph was taken by Holocaust survivor Max Mannheimer (1920–2016), who was Rosi Frölich's chess partner for many years.[114] A few months after her death, Brandt spoke at a memorial service in Frankfurt am Main for his old friend.

To address the questions posed at the outset, Wolfstein and Frölich always observed the changes in the twentieth century under the most extreme conditions. When the Stalinists came to power, they were marginalized from the party. When Hitler came to power, they had to leave the country, and later their place of escape, head over heels each time. In the United States, their seemingly safe place of exile, they were always exposed to the sword of Damocles by the grassroots of anti-communism. Therefore, they also broke off contact with some former friends, especially Jacob and Herta Walcher. They kept in contact with others, such as the Dunckers, Fritz Lamm and Henry Jacoby, for the entire time, as well as with foreign SAPD groups in Cuba, the United Kingdom, Israel, Germany and Scandinavia. In the reconstruction of a post-fascist left in Europe, they finally positioned themselves on the left wing of West German social democracy after many years of strife and doubt. The SED, a new SAPD, or the KPD were never an option for them. But through their network of numerous friends and former comrades that could overcome all transnational obstacles, they actively helped shape post-war German society in detail. This is reason for the creation of the double Wolfstein–Frölich biography, and it is also the reason to continue with academic work on this double biography in the future.

Works Cited

Archival Sources
Foundation of the Archives of Parties and Mass Organizations of the GDR in the Berlin Federal Archives (SAPMO)
Gedenkbuch: Opfer der Verfolgung der Juden unter der nationalsozialistischen Gewaltherrschaft in Deutschland 1933–1945:
www.bundesarchiv.de/gedenkbuch/de974228. Accessed May 28, 2017
www.bundesarchiv.de/gedenkbuch/de1183519. Accessed May 28, 2017
www.bundesarchiv.de/gedenkbuch/de296712. Accessed May 28, 2017

---

[113] Beate Brunner, *Ein Gespräch mit Max Diamant*, "…begleitete mich ein ganzes Stück meines Lebens," in Ahland and Brunner, *"Sie wollte und konnte nie etwas Halbes tun,"* 41–45, here 42–43.

[114] Correspondence between Frank Ahland and the author, Dortmund, Feb. 18, 2017.

SAPMO, DY 79 (Duncker-Archive), 1611, 1613
SAPMO, NY 4002, 48 (Estate Rosa Luxemburg)
SAPMO, NY 4087, 54–57 (Estate Jacob and Herta Walcher)
SAPMO, NY 4445, 171, 184, 250, 262 (Estate Hermann and Käte Duncker)

Records of the Central Intelligence Agency (CIA Archives), National Archives and Records Administration, College Park, MD
Information Report from June 29, 1948, "sanitized" copy of CIA-RDP93-00415R003200030003-9

Columbia University, New York, Butler Library
Varian Fry Collection I 1D

Institute for City History of Frankfurt am Main
Civil registry records, No. 437/V (1953), Mar. 21, 1953
Death records, 1953, No. 437/V
S1/452, No. 8 (Estate Alfhart)

International Institute of Social History, Amsterdam
Fritz Brupbacher Papers/61

Leipzig City Archive
Birth Record No. 460/1884 (Volkmarsdorf)
Civil Registration of Neusellerhausen, 1882–1891, A–L, PoA, No. 785, F, cont. No. 40
Civil Registration of Volkmarsdorf, 1885–1888, A–G, PoA, No. 1039, F, cont. No. 184
F 2535, Questionnaire

Russian State Archive of Socio-Political History, Moscow
Fond 340, Opis 4, Folder 271

Salomon-Ludwig-Steinheim Institute, Essen
Gidal Photo Archive 3875 (Portrait of Rosi Wolfstein, 1921)

State Archives Hamburg
Reparation Office, 47133

Published Primary Sources
Abtrünnig wider Willen: Aus Briefen und Manuskripten des Exils, ed. Peter Lübbe. Munich: Oldenbourg, 1990.
Die Gründung der KPD: Protokoll und Materialien des Gründungsparteitages der Kommunistischen Partei Deutschlands 1918/1919, ed. Hermann Weber. Berlin: Dietz, 1993.

Duncker, Käte and Hermann Duncker. *Ein Tagebuch in Briefen*, ed. Heinz Deutschland. Berlin: Dietz, 2016.

Entscheidung für die SPD: Briefe Aufzeichnungen linker Sozialisten, ed. Helga Grebing. Munich: Oldenbourg, 1984.

Frölich, Paul. *Im radikalen Lager: Politische Autobiographie, 1890–1921*, ed. Reiner Tosstorff. Berlin: BasisDruck, 2013.

Jacoby, Henry. "Begegnung mit Paul Frölich." *Internationale wissenschaftliche Korrespondenz* 2 (1983): 181–186.

——. *Davongekommen: 10 Jahre Exil 1936–1946. Prag, Paris, Montauban, New York, Washington: Erlebnisse und Begegnungen.* Frankfurt am Main: Sendler-Verlag, [1982].

Luxemburg, Rosa. *Gesammelte Werke*, vol. 7/1, *1907 to 1918*, eds. Annelies Laschitza and Eckard Müller. Berlin: Dietz, 2017.

Minute Book of the German Reichstag. Berlin: Bureau of the Reichstag, 1924.

"Telegraphische Zeichenkunst." *Deutsche Postzeitung* VII (Nov. 16, 1896), No. 22: 497.

Secondary Works

Ahland, Frank. *Rosi Wolfstein in Witten*. Witten: self-published, 2007.

"Alma Rosali (genannt Rosi) Wolfstein." In *"…vergessen kann man das nicht": Wittener Jüdinnen und Juden unter dem Nationalsozialismus*, eds. Martina Kliner-Lintzen and Siegfried Pape, 293–294. Bochum: Winklerverlag, 1991.

Altieri, Riccardo. "Paul Frölich, American Exile, and Communist Discourse about the Russian Revolution." *American Communist History* 17, no. 2 (2018): 220–231.

Anon. "Brandt—Nr. F 2019." *Der Spiegel* 36 (1976): 76–79.

Benz, Michael. *Der unbequeme Streiter Fritz Lamm. Jude, Linkssozialist, Emigrant 1911–1977: Eine politische Biographie.* Essen: Klartext, 2007.

Brunner, Beate. "'Alles kritisch nachprüfen…' Rosi Wolfstein—eine der bedeutendsten Frauen der Arbeiterbewegung." In *Wittener Frauengeschichte(n): Dokumentation anläßlich einer frauengeschichtlichen Stadtrundfahrt*, ed. Arbeitskreis Frauengeschichte, 39–41. Witten: Laube, 1992.

——. *Ein Gespräch mit Max Diamant*: "…begleitete mich ein ganzes Stück meines Lebens." In *"Sie wollte und konnte nie etwas Halbes tun": Die Sozialistin Rosi Wolfstein-Frölich 1914 bis 1924*, eds. Frank Ahland and Beate Brunner, 41–45. Witten: Rosi-Wolfstein-Gesellschaft e.V., 1995.

Degen, Bernard and Julia Richers, eds. *Zimmerwald und Kiental: Weltgeschichte auf dem Dorfe*. Zurich: Chronos Verlag, 2015.

Dischereit, Esther. "'…eigentlich könnte es doch viel besser und anders sein.'" In *"Sie wollte und konnte nie etwas Halbes tun": Die Sozialistin Rosi Wolfstein-Frölich 1914 bis 1924*, eds. Frank Ahland and Beate Brunner, 22–28. Witten: Rosi-Wolfstein-Gesellschaft e.V., 1995).

Engel, Gerhard. *Johann Knief—ein unvollendetes Leben*. Berlin: Dietz, 2011.

Franck, Sebastian [= Henry Jacoby]. "Paul Frölich ist tot." *Funken. Aussprachehefte für internationale sozialistische Politik* 3 (Apr. 1953) No. 11: 1.

Fritz, Bernd Dieter. *Die Kommunistische Arbeitsgemeinschaft (KAG) im Vergleich mit der KPO und SAP: Eine Studie zur politischen Ideologie des deutschen "Rechts"-Kommunismus in der Zeit der Weimarer Republik.* Ph.D. thesis, Bonn, s.n., 1966.

Frölich, Paul. *1789—Die große Zeitenwende. Von der Bürokratie des Absolutismus zum Parlament der Revolution.* Frankfurt am Main: Europäische Verlagsanstalt, 1957.

——. *Rosa Luxemburg: Gedanke und Tat.* Paris: Éditions nouvelles internationales, 1939.

——. *Zur Stalin-Legende.* Munich: E. W. Schumm, [1949].

[Frölich, Paul]. *Was kommt nach Hitler? Probleme der deutschen Revolution*, ed. the SAPD. Brussels: WUYTS, 1937.

"Frölich, Paul." In *Biographisches Handbuch der deutschsprachigen Emigration nach 1933.* Institut für Zeitgeschichte (Munich)/Research Foundation for Jewish Immigration (New York), 203–204. Munich: De Gruyter, 1980.

——. In *Biographisches Staatshandbuch: Lexikon der Politik, Presse und Publizistik*, vol. 1, ed. Wilhelm Kosch, 363. Berne: Francke, 1963.

——. (*1884–†1953). In *Deutsche Kommunisten: Biographisches Handbuch 1918 bis 1945*, eds. Herrmann Weber and Andreas Herbst, 271–272. Berlin: Dietz, 2008.

——. In *Lexikon Linker Leitfiguren*, ed. Karljosef Kreter, 132–134. Frankfurt am Main: Büchergilde Gutenberg, 1988.

"Frölich, Rose." In *Biographisches Handbuch der deutschsprachigen Emigration nach 1933.* Institut für Zeitgeschichte (Munich)/Research Foundation for Jewish Immigration (New York), 203–204. Munich: De Gruyter, 1980.

Fry, Varian. "The Massacre of Jews in Europe." *The New Republic*, Dec. 21, 1942: 816–820.

Grebing, Helga. *Lehrstücke in Solidarität: Briefe und Biographien deutscher Sozialisten.* Stuttgart: DVA, 1983.

Hayden-Roy, Patrick. *The Inner World and the Outer World: A Biography of Sebastian Franck.* New York: Peter Lang, 1994.

Hedeler, Wladislaw. "Vier Bemerkungen zu einem Lebenslauf." In *"Sie wollte und konnte nie etwas Halbes tun": Die Sozialistin Rosi Wolfstein-Frölich 1914 bis 1924*, eds. Frank Ahland and Beate Brunner, 19–21. Witten: Rosi-Wolfstein-Gesellschaft e.V., 1995.

Heid, Ludger. "Wolfstein-Frölich, Rosi (Rose). Partei- und Gewerkschaftspolitikerin." In *Jüdische Frauen im 19. und 20. Jahrhundert: Lexikon zu Leben und Werk*, eds. Jutta Dick and Marina Sassenberg, 403–406. Hamburg: Rowohlt, 1993.

Hobsbawm, Eric. *The Age of Capital: 1848–1875.* New York: Vintage Books, 1975.

——. *The Age of Empire: 1875–1914.* London: Weidenfeld & Nicolson, 1987.

——. *The Age of Extremes: The Short Twentieth Century, 1914–1991*. New York: Vintage Books, 1994.

——. *The Age of Revolution: Europe 1789–1848*. New York: World Publishing, 1962.

Jacobs, Reinhard. *Terror unterm Hakenkreuz: Ort des Erinnerns in Niedersachsen und Sachsen-Anhalt*. Berlin: Otto-Brenner-Stiftung, 2001.

Keßler, Mario. *A Political Biography of Arkadij Maslow, 1891–1941: Dissident Against His Will*. London: Palgrave Macmillan, 2020.

——. *Ruth Fischer: Ein Leben mit und gegen Kommunisten (1895–1961)*. Cologne: Böhlau, 2013.

Keßler, Mario and Heinz Deutschland. *Hermann Duncker: Sozialdemokratischer "Wanderprediger," Spartakist, Gewerkschaftslehrer*. Hamburg: VSA-Verlag, 2001.

Kinner, Klaus. "Paul Frölich." In *Demokratische Wege: Deutsche Lebensläufe aus fünf Jahrhunderten*, eds. Manfred Asendorf and Rolf von Bockel, 196–197. Stuttgart: Springer, 1997.

Klemm, Bernd. "Paul Frölich (1884–1953). Politische Orientierung und theoretische Reflexionen von Linkssozialisten nach dem Zweiten Weltkrieg. Sechs Briefe Paul Frölichs aus der Emigration (1946–1949) an ehemalige KPO/SAP-Mitglieder in Berlin, Duisburg, Offenbach, Wesel, La Habana/Cuba und Stuttgart." *Internationale wissenschaftliche Korrespondenz* 2 (1983): 186–229.

Kritidis, Gregor. *Linkssozialistische Opposition in der Ära Adenauer: Ein Beitrag zur Frühgeschichte der Bundesrepublik Deutschland*. Hanover: Offizin, 2008.

Langkau-Alex, Ursula. *Deutsche Volksfront 1932–1939: Zwischen Berlin, Paris, Prag und Moskau*, 3 vols. Berlin: Akademie-Verlag, 2004–2005.

Lenz, Gertrud. "Gertrud Meyer: Eine politische Biographie." Ph.D. thesis, Universität Flensburg, 2010.

Luban, Ottokar. "Rosi Wolfsteins antimilitaristische Aktivitäten 1916/17: Neue Quellenfunde." *Mitteilungsblatt des Instituts für soziale Bewegung* 44 (2010): 123–133.

Massmann, Ernst. "Frölich, Paul." In *Geschichte der deutschen Arbeiterbewegung: Biographisches Lexikon*, eds. Rudolf Grau et al., 145–146. Berlin: Dietz, 1970.

Meyer, Angelika. "'Gesucht von der Gestapo': Varian Fry und die amerikanische Fluchthilfeorganisation 'Emergency Rescue Committee.'" In *Ohne zu zögern. Varian Fry: Berlin—Marseille—New York*, ed. Aktives Museum Faschismus und Widerstand, Berlin, 126–149. Leipzig: Messedruck, 2008.

"Sie wollte und konnte nie etwas Halbes tun": Die Sozialistin Rosi Wolfstein-Frölich 1914 bis 1924, eds. Frank Ahland and Beate Brunner. Witten: Rosi-Wolfstein-Gesellschaft e.V., 1995.

Steinacker, Christian. "Rosi Wolfstein—Ein Leben in der Arbeiterbewegung." *StadtMagazin Witten* 88 (Dec. 2013–Jan. 2014): 7.

"Steinberg, Helene." In *Jüdische Familien in Münster 1918–1945*, vol. 1, *Biographisches Lexikon*, eds. Gisela Möllenhoff and Rita Schlautmann-Overmeyer, 429. Münster: Westfälisches Dampfboot, 2001.

Teetz, Christiane. *Otto Stolten und die Sozialdemokratie in Hamburg bis zum Ende der Kaiserzeit*. Münster: Lit-Verlag, 2004.

Ulrich, Volker. "Weltkrieg und Novemberrevolution: die Hamburger Arbeiterbewegung 1914 bis 1918." In *Hamburg im ersten Viertel des 20. Jahrhunderts: die Zeit des Politikers Otto Stolten. Sieben Abhandlungen*, ed. Heinrich Erdmann, 118–194. Hamburg: Landeszentrale für politische Bildung, 2000.

Vinschen, Klaus-Dieter. "Rosi Wolfstein-Frölich." In *Juden und deutsche Arbeiterbewegung bis 1933: Soziale Utopie und religiös-kulturelle Traditionen*, eds. Ludger Heid and Arnold Paucker, 165–176. Tübingen: Mohr Siebeck, 1992.

Weber, Herrmann. "Rosi Wolfstein: Eine zweite Rosa Luxemburg." In *Wittener Biografische Porträts*, eds. Frank Ahland and Matthias Dudde, 119–124. Witten: Ruhrstadt-Verlag, 2000.

"Wolfstein (Frölich), Rosi." In *Deutsche Kommunisten: Biographisches Handbuch 1918 bis 1945*, eds. Herrmann Weber and Andreas Herbst, 1043–1044. Berlin: Dietz, 2008.

Web

Becker, Peter von. "Der amerikanische Engel Fluchthelfer Varian Fry: eine Erinnerung zum 100." *Der Tagesspiegel* (online), Oct. 14, 2007. www.tagesspiegel.de/kultur/der-amerikanische-engel-fluchthelfer-varian-fry-eine-erinnerung-zum-100-/1068236.html. Accessed Nov. 28, 2017.

Föhl, Thomas. Family profile of Paul Wolfstein. www.geni.com/people/Paul-Wolfstein/6000000050839443417. Accessed Nov. 28, 2017.

Gutknecht, Christoph. "Viel Glück und viel Segen: Wie aus der hebräischen Redewendung 'Hazloche un Broche' 'Hals- und Beinbruch' wurde." *Jüdische Allgemeine* (online). July 20, 2015. www.juedische-allgemeine.de/article/view/id/22853. Accessed Nov. 28, 2017.

Interviews

Mail from Frank Ahland to the author, Dortmund, Feb. 18, 2017.

Telephone information from Paul Frölich's daughter, Edda Tasiemka (London), June 28, 2017.

10

Ossip K. Flechtheim (1909–1998)

Political Scientist and Futurologist between Europe and North America

Mario Keßler

The political scientist Ossip Kurt Flechtheim (1909–1998) lived in different countries on both sides of the Atlantic: Germany, France, Switzerland and the United States. He specialized in various fields of research—contemporary history, political science and future studies—and he taught and wrote in several languages. Flechtheim belonged to three different parties of the left: before 1933 he was a member of the Communist Party of Germany (KPD). After his return to Berlin in 1952 he joined the Social Democratic Party (SPD), which he then left in 1962. From 1979 until his death Flechtheim was a member of the Alternative Liste that was part of the ecological Green Party.[1]

Flechtheim's work, which includes nearly twenty books and a great number of edited volumes, is devoted to crucial problems of the twentieth and the twenty-first centuries: war and peace, democracy and dictatorship, fascism and anti-fascism, the north–south conflict, and capitalism and communism in its various forms. The following paragraphs give a biographical overview and try to explain how Flechtheim's life's path between Europe and America influenced his thinking as a versatile scholar and radical socialist.

Like other radical left intellectuals, Flechtheim's life was determined by exile, and he therefore had to adjust his life to different environments, broadening his network and intensifying his own standing within a global radical community alike. The present chapter aims to point to some aspects in Flechtheim's life as a radical migrant, whose knowledge gained from these experiences, as it became more globalized and shaped according to different cultural encounters. Flechtheim consequently represents a transatlantic radical, as they were "created" by the rise of fascism in general, and National

---

[1] This essay is mainly based on Mario Keßler, *Ossip K. Flechtheim: Politischer Wissenschaftler und Zukunftsdenker (1909–1998)* (Cologne: Böhlau, 2007). The author is indebted to Professor Renate Bridenthal (New York) for her advice and help.

Socialism in particular, the rule of the Nazi dictatorship in Germany, World War II and the Cold War. These transnational events consequently determined Flechtheim's life as a radical on both sides of the Atlantic—a life that can be closely linked to the development of international socialism. And his life offers more than just an interesting biography.

The Making of a Socialist Scholar

The benchmarks in Ossip Flechtheim's life are the watersheds of Germany's modern history. He was born in Nikolayev, Ukraine, on 5 March 1909. In 1910, the family moved to Germany, at first to Münster, Westphalia, his father's birthplace, and then to Düsseldorf.

Ossip Flechtheim's father Hermann (1880–1960) was a grain dealer and owned a small factory. His mother Olga, née Farber (1884–1964), was born in Moscow. The parents spoke to their son both in German and in Russian, thus giving him a multicultural background. Ossip's uncle Alfred (1878–1937) was a Berlin-based art dealer of international reputation. The Flechtheims represented the synthesis of humanistic education and enlightenment that characterized the Jewish educated middle and upper class in Germany. Growing up with a profound knowledge of German and Russian literature, Ossip Flechtheim became, at an early stage, immune to the nationalist climate that dominated imperial Germany and particularly its institutions of higher learning. "There was no room for patriotism in our family," as Flechtheim emphasized decades later.[2] The hope for a German-Jewish symbiosis did not lead the Flechtheims to identify with German nationalism. It was this attitude that was also at the root of Ossip Flechtheim's mistrust for and lack of interest in political Zionism, although he never kept his Jewish origin a secret. "I was and I remained Jew and German, European, *Weltbürger*, and a citizen of a coming better world," as he emphasized later.[3]

At his high school in Düsseldorf, Flechtheim became a close friend with Hans (later John H.) Herz (1908–2005). This friendship would last throughout their lives. Both families were secular Jews and supported the democratic experiment on German soil, the Weimar Republic.[4]

---

[2] Ossip K. Flechtheim, "In unserer Familie war kein Platz für Patriotismus," in *Die andere Erinnerung: Gespräche mit jüdischen Wissenschaftlern im Exil*, ed. Hajo Funke (Frankfurt am Main: Fischer Taschenbuch-Verlag, 1989), 422.

[3] Ossip K. Flechtheim, "Heute noch skeptischer als 1962," in *Fremd im eigenen Land: Juden in der Bundesrepublik*, eds. Henryk M. Broder and Michel R. Lang (Frankfurt am Main: Fischer, 1979), 132.

[4] See Herz's autobiography, *Vom Überleben: Wie ein Weltbild entstand* (Düsseldorf: Droste, 1984), 41 and *passim*.

In 1927, after graduating from high school with distinction, Flechtheim went to Freiburg with Herz, where both became university law students. Unlike his friend, Flechtheim became a member of the German Communist Party. In 1928, Flechtheim studied for one semester in Paris at the Sorbonne. At the University of Berlin, where he continued to study, Flechtheim worked with the Communist Students' League. There he got in contact with people who later became famous as scholars and political writers. Among them were Richard Löwenthal (1908–1991), at this time National Chairman of the Communist Students' League, and the future Bismarck biographer Ernst Engelberg (1909–2010), who succeeded Löwenthal as chair.

In 1931, Flechtheim traveled to Soviet Russia for the first time (it was only in 1964 that he was able to visit the country again). Since he spoke Russian fluently, Flechtheim was able to communicate with various people. "All in all, my impression was rather positive," he noted decades later. There was "still much enthusiasm and hope, although the economic situation was very difficult." It seemed to Flechtheim that the Soviet Union was a country obviously moving towards socialism, although Joseph Stalin's (1878–1953) negative impact on the politics of the KPD and the Communist International could hardly be neglected.[5]

As a communist student, Flechtheim turned to those party circles that doubted the Stalinist notion that a proletarian revolution was under way in Germany. They also opposed the designation of Social Democrats as Social Fascists. However, this new theory of "Social Fascism" found a positive echo among the KPD rank-and-file, because of the enormous amount of suffering and despair that virtually every social stratum was subjected to during the Great Depression of the early 1930s. Germany, and the world at large, was completely unprepared for that degree of economic downfall. The political climate in Germany provided suitable conditions of growth for revolutionary illusions, but also for fascist ideas, while the republican order became more and more discredited.

A small group of Communists and Social Democrats formed a clandestine organization called Neu Beginnen (New Beginnings), often called Die Organisation or Org.[6] The group sought to work inside the Communist and the Social Democratic Parties in order to prevent internecine warfare, which,

---

[5] Flechtheim, "Kein Platz für Patriotismus," 428. Around the same time, Isaac Deutscher (1907–1967), who would later become the biographer of Joseph Stalin and Leon Trotsky (1879–1940), was in the Soviet Union for around six months. Deutscher's time in the Soviet Union made him a critique of the emerging Stalinist order.

[6] For the politics of Neu Beginnen, see Jan Foitzik, *Zwischen den Fronten: Zur Politik, Organisation und Funktion linker politischer Kleinorganisationen im Widerstand 1933 bis 1939/40* (Bonn: J.H.W. Dietz, 1986); Terence Renaud, "Restarting Socialism: The New Beginning Group and the Problem of Renewal on the German Left, 1930–1970" (Ph.D.

as Neu Beginnen predicted correctly, would help the Nazi Party to gain power. Unlike many Communists and Social Democrats, the Neu Beginnen members clearly saw that Nazism was not a temporary phenomenon. Richard Löwenthal, who already had been expelled from the KPD, was among the founders of Neu Beginnen. Flechtheim, still a KPD member, joined this group. There he found comrades such as Robert Jungk, who became like Flechtheim one of the founders of the discipline of futurology and one of the latter's closest friends.[7]

On 30 January 1933, Hitler became German chancellor. This date saw the destruction of communist as well as social democratic illusions regarding the impact of the Nazis' seizure of power. The enmity between the two workers' parties made the victory of the Nazis possible. No serious attempt was made to offer open opposition.

It was at this time, right after the beginning of the Nazi rule, that Flechtheim left the KPD to invest all his political energy in Neu Beginnen's underground work. In an illegal manifesto, Neu Beginnen stated that "the collapse of German Social Democracy dates not from its passivity in the final crisis of 1933, but from the opportunity it missed in [the ill-fated revolution of] 1918. It bitterly paid for the illusion … that a working class may securely enjoy the fruits of political democracy, while the reality of power remains in the hands of the possessing class."[8] Under difficult circumstances, Flechtheim managed to continue his university studies. In 1934, he submitted his dissertation on "Hegel's Theory of Criminal Law" at the University of Cologne.[9]

After the Nazis' seizure of power, Flechtheim had no chance to get a position in public service or even to work as a registered lawyer. He had to dissolve his parents' household in Düsseldorf and made a very modest living from limited and part-time working as an associate in the legal profession. In September 1935, Flechtheim was arrested. When interrogated, he was able to play down his clandestine activities for Neu Beginnen, thus being released from prison after twenty-two days. He went to Brussels to meet his comrades, who told him that there was no future for him in Nazi Germany.[10]

---

thesis, University of California at Berkeley, 2015). The dissertation will soon be published as *New Lefts: The Making of a Radical Tradition, 1930–1970.*

[7] The term used today is future studies. See also Ziauddin Sardar, *Rescuing All Our Futures: The Future of Futures Studies* (Westport, CT: Praeger, 1999).

[8] Miles [i.e., Walter Löwenheim], *Socialism's New Beginning: A Manifesto from the Underground Germany* (New York: League for Industrial Democracy, 1934), 5.

[9] Ossip K. Flechtheim, *Hegels Strafrechtstheorie* (Berlin: Duncker & Humblot, 1975).

[10] See Flechtheim's curriculum vitae, undated (*c.*1940) in his Collected Papers at Deutsche National Bibliothek, German Exile Archive 1933–1945, Frankfurt am Main (cited henceforth as Flechtheim Papers) and Flechtheim, "Kein Platz für Patriotismus," 430.

From Brussels, Flechtheim went to Switzerland. He was fortunate enough to get a fellowship from the Institut universitaire de haute études internationales, the graduate school of the League of Nations in Geneva. Its directors, William Rappard (1883–1958) and Carl Jacob Burckhardt (1891–1974), hired a number of excellent university professors who had been dismissed in Germany, Austria or Italy. Among them was Hans Kelsen (1881–1973), Flechtheim's law teacher from his Cologne days.

Like Flechtheim, John H. Herz and Ernst Engelberg worked as research fellows in Geneva. It was Hans Kelsen who advised him to investigate the origins of contemporary Soviet ideology in relation to Soviet legal theory, but also within the framework of international communist politics. Thus, Flechtheim submitted a thesis on "Bolshevism and its Revolutionary Ideological Origins."

In his early writings on the subject, Flechtheim refuted the traditional approach that depicted Soviet and international communism as a theory of conspiracy. He saw the reason for the seductiveness of communist ideology in the fact that it combined characteristics of a powerful mass movement with that of a centralized "World Party" and with that of an illegally and effectively operating organization. Flechtheim emphasized that the social nature of Soviet society should be problematized as central to the analysis. He did not see Stalinist bureaucracy, the winner of the social upheavals of the 1930s, as a new capitalist class in Marxist disguise, as many foreign observers did at this time. The new bureaucratic elites "do not acquire the produced surplus value. It rather burdens future development [through its existence]."[11] The Communist International, once founded to inspire communist revolutions outside the Soviet Union, changed its function: the Comintern's current main objective was, as Flechtheim stated, to support Soviet politics.

Flechtheim made clear that the political aims and ethical principles of communism were incompatible with those of fascism, but he did not exclude political cooperation between the two movements once and for all. If the Soviet Union found a political agreement with fascist powers, "the Communist International would be directed to support this line, even if such a situation seems to be unlikely at the moment or in the near future."[12] Only a few months after these lines were written, Germany and Soviet Russia concluded their treaty of 23 August 1939 after the West refused to make alliances with the Soviet Union. By then, Flechtheim had already left Europe for the United States.

---

[11] See Ossip K. Flechtheim, *Weltkommunismus im Wandel* (Frankfurt am Main: E.V.A., 1965), 113. This collection contains several of Flechtheim's essays and papers from the 1930s.

[12] Ibid., 151.

Transatlantic Scholarship: From Europe to America and Back

Early on in 1939, Flechtheim saw clearly that the Swiss authorities would not allow him to stay in their country. While still in Geneva, he established contacts with the Institute of Social Research. Its director, Max Horkheimer (1895–1973), anticipating the Nazi takeover in Germany, had been wise enough to transfer the institute's estates from Frankfurt to Geneva as early as 1932. Horkheimer offered Flechtheim a fellowship at the institute, which provided the German academic refugee with a chance to go to New York when the institute was transferred there in 1939.

In February of that year, Flechtheim arrived in New York. On 5 July he applied for the First Papers to become an American citizen.[13] At the institute he cooperated closely with Franz L. Neumann (1900–1954), another refugee scholar from Germany. Neumann's book *Behemoth*, the groundbreaking study of Nazi Germany, profited from Flechtheim's expertise. Flechtheim, as Neumann wrote, had "spent much time in research on the history of the Weimar Republic,"[14] a subject about which he was to write extensively in the coming years. Next to Neumann, it was Erich Fromm, whose psychoanalytical approach to analyzing political and social trends, influenced Flechtheim the most. His academic start in the United States was facilitated by grants from the Oberlander Trust and the Emergency Committee in Aid of Displaced Foreign Scholars.[15] These grants enabled Flechtheim to support his parents who had managed to escape from Germany to Guatemala.[16]

With Thomas Mann's recommendation, Flechtheim succeeded in finding his first academic position at an American university.[17] In 1940, he became an instructor at Atlanta University, Georgia, and later was promoted to Assistant Professor of Government. At Atlanta University, Flechtheim taught in English for the first time. He offered the whole program of the newly established discipline of political science, teaching courses in American and general government and politics, the history of political theories, constitutional history, an introduction to social philosophy and comparative

---

[13] Flechtheim Papers: curriculum vitae (undated).

[14] See Franz L. Neumann, *Behemoth: The Structure and Practice of National Socialism* (New York: Octagon Books, 1963), xiv.

[15] See Flechtheim Papers: Statement regarding educational background and experience (undated), and New York Public Library, Manuscript and Archives Division: Emergency Committee in Aid of Displaced Foreign Scholars, Box No. 15, File Ossip K. Flechtheim (cited henceforth as Flechtheim, NYPL)

[16] See Flechtheim Papers: letter from Hermann Flechtheim, Guatemala City, to his son, Sept. 21, 1940.

[17] See Flechtheim, NYPL, List of References.

economic policy. He also taught the modern history of Germany, Russia and Western Europe.[18]

Atlanta University, a so-called historically black college, was a completely new experience for Flechtheim. Unlike most other universities, a number of black colleges opened teaching positions for refugee scholars from Europe.[19] It was at Howard University in Washington, D.C., the most renowned black institution of higher learning, where John H. Herz started his long academic career in the United States at the same time. "The helping hand stretched out by black colleges and black scholars should not be forgotten at a time when, alas, Jewish–black relations have become strained," as Herz wrote half a century later in a letter to the editors of the *New York Sunday Times*.[20]

At Atlanta University, almost all students and most faculty members were African American. The racial segregation at institutions of higher learning reflected the social reality in the American South. Compared to mainstream universities, the financial situation of these black colleges was difficult. The intellectual climate, however, was competitive. For most African American students, graduating with high marks was, as the historian Howard Zinn (1922–2010) wrote, a "life and death matter."[21] To get even low-paid employment the students had no choice but to finish school with much better grades than their white competitors in the job market if they were not to join the masses of unemployed African Americans who found no exit from poverty and inequality.

Flechtheim, himself a victim of racial and political persecution, was and remained sensitive to racism. He learned a lot from his experienced colleague and neighbor, the African American historian and sociologist W. E. B. Du Bois (1868–1963), who had visited Nazi Germany in 1936 as an Oberlander Trust Fellow. Du Bois, well acquainted with German language and culture since his student days in Berlin in the 1890s, was shocked about the Nuremberg Laws but did not abjure his belief in the humanistic heritage of Germany. Like many others, he saw the anti-Jewish legislation—and Nazi rule as a whole—as a temporary phenomenon. Nazi anti-Semitism would not come to a degree of "illegal caste and lynching," as was the case with anti-black racism in the United States. Like many of his contemporaries, Du Bois had left Germany with no intimation that the Nazi regime would

[18] Flechtheim Papers: Statement regarding educational background and experience. Flechtheim had asked the writer for a letter of recommendation on his behalf.

[19] See Gabriella Simon Edgecomb, *From Swastika to Jim Crow: Refugee Scholars at Black Colleges* (Malabar, FL: Krieger Publishing Company, 1993).

[20] John H. Herz, "Letter to the Editor," *New York Sunday Times*, Apr. 3, 1994.

[21] Howard Zinn, *You Can't be Neutral on a Moving Train: A Personal History of Our Times* (Boston: Beacon Press, 1994), 18. Zinn taught at Atlanta University two decades after Flechtheim.

soon launch a war of extermination.[22] It was only the start of the systematic annihilation of the Jews during World War II that forced him to correct this misperception.

From the very beginning of his acquaintance with Flechtheim, who was more than forty years his junior, Du Bois helped his younger colleague to become integrated into Atlanta's academia, and Flechtheim put Du Bois's name on his list of references for future job applications.[23] Du Bois asked Flechtheim to write for the newly established journal *Phylon: The Atlanta University Review of Race and Culture.* The journal took its name from the Greek word for "race." It was intended to become an interdisciplinary journal at the service of black scholars and their intellectual allies. The discrimination against the black population led Flechtheim to conclude that the process of the United States becoming a full-fledged democracy would only be completed when African American citizens had been guaranteed equal rights.[24]

It was during a visit to New York that Flechtheim met his future wife, Lili Faktor (1917–2004). At the end of 1942, the two married. As a husband, Ossip also hoped that his married status would exempt him from being drafted into the army. In Atlanta, Lili worked as a secretary, but also enrolled at Atlanta University, where she took extramural courses in English and philosophy. She was one of the very few white students at the university. In September 1946, she gave birth to Marion Ruth, their only child.

After his non-tenured employment at Atlanta University ended in 1943, Ossip Flechtheim was lucky enough to find a part-time teaching position at Bates College in Lewiston, Maine. There he taught until 1946. He also taught at Bowdoin College in Brunswick, Maine. From 1947 to 1951, Flechtheim was a non-tenured Assistant Professor of Political Science at Colby College in Waterville, Maine. In 1951, he was offered a visiting professorship at the College for Political Education in West Berlin. As early as the summer of 1945, Flechtheim went back to Germany to work as a guest lecturer at the University of Heidelberg.

During the academic year of 1946/47 he was on leave from Bates College in order to work as a senior legal advisor in Robert M. W. Kempner's office during the Nuremberg Trials, where Kempner (1899–1993) was American chief prosecutor. During this time Flechtheim found the opportunity to

<hr>

[22] David Levering Lewis, *W. E. B. Du Bois*, vol. 2, *The Fight for Equality and the American Century, 1919–1963* (New York: Henry Holt and Co., 2000), 420–421.

[23] See Flechtheim Papers: Statement regarding educational background and experience.

[24] See Ossip K. Flechtheim, "Das Dilemma der Demokratie," in *Eine Welt oder keine? Beiträge zur Politik, Politologie und Philosophie* (Frankfurt am Main: E.V.A., 1964), 111 and 121.

collect material for a book on the German Communist Party that he submitted as a D.Phil. dissertation at the University of Heidelberg. In 1948, the book was published in Germany. *Die KPD in der Weimarer Republik* [The Communist Party of Germany in the Weimar Republic] set a high scholarly standard. It was also to become a popular work on the subject.[25]

In this book Flechtheim analyzed the growth and destruction of Germany's third largest political force during the years 1918 to 1933. Before the Nazis destroyed it, the KPD was comprised of hundreds of thousands of members and millions of voters all over Germany and constituted the largest section of the Communist International outside the Soviet Union. The party was not powerful enough to realize its self-proclaimed aim to establish a "Soviet Germany," but obviously, as Flechtheim wrote, it was strong enough "to shake the newly established bourgeois republic to its foundations."[26] Unlike the fashionable Cold War literature of that time, such as Franz Borkenau's (1900–1957) *European Communism* or Ruth Fischer's (1895–1961) *Stalin and German Communism*, Flechtheim did not tell a conspiracy story. Instead, he saw the KPD as

> *the* party of strategy turns and changes par excellence. Its course was everything but straight and its leadership was replaced time and again because of real or pretended failure. While the party moved from defeat to defeat, segments of its ideology were opportunistically adjusted to the demands of the day, thus clashing with other ideological elements.[27]

Most of Flechtheim's central statements, far from hysterically anti-communist, have stood the test of time and are acknowledged in current serious historiography. He strictly distinguished Karl Liebknecht's (1871–1919) and Rosa Luxemburg's (1871–1919) ideas of council democracy from the authoritarian dictatorship that was established in Soviet Russia and in the Soviet Zone of Germany after 1945. He argued that had dictatorship succeeded in establishing a planned economy in Germany as envisaged by the communist movement as one of its goals, such a system would flout all "rational, libertarian and humanistic ideas of the communist tradition."[28]

Flechtheim analyzed the twisted road of the early KPD between syndicalism and Social Democratic reform policy. Criticizing the KPD, he did not ignore the political failures of the SPD, the German Social

---

[25] Ossip K. Flechtheim, *Die Kommunistische Partei Deutschlands in der Weimarer Republik* (Offenbach: Bollwerk-Verlag, 1948). Quotes are cited henceforth from the newer edition: *Die KPD in der Weimarer Republik*, ed. and introd. Hermann Weber (Frankfurt am Main: E.V.A., 1976).

[26] Flechtheim, *Die KPD in der Weimarer Republik*, 71.

[27] Ibid., 74 (emphasis in original).

[28] Ibid., 327.

Democratic Party. Flechtheim was among the first non-communist writers to challenge the conventional wisdom that there was no alternative to the cooperation between the SPD leaders and the old military elites, except an alleged Bolshevik dictatorship by the communists. His book inspired international research on the democratic potential of workers' and soldiers' councils during the time of the German Revolution of 1918–1919. The book shows in detail how Stalin was able to suborn the leadership of the Communist International and of the KPD after 1923. At a time when all strength was needed to counter the offensive of the reactionary forces, the KPD attacked the Weimar Republic and, most harshly, the "rightists" and "conciliators" in its own ranks. The result was a series of ultra-radical campaigns that isolated the KPD from all possible allies.

In the early 1930s, the KPD seemed to grow stronger when its membership increased. The KPD became the party of the unemployed, capable of organizing mass demonstrations, but incapable of organizing a successful struggle for power. As soon as workers lost their jobs, they transferred their votes from the SPD to the KPD, because the communist polemics against the former party seemed justified. The young jobless workers were attracted by the voluntarism of the communists that provided them with the vision of a sudden and ultimate change.

However, the Nazi movement grew much more quickly, enjoying support from people who had previously voted for the bourgeois parties. The Nazis' combination of pseudo-socialist and anti-Semitic propaganda had an inherent logic, while the workers' parties' internecine warfare with its ideological confusion disoriented and alienated people. Thus, Nazism gloried in the mobilization of masses.

As early as 1945, Flechtheim wrote a text entitled "Teaching the Future." Published in the *Journal for Higher Education* and reprinted in *Forum*, the essay called for the development of courses dealing with the future.[29] This attitude would include the future as an open dimension, thus enlarging the sphere of human action. "A serious investigation into the future— 'futurology' as a science—is scarcely a generation old; it is, historically speaking, still in its swaddling clothes," Flechtheim wrote.[30] "What I then called the new futurological approach," as he explained much later,

> was the attempt to discuss the evolution of man and his society in the hitherto forbidden future tense. I held that, by marshalling the ever growing resources of science and scholarship, we could do more than

---

[29] Ossip K. Flechtheim, "Teaching the Future," *Journal for Higher Education* 16 (1945): 460–465; Ossip K. Flechtheim, "Teaching the Future," *Forum* 104 (1945): 307–311.

[30] Ossip K. Flechtheim, "Teaching the Future," as quoted from the reprint in Flechtheim's *History and Futurology* (Meisenheim: Hain, 1966), 64–65.

employ retrospective analysis and hypothetical predictions; we could try to establish the degree of credibility and probability of forecasts.[31]

He argued that universities ought to teach about the future as a serious subject. Flechtheim was in search of a logical approach to the future in the same way that history is a search for the logic of the past.

While at Colby College, Flechtheim edited the textbook *Fundamentals of Political Science* that was published in 1952. There he emphasized that the subject is not the science of power, as such, nor is it confined to the science of statehood. He argued that the state constitutes a transitional type of social organization characteristic only of the world-historical age of civilizations, an institution that replaced the organizations based upon the authority of custom that were typical of primitive societies, and possibly foreshadowing a social organization based exclusively upon the authority of reason. Besides power, the state has other aspects. "Political science, therefore, is that specialized social science that studies the nature and purpose of the state in so far as it is a power organization and the nature and purpose of other 'unofficial' power phenomena that are apt to influence the state."[32]

Flechtheim made clear that political science cannot prescribe a course of action for the people, nor can it lay down anyone's life plan. Unlike old-fashioned authoritarian ethics, and unlike modern ideological master plans, it cannot speak in terms of a simple and categorical "Thou shalt" or "Thou shalt not." Political science should not convey the false impression that it can relieve the individual of the responsibility of choice. This, according to Flechtheim, was fallacious for three reasons:

> First, it has as its subject matter the study of choices among various values. It deals with the struggle between contradictory goals. The political scientist, himself a living human being, and hence a holder of values, finds it tempting to introduce his personal preferences into his study and thus to become a partisan. Second, political science cannot yet provide the average person with so much reliable, quantitative, testable, and hence convicting knowledge that he could make his own choice without much effort. … Third, political science is a pure and an applied science all in one. … Though the pure and the applied political scientist is one and the same person, little agreement exists among political scientists on which values political science as an applied science is to serve.[33]

---

[31] Ossip K. Flechtheim, "Discussion on Future Research," in *Mankind 2000*, eds. Robert Jungk and Johan Galtung (Oslo and London: Universitetsforlaget/Allen & Unwin, 1969), 336.

[32] Ossip K. Flechtheim, "Delimitation of the Field," in Ossip K. Flechtheim et al., *Fundamentals of Political Science* (New York: Ronald Press, 1952), 17.

[33] Ossip K. Flechtheim, "The Crisis of Our Civilization," ibid., 561–562.

Flechtheim concluded that political science can be adequately performed only if the political scientist enjoys a considerable amount of independence and professional security in a society that allows freedom for the expression of intellectual doubt and which provides the scholar with a social network where he can pursue his studies.[34]

During that time, Lili Flechtheim continued and finished her studies in sociology, economics and psychology. She graduated with distinction from Colby College, after which she found employment as a social worker. In 1951, this harmonious period of life ended for the family when Ossip Flechtheim was denied tenure at Colby College. All his academic credentials, his output of publications and the variety of courses he offered as a teacher did not help him in the time of Cold War politics that affected American academia: the conservative college administration mistrusted him. While he was in Berlin, college president Julius Seelye Bixler (1894–1985) and dean Ernest Cumming Marriner (1894–1983) had selected another candidate for the vacant position in the political science department. They informed Flechtheim that his contract could only be extended for one more year.

He reacted angrily. Given these conditions, Flechtheim would "not for a minute" consider returning to Colby. He referred to his credentials as a writer and teacher. In Germany, Flechtheim wrote, he would certainly have a good chance to get a chair at one of its best universities. He would, however, gladly return to Colby, if the college were to consider a tenure position as a serious offer.[35] Marriner responded that Flechtheim had to decide quickly whether he would return for a year or give up his position.[36] But before Flechtheim had answered, he received a letter from the president of the college. President Bixler informed him that his contract at Colby College had ended. It would be best for Flechtheim to look for an academic position in Germany.[37]

Flechtheim informed Ralph E. Himstead, General Secretary of the American Association of University Professors (AAUP), about the case. He complained that all his colleagues who had been denied tenure at Colby College were either liberals or Jews, not only those who had been suspected of sympathizing with communists. Flechtheim's own political position was, as he wrote, "definitely left of the center and decidedly anti-totalitarian," as his book about the KPD would testify.[38] The AAUP's

---

34 Ibid., 565–566.

35 Flechtheim Papers: Flechtheim to E. C. Marriner, Feb. 3, 1952.

36 Flechtheim Papers: Marriner to Flechtheim, Feb. 20, 1952.

37 Flechtheim Papers: Bixler to Flechtheim, Mar. 20, 1952.

38 Flechtheim Papers: Flechtheim to Himstead, Mar. 31, 1952. See also his letter to Warren C. Middleton, Washington Bureau, American Association of University Professors, ibid., Mar. 31, 1952.

response stated only that there was hardly anything that the organization could do for Flechtheim.[39] Colby College's paper refused to report about his case.[40]

Flechtheim had a communist past, and in the age of McCarthyism there was no way to whitewash the red badge. He had no other alternative than to look for an academic appointment in Germany. It was Franz Neumann who, in the end, saved Flechtheim's academic career. Neumann, a political science professor at Columbia University, worked at this time as an advisor for the newly established Free University of Berlin. He and social democratic politician (and later West Berlin's mayor) Otto Suhr (1894–1957) had, in 1951, suggested that Flechtheim apply for the visiting professorship in Berlin. At that time, Suhr was director at the Deutsche Hochschule für Politik (DHfP, German College for Political Education). The DHfP, whose predecessor had been founded after World War I in Berlin, would adopt a set of principles and practices that had proved successful in the United States.[41] Nonetheless, it was obvious that American occupation officials "could not force their own brand of democracy down Germans' throats" and that the best strategy was to help Germans find their own way to establish a new political culture.[42]

Neumann became a key figure in the reestablishment of academic education in West Berlin. He was "ombudsman" at Columbia for the partnership with the newly established Free University, visiting consultant for German university reforms for the State Department and intermediary in financial matters for the Ford Foundation. One of his top priorities was to establish the DHfP and to recruit faculty members, particularly from among refugee scholars who had, in the United States, become accustomed to the practice of "Western liberal democracy." On the other hand, those refugee scholars contributed to a more critical self-understanding of American democratic theory, as was shown in Flechtheim's *Fundamentals of Political Science*.[43]

Flechtheim's academic expertise made him eligible for a permanent position at the DHfP. In September 1952, after his year as a visiting

---

[39] Flechtheim Papers: Middleton to Flechtheim, July 24, 1952.

[40] Ibid.; Sarah E. Packard, editor Colby Echo, to Flechtheim, May 24, 1952.

[41] The Deutsche Hochschule für Politik had already received U.S. funding in the 1920s and thereby could be considered a transatlantic institution from early on.

[42] Richard L. Merritt, "American Influences in the Occupation of Germany," *Annals of the American Academy of Political and Social Science* 428 (1976), 91.

[43] See Hubertus Buchstein, "Ernst Fraenkel, Otto Suhr und Franz L. Neumann: Die Entstehung der neopluralistischen Demokratietheorie an der Freien Universität Berlin," *Zeitschrift des Forschungsverbundes SED-Staat* 24 (2008): 40–56; Hubertus Buchstein and Gerhard Göhler, "Die ersten fünfzehn Jahre—Von der Deutschen Hochschule für Politik zum Otto-Suhr-Institut," *Leviathan* 17 (1989): 127–139.

professor, Flechtheim was regularly appointed as Full Professor. His parents
returned from Guatemala to West Germany. Lili Flechtheim did not want
to return to Germany—the land from which the Nazis had started to destroy
Europe—but did. After the family's final return, it took her years to feel at
home again in the country and the city of her birth.

In 1957, Flechtheim received his habilitation degree for his works on
comparative party politics.[44] Two years later, the DHfP became part of
the Free University and henceforth bore the name Otto Suhr Institute. On
1 January 1959, Flechtheim was appointed Associate Professor of Political
Science at the Otto Suhr Institute and in 1961 he became Full Professor
for the Sociology of Political Parties.[45] Together with two other former
refugees, Richard Löwenthal and Ernst Fraenkel (1898–1975), he belonged
to the leading scholars of political science in West Berlin from the 1950s
to the 1970s.

Professor in West Berlin

During his first years as a professor in Berlin, Flechtheim's work focused
mainly on the sociology of political parties. He initiated a collective research
project that resulted, among other works, in a multi-volume documentary
collection on party politics in West Germany.[46] He also continued to write
on the history and politics of international, namely Soviet, communism.[47]

It was not only Flechtheim's contributions to research on communism and
to political science that made his name known to generations of scholars and
political analysts. He was also one of the first, if not the first, to urge the
introduction of "future" into education.[48] Here, he worked particularly as a
bridge-builder between academic discourses in the United States and West

[44] He did not submit a special thesis but was habilitated with his works on German and
Soviet party politics that included his book on the KPD in the Weimar Republic. See Free
University of Berlin Archives, Akte [File] Ossip K. Flechtheim: Habilitation (unpag.).

[45] Since the DHfP had no full university status, Flechtheim had to undergo the habilitation process in order to be admitted permanently to the Free University. See Flechtheim
Papers, File: Diplome und Zeugnisse.

[46] *Dokumente zur parteipolitischen Entwicklung in Deutschland*, ed. Ossip K. Flechtheim, 9
vols. (Berlin: Wendler, 1962–1970).

[47] See his works *Weltkommunismus im Wandel* (n. 10); *Bolschewismus 1917–1967: Von der
Weltrevolution zum Sowjetimperium* (Vienna: Europa-Verlag, 1967); *Von Marx bis Kolakowski:
Sozialismus oder Untergang in der Barbarei?* (Cologne: E.V.A., 1978); *Rosa Luxemburg zur
Einführung* (Hamburg: SOAK, 1985); *Karl Liebknecht zur Einführung* (Hamburg: SOAK,
1985); with Hans-Martin Lohman, *Marx zur Einführung* (Hamburg: SOAK, 1988).

[48] See for the context Elke Seefried, *Zukünfte: Aufstieg und Krise der Zukunftsforschung
1945–1980* (Berlin: De Gruyter Oldenbourg, 2015).

Germany. Alvin Toffler (1928–2016), the renowned American scholar in the field, wrote in 1972: "The founding father of modern futurism, if there is one, may well be a mild-mannered German professor who, as early as the mid-1940s, began speaking and writing about the need for what he termed 'futurology.'"[49] Flechtheim laid down an agenda that has been followed in much research and in various activities in the field around the globe. He argued that futurology embraces all types of prognoses, projections, linear programming etc., as well as all planning procedures in economics, education, traffic etc. Flechtheim understood futurology as an assessment of goals, norms and values pertaining to the future. He considered it a broadly systematic science in contrast to a specialist discipline.[50]

It was not before 1970 that Flechtheim summarized his deliberations on how to do research on the future in a large book, and *Futurology: The Struggle for the Future* became his main work. As he wrote in the preface, Flechtheim had hesitated to write a summing-up of his thoughts. The struggle for tomorrow would allow only provisional conclusions.[51]

In this book, Flechtheim anticipated three tendencies of converging developments for the foreseeable future, i.e., before the end of the twentieth century.

> The most clearly negative kind of convergence is the collective death of mankind or, at least, the downfall of modern civilization. The second alternative would stabilize bureaucratic-technological regimes. Armament and the arms race, even with air-space weapons, were further reinforced. Eventually this would produce a state of affairs which one might best describe as neo-Caesarism. The third and least likely alternative of development in the 20th and 21st centuries would lead to a solidaric world federation. This would include the planning of humankind's future in the service of peace, welfare, and creativity.[52]

Flechtheim was clearly distinct from status quo scholars like Herman Kahn (1922–1983) or Anthony J. Wiener (1933–2012). He considered their futurological philosophy as definitely conservative because they assumed that all development in the technical, commercial and social spheres would take place within the existing Western social and economic order.

---

[49] Alvin Toffler, Introductory Note to Ossip K. Flechtheim, "Futurology: The New Science of Probability?", in *The Futurists*, ed. Alvin Toffler (New York: Random House, 1972), 264.

[50] See Flechtheim, "Is Futurology the Answer to the Challenge of the Future?", in Jungk and Galtung, *Mankind 2000*, 264.

[51] Ossip K. Flechtheim, *Futurologie: Der Kampf um die Zukunft* (Cologne: Verlag Wissenschaft und Politik, 1970), 9.

[52] Ibid., 37.

Flechtheim insisted that a continuing power policy as instigated by the two superpowers could result in a barbaric war if there was no nuclear disarmament.[53] After that war the world would relapse into barbarism, not unlike the situation in Europe in the aftermath of the destruction of the Roman Empire.

It is not surprising that Flechtheim saw the political philosophy of contemporary Soviet communism not as an alternative but as parallel thinking to right-wing conservatism in the West. Both favored technological modernization without human emancipation, thus disparaging democratic as well as socialist principles. The collective mentality of the Communist Party elite was, as Flechtheim pointed out, similar to conservative decision-makers. The conservatives would prefer to put the clock back to a social order without strong trade unions as protectors of the welfare state. Communist Party bureaucrats also opposed independent political organizations of the workers, such as workers' councils.

However, Flechtheim clearly predicted that a "retreat to *laissez-faire* capitalism," particularly in Eastern Europe, "would cause an immense catastrophe." It would be a historical tragedy should Eastern Europe, disappointed by the Soviets' iron rule, dismantle all modest achievements of the communist system and prefer a comeback of the capitalist order.[54] Although "barbarism" was one of the options he envisaged, Flechtheim's attitude left no room for fatalism. He insisted that "no trough ever declines to the low level of the predicting one, each crest out-tops its last precursor."[55]

Flechtheim's concept of futurology was based on the process of social evolution that was emerging in Eastern and Western Europe. This concept would integrate the growing permissiveness, liberalism and individualism of Western societies with an enlightened interpretation of socialism. It would lead to a Third Road beyond capitalist and communist systems and would mean a new democratic alternative to existing societies. It would also transcend commonly received notions of democracy. Flechtheim insisted that this new type of democracy was born in Czechoslovakia in 1968—in later years, he would also refer to the democratic and socialist experiment in Chile under Salvador Allende (1908–1973). Significantly enough, the Czechoslovak reform movement included a team of scholars under the

---

[53] In 1963, Flechtheim nominated Bertrand Russell (1872–1970), who was already Nobel Laureate in the field of literature, for the Nobel Peace Prize, "as a philosopher, teacher and writer promoting Peace and preventing the spread of nuclear weapons." See The Nobel Peace Prize, Nomination Database. www.nobelprize.org/nomination/redirector/?redir=archive/show.php&id=17187.

[54] Flechtheim, *Futurologie*, 321.

[55] Ibid., 320.

auspices of the Academy of Sciences that even used the term "futurology" in their social prognosis.[56] The Soviet tanks in Prague demonstrated, as Flechtheim pointed out, that there was no *automatic* development towards convergence in the positive sense. Given the Soviet invasion of Czechoslovakia and the American war in Vietnam, a negative kind of convergence could be the one that mankind would have to reckon with.[57]

This negative convergence would imply a

> post-republican and post-democratic, even post-fascist regime under democratic disguise. A modern Caesarian dictatorship would be based on pseudo-democratic campaigns, such as plebiscites. The dictators, rather more charismatic than traditional leaders, would rule a society in which only relics of rationality and legality would remain.[58]

All cultural and environmental problems would be neglected. What kind of resistance would this society cause? Among the "have-nots" in underdeveloped countries, resistance could be expressed in terrorist forms not unlike those of the nineteenth century but using modern technology. All these oppressed people "know very well that ten trucks filled with dynamite and exploding in the tunnels and under the bridges of Manhattan would cause more damage there than in any other place in the world."[59]

Flechtheim reminded his readers of a possible alternative. There is today, as he wrote, a whole range of technological means at our disposal that earlier generations did not possess. These means should make it possible to enjoy a higher standard of living and particularly a higher standard of education. This would require, but also enable, a new kind of social participation based on fundamental human rights and democratic procedures. Flechtheim predicted the re-emergence of Rosa Luxemburg's old idea of democratically elected councils in cooperation with parliamentary bodies. These councils could be formed in a process of non-violent mass action for democracy and social justice. In an interview for Radio Free Europe, Flechtheim repeated "the Third Road, which to my mind is the only sane road for the future, presupposes a coming together of the neo-conformists on our [Western] side with the revisionists in the East." He reminded intellectuals of their particular responsibility in the struggle of ideas to envisage a project of the future "which neither the East nor the West

---

[56] See Ossip K. Flechtheim, "Vorwort," in *Technischer Fortschritt und Industrielle Gesellschaft*, eds. Radovan Richta et al. (Frankfurt am Main: Makol, 1972).

[57] For Flechtheim's critique of the American war in Vietnam, see his essays "Für und Wider des Krieges in Vietnam," *Der Tagesspiegel*, Dec. 31, 1965 and "Amerikanisches Engagement in Vietnam—aus der Sicht Berlins," *Der Tagesspiegel*, Jan. 8, 1966.

[58] Flechtheim, *Futurologie*, 322.

[59] Ibid., 325–326.

could claim as its own."[60] From 1968 to 1974, Flechtheim edited the German journal *Futurum*, a scholarly journal devoted to studies of the future.[61]

In the meantime, his futurology book and his other writings found numerous responses in East Germany and the Soviet Union. In the 1960s, state and party leaders in the Soviet Union and other Eastern Bloc countries, including the German Democratic Republic, became aware of the discussions about the new discipline of futurology. The official position was that Marxism–Leninism was considered the combined science of politics, sociology, economics and philosophy. For that reason, no other form of social science was possible. However, at the same time, Soviet and East German officials became concerned with the effectiveness of the existing models of central economic planning. A general orientation towards the implementation of more "scientific" methods led to a focus on cybernetic theory. It was Walter Ulbricht (1893–1973) himself who emphasized the necessity of promoting research on the future and used the name of *Prognostik* (prognostics) for the new discipline.[62]

The term remained controversial in the Soviet Union, since Marxism–Leninism stood in the tradition of criticizing "Utopian Socialism" as opposed to the rational-based theory of Marx and Engels. In the Soviet Union, Igor Bestuzhev-Lada (1927–2015) was chief among those who saw research on the future not in contrast to but as an inherent component of Marxist–Leninist thinking. In the GDR, a group of scholars from the party-led Institute of Social Sciences published a book that emphasized the need to study future developments in order to anticipate possible missteps on the path to communism.[63] In 1968, an Institute for Research on Public Opinion was established in East Berlin. Utopian aspects were particularly visible in a number of movies and a remarkable output of science fiction literature.[64] Soon after Ulbricht's dismissal from his post as

[60] Ossip K. Flechtheim, "Marxism and the Third Road," in *Can We Survive Our Future?*, eds. George R. Urban and Michael Glenny (New York: St. Martin's Press, 1971), 381.

[61] See the selection of essays from this journal in Ossip K. Flechtheim, ed., *Futurum* (Munich: Minerva, 1980). Flechtheim's principal essays on the subject are collected in his *Zeitgeschichte und Zukunftspolitik* (Hamburg: Hoffmann & Campe, 1974), republished in a slightly revised form as *Vergangenheit im Zeugenstand der Zukunft* (Berlin: Dietz, 1991).

[62] See Walter Ulbricht, *Die gesellschaftliche Entwicklung in der Deutschen Demokratischen Republik bis zur Vollendung des Sozialismus* (Berlin: Dietz, 1967), 92.

[63] See "Autorenkollektiv unter Leitung von Wolfgang Eichhorn und Günter Kröber," in Adolf Bauer, *Philosophie und Prognostik: Weltanschauliche und methodische Probleme der Gesellschaftsprognose* (Berlin: Dietz, 1968).

[64] See Sonja Fritzsche's excellent essay "East Germany's 'Werkstatt Zukunft': Futurology and the Science Fiction Films of 'Defa-Futurum,'" *German Studies Review* 29, no. 2 (2006): 367–386.

First Secretary of the Socialist Unity Party in 1971, pronounced interest in prognostics and public opinion withered away from the agenda of high political priorities.[65]

Flechtheim's book on futurology was published during the blossoming of futurist trends in East Germany. It was partly criticized and partly welcomed. Jürgen Kuczynski (1904–1997) emphasized this ambivalent position when he, in the widely read journal *Die Weltbühne*, wrote that Flechtheim, as a scholar and political person, should be considered as an "ideological enemy" and likewise as a "companion in the struggle against monopoly capital and war-mongers." Despite Flechtheim's relative merits, the futurology book as well as his other monographs remained forbidden in the GDR, and Kuczynski's suggestion that East German readers should not consult it, unless they were attempting to "repudiate" its main thesis, had a slightly cynical undertone.[66]

Frank Fiedler (1928–2007) and Werner Müller (1922–2006), two philosophy professors from Leipzig, rejected the term "futurology" and stressed that "Marxism–Leninism" (which in fact justified the one-party dictatorship) should be considered as the single instrument for predicting the future. However, they emphasized the need to establish a dialogue with scholars such as Flechtheim whose "humanistic approach" they praised.[67] Alfred Bönisch (b. 1932), from the Institute of Social Sciences, wrote: "Flechtheim and other bourgeois professors can play a very positive role through their appeal to the public and their engagement for peace and disarmament."[68] Manfred Krautz and Dieter Grohmann, as well as the Soviet authors Georgi Shakhnazarov (1924–2001) and A. L. Gaisudis, considered Flechtheim's scholarly work as an alternative to Cold War ideologues within the realm and (as they saw it) the limits of non-Marxist thinking.[69]

---

[65] See Heinz Niemann, *Meinungsforschung in der DDR: Die geheimen Berichte des Instituts für Meinungsforschung an das Politbüro der SED* (Cologne: Bund-Verlag, 1993), and Heinz Niemann, *Hinterm Zaun: Politische Kultur und Meinungsforschung in der DDR* (Berlin: Edition Ost, 1995). See also Jens Gieseke, "East German Popular Opinion: Problems of Reconstruction," in *The Silent Majority in Communist and Post-Communist States*, eds. Jens Gieseke and Klaus Bachmann (Frankfurt am Main: Peter Lang, 2016), 59–77.

[66] Jürgen Kuczynski, "Futurologische Strömungen," *Die Weltbühne* 66, no. 6 (1971): 163.

[67] Frank Fiedler and Werner Müller, "Zukunftsdenken im Kampf der Ideologien—eine Kritik der 'Futurologie,'" *Die marxistisch-leninistische Philosophie und der ideologische Kampf der Gegenwart*, ed. Rolf Kirchhoff (Berlin: Dietz, 1970), 289. It was the general premise of all Soviet (and East) German works on futures research that Karl Marx was the first (and, as it was understood, infallible) scientific forecaster.

[68] Alfred Bönisch, *Futurologie: Eine kritische Analyse bürgerlicher Zukunftsforschung* (Berlin: Akademie-Verlag, 1971), 216.

[69] See Manfred Krautz, "Untersuchungen zur Futurologie im System des staatsmonopolistischen Kapitalismus Westdeutschlands" (Ph.D. thesis, Technical University Dresden,

Igor Bestuzhev-Lada considered clear differences between pro-capitalist futurologists, such as Kahn and Wiener, and critically minded scholars like Flechtheim, Robert Jungk (1913–1994) or Fritz Baade (1893–1974).[70] Flechtheim, Jungk and Baade indeed "represented a different current of futures thinking; for them the future was a utopia—not something to be predicted and foretold, but the hope for a better world."[71] They, as well as the Norwegian sociologist and "father" of peace research Johan Galtung, "were all shaped by a social philosophical and critical epistemology that was close to Critical Theory, and they were molded by an understanding of society that focused on human beings, an awareness of the development of time in history and a historical–dialectic approach to science, which reflected the role of the scientist in the cognitive process."[72] Thirty years after this debate, Bestuzhev-Lada included parts of Flechtheim's futurology book in a collection of principal essays on the subject that he published in Moscow.[73]

There were also much less nuanced judgments. Nikolai Gribachev, a Soviet *Pravda* journalist, and Thomas Pfau, an East German doctoral student, were among those who saw Flechtheim as a "silent crusader" and

---

1969); Dieter Grohmann, "Futurologie und Ethik: Eine kritische Analyse philosophisch-ethischer Probleme in der bürgerlichen Zukunftsforschung" (Ph.D. thesis, Martin Luther University Halle-Wittenberg, 1977); Georgi K. Shakhnazarov, *Fiasko futurologii (Kriticheskiy ocherk nemarksistkikh teorii obshchestvennogo razvitiya)* [The Fiasco of Futurology: A Critical Outline of Non-Marxist Theories of Social Development] (Moscow: Politizdat, 1979), 343; A. L. Gaisudis, "Kritika futurologii O. K. Flekhtkheima" [A Critique of O. K. Flechtheim's Futurology], *Filosofskie nauki* 16, no. 4 (1983): 140.

[70] See Igor Bestuzhev-Lada, "Bourgeois 'Futurology' and the Future of Mankind," *The Futurists*, 194–209.

[71] Jenny Andersson, "The Great Future Debate and the Struggle for the World," *American Historical Review* 117, no. 5 (2012): 1143.

[72] Elke Seefried, "Steering the Future: The Emergence of 'Western' Futures Research and its Production of Expertise, 1950s to Early 1970s," *European Journal of Futures Research* 2 (2013).

[73] Ossip K. Flechtheim, "Futurologiya: Borba za budushcheye" [Futurology: The Struggle for the Future], in *Vpered XXI vek: perspektivy, prognozy, futurologiya* [Towards the 21st Century: Perspectives, Outlooks, Futurology], ed. I. [Igor] V. Bestuzhev-Lada (Moscow: Akademia, 2000), 247–274. This was part of Bestushev-Lada's attempts to transform Soviet/Russian futures research from an ideological tool to a part of intellectual technology that would provide solutions for large-scale economic and ecological problems. See Egle Rindceviziute, "A Struggle for the Soviet Future: The Birth of Scientific Forecasting in the Soviet Union," *Slavic Review*, 75, no. 1 (2016): 52–76 (on Flechtheim, see p. 59); Egle Rindceviziute, "The Future as an Intellectual Technology in the Soviet Union: From Centralised Planning to Reflexive Management," *Cahiers du monde russe* 56, no. 1 (2017): 111–136; Stefan Guth, "One Future Only: The Soviet Union in the Age of Scientific-Technical Revolution," in *Reconfiguring the Future? Politics and Time from the 1960s to the 1980s,* ed. Elke Seefried, Special issue, *Journal of Modern European History* 13, no. 3 (2015): 355–376.

representative of the creeping counter-revolution that was determined to undermine the "Socialist Camp."[74] It should be noted that the most "violent" attack against Flechtheim came from Claus Koch, a West German writer who saw Flechtheim as an "accomplice of capitalist big business," while the general reception of Flechtheim's futurology book in the West was overwhelmingly positive.[75] In 1990/91, the young East German Egbert Joos cooperated with Flechtheim for the publication of the interview book *In Search of a Better World*.[76]

Politics for a Pluralist Left

As a political person Flechtheim was engaged in party politics for many years of his life. In 1952, right after his final return to Germany, he joined the SPD. Together with his friend Wolfgang Abendroth (1906–1985), professor of political science at Marburg University, he belonged to the minority of Social Democrats who firmly opposed the new party program that the SPD was to adopt in 1959 and that no longer defined the party as a working-class organization. In 1962, Flechtheim left the party.[77] This was not his retreat from political engagement, however. The years 1967–1968 were the time of student revolt in West Germany and especially in West Berlin. Students became politicized because of university overcrowding and traditional, highly authoritarian structures. They also opposed the introduction of emergency laws in the jurisdiction of the Federal Republic of Germany.[78]

Until 1967–1968 Flechtheim was considered to be most on the left among the faculty of the Free University. "A few months later there

[74] N. M. [Nikolai Matveevich] Gribachev, "Tikhye krestonostsy" [Silent Crusaders], *Pravda*, Sept. 29, 1967; Thomas Pfau, "Zur Kritik der sozialpolitischen Theorien des Ossip K. Flechtheim" (Ph.D. thesis, Martin Luther University Halle-Wittenberg, 1978).

[75] Claus Koch, "Kritik der Futurologie," *Kursbuch* 14 (1968): 2. For the reception of Flechtheim's *Futurologie*, see Keßler, *Ossip K. Flechtheim*, 169–172.

[76] See Ossip K. Flechtheim and Egbert Joos, *Ausschau halten nach einer besseren Welt: Biographie, Interview, Artikel* (Berlin: Dietz, 1991). During GDR times, Joos had submitted a well-balanced thesis on futurology. See his "Futurologie: Eine Theorie der Vergangenheit?" (Ph.D. thesis, Technical University Dresden, 1988).

[77] See William D. Graf, *The German Left since 1945: Socialism and Social Democracy in the German Federal Republic*, with an epilogue by Ossip K. Flechtheim (Cambridge: Oleander Press, 1976), 234–235.

[78] For an early critique of the emergency laws, see Ossip K. Flechtheim, "Notstandsgesetze würden die Freiheit des Bürgers dauernd bedrohen," *Westdeutsches Tageblatt*, Apr. 6, 1963. The Emergency Acts legislation, which came after long public debates adopted by the West German parliament in 1968, limited some of the basic constitutional rights under certain conditions, such as war, natural catastrophes or internal crises that would lead to a breakdown of public life. The legislation faced opposition from outside parliament.

were many teachers whose political standpoints were much more radically leftist. Suddenly I found myself in a center position and even 'right' of the center."[79] In a discussion with one of his most brilliant students, Rudi Dutschke (1940–1979), Flechtheim advised the students to refrain from any kind of physical violence that would only discredit and defeat the student movement.[80] But Flechtheim protested against rightist slanders that connected the student movement with terrorist or subversive activities. West Berlin would no longer remain a democratic alternative to the East, where students were persecuted just for political, non-violent actions. After his retirement from the university in 1974 Flechtheim founded the private Institute for Future Research. A good part of the institute's work was devoted to the risks of atomic energy plants, though Flechtheim expressed his skepticism less rigorously than did Robert Jungk. In 1980, he joined the Alternative Liste Berlin, the city's branch of the emerging West German Green Party.

The message of Flechtheim's last monograph *Can Future Still Be Preserved?* was, in 1987, that one should more fully explore the limits and potentialities of non-violent means of reform and revolution. As the destructiveness of weapons, the ecological crisis, hunger and starvation, mass manipulation and cultural crisis were bound to increase, the future of civilization could depend upon the rapid replacement of traditional means of coercion and deceit by more rational and humane procedures. In 1987, two years after a fundamental reform process in the Soviet Union had started, Flechtheim was more optimistic than years earlier about the chances of a development towards a democratic socialism. If the Soviet Union and her allies could achieve more democratic societies, socialist forces in the West would benefit greatly. It would help them to resist the growing power of big multinational enterprises, particularly mass media groups. To preserve democracy and its political culture, the nationalization of press syndicates as well as of the arms industry would be a viable alternative to the excesses of private capitalism.[81]

Flechtheim felt no Cold War triumphalism when the Berlin Wall came down and East European communism imploded. He immediately sought contact with the renewed East German left. Flechtheim was shocked to witness that almost all East German social scientists, despite their political past and scholarly qualifications, had been dismissed from academia in the post-unification "purge" of the early 1990s. The arrogance and behavior of

---

[79] Flechtheim, "Kein Platz für Patriotismus," 434.

[80] See Jürgen Miermeister, *Rudi Dutschke mit Selbstzeugnissen und Bilddokumenten* (Reinbek: Rowohlt, 1986), 116.

[81] Ossip K. Flechtheim, *Ist die Zukunft noch zu retten?* (Hamburg: Hoffmann & Campe, 1987).

many West Germans reminded him of the darkest past in German history.[82] Flechtheim, already ill and frail, demonstrated his solidarity with the East German left, a minority within the minority, by joining the curators of the Rosa Luxemburg Foundation, at that time a small independent institute closely related to the PDS (Partei des Demokratischen Sozialismus), the reformed Communist Party.[83]

On the occasion of his 80th birthday, the Free University of Berlin awarded Flechtheim with an honorary doctorate.[84] But in the early 1990s, Flechtheim's health deteriorated rapidly. He withdrew from any public activity. Together with his wife Lili, who survived him by six years, he went to a rest home in Kleinmachnow near Berlin. There he died on 4 March 1998, one day before his 89th birthday. On the occasion of his 100th birthday in 2009, several conferences were held in Germany. A new collection of essays, mostly written by friends and former students, portrayed him as a researcher of communism and political scientist who transcended the narrow ideological barriers of the Cold War. Contributors discussed Flechtheim's pioneering role in the research of the future that described the value of systematic future studies to society.[85] In the English-speaking world, the political thinker Ossip Flechtheim has yet to be recovered.[86]

Reflecting on the history and future of socialism, Flechtheim remembered those socialists who started fighting fascism right after they had been defeated and persecuted. He quoted Joseph Buttinger (1906–1992), the

[82] See Ossip and Lili Flechtheim's correspondence in the hitherto enclosed section of Ossip K. Flechtheim's papers. Ms Marion Timm was kind enough to provide me with this material.

[83] Flechtheim's work was now widely acknowledged in East Germany and even the (former) Soviet Union. Among others, the Soviet-Russian philosopher Vadim Semyonov referred in 1997 to Flechtheim's "challenges" and mentioned "the economic crisis, imbalanced North–South relations, the crisis of society, and problems of ecology" as crucial problems of present times and the immediate future. He emphasized that there is not only a crisis of socialism "but of the world at large." V. Semyonov, "Sovremennii krizis i put' v budushchee: diagnoz i prognoz" [Contemporary Crisis and the Way Towards a Future: Diagnosis and Prognosis], *Al'ternativy* 1, no. 1 (1996): 41.

[84] See "Pioneer Futurist Honored in Berlin," *The Futurist*, 23, no. 4 (1998), 43.

[85] See Siegfried Heimann, ed., *Ossip K. Flechtheim, 100 Jahre* (Berlin: Humanistischer Verband Deutschlands, 2009).

[86] The exceptions are Lora Wildenthal, *The Language of Human Rights in West Germany* (Philadelphia: University of Pennsylvania Press, 2013), 70–72 and Jenny Andersson, *The Future of the World: Futurology, Futurists, and the Struggle for the Post-Cold War Imagination* (Oxford: Oxford University Press, 2018), 44–46 (on Flechtheim). Wildenthal investigates Flechtheim's contribution to the founding of the West German branch of the International League of Human Rights and the Humanist Union, while Andersson discusses Flechtheim's early writings in the United States as part of his transition from a moral to a rational and scientific approach. Unfortunately, Andersson's book contains numerous printing errors.

1934 leader of the illegal Austrian socialist movement who wrote about his companions that, in the deepest sense, they had not failed.[87]

> Their socialism lives on, like seed beneath the snow. In every country they have brothers, including some of other name, brought-up in other schools. Everywhere, individually or in small groups, they search for a new way. Gradually they will be joined by other men, thrust into thought and action by the course of social disaster. They will not be units of a mighty host in the near future. But even if their spirit cannot prevail in politics for many years, the needs of the time will call them, sooner or later. Going his way, even the loneliest will some day encounter brothers, at home or abroad. And wherever in the world they meet, however different their tongues, they will know and embrace one another, and wonder what made them think they were alone.[88]

Works Cited

Archival Sources
Deutsche National Bibliothek, German Exile Archive 1933–1945, Frankfurt am Main
Ossip K. Flechtheim, Collected Papers

Free University of Berlin Archives
Akte [File] Ossip K. Flechtheim

New York Public Library, Manuscript and Archives Division
Emergency Committee in Aid of Displaced Foreign Scholars, Box No. 15, File
Ossip K. Flechtheim

Secondary Works
Andersson, Jenny. *The Future of the World: Futurology, Futurists, and the Struggle for the Post-Cold War Imagination*. Oxford: Oxford University Press, 2018.
——. "The Great Future Debate and the Struggle for the World." *American Historical Review* 117, no. 5 (2012): 1411–1438.
"Autorenkollektiv unter Leitung von Wolfgang Eichhorn und Günter Kröber." In Adolf Bauer, *Philosophie und Prognostik: Weltanschauliche und methodische Probleme der Gesellschaftsprognose*. Berlin: Dietz, 1968.
Bestuzhev-Lada, Igor. "Bourgeois 'Futurology' and the Future of Mankind." In *The Futurists*, ed. Alvin Toffler, 194–209. New York: Random House, 1972.

---

[87] Ossip K. Flechtheim, *Bolschewismus 1917–1967: Von der Weltrevolution zum Sowjetimperium* (Vienna: Europa-Verlag, 1967), 15.

[88] Joseph Buttinger, *In the Twilight of Socialism: A History of the Revolutionary Socialists of Austria*, trans. E. B. Aston (New York: Praeger, 1953), 550.

Bönisch, Alfred. *Futurologie: Eine kritische Analyse bürgerlicher Zukunftsforschung.* Berlin: Akademie-Verlag, 1971.

Buchstein, Hubertus. "Ernst Fraenkel, Otto Suhr und Franz L. Neumann: Die Entstehung der neopluralistischen Demokratietheorie an der Freien Universität Berlin." *Zeitschrift des Forschungsverbundes SED-Staat* 24 (2008): 40–56.

Buchstein, Hubertus and Gerhard Göhler. "Die ersten fünfzehn Jahre—Von der Deutschen Hochschule für Politik zum Otto-Suhr-Institut." *Leviathan* 17 (1989): 127–139.

Buttinger, Joseph. *In the Twilight of Socialism: A History of the Revolutionary Socialists of Austria.* Trans. E. B. Aston. New York: Praeger, 1953.

Edgecomb, Gabrielle Simon. *From Swastika to Jim Crow: Refugee Scholars at Black Colleges.* Malabar, FL: Krieger Publishing Company, 1993.

Fiedler, Frank and Werner Müller. "Zukunftsdenken im Kampf der Ideologien— eine Kritik der 'Futurologie.'" In *Die marxistisch-leninistische Philosophie und der ideologische Kampf der Gegenwart*, ed. Rolf Kirchhoff, 253–272. Berlin: Dietz, 1970.

Flechtheim, Ossip K. "Amerikanisches Engagement in Vietnam—aus der Sicht Berlins." *Der Tagesspiegel*, Jan. 8, 1966.

——. "Discussion on Future Research." In *Mankind 2000*, eds. Robert Jungk and Johan Galtung, 336–337. Oslo and London: Universitetsforlaget/Allen & Unwin, 1969.

——. ed. *Dokumente zur parteipolitischen Entwicklung in Deutschland*, 9 vols. Berlin: Wendler, 1962–1970.

——. *Eine Welt oder keine? Beiträge zur Politik, Politologie und Philosophie.* Frankfurt am Main: E.V.A., 1964.

——. "Für und Wider des Krieges in Vietnam." *Der Tagesspiegel*, Dec. 31, 1965.

——. *Futurologie: Der Kampf um die Zukunft.* Cologne: Verlag Wissenschaft und Politik, 1970.

——. "Futurologiya: Borba za budushcheye" [Futurology: The Struggle for the Future]. In *Vpered XXI vek: perspektivy, prognozy, futurologiya* [Towards the 21st Century: Perspectives, Outlooks, Futurology], ed. Igor V. Bestuzhev-Lada, 247–274. Moscow: Akademia, 2000.

——. "Futurology: The New Science of Probability?" In *The Futurists*, ed. Alvin Toffler. New York: Random House, 1972.

——. ed. *Futurum.* Munich: Minerva, 1980.

——. *Hegels Strafrechtstheorie.* Berlin: Duncker & Humblot, 1975.

——. "Heute noch skeptischer als 1962." In *Fremd im eigenen Land: Juden in der Bundesrepublik*, eds. Henryk M. Broder and Michel R. Lang. Frankfurt am Main: Fischer, 1979.

——. *History and Futurology.* Meisenheim: Hain, 1966.

——. "In unserer Familie war kein Platz für Patriotismus." In *Die andere Erinnerung: Gespräche mit jüdischen Wissenschaftlern im Exil*, ed. Hajo Funke, 422–439. Frankfurt am Main: Fischer, 1989.

——. "Is Futurology the Answer to the Challenge of the Future?'" In *Mankind 2000*, eds. Robert Jungk and Johan Galtung, 264–269. Oslo and London: Universitetsforlaget/Allen & Unwin, 1969.

——. *Ist die Zukunft noch zu retten?* Hamburg: Hoffmann & Campe, 1987.

——. *Karl Liebknecht zur Einführung.* Hamburg: SOAK, 1985.

——. *Die KPD in der Weimarer Republik*, ed. and introd. Hermann Weber. Frankfurt am Main: E.V.A., 1976.

——. "Marxism and the Third Road." In *Can We Survive Our Future?*, eds. George R. Urban and Michael Glenny. New York: St. Martin's Press, 1971.

——. "Notstandsgesetze würden die Freiheit des Bürgers dauernd bedrohen." *Westdeutsches Tageblatt*, Apr. 6, 1963.

——. *Rosa Luxemburg zur Einführung.* Hamburg: SOAK, 1985.

——. "Teaching the Future." *Forum* 104 (1945): 307–311.

——. "Teaching the Future." *Journal for Higher Education* 16 (1945): 460–465.

——. *Vergangenheit im Zeugenstand der Zukunft.* Berlin: Dietz, 1991.

——. *Von Marx bis Kolakowski: Sozialismus oder Untergang in der Barbarei?* Cologne: E.V.A., 1978.

——. *Weltkommunismus im Wandel.* Frankfurt am Main: E.V.A., 1965.

——. *Zeitgeschichte und Zukunftspolitik.* Hamburg: Hoffmann & Campe, 1974.

Flechtheim, Ossip K. and Egbert Joos. *Ausschau halten nach einer besseren Welt: Biographie, Interview, Artikel.* Berlin: Dietz, 1991.

Flechtheim, Ossip K. and Hans-Martin Lohman. *Marx zur Einführung.* Hamburg: SOAK, 1988.

Flechtheim, Ossip K. et al. *Fundamentals of Political Science.* New York: Ronald Press, 1952.

——. *Grundlegung der Politischen Wissenschaft.* Trans. Lili F. Flechtheim and Heiner Randemann. Meisenheim: Hain, 1958.

Foitzik, Jan. *Zwischen den Fronten: Zur Politik, Organisation und Funktion linker politischer Kleinorganisationen im Widerstand 1933 bis 1939/40.* Bonn: J.H.W. Dietz, 1986.

Fritzsche, Sonja. "East Germany's 'Werkstatt Zukunft': Futurology and the Science Fiction Films of 'Defa-Futurum.'" *German Studies Review* 29, no. 2 (2006): 367–386.

Gaisudis, A. L. "Kritika futurologii O. K. Flekhtkheima" [A Critique of O. K. Flechtheim's Futurology]. *Filosofskie nauki* 16, no. 4 (1983): 140–141.

Gieseke, Jens. "East German Popular Opinion: Problems of Reconstruction." In *The Silent Majority in Communist and Post-Communist States*, eds. Jens Gieseke and Klaus Bachmann, 59–77. Frankfurt am Main: Peter Lang, 2016.

Graf, William D. *The German Left since 1945: Socialism and Social Democracy in the German Federal Republic*, with an epilogue by Ossip K. Flechtheim. Cambridge: Oleander Press, 1976.

Gribachev, Nikolai Matveevich. "Tikhye krestonostsy" [Silent Crusaders]. *Pravda*, Sept. 29, 1967.

Grohmann, Dieter. "Futurologie und Ethik: Eine kritische Analyse philosophisch-ethischer Probleme in der bürgerlichen Zukunftsforschung." Ph.D.
thesis, Martin Luther University Halle-Wittenberg, 1977.

Guth, Stefan. "One Future Only: The Soviet Union in the Age of Scientific-
Technical Revolution." In *Reconfiguring the Future? Politics and Time from the
1960s to the 1980s*, ed. Elke Sefried. Special issue, *Journal of Modern European
History* 13, no. 3 (2015): 355–376.

Heimann, Siegfried, ed. *Ossip K. Flechtheim 100 Jahre.* Berlin: Humanistischer
Verband Deutschlands, 2009.

Herz, John H. "Letter to the Editor." *New York Sunday Times*, Apr. 3, 1994.

———. *Vom Überleben: Wie ein Weltbild entstand.* Düsseldorf: Droste, 1984.

Joos, Egbert. "Futurologie: Eine Theorie der Vergangenheit?" Ph.D. thesis,
Technical University Dresden, 1988.

Keßler, Mario. *Ossip K. Flechtheim: Politischer Wissenschaftler und Zukunftsdenker
(1909–1998).* Cologne: Böhlau, 2007.

Koch, Claus. "Kritik der Futurologie." *Kursbuch* 14 (1968): 1–17.

Krautz, Manfred. "Untersuchungen zur Futurologie im System des staatsmonopolistischen Kapitalismus Westdeutschlands." Ph.D. thesis, Technical
University Dresden, 1969.

Kuczynski, Jürgen. "Futurologische Strömungen." *Die Weltbühne* 66, no. 6
(1971): 161–163.

Kühne, Tobias. *Das Netzwerk "Neu Beginnen" und die Berliner SPD nach 1945.*
Berlin: Verlag für Berlin-Brandenburg, 2018.

Lewis, David Levering. *W. E. B. Du Bois*, vol. 2, *The Fight for Equality and the
American Century, 1919–1963.* New York: Henry Holt & Co., 2000.

Merritt, Richard L. "American Influences in the Occupation of Germany."
Annals of the American Academy of Political and Social Science 428 (1976):
91–103.

Miermeister, Jürgen. *Rudi Dutschke mit Selbstzeugnissen und Bilddokumenten.*
Reinbek: Rowohlt, 1986.

Miles [Walter Löwenheim]. *Socialism's New Beginning: A Manifesto from the
Underground Germany.* New York: League for Industrial Democracy, 1934.

Neumann, Franz L. *Behemoth: The Structure and Practice of National Socialism.*
New York: Octagon Books, 1963.

Niemann, Heinz. *Hinterm Zaun: Politische Kultur und Meinungsforschung in der
DDR.* Berlin: Edition Ost, 1995.

———. *Meinungsforschung in der DDR: Die geheimen Berichte des Instituts für
Meinungsforschung an das Politbüro der SED.* Cologne: Bund-Verlag, 1993.

The Nobel Peace Prize, Nomination Database. www.nobelprize.org/nomination/
redirector/?redir=archive/show.php&id=17187. Accessed Oct. 7, 2018.

Pfau, Thomas. "Zur Kritik der sozialpolitischen Theorien des Ossip
K. Flechtheim." Ph.D. thesis, Martin Luther University Halle-Wittenberg,
1978.

"Pioneer Futurist Honored in Berlin." *The Futurist* 23, no. 4 (1998): 43.

Renaud, Terence. "Restarting Socialism: The New Beginning Group and the Problem of Renewal on the German Left, 1930–1970." Ph.D. thesis, University of California at Berkeley, 2015.

Rindceviziute, Egle. "The Future as an Intellectual Technology in the Soviet Union: From Centralised Planning to Reflexive Management." *Cahiers du monde russe* 56, no. 1 (2017): 111–136.

——. "A Struggle for the Soviet Future: The Birth of Scientific Forecasting in the Soviet Union." *Slavic Review* 75, no. 1 (2016): 52–76.

Sardar, Ziauddin. *Rescuing All Our Futures: The Future of Futures Studies* (Westport, CT: Praeger, 1999).

Seefried, Elke. "Steering the Future: The Emergence of 'Western' Futures Research and its Production of Expertise, 1950s to Early 1970s." *European Journal of Futures Research* 2 (2013).

——. *Zukünfte: Aufstieg und Krise der Zukunftsforschung 1945–1980.* Berlin: De Gruyter Oldenbourg, 2015.

Semyonov, V. "Sovremennii krizis i put' v budushchee: diagnoz I prognoz" [Contemporary Crisis and the Way towards a Future: Diagnosis and Prognosis]. *Al'ternativy* 1, no. 1 (1996): 41–50.

Shakhnazarov, Georgi K. *Fiasko futurologii (Kriticheskiy ocherk nemarksistkikh teorii obshchestvennogo razvitiya)* [The Fiasco of Futurology: A Critical Outline of Non-Marxist Theories of Social Development]. Moscow: Politizdat, 1979.

Son, Hyeonju. "The History of Western Future Studies: An Exploration of the Intellectual Traditions and Three-Phase Periodization." *Futures* 66 (2016): 120–137.

Ulbricht, Walter. *Die gesellschaftliche Entwicklung in der Deutschen Demokratischen Republik bis zur Vollendung des Sozialismus.* Berlin: Dietz, 1967.

Wildenthal, Lora. *The Language of Human Rights in West Germany.* Philadelphia: University of Pennsylvania Press, 2013.

Zinn, Howard. *You Can't be Neutral on a Moving Train: A Personal History of Our Times.* Boston: Beacon Press, 1994.

11

Concluding Remarks

Frank Jacob

Radicals in the nineteenth and twentieth centuries would, due to their pure existence in such an identity, come into conflict with the nation states they were active in, whether it be as citizens or exiles. Anarchists would contest any state, as its rejection was "an organising principle,"[1] and socialists and communists were usually persecuted for challenging the existent social order.[2] Owing to the existence of radical core values, e.g., anti-statism, or key events of global history, e.g., suppressed or failed revolutions, anarchists, socialists and communists were forced to move. They were considered "dangerous foreigners" while being in exile, often forced to reframe or rebuild their own radical networks from scratch. Regional exchanges and movements between radicals would eventually establish a global network of radicalism, in which individuals exchanged ideas, strategies, publications or simply stories about different political and social environments.[3] This was made possible by the already existent transportation and communication networks, as they were used by non-radical individuals as well.[4]

As the present volume shows, once existent, radical networks could be used as an asset for those who sought to gain support from exile communities, although the latter ones did not always demand or support

---

[1] Carl Levy and Matthew S. Adams, "Introduction," in *The Palgrave Handbook of Anarchism*, eds. Carl Levy and Matthew S. Adams (Cham: Palgrave, 2019), 1.

[2] See Christian Gerlach and Clemens Six, eds., *Palgrave Handbook of Anti-Communist Persecution* (Basingstoke: Palgrave Macmillan, 2020).

[3] Carl Levy, "Anarchism and Cosmopolitanism," *The Palgrave Handbook of Anarchism*, 128.

[4] On the impact of transportation and communication networks see, among others, the following: James Dobson, *Modernity and Autobiography in Nineteenth-Century America: Literary Representations of Communication and Transportation Technologies* (Cham: Palgrave Pivot, 2017); Wolfgang Schivelbusch, *Geschichte der Eisenbahnreise: Zur Industrialisierung von Raum und Zeit im 19. Jahrhundert*, 6th ed. (Frankfurt am Main: Fischer, 2015).

such radical networks.[5] For radical purposes at home, yet only for as long as these immigrant communities in the foreign environment could truly identify with the cause for which support was sought, its members could become part of a larger transnational cause, while remaining also active on the local level. When Yekaterina Breshkovskaya, the "grandmother" of the revolutionary movement in Russia, visited the United States to ask for financial support, she was able to do so because the Eastern European immigrant communities supported her. Nevertheless, she was also lucky that perceptions of her were positive and that her visit turned out to be a "mass media spectacle" (see Lutz Häfner's chapter in this volume). In later years, and under different circumstances, the "priestess of anarchy,"[6] Emma Goldman, could not succeed in gaining sufficient financial support for her work, because the attention to and attractiveness of anarchism had declined after World War I and the Russian Revolution.[7] In contrast to Goldman, Breshkovskaya was also more successful at the beginning of the 1900s because, as Häfner emphasizes in the present volume, she "was polyvalent and could be seen as a Russian martyr, an international heroine, a socialist-revolutionary living icon and a role model for the American suffragettes." It is therefore clear that the value of the networks, once in existence, depended on their valuation at both ends and the radical exile communities could turn into uninterested second-generation natives, who showed no more interest in the radical ideas of those who had arrived from foreign shores before them. Support was only granted if deemed necessary by the radicals at the other end, and exchange was only possible if individuals were actually actively using the available connections. Otherwise a network could be dismantled again, especially when former immigrant communities disappeared as a consequence of individual integration and social advances by a critical mass.

The networks, like the "transatlantic Italian anarchist network across South America and Italy, France and other countries" presented by Carlo Romani and Bruno Corrêa de Sá e Benevides in the present volume, were constantly redefined by the radicals who were on the move, and the experiences they gathered in their respective environments of asylum must

---

[5] For a theoretical discussion of solidarity in internationalist settings, see David Featherstone, *Solidarity: Hidden Histories and Geographies of Internationalism* (London: Zed, 2012), 15–39.

[6] Emma Goldman, "What Is There in Anarchy for Woman?," *St. Louis Post-Dispatch Sunday* Magazine, Oct. 14, 1897: 9, printed in *Emma Goldman: A Documentary History of the American Years*, vol. 1, *Made for America, 1890–1901* (Urbana: Illinois University Press, 2008), 289.

[7] Levy, "Anarchism and Cosmopolitanism," 126–127. On Goldman's view of the Russian Revolution and the attempt to criticize Bolshevism, see Frank Jacob, *Emma Goldman and the Russian Revolution: From Admiration to Frustration* (Berlin: De Gruyter, 2020).

also be taken into consideration when discussing transatlantic radicalism, especially with regard to the political left that in itself already consisted of a specific radical diversity. Regional identities therefore also shaped radicalism within the Atlantic world,[8] and the connections must at least be considered as being twofold, if not more divided, according to the necessities of further and ideally not Eurocentric research, and in accordance with different potential categories, such as gender or age.[9] Radicalism per se must consequently also be considered a process, in which transnationalism can play an important role, but is also losing its momentum if the very active and mobile radicals disappear as a connection between radical communities, e.g., on the two sides of the Atlantic.

The migration of radicals of the political left in the Atlantic world was also very much related to the migrants' knowledge that they provided for the radical milieus that would be established or that already existed. It was Spanish migrants, as James Michael Yeoman highlights, that radicalized the Panama Canal Zone when they brought with them radical periodicals, which would also be shipped to the region due to this immigrant community's existence. The activity of publishers from Spain, like Rodríguez, who was in charge of *Tierra y Libertad*, had an important impact on far away spaces of radicalism. The radical press, like *Man!* (see Hillary Lazar's chapter), were often related to migration issues, and the U.S. State would try to get rid of the political menace that such publications presented by deportation as a means to limit existent radical exchange networks. Nevertheless, it was hard to contain ideas related to anarchism, socialism or communism in the Atlantic world, as it was first and foremost individual bonds that could be intellectually transnational without an actual border crossing, as Steven Parfitt highlights with regard to the transatlantic political activism of Terence Powderly (1849–1924).

That such individual initiatives could lead to the genesis of new networks beyond party- or union-related networks is emphasized by Frank Jacob when he discusses the impact of a summer trip by Herbert S. Calvert (1889–1981) to Siberia. The Kuzbas Autonomous Industrial Colony, however, was as utopian as the belief that Lenin would actually lead Russia to a truly free and communist society. In the end, the failure of Kuzbas just embittered the hopes and dreams of those who really had believed in a worker's utopia in the Soviet Union. Yet not all individuals got on the move due to their own ambitions.

---

[8] Ángel J. Cappelletti, *Anarchism in Latin America*, trans. Gabriel Palmer-Fernández (Chico, CA: AK Press, 2017), 10.

[9] Sheila Rowbotham, *Rebel Crossings: New Women, Free Lovers, and Radicals in Britain and America* (London: Verso, 2016).

As stated before, many radicals were exiled, especially during the Hobsbawmian age of extremes, in which the rise of fascism led to a transnational "defensive gathering" in Spain, before the leftist radicals had to leave their homes due to their defeat and the uncontested rise of right-wing radicalism in Europe. Many anarchists, socialists and communists had to leave the "Old World" to seek refuge in the United States or other free parts of the world. As Georg Leidenberger correctly argues, "Hannes Meyer's life amidst the German-speaking communist exile community in Mexico illustrates the multivalence of the exile experience of the European Left," and in this volume he provides one example of the problems leftist exiles had to deal with on the other side of the Atlantic where their unwilling journey often ended, sometimes only temporarily, sometimes forever. Like Meyer in Mexico, Paul Frölich and Rosi Wolfstein-Frölich, as Riccardo Altieri shows, "were one part of a much bigger exile network in the United States, which was connected to many emigrants not only in the transatlantic world but also back home in Europe." They shared this experience with many others, the most well-known of whom is probably Bertolt Brecht.[10]

During their exiles, the leftist radicals were also confronted with challenging new perspectives as global events did not stop in the meantime, and, embedded in the local political discussions, Wolfstein and Frölich needed to position themselves towards Stalinism while preparing themselves for a return to their German home and the "reestablishment of a post-1945 line for a Marx-oriented new-line Socialism in Germany." In addition, Ossip K. Flechtheim and others were experiencing new things in their post-migrant environments, finding no less reason to continue, but maybe also transform their own radical perspectives.

Considering that people could use the globalized transportation and communication networks of the nineteenth and twentieth centuries, this availability must also have created an overlap between the different networks, and it would be fruitful to take a closer look at such possible overlaps. However, this, and many other valuable approaches to further intensify the study of transatlantic radicalism, should be answered in further studies, which will hopefully have been stimulated by the present volume, whose editors wanted not only to answer some questions related to the role of migrant individuals and their radical identities within the networks of the Atlantic world but also to arouse a more intensified interest in the study of politically leftist radicalism in the nineteenth and twentieth centuries from a transnational perspective.

---

[10] James K. Lyon, *Bertolt Brecht in America* (Princeton, N.J.: Princeton University Press, 2014).

Works Cited

Cappelletti, Ángel J. *Anarchism in Latin America*, trans. Gabriel Palmer-Fernández. Chico, CA: AK Press, 2017.

Dobson, James. *Modernity and Autobiography in Nineteenth-Century America: Literary Representations of Communication and Transportation Technologies.* Cham: Palgrave Pivot, 2017.

Gerlach, Christian and Clemens Six, eds. *Palgrave Handbook of Anti-Communist Persecution.* Basingstoke: Palgrave Macmillan, 2020.

Goldman, Emma. "What Is There in Anarchy for Woman?" *St. Louis Post-Dispatch Sunday* Magazine, Oct. 14, 1897: 9, repr. in *Emma Goldman: A Documentary History of the American Years*, vol. 1, *Made for America, 1890–1901*, 289–292. Urbana: Illinois University Press, 2008.

Jacob, Frank. *Emma Goldman and the Russian Revolution: From Admiration to Frustration.* Berlin: De Gruyter, 2020.

Levy, Carl. "Anarchism and Cosmopolitanism." In *The Palgrave Handbook of Anarchism*, eds. Carl Levy and Matthew S. Adams, 125–148. Cham: Palgrave, 2019.

Levy, Carl and Matthew S. Adams. "Introduction." In *The Palgrave Handbook of Anarchism*, eds. Carl Levy and Matthew S. Adams, 1–23. Cham: Palgrave, 2019.

Lyon, James K. *Bertolt Brecht in America.* Princeton, N.J.: Princeton University Press, 2014.

Rowbotham, Sheila. *Rebel Crossings: New Women, Free Lovers, and Radicals in Britain and America.* London: Verso, 2016.

Schivelbusch, Wolfgang. *Geschichte der Eisenbahnreise: Zur Industrialisierung von Raum und Zeit im 19. Jahrhundert*, 6th ed. Frankfurt am Main: Fischer, 2015.

List of Contributors

Riccardo Altieri is a historian and wrote his Ph.D. thesis in Contemporary History at the University of Potsdam, Germany (2017–2021). His research fields are Jewish History and Labour History. Most recently, Altieri has published an anthology on *Klassismus und Wissenschaft* (BdWi, 2020) and a short biography of *Rosi Wolfstein* (Hentrich & Hentrich, 2021).

Bruno Corrêa de Sá e Benevides is a Ph.D. student in History of the Sciences and Health at Casa de Oswaldo Cruz, Fundação Oswaldo Cruz (Fiocruz), Brazil. His main fields of research include the history of psychiatry and criminology as well as the histories of anarchism and revolutions. Bruno's recent works include the papers "'I Have No Homeland': The First World War According to the Libertarian Propaganda of Angelo Bandoni" (Cantareira Review, 2021) and "Moral Insanity, Political Crime and Anarchism: Medicalization in Brazil in the First Decades of the 20th Century" (Fênix Journal, 2021).

Lutz Häfner is Professor at the University of Bielefeld, Germany. He received his Ph.D. in Modern Eastern European History from Hamburg University, Germany, and obtained his habilitation at the University of Bielefeld. His main fields of research include modern Russian and German History as well as the histories of socialism and revolutions.

Frank Jacob is Professor for Global History of the Nineteenth and Twentieth Centuries at Nord Universitet, Norway and received his Ph.D. in Japanese Studies from Erlangen University, Germany. His main fields of research include modern Japanese and German History as well as the histories of anarchism and revolutions. Jacob's recent works include *Emma Goldman and the Russian Revolution* (De Gruyter, 2020), *Rosa Luxemburg: Living and Thinking the Revolution* (Büchner, 2021) and *Mut zur Freiheit: Ein Essay zur Revolution im 21. Jahrhundert* (Transcript, 2021).

Mario Keßler was, until his retirement in March 2021, Professor at the Leibniz Center for Contemporary History in Potsdam, Germany. He taught at the University of Potsdam and at Yeshiva University, New York and held many visiting professorships as well as scholarships at other universities, mainly in the United States. His main fields of research include twentieth-century German and European History, modern antisemitism, European labor movements and the history of historiography. His recent book publications include *Abgründe und Aufbrüche: Neue Studien und Kritiken* (Trafo, 2020), *A Political Biography of Arkadij Maslow, 1891–1941: Dissident Against His Will* (Palgrave MacMillan, 2020) and *Westemigranten: Deutsche Kommunisten zwischen USA-Exil und DDR* (Böhlau, 2019).

Hillary Lazar is a Doctoral Candidate in Sociology at the University of Pittsburgh and holds an MA in History from San Francisco State University. Her research focuses on historical and contemporary anarchism, movement evaluation and the politics of emotions. She has been published in *Anarchism: A Conceptual Approach, Socialism and Democracy* (Routledge, 2018), *Perspectives on Anarchist Theory*, and has forthcoming work in *Research in Political Sociology*. Hillary is a member of the Institute for Anarchist Studies' Speakers Bureau, part of the *Perspectives* editorial collective and on the advisory board for Anarchist Agency.

Georg Leidenberger received his Ph.D. in U.S. history from the University of North Carolina at Chapel Hill and is Professor at the Universidad Autónoma Metropolitana in Mexico City. He co-edited *100 years Bauhaus: Variety, Conflict and Impact* [*100 Jahre Bauhaus: Vielfalt, Konflikt, Wirkung*] (Metropol, 2019) and is currently working on a book entitled *The Other Bauhaus: Architect Hannes Meyer and Left-Wing Modernism. A Biography*.

Steven Parfitt is between careers, after being let go by Loughborough University during the COVID-19 pandemic. He has a Ph.D. in History from the University of Nottingham, and has published a book, *Knights Across the Atlantic: The Knights of Labor in Britain and Ireland* (Liverpool University Press, 2016). In addition to more than a dozen journal articles and book chapters on various topics in global labor history, he has published numerous articles in publications including the *Guardian, Jacobin, In These Times* and *Open Democracy*. He is currently compiling the work of Emma Paterson, a pioneering woman trade unionist, for a volume with Trent Editions.

Carlo Romani holds a Ph.D. in Cultural History (from the University of Campinas, 2003) and is Associate Professor of Contemporary History at Universidade Federal do Estado do Rio de Janeiro, Unirio (since 2010). His main fields of research in Global History include the history of anarchism, transatlantic migration to South America and border studies in the Amazon region. Recent works include "Anarquismo italiano, transnacionalismo e emigração ao Brasil: Contribuições ao debate teórico" (*Crítica Histórica*, 2019), "História imperial, ciência e poder: A disputa de fronteira anglo-brasileira" (*RBH*, 2019) and the book *Fronteiras e Territorialidades: miradas sul-americanas da Amazônia à Patagônia* (Intermeios, 2019).

James Michael Yeoman is an independent researcher affiliated to the University of Sheffield, where he received his Ph.D. in 2016. His research focuses on the history of anarchism and anarchist movements, above all the interactions between ideology, political economy and culture, and between the local, regional, national arenas. His publications on the Spanish anarchist movement include *Print Culture and the Formation of the Anarchist Movement in Spain, 1890–1915* (Routledge, 2020) and "The Spanish Civil War" in *The Palgrave Handbook of Anarchism* (Palgrave Macmillan, 2018). His ongoing research into transnational connections between radical movements across Europe and Latin America include "*Salud y Anarquia desde Dowlais*: The Translocal Experience of Spanish Anarchists in South Wales, 1900–1915" (*International Journal of Iberian Studies*, 2016), which appears in a special issue on transnationalism and Spanish anarchism co-edited by Yeoman and Danny Evans (Liverpool Hope University).

Index

Acción Libertaria (Gijón) 89,
92–93n53, 102–103n120
Alianza Internacional Giuseppe
Garibaldi 180, 186
American Civil Liberties Union 116,
157, 164
American Socialist Party 4, 8
anarchism 3–10, 13, 57n1, 58, 63,
65, 67–73, 77–78, 83, 85, 88,
94–97, 101, 105, 109,10, 112,
250–251
anarchists 8–11, 14–15, 30, 33,
42, 58–60, 62–65n27, 67–72,
75–78, 83, 85, 90, 98, 100,
104–105, 110–113, 122, 124,
130, 135, 143, 249, 252
Arbeiter-Zeitung (Workers' Daily) 6
Archibald, James P. 136, 142, 145
Argentina 57, 59, 61, 63, 65–66,
69–70, 73, 75, 83–85, 89, 92,
104
Atlanta University 226–228
Atlantic 1–3, 5–7, 9, 11, 14–15, 61,
83–86, 88, 90, 97, 105–106,
133–135, 137, 140–141,
143–146, 148, 171, 221–222,
251–252
Autonomous Industrial Colony 152
Aveling, Edward 3
L'Avvenire 63, 65–66

Bandoni, Angelo 60, 64–65, 69–72,
75, 77
Battaglia, La 60–62, 65, 72n50,
73–75
Bebel, August 12
Berger, Victor L. 4
Berlin 30, 178, 192, 195, 198–199,
201n60, 207, 221–223,
227–228, 232–234, 238,
241–243,
Boni, Tobia 60, 64–65
Borodin, Mikhail 154
Brandt, Willy 200, 213–14
Brazil 57, 59, 61–66, 69, 71–74,
76–77, 79, 84, 92, 104
Brazilian labor movement 15, 57, 64
Brecht, Bertolt 13, 28, 33, 252
Breshko-Breshkovskaya, Ekaterina
Konstantinova 14, 25
Buenos Aires 6, 63, 65–67, 69,
70n42, 72, 86n11
Burckhardt, Carl Jacob 225
Burt, Thomas 132, 141, 145

Cafiero, Carlo 58
Cahan, Abraham 4
California 113, 115, 117, 119,
122–124, 153
Calvert, Herbert S. 151, 154–157,
166–167

capitalism 12, 97, 152, 154, 221, 236, 242
Cecilia Colony 62
Cerchiai, Alessandro 60, 65, 68, 74, 77
Chaikovskii, Nikolai Vasil'evich 39, 46
Chicago 4, 6, 13, 25–26, 38–39, 41–42, 45n123, 47, 72, 110, 114, 119, 130, 134–135, 138, 146–147
Clan na Gael 136
Columbus, Christopher 1
commodities 1
communism 3,152, 157, 171, 173–174, 201, 205, 221, 225, 229, 234, 236, 238, 242–243, 251
Communist Party of Germany (KPD) 191–192, 221, 229
Confederación Nacional del Trabajo (CNT) 88
Costa, Andrea 58

Damiani, Gigi 60, 62–63, 65, 68–69, 75–77
Davaud, Abel 143–145
Davitt, Michael 132, 134–136, 142, 145, 147
Denny, A. G. 141
deportation 77, 109–110, 115–117, 120–121, 123–124, 164, 251
Du Bois, W. E. B. 227–228
Duby, Gertrude 172, 178n26, 180, 185
Duncker, Hermann 178, 192, 210
Duncker, Käte 181–182, 206, 209
Duncker, Wolfgang 180–181

Eisler, Hanns 13
Engelberg, Ernst 223, 225
Engels, Friedrich 3, 130, 238
European expansion 1

exchange 1–2, 5, 14, 69–70, 85, 90, 96, 105, 124, 139, 161, 181, 183, 212, 250–251
exile 2, 6, 8n41, 11, 14, 16, 28–33, 38, 71, 85n8, 96, 153, 172–175, 178, 183–188

fascism 77, 113–114, 124, 173, 185, 211, 221, 223, 225, 243, 252
Federal Republic of Germany (FRG) 192, 213, 241
Federation of Free Groups and Individuals of the Isthmus of Panama (FAILP) 94–95
Ferrero, Vincenzo 109–110, 112, 115–117, 118n44, 119–122, 124
First International 7, 139
First Trade Union International Congress 154
Flechtheim, Ossip Kurt 16, 221–244, 252
foreign policy 121, 125
France 59, 70–71, 75, 78, 83, 92, 120, 131–132, 141, 143–147, 171, 173, 174n8, 178, 200, 221, 250
Freies Deutschland (journal) 175–176n20, 179, 185, 187n65
Freies Deutschland (organization) 175–176, 179n33, 184, 186
Friedeberg, Erwin 178, 180
Frölich, Paul 16, 191–193, 195–214, 252
Frölich, Rose 192n4, 213
    see also Wolfstein, Rosi
futurology 224, 230, 235–241

Geneva 34, 176, 178, 225–226
German Democratic Republic (GDR) 184n57, 192, 238
German Social Democracy 214, 224

Germany 4, 11, 13–14, 34, 113,
141, 175–176, 178, 181,
191–192, 199–200, 204,
206, 209–210n101, 212–214,
221–229, 232–235, 238–239,
241, 243, 252
Germinal 64–66, 69–70n42, 71–72,
77, 100
Goldman, Emma 10, 26, 42, 111,
118n144, 164, 250
Goldschmidt, Alfons 175, 177–178,
180, 183
Graham, Marcus (Shmuel) 109, 112
Great Depression 122, 223
Green Party 221, 242
Guerra Sociale 71, 75

Hardie, Keir 3
Hayes, John 144
Haywood, William "Big Bill" 153,
156, 159, 162–167
Herz, Hans (later John H.) 222–223,
225, 227
Hillquit, Morris 4
Hitler, Adolf 185, 199, 201,
203–204, 212, 214, 224
Horkheimer, Max 226

immigrant 6, 15, 73, 76, 109, 111,
114–115, 119, 121–124, 153,
173, 187, 250–251
Independent Social Democratic Party
(USPD) 196
individualism 15, 91, 95, 98, 236
Industrial Workers of the World
(I. W. W.) 4, 119, 123, 147, 153
Institute of Social Research 226
Instituto de Planeación y Urbanismo,
IPU (Institute of Planning and
Urbanism) 177
International Group, the 109–110,
112–116, 119–21, 123–124
International May Day 4

Isthmian Canal Commission (ICC)
84
Italian immigrants 60–62, 72
Italian-Brazilian anarchism 71, 73
Italy 6, 11, 15, 58, 60, 62–63n21,
64–75, 77–79, 95, 99, 116–117,
120, 131, 141–142, 173, 187,
225, 250
IWA (International Workingmen's
Association) 58–59

Katz, Leo 172–173, 179–180
Kautsky, Karl 12
Kelsen, Hans 225
Kemerovo 15, 155–156, 160, 163,
165
Kempner, Robert M. W. 228
Kisch, Egon 172, 175
Knights of Labor 15, 129–137, 139,
141–143, 145–147
Kuzbas Autonomous Industrial
Colony 15, 151, 251
see also Autonomous Industrial
Colony; Kuzbas colony
Kuzbas colony 151, 161
Kuznetsk Basin 152, 155

Lang, Fritz 13
Latin America 6, 70, 105
Lenin, Vladimir 151, 153n12,
154–156, 166, 196, 205–206,
251
Leon, Daniel de 4
El Libertario (Gijón) 102–103
Liebknecht, Karl 229
Liebknecht, Wilhelm 3
Liga Pro-Cultura Alemana (League
for German Culture) 175
Local Assembly 300 140
Lombardo Toledano, Vicente 171,
173, 177, 181–182, 186
Löwenthal, Richard 223–224, 234
Luxemburg, Rosa 195, 201, 208, 243

McKinley, William 10, 110
Malatesta, Errico 10–11, 58, 78
Man! 15, 109–118, 120–121,
    123–124, 251
Mann, Thomas 156
Marx, Eleanor 3
Marxism *see* Marxists
Marxists 9, 143, 146, 208, 238–239
Méndez, Leopoldo 175n13, 186
Merker, Paul 172–173, 174n8, 175,
    184–185, 187n65
Meyer, Hannes 16, 171–173,
    175–188, 252
Meyer-Bergner, Lena 176
migration 7, 10n7, 11, 59, 85, 88, 90,
    251, 257
Modotti, Tina 180, 186
Montevideo 65–67, 69, 72
Moscow 16, 25, 29–30, 154,
    156, 158, 166, 176n21, 204,
    208–209, 211, 222, 240
Most, Johann 4, 93, 164n71

National Socialism 208, 222
network 7, 10, 15, 57, 59–61,
    65–70, 73–74, 76–79, 83, 90,
    94, 105, 109, 111–112,
    114–115, 121, 124, 134, 136,
    172, 179, 191–192, 200–202,
    205–206, 212–214, 221, 232,
    249–250
    see also press networks
Neu Beginnen (New Beginnings)
    223–224
Neumann, Franz L. 226, 233
New Economic Policy (NEP) 151,
    166
New York City 4, 35n60, 38, 39n81,
    45n124, 114, 119, 178n25
Nolan, Mary 2, 12
Nuremberg Laws 227

October Revolution 206

Panama 84–88, 90–98, 100,
    102–105, 251
Panama Canal, construction of 84
    see also Isthmian Canal
    Commission (ICC)
Paris 4, 10, 34, 72, 89, 138, 142–146,
    164, 174n8, 178, 200–201, 203,
    213, 223
Partido Liberal Mexicano (PLM) 101
People's Commissariat for Internal
    Affairs (NKVD) 205
periodicals 1n4, 10, 29, 66, 70,
    71, 83, 94, 96n69, 102–103,
    111–112, 114, 251
police 27–28, 33, 42, 58n7, 59, 63,
    66, 69, 72
    Argentinian police 66, 69
    Brazilian police 66, 69
    Italian police 58n7, 59, 69, 72
Powderly, Terence 15, 129–147, 251
press networks 2, 14, 105
El Productor 6
Propaganda Libertaria, La 75

radical ideas 3, 6, 166, 250
radicalism 1, 2, 4–9, 11–16, 110, 124,
    129, 154, 183n48, 209, 249,
    251–252
Rappard, William 225
Regler, Gustav 172–173, 179
remittances 91, 105
Renn, Ludwig 173, 175, 180
repression 9, 35, 70–71, 76–77,
    109–110, 113, 121, 124–125
revolution 5, 7, 9, 23, 27, 42, 67, 89,
    99, 101, 137, 143, 155, 174, 201,
    223–224, 230, 241–242
    see also Russian Revolution
revolutionary ideas 15, 152n6
Riga 4
Rio de Janeiro 63, 69, 72–73, 76–77
Ristori, Oreste 60, 65–68, 73–74, 77
Rivera, Diego 182

Rodríguez, M. D. (pseud.
	Intransigente) 85–91, 94, 96–97,
	99–105
Roosevelt, Theodore 10, 203, 10
Rühle, Otto 179, 183n49, 184
Rühle-Gerstel, Alice 179, 183n49
Russian Revolution 10n51, 25, 40,
	44, 46, 151n4, 151n7, 154, 157,
	160, 250
Russian Revolution of 1905 41, 49
Russian Revolution of 1917 74, 208
	see also October Revolution
Rutgers, Sebald J. 154, 156–158, 166

Sallitto, Domenico 109–110,
	115–116, 118–122, 124
Sanial, Lucien 146
Santos 69, 72
São Paulo 15, 57–58, 60–77
Sassi, Attilio 69
	see also Sassi, Vincenzo
Sassi, Vincenzo 67–68
Seghers, Anna 172–173, 175, 179
Serantoni, Fortunato 66
Siberia 16, 38, 46, 151–153, 155,
	157–158, 165–167
Social Democratic Party of Germany
	(SPD) 3, 192, 195–198, 206–209,
	213, 221, 229–230, 241
socialism 3, 4, 7, 10, 12, 37, 43, 58,
	64, 68, 85, 208, 212, 222–223,
	226, 236, 238, 242–244
Socialist Revolutionaries 25, 29–31,
	49
Socialist Revolutionary Party (SR
	Party) 23, 25, 35, 42, 44–47
Socialist Unity Party of Germany
	(SED) 206, 209, 214
Socialist Workers Party of Germany
	(SAPD) 199–201, 203,
	206–207, 209, 214
Society of Friends of Russian
	Freedom 26, 33, 45–46

solidarity 2, 83, 87, 101, 109, 111,
	115, 120–121, 124, 160, 243
Sombart, Werner 12
South America 4, 57, 59, 62, 68–69,
	78, 156, 250, 257
Soviet communism 171, 234, 236
Soviet Russia 15, 151–154, 156–160,
	162, 164, 166, 223, 225, 229
Spain 6, 73, 75, 83–85, 88–93,
	95–96, 102–105, 120, 204,
	251–252, 257
Spanish anarchist movement 257
Stalin, Joseph 204–206, 212, 223n5,
	229–230
Steinmetz, Charles P. 153
Stephens, Uriah 133
Stibi, Georg 172–173, 174n8, 175,
	187n65
St. Petersburg 11, 34, 39, 50
Sulzbacher, Fritz 178, 183
Sylvis, William 138
syndicalism 8n41, 13, 63n21, 64n26,
	68–69, 88–89, 97, 102, 112, 229

Taller de Gráfica Popular, TGP
	(Workshop of Popular Print
	Art) 175n13, 186, 187n65,
	188
terrorism 9, 14, 23n1, 25–25, 27–31,
	34–35, 37n70, 44, 47–50, 102
Third International Congress of the
	Communist International 154
Tierra y Libertad (Barcelona) 83–85,
	88–96, 101–103, 105, 251
transatlantic public sphere 14, 23
transatlantic radicalism 2, 5–6, 12,
	15, 129, 251–252
transnationalism 7, 13, 15, 70, 85,
	94, 251
Transylvania 4
Trotsky, Leon 173, 182–183, 186n61,
	208, 223n5
Tuscany 60, 70–72, 74, 79

Uhse, Bodo 172, 175, 178
Ukraine 222
El Único (Colón, Panama) 85n11,
    95–102, 104
United States 3–6, 11–16, 24–26,
    29, 32, 35–36, 38–42, 44,
    46, 48–49, 72, 75, 83–84,
    92, 100, 104, 109, 111, 116,
    121–123, 129–130, 132–140,
    142, 144–147, 151, 152n7, 153,
    156–157, 162–166, 172, 174n8,
    178n25, 180–181, 191, 201,
    203n63, 204, 207n88, 212,
    214, 221, 225–228, 233–234,
    243n86, 250, 252
Universidad Obrera (Workers'
    University) 171n1, 177, 181
University of Heidelberg 228–229

Vandervelde, Émile 12
Vezzani, Felici 63, 66

Weimar Republic 197, 209, 222, 226,
    229–230, 234n44
Weydemeyer, Joseph 4
Wolfstein, Rosi 16, 191, 193–197,
    199–201, 206–209, 210n101, 212
    see also Frölich, Rose
working class 3, 15, 57–58, 63–64,
    73, 76, 85, 98, 104, 129, 131,
    134, 147, 152–153, 166, 194,
    206, 211, 224, 241
World War I 5, 7, 11, 29, 75, 122,
    131, 153, 191, 194n14, 196,
    233, 250
World War II 2, 13, 16, 122, 172,
    178, 186n61, 191, 200, 222, 228